THE CHIEF MINISTERS OF ENGLAND
920–1720

ST. EDWARD'S OR THE PAINTED CHAMBER
'N THE OLD PALACE OF WESTMINSTER

This historic place, the bedchamber and treasury of the Saxon Kings, the *curia regis* of the Normans, the council-room of the Plantagenets, the hall of assembly of the early Parliaments, was for five centuries the actual seat and centre of the English government. In it Edward the Confessor died, Simon de Montfort was married, the victories of Crecy and Agincourt were announced, the death warrant of Charles I. was signed, Chatham lay in state. From Earl Godwin to Earl Grey every First Minister of the Crown has played his part within its walls.

Eighty feet long, thirty wide and forty high, it lay east and west from the river garden to Old Palace Yard, across the Lords' lobby of to-day. Its noble proportions, the frescoes and tapestries that adorned it, the traditions which it enshrined, had made it one of the marvels of mediæval England. After standing for eight hundred years and surviving the fire of 1834, it was pulled down to make way for the present Houses of Parliament.

THE
CHIEF MINISTERS
OF ENGLAND
920–1720

BY

CHARLES CLIVE BIGHAM,
2d VISCOUNT MERSEY

Essay Index Reprint Series

BOOKS FOR LIBRARIES PRESS, INC.
FREEPORT, NEW YORK

First Published 1923
Reprinted 1967

LIBRARY OF CONGRESS CATALOG CARD NUMBER:
67-30222

PRINTED IN THE UNITED STATES OF AMERICA

PREFACE

HISTORY has been called the art of impressing general truths by means of particular incidents. These scant epitomes of the lives of those men who have held the destinies of England in their hands may perhaps serve to illustrate the strength, character and understanding of a nation which for centuries has shown and still shows the world how to excel in peace and war, in trade and justice, in liberty and government.

CONTENTS

LIST OF ILLUSTRATIONS

ix

From photographs by Mr. Emery Walker.

THE
CHIEF MINISTERS OF ENGLAND
920–1720

INTRODUCTION

THE PLACE OF CHIEF MINISTER

KINGS, since first they reigned, have taken ministers to help them. The camp, the chase, the banquet and the bower claimed most of their days, and neither instinct nor training fitted them for the conduct of affairs or the detail of government. At first those on whom they devolved their business were men of their own free choice, and in the East climate and temperament have maintained this custom, and there the vizier still flourishes. But in the colder regions of the West another breed and another creed led to a different system. There the people had more mettle, and unless the prince was of a virile type he risked losing his throne to a too potent mayor of the palace—such was the lot of the Merovingians in France.

In England the early Kings were as a rule cautious. The free institutions of the race did not encourage the concentration of too much power in the hands of a single servant, nor did the higher dignities of the Saxon court or the Norman curia lend themselves to a plurality of functions and an engrossing of control. Ministers there always were, though it was only now and again that one of them became supreme. But if the prince was weak, or if he was often abroad, it was sometimes safer to commit the care of the realm to one individual rather than to several—a viceroy was better than a committee—and when the holder of such a charge was a man of mark, when he enjoyed in a special degree and for a considerable period the Sovereign's favour, then he overtopped his colleagues and became a Chief Minister.

1

Insensibly the custom of having such an officer grew, and by the time that the nation was a conscious whole the idea of one particular statesman bearing the principal burden of government and wielding the principal power was already understood. Nearly always he was the friend of the King, rarely the champion of the people. His duties were arduous, his tenure insecure, his favour fleeting, his fate hazardous. Officially his post was never recognized nor were his privileges defined, though his penalties were only too well known. To run such risks required great rewards, and while few Chief Ministers abjured rank and riches, many met with an unhappy end. Yet they went on increasing in frequency, gradually forming a tradition which influenced those who worked with and those who came after them. At last they became a regular feature of the government until they were replaced by the modern Premiers.

The development of their position is illustrated by the historical sequence of the different offices of State which they held in successive epochs. Without laying too much stress on apparent analogies, these progressive changes coincide in the main with the advance of the constitution. Sometimes the place conferred power on the man, sometimes the man increased the power of his place. But as a general rule, during each phase of political evolution, the Chief Minister, whenever there was one, was associated with the same department of government.

In Saxon times the Justiciar was definitely the first man under the King: he was the *Capitalis Justicia*, the lieutenant of the kingdom. A captain-general, a chief justice, often a treasurer, he united in his own person all the cardinal attributes of rule. His duties were enlarged and his control confirmed by the Norman and early Angevin Kings, whose continual absence on the Continent made some such a deputy necessary.

But as the foreign provinces dropped away and security at home became the predominant interest, as the parliamentary idea widened, law began to have as much importance as administration. The chief exponent of the law was the Chancellor, the head of the royal clerks, the Keeper of the King's Great Seal, the chief dispenser of his patronage, and after the middle of the thirteenth century the Justiciar sinks into a judge, and the Chancellor assumes the higher place. His authority is seldom so complete as that of his predecessor, for it is shorn of its military and viceregal functions, but he presides in the Council and in Parliament, and when his influence there approaches his favour with the King, he probably becomes Chief Minister.

For three centuries the chancellorship remains pre-eminent, practically always in the hands of churchmen; but after Wolsey " no Chancellor combined the direction of the Great Seal with that of foreign policy, . . . though Gardiner recovered some shreds of his power,"* and for a few years Clarendon faintly revived it.

After the Reformation, the firmer establishment of the Legislature, and the expansion of trade and wealth, the Chancellor is displaced by the Treasurer, who typifies the power of the purse. From the time of Somerset onwards the man at the head of the exchequer is usually the most prominent member of the government; and two generations later the practice has already begun of putting the Lord Treasurer's place into commission, to divide its duties and diminish its power. But a First Lord of the Treasury does not enjoy at his own board or in council a consideration or a control equal to that of a Lord Treasurer, and it is only after the institution of Cabinet government that he attains to the later position of a Premier.

These three periods of the Justiciar, the Chancellor and the Treasurer are not entirely unbroken or always regular. At times of crisis or of crucial changes in the State, the Chief Minister often assumes an office of special authority. Simon de Montfort is High Steward during the Barons' War and the first Parliament; Suffolk, Warwick and Buckingham are Lord High Admirals in the Wars of the Roses and the wars with France; Thomas Cromwell is Vicar-General during the Reformation; Strafford is Lord-Lieutenant of Ireland in the effort to reduce England and

* Pollard, *Eng. Hist. Rev.*, 148, 533.

Scotland by force of arms. Again, after a period of anarchy, the chief control tends to revert to the lawgivers: Becket is Chancellor after the wars of Stephen, and Clarendon after the Great Rebellion.

Throughout this process the legal idea is always present: the Justiciar presides at common law, the Chancellor in equity, the Treasurer at the exchequer, while the Steward, the Privy Seal, the Marshal, and the Admiral each have a court of their own.* Thus law and finance remain constant features in the English polity, and the President of the Council rarely attains to the dignity that foreign countries accord him: he only holds a second place.

There were many Justiciars, many Chancellors and many Treasurers who were never Chief Ministers; but it is rarely difficult to distinguish who did and who did not hold the place, for there are certain conditions inherent to it. Its holder fills one of the great offices of State, he enjoys the special confidence of the Sovereign, he is paramount over his colleagues in the Council, and history seldom denies him the name. Often there is no Chief Minister for many years: strong rulers, such as William I. and III. or Oliver Cromwell, could do without them; weak ones, like Stephen, Edward II., or Richard II., could never maintain them. Thus Gaveston and the Despencers, the Dudleys and Carr, cannot aspire to the title. They had the prince's ear, as had her priests with Mary or his mistresses with Charles; but they held no predominance in the hierarchy of the State, and they owed it no responsibility. Others, like Longchamp and Glanvil, More and Gardiner, though they bulked large in their time, confined their attention to particular business, and never held an acknowledged control over their fellows. Nor do the junior members of the royal house, Thomas and John of Lancaster, Humphrey and Richard of Gloucester, John of Bedford or Richard of York, come within the category; at times they replaced the King in Council, and their relationship to him gave them high consideration with Parliament, but they never acted as the heads of a public office or definitely led the government.

* Angliæ Notitia, i. 144.

The roll, therefore, is not arbitrary, but determined by rules that are comparatively fixed, and although one or two other ministers with doubtful claims might perhaps be added to it, hardly any of those here included have rights open to dispute. Such as they are—good, bad and indifferent—all have filled the place and exercised the power of first servant of the Crown.

In early days the classes from which they were drawn were strictly limited: the ecclesiastic, schooled in law and learning, with the prestige of Rome behind him; or the noble, born and bred a ruler and a fighter, in touch with the feeling of the country. The former was guided by his education, the latter by his birth. Then as the Church lost and Parliament gained in prestige, its members monopolized the place, and from the Reformation onwards every Chief Minister, except Somerset and Buckingham, began his career in the House of Commons. These latter were all country gentlemen of a higher or lower degree of quality and fortune, but all men connected with the land.

The duties of a Chief Minister outside his own department were largely determined by himself, but in the main they were those of supervision. " Think it more honour," says Bacon, " to direct in chief than to be busy in all." His authority depended on his own personality and on his favour with the Sovereign, while as time went on his influence was modified by his relations with Parliament; but, with few exceptions, from the tenth to the eighteenth century all the Chief Ministers were chosen, maintained and dismissed by the Crown alone. " Kings must be answerable to God Almighty, to whom they are but vassals, for their actions; but Ministers, whose eyes, ears and hands they are, must be answerable to God and man."

" The choyce of Counsellours," says Hobbes, " is proper to Monarchy, and the most able Counsellours are those that have least hope of benefit by giving evill counsel, and most knowledge of those things that conduce to Peace and Defence of the Commonwealth." Over the varying fortunes of a thousand years few States can better the record of England in her principal public servants.

CHAPTER I

THE SAXONS

DUNSTAN, GODWIN AND HAROLD

IN the year 901 Alfred the Great died, leaving to his son and successor, Edward the Elder, the task of consolidating his dominions and confirming his rule. The seven Saxon kingdoms, called the Heptarchy, had existed for several centuries in a loose federation, but now at last they settled down into one state under the sceptre of a single prince. Edward's predecessors, though they had styled themselves Bretwaldas and even Autocrats of Britain, had never yet taken the title of King of the English. It was reserved for him to assume that dignity, and with it to transmit to his successors the peculiar and indigenous authority, independent of any Papal or Imperial suzerainty, that has always distinguished the island throne.

Isolated though it was, Edward's court was not barbaric or unlettered. His great-grandfather Egbert had been brought up at the court of Charlemagne, his father Alfred had visited Rome, and from them he had inherited certain conceptions of regularity, certain traditions of ceremonial, which, blended with the customary rites of his Teuton ancestors and fostered by the care of the Catholic Church, have descended through a thousand years to his posterity. The cries of assent by which the Westminster boys still greet the new King when he is presented to the people at his coronation, the ermine bars on the peers' robes, the waxen effigies in the Abbey, may well derive some part of their origin from tribal elections in Saxon forests, from the striped togas of Byzantine senators, and from the *jus imaginum* of the patricians of Rome.

6

From an MS.

DUNSTAN
ARCHBISHOP OF CANTERBURY
AT THE FEET OF CHRIST

To face page 6

Since their establishment in England in the fifth century the Saxons had adapted themselves to a humid climate, a fertile soil and an easy life. Their days were spent in the open air, in sport or pastoral pursuits, supplemented for the upper classes by copious meals and hard drinking. To hold land, with all its amenities, was the aim of everyone, for on that both comfort and consideration depended. The ownership of a gate, a kitchen, a brewery and a church, raised a man from the servile condition, and the possession of a certain number of hides made him a thane. Moot and mark, sac and soc, strond and streame, toll and team, wassail and witan, comprised Saxon interests, and their system, while recognizing the French feudal maxim that " *la vraie noblesse est fondée dans la terre,*" yet admitted the paramount claim of riches, as the English idea of aristocracy has always done. Commerce as yet occupied a minor place in their scheme, and except in one or two ports and trading centres, they mixed but little with their neighbours from overseas, content to enjoy domestic bliss at home. Thus, when hordes of hardy Norsemen, packed in their long black galleys, and driven by hunger, greed and the love of adventure, poured down on them, the softer Saxons readily went under; and it was only the genius and devotion of Alfred, the energy and courage of his son, that deferred their complete subjection to a later date.

The Saxon Church, humble and poor, had at first flourished in comparative independence, and the chains which the Popes gradually riveted upon it were largely due to the later foundation of abbeys and monasteries, owning allegiance only to Rome and exempt from the jurisdiction of the English bishops.

The King was still the elected chief of a free state, though by custom and respect the election was confined to the House of Cerdic, the most potent and most eminent of the Saxon royal families. He ruled by the advice of the Witenagemot, an assembly of wise men which met at stated intervals, usually on the greater festivals of the Church, and consisted of the principal prelates and alder-

2

men and of a certain number of the more prominent
thanes. It concerned itself with larger questions of policy,
while the local administration was carried on by the
bishops, earls and reeves. The central direction of
affairs, however, lay with the permanent members of the
royal household, the " gesiths " or companion thanes of the
King—the " *comites* " of the French monarchs—who were
always on the spot. The dignified offices that they filled,
the important duties that they discharged, had to be
honoured and rewarded, and gradually these thanes became
a titled nobility, distinct from the territorial rulers of the
shires. The Witenagemot and the royal officials thus
provided a system on which the Normans could graft their
Great Council and their Curia, while the county earls,
the councillors and the court thanes bore some faint
resemblance to the later feudal idea of peers by tenure,
writ and patent.

The business of state was not at first too onerous for
the King himself to transact, but whenever pleasure,
absence or incompetence made him need assistance, convenient helpers were to hand among his court. The greater
earls were engaged in their own governments, and might
easily become too powerful, so the King's tendency was
rather to employ priests, who were men of letters, or
friends, who owed all to his favour. The government,
however, was rarely strong, for its chief was continually
changing. In the two centuries that elapsed between the
accession of Egbert and that of Edward the Confessor no
less than twenty princes sat upon the throne. Sixteen of
these were of the House of Cerdic, and they gradually
diminished in character, vigour and prestige. They move
swiftly across the stage, the phantoms of history, best
known by their nicknames—Edward the Elder, Edward the
Martyr and Edward the Confessor, Edmund the Magnificent and Edmund Ironside, Edgar the Peaceable, Edwy
the Unruly and Ethelred the Unready. Removed from
the progress of the Continent, they were often ignorant and
idle, ready to sink to the position of puppets, and to let
their effective functions slip into the hands of an ambitious

subject. When they were without a strong minister to
guide them their realm fell an easy prey to the savage
pirates of the North, and in the last half-century of their
rule England was twice conquered, once by the Danes and
once by the Normans. But though the later princes often
lacked the talent to govern or the spirit to lead, the body
of the people remained sound, and after the dogged character and lethargic strength of the Saxon yeoman had
been inspired anew by the dash and daring of the Norman
knights, a nation grew up which comprised all the qualities of success; the " dullness of the creeping Saxons " was
cast off, and from the clash and stir of the Middle Ages no
people emerged better bred and better armed than the
English.

In the last century and a half of Saxon rule three
Chief Ministers appear. They are the first of their kind
in England, but in genius, authority and permanence they
rank among the greatest.

I.—DUNSTAN

Dunstan, the " Hill Stone " as his name signifies in Saxon,
was born near Glastonbury about the year 920, when
Edward the Elder was King of England.* His father was
Herstan, a wealthy thane of Wessex, his mother Cyne-
dreda, a noble Saxon lady. He was nephew to Athelm,
Archbishop of Canterbury, and was related by blood to
several of the leading prelates and to the royal house of
Cerdic. His breeding, his upbringing, and his future
circumstances were thus assured. His health, however,
was poor, though his energy was intense. As a boy he
suffered from brain fever, losing most of his hair, and his
highly strung nerves made him continually subject to
hallucinations and dreams. Once as a child he climbed
over the roof of a church in his sleep, and his escape without
injury was regarded as a miracle.

* Many accounts say in 924, but an earlier date seems probable.

His early days were passed in the pleasant Somerset-
shire country of his home—

> "the island valley of Avilion,
> Where falls not hail, nor rain, nor any snow,
> Deep meadowed, happy, fair with orchard lawns."

For his education he was sent to the famous monastery
that lay near. There a little colony of Irish priests had
long maintained a tradition of learning, teaching young
nobles the few liberal sciences that they possessed. Dunstan
was small and delicate, sedate in his ways, but precocious
and hardworking. Unable to excel in the ordinary sports
of his schoolfellows, he devoted himself to study. "He
strove," says Osbern, "to take part in the society of his
elders, declining the games of youth."* His ambition and
application gained him rapid success. Not only did he
read the Fathers of the Church and such of the classical
poets and historians as were available, but he ventured on
mathematics and even astronomy. His hands were as
busy as his mind, and he became a painter, an illuminator,
an excellent musician, and a skilful craftsman in metal.
It has been suggested that conjuring and ventriloquism
were also among his accomplishments.

When he was about sixteen Dunstan went on to the
court of King Athelstan, "Alfred's golden-haired grandson." He was of the highest promise, but his pro-
ficiency got him more foes than friends. Clever and good-
looking, his abilities were too patent and too exceptional
not to arouse jealousy, and he had not learnt as yet how
to become popular. He was always in the bower and
rarely in the field. On one occasion when he had gone to
help some young ladies in designing a stole, he hung his
harp on the wall. Suddenly it began to play by itself—
by what art is not determined—

> "St. Dunstan's Harp fast by the Wall
> Upon a Pin did hang-a
> The Harp itself with Ly and all
> Untouched by hand did twang-a."

---

* Mem. Dunst., 77.

The whole company was terrified and fled. "The damsels rushed out shrieking, with their mother and the servants, crying out that the man was too wise, that he knew more than he ought."*

It was soon rumoured that magic was one of his attainments, and that he practised the black art. Such charges in the tenth century were as serious as they were hard to rebut: Pope Sylvester himself nearly fell a victim to them. Athelstan was a prince of character and talents, favourably disposed to so well-connected and able a youth as Dunstan, but he was not proof against the prejudices of his age. He looked askance at the handsome young sorcerer, and Dunstan thought it best to leave the court. His exit was unfortunate. He was followed, bound hand and foot, and flung into a muddy pond—perhaps to see if he would sink or swim. Some dogs, it is said, rescued him, and in great misery and bitterness of spirit he took refuge with his cousin, the old Bishop of Winchester.

Here he was pressed to become a monk, but for a long time he resisted, for he was in love. Then an attack of illness prostrated him, and changed his views. He determined to embrace a religious life, and went off abroad to Fleury to make his profession. He came back thoroughly imbued with the ascetic spirit, and going home to Glastonbury he adopted the strenuous rôle of an anchorite. He dug himself an underground cell—a "Little Ease," Fuller calls it—where he passed long months in prayer, contemplation and work, wrestling with the flesh, and subduing his passions by the hard labour of a smith. "When it was so," says the Golden Legend, "that Saynt Dunstan was wery of prayer, then used he to werke in Goldsmyth's works with his owne handes for to eschewe ydelnes." His sanctity grew famous, legends began to gather round his name, and honestly or not, he encouraged a belief in his own supernatural powers. Evil spirits, he averred, assailed and tempted him in the form of foxes, wolves, bears and lovely maidens; but he repelled them all, and even caught hold of the devil's nose with a pair

* Mem. Dunst., 80.

of blazing tongs, making him howl with pain. "What has the bald fellow done?" " *Quid fecit iste calvus* " is said to have been Satan's wail of anguish, though history omits to state in what language he spoke.

Such tales enhanced Dunstan's reputation for piety, and also brought him more material gains. Ethelfleda, a rich widow of the royal kin, came to visit him. She sought his counsel, lodged near him, and becoming his disciple, left him her property at her death. His father's lands soon descended to him, and Dunstan found himself a wealthy man. His holiness, his learning, his riches and his generosity pointed him out as the obvious chief of his native monastery, and in 944, when still a young man, the King made him the first abbot of Glastonbury.*

King Edmund had now succeeded his brother Athelstan. His Chancellor, Thurketell, and Odo, the Archbishop of Canterbury, both knew Dunstan, and appreciated his influence and energy. He was recalled to court, and began to recover his position. Attempts were again made to oust him, both sorcery and wantonness being this time laid to his charge. But Dunstan had now potent friends, and had become a warier and stronger man. After a temporary withdrawal he returned and supported Odo in his new policy of reforming the Church by substituting clerks for canons. It was not popular, but it succeeded. The married priests were expelled, the monks were introduced, celibacy was enforced, and the ecclesiastical practice of England was brought into line with that of the Continent.

In 946 King Edmund was murdered. Edred, his brother and successor, was a personal friend of Dunstan's; and the young abbot was now made " keeper of the King's hoard." Archbishop Odo was getting old, Thurketell was soon to retire to the monastery of Croyland, and Dunstan became the actual if not the nominal Chief Minister. He was thus fairly embarked upon his career as a statesman, and for the next thirty years, with few intervals, he was to be the real ruler of the kingdom.

* Dugdale calls Britweld the first abbot; Monast. Angl., i. 12.

Already Treasurer, he next became "custodian of the royal archives" and Chancellor. In 953, when the bishopric of Winchester was offered him, he refused it, though the saints, he said, admonished him for doing so. "While thy son liveth," he told the Queen, "the mitre shall not cover my brows."* But he did not neglect the Church; and he enlarged and embellished his abbey, which was soon considered the principal seat of learning in the country. Education was always one of his first interests, while his general policy was identified with that of the aged primate, whose mind he was content to guide, and whose seat he was clearly destined to fill.

Edred's death in 955 shook Dunstan's position, and for a year or two he was under a cloud. The new King, Edwy, was a weak and dissolute youth, and at his coronation feast an incident occurred the rights of which are not clearly known. The King had left his nobles and retired to an inner chamber to pass the time, probably injudiciously, with two ladies, variously described as his wife, his mistress, and his mother-in-law. The thanes took offence at this desertion, and Dunstan, as a bold man, was given the task of recalling Edwy to the banquet. By force rather than persuasion the abbot fulfilled his mission; "blaming the women's folly, with his own hand he dragged up the unwilling King from the harlot's couch and, placing the crown on his head, led him out."† But his success cost him his place, and he had to flee the country, barely escaping the messengers who were sent to blind him. Behind this tale lay, it seems, the support accorded by Edwy to the married priests and the refusal of Dunstan to recognize the King's marriage.

Dunstan now took refuge in Flanders, at the court of Count Arnulf of Ghent, a grandson of King Alfred's. There he was assigned the monastery of Blandin as a residence, and he soon became still further attached to the principles of the Benedictines. From his vantage ground he kept in touch with his friends in England, who were now bearing the brunt of Edwy's displeasure and the Queen's revenge. Dunstan's

* Adams, 100. † Mem. Dunst. Auct. B., 33.

party had their lands sequestered and their abbeys plundered, while the monks were forced to make way for the secular clergy. But the change was not for long. His followers rallied round Edgar, Edwy's younger brother, and made him under-king of the country north of the Thames. Elgiva, the Queen, was caught, branded and hamstrung, and on her death the party of Edwy began to lose strength.

In 957 Dunstan was recalled by Edgar and made Bishop of Worcester, and shortly afterwards he also received the see of London *in commendam*. Two years later Archbishop Odo was gathered to his fathers. The first prelate who was nominated to succeed him perished in an Alpine snowstorm on his journey to Rome, and a second candidate was induced to retire. Then Edwy died, Edgar succeeded to the throne, and in 959 Dunstan was translated to the primacy.

While still under forty Dunstan thus found himself the most powerful man in England. He was Chancellor and Archbishop, he was exceptionally learned and rich, and he was already a reputed saint. He went to Rome to receive the pallium from the Pope, and on his return resumed his rule with energy and discretion. The King deferred to him in all matters of State, and though in private life Edgar was a profligate—Baker chronicles his amours with gusto—the penances that Dunstan imposed seem to have been well tempered with mercy. Yet at times the Archbishop could be a stern judge, and he did not hesitate, when a wealthy thane had invoked the aid of Rome against him, to withstand even the Pope. His sway was unquestioned—"There was no one in the whole realm of the English who moved hand or foot without his order"*—but it was comprehensive, peaceful and beneficent. During the sixteen years of Edgar's reign, "Northumbria was divided up into earldoms instead of kingdoms; the Danes were subdued or conciliated; the sovereignty of the Anglo-Saxon King over the Scots was established; the navy was placed in such a state of

* Osb., 95.

efficiency that no enemy ventured to attack the coast . . . piracy was abolished, trade was encouraged, family feuds were suppressed . . . regular circuits were established for the administration of justice . . . standard measures were made."* On one occasion, to illustrate his power, Edgar even forced eight vassal kings to row him along the River Dee.

But this era of triumph was not to last. In 975 the King died, and there was some difficulty in proclaiming his young son Edward. Elfrith, the new King's stepmother, had determined that her own child should succeed, and the weight of her power was thrown against Dunstan. The Archbishop's influence began to decline, and the secular party again raised its head. Latterly he had been much more conciliatory to the married priests and had not treated them with undue severity. Now, however, he was compelled again to take sides, and it was during the disputes between the rival leaders that the best known of his miracles are said to have occurred. At Winchester, when the policy opposed to Dunstan's was mooted, a crucifix hanging in the church exclaimed twice: "Let it not be done" —*Absit ut hoc fiat.* In 977 the matter was again argued in a meeting of the Witan at Calne, and on this occasion the floor of an upper chamber, in which the magnates were assembled, fell bodily in, and many were killed or maimed. Dunstan, however, and his attendants remained safely seated on a beam, and were quite uninjured. His critics have seen in these events mechanical tricks, his apologists Divine providence.

In 979 Edward was murdered by the arts of Elfrith, and in the following year Dunstan crowned the unlucky Ethelred. Of this prince he never had any opinion, owing, it is said, to an unpleasant accident at his baptism which had caused the Archbishop to rate him as a poltroon.† At the coronation Dunstan foretold an evil reign, and then, as Ethelred paid little attention to his advice, he gradually retired from politics. He now confined himself to the work of his province and his diocese, and under his

* Hook, i. 409.   † Fuller, Hist., i. 135.

rule Canterbury grew steadily in temporal power, the archbishop gradually displacing the Kentish earldorman. In
his later days he turned again to building, to prayer,
teaching and harmony. The chroniclers show him as a
venerable and lovable figure surrounded by penitents and
children engaged in writing music and correcting books.
But, politically, his credit had sunk low, and on May 19,
988, he died " not so much of old age as of grief and
vexation " at his fall.*

He was buried in his own metropolitan church, though
Glastonbury in subsequent ages used to claim his body.
He was not yet seventy, though for more than a generation
he had been primate. He had lived under eight Kings,
served seven, and crowned three. Twice he had been
banished the court, once driven into exile, often he had
been near death. To a delicate constitution and a nervous
mentality such experiences equalled many years, and he
had never spared himself.

> " A fiery soul which working out its way
> Fretted the pygmy body to decay."

There are one or two portraits of him in illuminated
missals, how far authentic it is hard to say. A drawing of
him in the Bodleian Library is perhaps by his own hand.
Of his script there are two examples—*qui textus Dunstani
dicitur* † — though the literary productions formerly
assigned to him are now discredited. But the tune,
" *Gaudent in cœlis animæ sanctorum*," the chant which
his harp is said to have played on the wall, is still believed
to have been his own composition.

Of the histories of Dunstan one or two are almost contemporary. Like later accounts they are coloured with
fantastic legends and disproportionate praise or blame,
but from all there emerges a clear picture. It is that of a
practical man—in private life kind, conciliatory, studious,
liberal and " easily moved to tears "; in public affairs a
wise counsellor, a firm ruler, a formidable ally or opponent.
" His whole work," says Osbern, " was devoted to his

* Rapin, i. 118.   † Dugdale, Monast. Angl., i. 15.

country, and more to withstanding her damage than his own danger."* To weld together Danes and Saxons, to make the clergy real teachers and leaders of the people, to ensure peace to his country—such was his policy. In his life-time he succeeded, but immediately after his death the Northmen burst upon England, the Danegeld was instituted, and Danish and Norman dynasties soon ousted the ancient race of Cerdic. For nearly three centuries his countrymen magnified the golden days of Dunstan, and the peaceful Saxon prelate thus became a national hero. He was canonized by the Roman Church as a Confessor, and in 1017 the observance of Saint Dunstan's Day, May 19th, was enjoined by Canute. The proverb with which it is associated—"Before Dunstan no summer; after Dunstan no winter"—marks a division in the seasons of the year—perhaps a division in the history of England.

Dunstan is one of the most striking figures in early English annals—an historical personage of the first importance. "His position is in the front rank of ecclesiastical statesmen, such as Becket, Wolsey, Laud, Richelieu and Mazarin. . . ." With many and great faults he was "a good and virtuous man."† "The noblest tribute to his rule," says Green, "lies in the silence of our chroniclers."‡

His days are distant, and his records, plentiful in volume, are scanty in substance, but it is not difficult to form some idea of the man. A well-born, forward and imaginative child, nurtured in the very home of national traditions—whither Joseph had brought the Holy Grail, where Arthur was buried, where St. Patrick had taught— he flung himself with youthful ardour into study and handicraft. Then he moved on to the Saxon court, but there his arts were eyed with little favour, and bred only envy. Neither a hunter, a fighter nor a trencherman, his delicate mind and body sought the society of women. The worst construction was put upon his acts, and unpopularity and ostracism followed. He fled to solitude,

* Osb., 110. † Hook, i. 402, 403. ‡ Green, i. 95.

and almost succumbed to illness. When he recovered he had become an enthusiast, but an enthusiast with a harder and a more material ambition. He turned his talents to more practical uses, and his visions moved hand in hand with his dexterity.

The legends of Orpheus and Amphion, of Vulcan and Venus, were perhaps unknown to him, but those of the saints were always in his mind. His imagination was exalted, and miracles came when they were expected. How much of the devil-mongering and the seraphic psalms was true and how much false it is difficult to say. When the crucifix spoke at Winchester, was it Dunstan's ventriloquism? When the floor collapsed at Calne, was it Dunstan's mechanics? The answers are lost in the limbo of ages. But whatever the means, the ends were not ignoble, for the man's spirit was alive and his conscience sound. When power came to him he showed himself made of true metal; in Stubbs' words, " a constructor not a destroyer, a consolidator not a theorist— his career was the very counterpart of that of Gerbert, the student, the practical workman, the statesman, the reformer and the patriot."* Promotion of intercourse with the Continent and the advancement of learning were the keynotes of his policy.

After the lapse of a thousand years his name still lives among his countrymen. A saint and a sorcerer, a sage and a seer, a Chancellor and a craftsman, a subject of the "Ingoldsby Legends" and a patron of the Goldsmiths' Company, he is the hero of countless popular tales and the first national minister in England. Pious, learned, bold and adroit, he served his country well, and by his insistence on order, restraint and education, he advanced it in the comity of nations and left a notable example for those who followed him as its leaders.

* Mem. Dunst., cviii.-cxx.; Traill, i. 236.

II.—GODWIN.

Godwin, the "Well-loved," was born about the year 988, probably in Wiltshire. The history of his origin is exceptionally confused, and though the different accounts have been collated by many experts the result remains uncertain. It is clear, however, that he was the son of one Wulnoth, who was probably a South Saxon noble, but perhaps only a yeoman in comfortable circumstances and connected with families of some repute.

Of Godwin's childhood nothing is known, but a tale found in nearly all the chroniclers says that in July 1016, after Canute's defeat by Edmund Ironside near Sherstone, the Danish earl Ulf, who had lost his way, met Godwin wandering in the forest. Ulf asked him for shelter and offered him a golden ring. After some demur Godwin took him to his father Wulnoth's house, fed and lodged him, and next day rode with him to Canute's ships at Southampton.*

Godwin was a young man of good appearance and address: Ulf was grateful to him and presented him to Canute: the latter was attracted by his manner or discerned his merits, and attached him to his court. Within a year Canute had become King of England. Godwin was a man after his own heart, pleasant, brisk and efficient. In a short time he had risen to the rank of a military leader and a councillor, and before 1018 he had been made an earl, probably of Kent. In 1019 he accompanied Canute to Denmark, and in one of the expeditions against the Wends he led the English contingent with remarkable courage and success. Canute promoted him still further, married him to Gytha, the sister of Earl Ulf, who was his own brother-in-law, and in 1020 appointed him Earl of the West Saxons—a title which no man had borne before.†

This office gave Godwin control over all the shires of the old Wessex kingdom, and there he enjoyed an

* Turner, i. 285 *et seq.* † Freeman, Norm. Conq., i. 425.

almost independent position. Green calls him "the
Viceroy or Justiciar of the King," and by some writers
he is also styled Treasurer.* Whatever his exact dignity
may have been, he soon became Canute's principal minister,
his deputy when he was abroad, and the first subject in the
realm. His wealth increased greatly, and his possessions
extended into nearly every county of the south and
centre of England.† He was apt, active and sagacious.
In the " *Vita Edwardi* " he is described as " most cautious
in counsel, most agreeable from his even manners, incomparable in his attention to business, affable and cheerful
to all " . . . and William of Malmesbury lays stress on
his eloquence—*Mirus dicere, mirus populo persuadere, quæ
placerent.*‡

For the next fifteen years Godwin prospered exceedingly. He kept England quiet while Canute, fought
in Scandinavia. The father of seven sons, he became
the richest and most powerful of all the earls, the
national representative of the Saxons, their constant
shield and protector with the Danish King, and that
King's loyal and trusted lieutenant. The country was
at peace, the people contented, the minister popular,
though to some he seemed " almost more Dane than
Saxon."

In 1035 Canute died. He had married Emma, the
Norman widow of Ethelred II., by whom she already
had two sons, Edward and Alfred. To Canute late in
life she bore Hardicanute. By Elgiva, an earlier wife or
concubine, Canute had had another child, Harold, though
the latter was held by many not to be his son. Thus
there were several possible claimants to the crown.

Canute's British dominions were at first divided between
his own two children. Harold was the candidate of
the Danes and the North of England, Hardicanute of the
Saxons and the South. Godwin in Winchester supported
Emma and her son Hardicanute, acting as their minister

---

* Green, i. 103.
† Freeman, i. 426.
‡ Edw. Conf., 392; Freeman, i. 409, note.

and treasurer—*regias gazas custodiens.** Terms, however, were arranged, and though Hardicanute kept Wessex,
Harold became in effect the King.

The next year the two Saxon ethelings, Edward and
Alfred, came over from Normandy and tried to recover
their inheritance. They were invited, it was said, by their
mother, but their venture had no success. Many of their
followers were captured and killed, and though Edward
escaped, Alfred was seized, blinded, and soon afterwards
died at Ely. In this business Godwin took an important
part, and there are various versions of it. Some say that
he met Alfred at Guildford, swore fealty to him, and then,
having seized him in the night, sent him to the King and
massacred five hundred of his men. Others absolve
him from all but a proper defence of the land against
foreign invaders, and place the blame for the treatment
of Alfred on Harold.† Queen Emma's share in the
affair is dark and dubious.

The " Saxon Chronicle," speaking of Alfred, says:

> " But Godwine him then let
> And him in prison set;
> And his companions he dispersed;
> And some divers ways slew,
> Some they for money sold
> Some cruelly slaughtered."‡

It seems probable that Godwin, anxious to conciliate
Harold's favour, allowed his messengers to carry off Alfred,
and did not concern himself with what happened afterwards. But whatever the exact truth, for the rest of
his life the crime was imputed to him, and it seriously
affected his future.

Four years later, when Harold was dead and Hardicanute had succeeded to the throne of the whole kingdom,
he accused Godwin of being the cause of Alfred's murder.
Godwin appeared before the Witan to clear himself,
and the Danes then swore that what he had done had
been at Harold's orders. Godwin was formally acquitted,
but it is significant that he at once made a magnificent

---

* Thierry, i. 235, note.   † Duchesne, 173.
‡ Anglo-Saxon Chron., 95.

present to the King—" a ship with a beak of gold, manned
with eighty chosen warriors, splendidly equipped."* As a
rule he was a receiver rather than a giver of gifts.

In 1042 Hardicanute died in a fit at dinner, and by
Godwin's influence the etheling Edward, afterwards called
the Confessor, was chosen King—" *Eall folc geceas
Eadward to cynge.*" Delicate, white-haired, gentle and
religious, Edward had been bred and educated in
Normandy. His mother was a Norman; his cousin was
Duke of Normandy; and his sympathies lay very largely
in that country. Godwin feared the connection, and one
of his conditions had been that Edward should wed his
daughter Edith. Her beauty, her intellect and her piety
are admitted even by the Norman writers—" *Sicut spina
rosam, genuit Godwinus Editham.*"† For reasons of
policy Edward consented to the union, but though the
marriage took place it is doubtful if it was ever con-
summated, and it certainly was never happy. Sober
saint as he was, Edward could be harsh in his own household, and his blameless wife had many burdens to bear.

Under the new reign the rest of Godwin's family throve.
His eldest son Sweyn was made earl of three shires in
Mercia; Harold, his second son, Earl of East Anglia;
Tostig, the third, was to marry the Count of Flanders'
daughter. They were all " *thaes Cynges dyrlingas,*"
" the King's darlings," and the influence of their father
remained supreme. " South of a line from the Wash
to the Severn, Godwin and his family were the virtual
rulers of all England."‡

But Edward hankered after his early friends, and
resented the domination of his wife's Saxon relations.
His English patriotism was doubtful, his character petu-
lant, irresponsible, almost childish. There was nothing
he would not promise from the exigency of the times.§
All his efforts were turned to bringing in Normans and
promoting them in his court—*Quiconque sollicitait en
langue Normande n'essuyait jamais un refus.*‖ In 1044

* Freeman, i. 516.   † Adams, 140.   ‡ *Ibid.*, 140.
§ Bell, xlii. 43.   ‖ Thierry, i. 254.

GODWIN

EARL OF WESSEX

WITH EDWARD THE CONFESSOR AND QUEEN EDITH

To face page 22

he succeeded in appointing Robert of Jumièges, a Norman abbot, to the see of London. Godwin, who hated Normans, had bitterly opposed this. The new bishop now assured the King that it was Godwin who was really responsible for the death of his brother Alfred, and the King was not disinclined perhaps to believe it. Other events also began to affect Godwin's influence. In 1046 his son Sweyn seduced the abbess of Leominster, for which he was outlawed. With some difficulty Godwin got the sentence set aside. A year later he tried to enlist Edward's help overseas for Swend, King of Denmark, who was a nephew of Godwin's wife. The Witan, however, refused, and a second request in 1048 met with no better result. Soon after this Sweyn suddenly returned to England and cruelly murdered his cousin Beorn, Earl of Hertford. For this act he was again outlawed and proclaimed " nithing," the worst disgrace that could be put upon a Saxon noble. Such scandals and rebuffs damaged Godwin's prestige, and the Norman party were not slow to turn them to advantage.

In 1050 the Saxon Archbishop of Canterbury died, and Robert of Jumièges, despite Godwin's opposition, was raised to the primacy. He had been a constant critic of the Earl's policy, and the nearness of their lands in Kent now provided more personal sources of quarrel. In the summer of the following year the King's brother-in-law, Count Eustace of Boulogne, was returning to France from a visit to the English court. On his journey he attacked the men of Dover, apparently without reason. They retaliated and slew several of his escort. Eustace complained, and Godwin was ordered by the King to " harry the town of Dover " as a punishment. This he refused to do, asking that the offenders should be judged by law. Edward was incensed at the reply, and summoning a Witan at Gloucester he accused Godwin of disobedience. Godwin then called the men of his shires together, while the King, aided by Siward and Leofric, the chief northern earls, collected troops to meet him. By mediation civil war was averted, but Godwin was directed to appear

3

unarmed at Westminster and to sue for pardon. He
came up to his house in Southwark, but there " his men
melted away ever the longer he stayed." Then one night
his friend Bishop Stigand warned him of danger: "the King
was waiting to entrap him and to break his power." On
hearing this, Godwin leapt to his feet, overturned the table,
called for his horses and rode off to the coast. There with
his wife and two of his sons he took ship for Flanders. He
was at once outlawed by Edward, who seized his goods
and lands, and at the same time Queen Edith was disgraced and banished the court. To the people at large, so
rapid a fall of so great a family seemed well-nigh incredible.

But Godwin was a man of wide experience and connection. He had not ruled England for thirty years for
nothing. He established himself in Bruges, and bided
his time. The King of France and the Count of Flanders
interceded for him. Then, as this was of no avail, he got
together some ships, and in conjunction with his son Harold,
who had gone to Ireland, he appeared off the coast of
Dorset. At first the King's fleet drove him away, but at
his second attempt he sailed along the southern littoral
from port to port, welcomed by all his people. " We will
live and die with Earl Godwin " was their cry. In September 1052 he entered the mouth of the Thames. This
time the King's squadron missed him, and he arrived off
Southwark to find all London in his favour. At the news
of his coming the Norman prelates and courtiers had fled
in terror, while his friends now came in from all sides to
support him. An assembly was held outside the city;
Godwin again made compurgation for his past misdeeds,
and Edward thought it best to compromise and to restore
him to favour.

But Godwin's absence had been big with fate, and his
triumph was to be short. While he had been in Bruges
William of Normandy had visited his kinsman, King
Edward, and had obtained a promise of the reversion of the
English crown. Fourteen years later he was to make it good.

His recent experiences had shaken Godwin, who was
ailing and ageing. At Easter next year, when dining with

the King at Winchester, he was suddenly seized with a fit. Later legends say that he had just called God to witness his innocence of Alfred's murder, and that he choked at the oath. But whatever the cause, the result was fatal. His sons carried him into the King's inner room, and there, three days later, he died. He was buried at Winchester. Of his sons Harold succeeded to his principal honours, but his male issue, so far as is known, is long extinct, though his name still lives in the Goodwin Sands.

Godwin was a man of consummate talents. " Shrewd, eloquent, an active administrator, he united vigilance, industry and caution with a singular dexterity in the management of men."* Originally chosen by Canute as a strong and useful link with the Saxons, he gradually became their champion against the oppression of the later Danish princes and the Normanizing tendencies of Edward. But while he was loyal to his countrymen, he was no less loyal to the King. Whether or not he was primarily concerned in the death of the etheling Alfred it is hard to say, but, if he was, he was only dealing with the King's enemies in the usual manner of the day.

The Saxon chronicles all celebrate his merits—especially his discretion, his wit and his temper, though they complain of his greed. There is a tale of his obtaining the village of Bosham, which illustrates his character. He went up to the archbishop, who owned the port but would not part with it, and said: " *Da mihi Bosham.*" The archbishop, misunderstanding " *Bosham* " for " *basium*," gave him the kiss of peace. Godwin then explained his mispronunciation to the primate, and got what he wanted. There is, indeed, little doubt that he was grasping. " Already master of the wealthiest part of England, by purchase, bargain, or suit, he added district after district to his house."†

> " *Par plaiz et par achatz*
> *De grant aver ont fait purchaz.*" ‡

Nor was he very liberal to the Church: " He did all too little penance for the property of God which he held

* Green, i. 103.   † *Ibid.*, i. 104.   ‡ Edw. Conf., 1137.

belonging to many holy places."* Among the higher classes he was not popular, for the long habit of rule had made him inconsiderate of others, while the wish to advance his family led him to discount their misdeeds. Edward always disliked his control, and was ready to listen to his enemies, while the Saxon earls and the Norman bishops were jealous of him.

The public policy that Godwin had to pursue throughout his life was one of defence: first against the rough rule of the Danes, and then against the more subtle influence of the Normans. This reacted on his character, and enhanced the faults of an already careful nature. Of Edward, the mild creature that he had set on the throne, he had little opinion. Edward had never treated his daughter well, and had abstained from giving him a grandchild to inherit the kingdom. Canute, a fierce warrior and a real ruler, had been content to take his advice—why should this simple saint think himself a better man than the Danish Viking?

Thus the years passed by, and in his old age Godwin became less conciliating, more inclined to engross power and riches. The appointment of a Norman to the primacy marked the beginning of his decline. Accidents alienated sympathy from him, his enemies were constant and active, and, like others, he made mistakes. But in the main he was "essentially cautious and fair, without levity or haste"—a statesman of broad views. The first great Englishman who was neither a prince nor a priest, he had guided the strength of Canute, moderated the harshness of his sons, and sustained the weakness of Edward. For over a generation he had maintained his country in peace, striving for her welfare and liberty, fortifying her for the tribulations that were to come.† The father, father-in-law and uncle of kings, he might have been a king himself. He was content to be a Chief Minister, but a Chief Minister of the highest order. Steadfast, skilful and strong, he was a father to his flock; he well deserved their gratitude, and in after years his unhappy countrymen often recalled with pride and regret their "*Dux felicis memoriæ.*"

* Anglo-Saxon Chronicle, 107.   † Freeman, Norm. Conq., ii. 353.

III.—HAROLD

Harold, afterwards Earl of Wessex and King of England, was born about 1022, the second son of Earl Godwin and his wife Gytha, a sister of the Danish Earl Ulf. Half a Saxon and half a Dane, of noble blood, splendid strength and brilliant beauty, he united in his person all the Saxon virtues. Of his early life nothing is known beyond a legend of a boyish fight with his brother Tostig, but long before he had come of age he was regarded as the hope of his family.

In 1044, directly after the accession of Edward the Confessor, his advancement began. The King was married to his sister, his father was the Chief Minister, and Harold, though only twenty-three years of age, was appointed Earl of the East Angles. It was a great position which he adorned and improved. His Danish blood recommended him to the inhabitants of a country where many came of Danish stock, while the example of his father and his own nature spurred him on to justify the choice. He was soon known as a just and kindly ruler, popular, generous and brave; and when in 1045 his elder brother Sweyn was banished, Harold received a part of the Mercian earldom. With Sweyn's lawless character he had no sympathy, and the latter's return from exile commended itself to him still less. With his younger brother Tostig, Harold had been sent in command of two of the King's ships against pirates, and during their expedition Sweyn murdered his cousin, Earl Beorn. This cruelty and deceit enraged Harold still more, and after burying Beorn at Winchester he declared himself definitely against Sweyn, " contending that he should not be held worthy."* Sweyn again fled abroad, and soon afterwards died. Thenceforward Harold was the eldest son and the active spirit of the family.

In 1051 came the King's quarrel with Godwin. Harold joined his father in Gloucestershire and went with him to the Witenagemot in London. But when Godwin escaped

* Anglo-Saxon Chronicle, 100.

to Flanders, Harold with his brother Leofwine rode off
to Bristol and crossed to Dublin. " As he went out from
Avonmouth he met with such heavy weather that with
difficulty he got away."* He spent the winter in Ireland
with Dermot, King of Leinster, keeping in correspondence
with Godwin in Bruges and his party in England. In
the spring he raised a force of Irish and Danish settlers
and descended on the north coast of Somerset. There,
near Porlock, he fought the local thanes, slaying thirty,
and then sailed round to Portland, where he joined his
father. Their combined fleet went on to London, the
King's Norman advisers took flight, peace was made,
and again the family of Godwin "sat down in their
possessions."

Next year, in April 1053, Godwin met his death at the
King's table at Winchester. Harold, who was present,
succeeded to his lands and his earldom of Wessex, resigning his own to Ælfgar. Eight years of experience and his
father's recent victory over Edward had made him the
most prominent man in the kingdom, while his own
natural talents and physical qualities fitted him to wield
all Godwin's power. " Tall and stalwart, comely and
gentle, he drew men's eyes and hearts towards him."†
From this time until his election as King some twelve
years later he was virtual ruler of the land. He is styled
dux, subregulus, Aldermannus totius Angliæ.‡

Harold was now thirty-one years of age. He was not
yet married, but by his mistress, " Edith of the Swan neck,"
a lovely lady of Norfolk, he already had several children.
His wealth was great, his territorial sway wide, his influence
with his younger brothers and his brother-in-law the King
was supreme. True to the policy of his house, he continued
to extend his control, but with more moderation and
diplomacy than his father. Thus his appointment as
Chief Minister was welcomed by the English, for his
qualities appealed to all. His record was sound, and his
name honoured; his rule had been just and pacific, and

* Anglo-Saxon Chronicle, 108.   † Low, 537.
            ‡ Dugdale, Orig. Jurid., 20.

he had few foreign sympathies. Some, it is true, accused him of being double-faced :—

> " *Grantz fu, e apertz e beus,*
> *Mes meins kil ne parut leus* " ;*

but the charge has little to support it.

Like his father, he opposed the influx of Normans, but he exercised discretion, and men of good character were allowed to hold office about the court, although the bishoprics and earldoms were reserved for natives. " The policy of Edward's reign was . . . the policy of Harold,"† but obedience and not dictation was his attitude to the King. He was a conciliator, a more modern and a more moderate man than his father. " If he erred, his error lay in too great a toleration of the dangerous intruders."‡

The first years of his ministry were years of war. Macbeth in Scotland and Griffith in Wales were disturbing the peace. Siward, the old Earl of Northumbria, had recently died, and Edward, with the approval of Harold and the Queen, had given the earldom to Tostig, Godwin's third son. Tostig was a closer friend of the King's than was Harold; but though a capable man he was idle and hard.

Harold himself dealt with the southern troubles, and in 1056 he made peace with the Welsh and fortified the border. A year later the Hereford earldom was added to his own, his authority thus extending across the kingdom.

About this time the etheling Edward came on a visit to the English court, and while there he suddenly died. This left an unknown prince in Hungary as heir to the throne. Nothing was done to recall him, and though the King was believed to have promised the succession to his kinsman, the Duke of Normandy, the idea was unpopular, and it was probably at this time that Harold's possible candidature was first publicly thought of.

In 1058 Harold went to Rome. It was the fashionable pilgrimage of the day, but he treated it in a serious manner,

---

* Edw. Conf., 4077-8.   † Freeman, Norm. Conq., ii. 359.
‡ *Ibid.*, ii. 361.

combining instruction and politics with religion. Like all Edward's court, he spoke French well, and he spent four months on his journey studying the characters and manners of the princes through whose lands he passed. " None of them," says the author of the " *Vita Edwardi*," " could afterwards mislead him."* At Rome he obtained from Pope Benedict the pallium for his friend, Archbishop Stigand. He also brought back with him various relics and treasures to decorate the magnificent shrine he was building at Waltham, for, unlike his father, he was a devoted bene- factor of the Church. In 1060 his new foundation was consecrated in the presence of the King and Queen.

In 1062 another rebellion broke out in Wales, and Harold again led an army against Griffith. This time his methods were less restrained than before. In company with Tostig he ravaged the land from dyke to sea, defeated the Welsh in a number of engagements, and by a merciless policy succeeded in reducing them to order. By the summer of the following year the outbreak was crushed, and Griffith's head and the beak of his ship were sent by Harold to King Edward. Cruel as was this expedition, its efficacy and the excellence of its strategy are admitted even by the Norman writers, who ascribe the tranquillity of Wales for the following century to its results.

After the campaign Harold reverted to his regular duties of government. With the exception of part of Mercia, his family were the lieutenants of all the provinces; both in military and civil affairs he was the King's principal representative and most trusted counsellor, and most men now looked to him as the natural successor to the throne.

In 1064 he went over to Normandy, it is not clear for what purpose, whether business or pleasure; perhaps it was as the result of an arrangement between Edward and William. Though he took his hawks and hounds, he did not intend to be absent for any long time; but off the coast of Ponthieu he was wrecked and taken prisoner by the local lord, Count Guy. Harold at once appealed to William, who was Guy's suzerain, and William sent to

* Edw. Conf., 410.

enforce his release. The duke was well aware of Harold's strength as a possible rival, and profited from his chance.

Harold joined William at Rouen, and with him fought in several forays against Count Conan of Brittany. His prowess and bodily strength in this campaign are shown in the Bayeux Tapestry, where, single-handed, he lifts sinking Normans out of a quicksand, " *Hic Haroldus Dux trahebat eos de arena.*"* At Bayeux he was knighted by William, and it is said that there or at Rouen he swore on some holy relics—more holy than he was aware—to support William's claim to the English crown at Edward's death, and to marry William's daughter. The tale is variously given, embellished by the Normans, excused by the Saxons; but in any event it seems that the oath was made under duress, for Harold was entirely in William's power.

After this damaging transaction Harold was allowed to return to England. Soon after his arrival he at last married, taking as his wife Aldgyth, the widow of King Griffith of Wales, and the sister of Edwin, Earl of Mercia, and of Morcar, who were grandsons of Leofric, Godwin's old rival. This strange alliance brought Harold into closer touch with the Mercians than he had hitherto been, while the quarrel with William that his action must necessarily entail made him more anxious to obtain their support. But it is not clear that he relinquished his mistress, Edith.

In the following year, 1065, the people of Northumbria revolted against Tostig. His rule had been extremely harsh; he had lived continually at the King's court, leaving his province for long periods; and latterly he had been a party to the murder of some northern thanes. Harold met the Northumbrian leaders at Northampton and " tried to arrange an accommodation, but they all unanimously refused, and outlawed Tostig and all who had taken part in his unjust government."† Tostig was then banished, apparently with Harold's assent (some chroniclers allege a long-standing rivalry between them), and Morcar, Harold's new brother-in-law, received the Northumbrian earldom. The whole of this business —the marriage with Aldgyth,

* Bayeux Tapestry, xxi.   † Florence of Worcester, 294.

the alliance with Edwin and Morcar, and the transfer of Northumbria to them—marks the first overt move of Harold for the English throne, and it coincides with the failing health of Edward.

A few months later the King came up to Westminster for the consecration of his lately-founded Abbey, and there, on January 5, 1066, he died in St. Edward's, afterwards the Painted Chamber. He left the crown, it is said, to Harold, entrusting the Queen to his care. *Porrecta manu ad fratrem Haroldum, " Hanc, inquit, cum omni regno tutandam committo "*—the gesture is shown in the Bayeux Tapestry, but the reference of the words is not so clear.

Harold's position was strong, and he held most of the cards in his hand. He had the apparent approval of his predecessor, he was on the spot, and he already ruled most of England. The Witan at once met to elect him King, and he was crowned on the same day. It has been suggested that there was some uncertainty as to the choice—" The English were moved by different wishes, though openly all wished well to Harold,"[†] but probably, as Lytton remarks, " All must have been settled long before the election."[‡]

For the moment matters looked secure, but there were plenty of clouds on the horizon. William was not a man to be set aside easily: Tostig was angry and in exile; Edwin and Morcar were bound to Harold by less strong ties than his brothers. A year earlier four of the great earldoms had been in the hands of the House of Godwin and only one in those of the House of Leofric. Now Leofric's grandsons held the two largest and most contiguous, while Harold had to reckon on the enmity of his brother. He was hampered also by his oath to William, by the fact that he was not of royal blood, and by the refusal of the men of the north to recognize him, although he had been crowned by their own archbishop. But he was a resolute man, he was confident in himself, and he began his reign with the confidence of his people.

* Freeman, Norm. Conq., iii. 14, note.   † Freeman, iii. 20.
‡ Lytton, " Harold," note P.

Bayeux Tapestry.

HAROLD
EARL OF WESSEX
CROWNED KING OF ENGLAND

To face page 32

In the following nine months events moved rapidly. William first sent over a herald to remind Harold of his promises. Harold absolved himself, saying that they had been given when he was not a free agent. To curb the disaffection in the north he then hastened to York and persuaded the thanes to agree to his election. In April he was back at Westminster, where the Easter festivities were marred by a comet " which shone for seven nights," and was looked upon as an evil omen. News next came that Tostig had allied himself with William and that a fleet was preparing in Normandy to enforce the duke's claims. Harold replied by " gathering as great a ship army and land army as no king here before had done."*

In May Tostig crossed over and ravaged the southern parts of England, but on Harold's approach he sailed up the east coast and was beaten off by Edwin and Morcar, the two northern earls. He then fled to Scotland, and Harold went back to London.

During the summer Harold occupied himself with making ready in every way for the expected invasion, while similar preparations went on in the Norman harbours. But by September the needs of the harvest and the expense of maintaining his troops in idleness compelled him to demobilize them, for " to assemble such a force was to bring labour to a standstill."† He therefore sent his men home and again returned to London, but only to hear now that Harold Hardrada, King of Norway, had landed with an immense force near York. The Norwegians had gone first with 300 ships to the Orkneys, and had then been joined by Tostig in the Tyne. They next sailed up the Humber, heavily defeated Edwin and Morcar, and captured York.

Harold was ill with the gout, but he had not a moment to lose. He went first to King Edward's shrine, where he was miraculously healed:—

" *Mais par Saint Aedward la gute*
A une nuit se asuaga tuite."‡

---

* Anglo-Saxon Chronicle, 117. † Green, i. 112.

‡ Edw. Conf., 21.

Then he turned to action. He sent his fleet up the coast and marched rapidly north himself, "resting neither day nor night."* On September 25 he met the men of Norway at Stamford Bridge. To Tostig he offered his old earldom, but to his ally only "seven feet of English ground." The battle was joined, and after a long day's fight the invaders were utterly beaten, both Tostig and the King of Norway, the last of the Vikings, being slain.

Harold, who had lost many men himself, celebrated his victory at York, and there, after dinner on October 1, he received the fatal tidings of William's landing at Pevensey with his Norman host. Again he posted south, and by October 5 he was in London. He had his body-guard of house carles with him, and a considerable array from the eastern and southern counties had joined him on the march; but the two northern earls, his brothers-in-law, had refused to follow him, and their defection meant a serious loss of numbers. His brother Gyrth urged him not to fight until his troops were all assembled, but rather to harry the country round William: but this Harold refused: "Never," he said, "will I burn an English village or an English house."†

On October 12 he left for Hastings, and halted his army on the last spur of the downs across the London road, just north of where Battle Abbey now stands. Two days later, "at the place of the hoar apple tree," was fought the fight of Senlac or Hastings, which was to determine the future of England. Harold's battle position was strong, and he had fortified it well. At their first attack the Normans were beaten off, though Harold's brothers, Gyrth and Leofwine, were killed; but by a simulated flight, William enticed the Saxon right wing into a pursuit. The heavily armed Norman cavalry was then able to engage the Saxon centre at better odds, and gradually to reduce them, though suffering severely themselves. The Saxons, who were all on foot, resisted manfully, shouting their battle cries:—

" *Olicrosse sovent crioent*
E Godemite reclamoent,"

---

* Freeman, iii. 361.   † Roman de Rou, 12080.

are the remarkable words of the contemporary Norman *trouvère*.* Harold, fighting valiantly with his two-handed axe, kept up the defence until the evening. Then, by a chance arrow shot upwards, he was wounded in the eye. He sank in an agony, and his fall caused a panic. A charge of Norman knights captured his Golden Dragon standard, and about twilight four of them rode in and despatched him. His death finished the battle, the Saxons dispersed, and the Conqueror " sat down to eat and drink among the dead."

The slaughter had been so great, the corpses so mangled, that Harold's body could not be found, though his mother offered to buy it at its weight in gold; at last his old love, Edith of the Swan neck, recognized it, and after being buried on the seashore it was finally entombed at Waltham. But for many years his countrymen believed that he was still alive, and legends told of him as a hermit and a wanderer into the twelfth century.

By both his mistress and his wife Harold left several children. Their names are known, but neither their history nor their descendants. His lands and wealth, all the vast possessions of the House of Godwin, were distributed to Norman knights; while his family, which had ruled England for half a century, had to flee the country.†

Harold was forty-four years of age at his death. His height, strength and beauty are testified to by all. He was fair-haired and blue-eyed, genial and dexterous, his manners engaging, his scholarship sufficient, his piety real. He was, it seems, over free in his amours, over jealous of his brothers—but except for these pitfalls, which were to be his ruin, he had a singularly fine character. The Norman chroniclers concur in his detraction, calling him a supplanter, a debaucher and an oath-breaker; the Saxons and the moderns unite in his praise. Yet circumstance was the key of his career. Dowered by fortune with every good gift, fate still played into his hands. The death of Sweyn left him his father's heir, that of the etheling Edward removed a rival, that of the King placed the

* Roman de Rou, 13119.   † Freeman, Norm. Conq., iv. 159, 245.

crown within his grasp. His claim by birth was as good or as bad as William's, his claim by election and service far better. But when he had laid his plans, with much in his favour, his brother and his wife's brothers brought about his fall: their envy had perhaps some excuse.

As a statesman and a captain Harold was a brilliant type of what the Saxon race could produce, inspired by all their love of liberty and courage, free from the inordinate slavery to feasting and hunting that had latterly been their curse. As a minister " he always faithfully obeyed his rightful lord in words and deeds, nor neglected anything which was needful to his Sovereign."* As a King he devoted himself to his country, for he realized that the good of his people was the first of his duties. Of all the Kings of England who have fallen in battle, none fell in a more national cause, a more dramatic setting or a more historic moment than the Last of the Saxons.

Such were the leaders who ruled England a thousand years ago. All of native blood, all wealthy and well born, all from the heart of the West Country, they were English to the core. Their tenure of office was long, their power great, their leading trait a sober, strong, almost insular care for their own country. They founded a caste, they supplied a pattern which has endured in the main to the present day, and though to many they are only dim and distant figures of romance, history knows them better as the earliest pioneers on the road of liberty and progress.

* Anglo-Saxon Chronicle, 116.

CHAPTER II

THE NORMANS

FLAMBARD, ROGER AND BECKET

WHEN the Conquest came England had already some slight experience of the Normans; but it had been by a system of peaceful penetration, and the Saxon people as a whole had formed little idea under the mild rule of the Confessor what their undiluted strength could be. Now the great house of Godwin had gone, the northern earls had gone, the exiled ethelings had gone, and the common folk had nothing to temper the stark blast of the Conqueror to their shorn bodies. In truth for them—

> "Evil went the battle play
> On the Pope Calixtus' day."

The first Norman princes were terrible men. Stalwart, corpulent, crimson faced, with flashing eyes, swollen in mind and body, they fought, rode, ate, drank and swore harder than any of their subjects. The Viking blood still ran hot in their veins. Their rage was shattering, their pride satanic, nothing could stand in their way. It was told of Rollo their ancestor that when ordered to do homage for his duchy to his suzerain, he had disdained to kneel, but roughly picking up the royal foot he had flung the French King on his back. The character of his descendants was little changed. Philip of France, jeering at the fleshy stomach and new royalty of his liegeman, the Bastard William, had asked " *Quant est-ce que ce gros homme accouchera ?*" The speech was reported to William as he lay sick in bed. " By the Holy Face of Lucca," he

cried, " I will do my churching in Paris and light many
hundred candles."*

The Conqueror himself was a statesman. He knew the
value of what he had won, and he was not going to
diminish it. When viceroys were needed he joined
two together, as Odo and Fitzosbern, but in truth he
was his own minister, trusting no weaker hand. Stern,
hard, inexorable at times, he was yet just, clear-sighted
and politic. But with his elder children there was a
throwback in blood to the tanner's daughter. Robert
Gambaron or Curthose, with his heavy shoulders and short
legs, was ever unstable and shiftless. His father appraised
him rightly and set him aside in the comparative safety of
Normandy—which he soon lost. The new inheritance,
England, William left to his second son. Dissolute,
cruel, greedy, caring only for money, sport and women,
William Rufus was yet a man. Once when hunting in
his favourite New Forest he got word of a revolt in Normandy. He turned his horse's head on the instant and
rode straight to the coast, followed only by some half-
dozen companions. At Southampton there were no
soldiers, no ships, and a hurricane was blowing. He
flung himself on board a fishing boat and bade the skipper
set sail for France. His courtiers urged him to collect
some troops, the sailors besought him to wait for better
weather. " Who loves me," he cried, " will follow me.
Kings never drown."† Despite all opposition he made
his way across. He landed, and with what forces he
could find moved straight upon his enemy. It was more
than enough. At the mere breath of his coming the
rebellion had faded away.

The Conqueror's third son, Henry, with the courage of
his race and the genius of his sire, possessed also a spirit
of progress, induced perhaps by his early poverty and
studies, for to the name of Beauclerk he had some real
claim. Like his father and his brother, he knew well what
feudalism meant as an administrative system; he had seen
plenty of it in Normandy, and he had no intention of

* Lingard, i. 501.   † *Ibid.*, i. 525-6.

allowing it to take root in England. As a theory of jurisprudence it might do well enough, but the practice of every baron being master in his own lands, wielding the high justice and the low, independent of the King and his courts, able to make war when and where he liked—to such a system Henry would never bow. With the aid of ministers chosen and raised to power by himself he gradually brought the Norman lords under some subjection and enforced a centralized rule upon England.

In his reign the *Magnum Concilium* or the assembly of the tenants in chief, the successor of the Witan, gradually lost what little power it had, and the *Curia Regis*, the Royal or Privy Council, began to take its place.

The royal authority, the royal justice, and the royal taxes were imposed on all, attention was paid to the common welfare, the abuses and extortions of old local courts were restrained and a genuine attempt was made to weld Saxons and Normans into a single people. The King set the example by wedding a Saxon princess, though for this the Norman barons laughed at him and used to call him and the queen Godric and Godgifu.

Henry left no legitimate son, and the Salic idea helped his nephew rather than his daughter, the Empress Maud.

But the hectic reign of Stephen, weakened by all the defects of a usurping and divided rule, checked Henry's reforms, and for a time the feudal magnates regained their power. Yet the foundations of order had been too firmly laid to be uprooted easily, and under the next King, Henry's grandson, the process of pacification went on. The Norman barons were not prolific, and by the beginning of the thirteenth century they had almost ceased to exist in England. The destruction of their power was largely the work of three of their own countrymen, three poor priests, who by a deft use of the shrewd weapons of the Church, the law and the exchequer, brought to their knees those mailed tyrants who had formerly been invulnerable and supreme.

I.—FLAMBARD

Ranulf, afterwards called Flambard, "the Devouring Flame," was born probably near Bayeux about 1060. His father was one Turstin, "a lying priest," while his mother, according to Orderic, was a reputed witch. His origin had thus little to recommend it.

He had, however, a handsome person, a cheery manner, and the determination to succeed. Early in life he attached himself as a hanger-on to the court of the Conqueror, some say as a groom, and there he earned an unenviable reputation as a common informer. He had no book-learning, but plenty of natural talent, and knowing that the Church was the quickest road to success for men of his limitations and arts, he took minor orders, learnt a little law, and came over to England.

William recognized his uses, and though he called him "a traitor and the son of a traitor," seems to have sent him as early as 1082 to Durham on some small mission; but he gave him no official place. Ranulf's intelligence, however, his impudence and activity, were not to be denied. They gained him his nickname of Flambard or Passeflambard, which was given him by Count Robert, the Steward of the Royal Household, who said that "he was like a burning flame because he pushed himself on regardless of others."*

He was next employed in the compilation of the general survey of England, from which he gained some profit, for his name is found in Domesday Book as the possessor of lands in Hampshire and other counties. About 1084 he got into the service of Maurice, the Bishop of London, and was probably helped by him to the deanery of Twynam, now Christchurch, in the New Forest. This preferment he subsequently lost, and for that reason seems to have left the bishop and again attached himself to the court. The Conqueror had just died. Flambard was a man whose temperament appealed to William Rufus, and that

* Freeman, Will. Ruf., i. 330.

prince rapidly showed his appreciation of the Norman clerk's peculiar arts. Sociable, openhanded, addicted to wine and women, Flambard was appointed a royal chaplain almost immediately after the Red King's accession, and he soon made his influence felt. He " gave the King new ideas," and in return was made a prebendary of Tottenham and Lincoln and a canon of Salisbury.

William II. was excessively prodigal and always needed money. Getting money was Flambard's forte. For a year or two Archbishop Lanfranc was there to restrain his wilder projects, but in 1089 the old Italian died and William at once installed Flambard at the treasury.* The new broom swept clean. Besides levying the regular feudal aids on the lay tenants in chief, he forced the prelates to pay in a similar manner. Bishops and abbots, like nobles, he regarded as holding their lands of the King; he made them redeem their succession to a new see or abbey by a fine, and during the vacancy of any ecclesiastical benefice he took its revenues for the Crown. Such a practice was new and illegal, but it found favour in the eyes of the King. Heavy duties were accordingly levied on baron and bishop alike, nor were lesser fry allowed to escape from the close meshes of Flambard's net. The success of his policy was so pronounced that he was next promoted to the place of Justiciar. " Till his time," says Freeman, " that post had not, as a distinct office, reached the full measure of its greatness. It was Flambard himself who raised it to the height of power and dignity which accompanied it when it was held by Roger of Salisbury. He was " to the post of Justiciar what Thomas of London two generations later was to the post of Chancellor: he was the man' who knew how to magnify his office."† According to Lord Campbell, Flambard also received the Great Seal in 1090,‡ and sometimes he is styled *Prefectus*. But whatever his position, for ten years he ruled England and squeezed the land as did no other minister before or since. Unlimited hatred pursued

---

* Freeman, Will. Ruf., ii. 536. † *Ibid.*, i. 333.
‡ Campbell, Chancellors, i. 45.

him, but he went on boldly with his taxes, while the King only laughed and said that " Flambard cared for nothing so long as he pleased his master."*

One of the first fruits of the new policy was that the see of Canterbury remained vacant for four years, during which the King drew its revenues. When at last the gentle Anselm was enthroned, Flambard appeared in his cathedral " harsh and blustering "† on the very day of the solemnity, with a suit against him on· behalf of the King.

From such exactions it was but a step to simony, which soon became rampant—prebends, abbeys and bishoprics being sold unblushingly to the highest bidder. Flambard was at the head of both legal and fiscal administration and could do practically what he liked, and " he drove the King's courts all over the land "—" *Rannulfe his capellane . . . ealle his gemot ofer ealle Englelande draf.*" His system was that the King should be every man's heir. For the privilege of succession, inheritance, marriage, induction, election, or translation, heavy fees had to be paid to the royal treasury. " The nobles were at the King's feet, for the policy of his minister loaded their estates with feudal obligations."‡ He became " the lawgiver of feudalism,"§ the embodiment of tyranny.

Many attempts were made to defeat his schemes. On one occasion he was decoyed into a boat on the Thames by Gerald, one of his own retainers, who begged him to come and visit his old master, the Bishop of London, then lying ill at Stepney. But when Flambard had taken his seat the boat was rowed rapidly to a ship that lay in midstream ready to put out to sea. Flambard was forced on board, hustled and threatened, and soon found himself out of sight of land, in the presence of a murderous crew of ruffians by whom his death was being debated. But his courage never left him. He had already succeeded in dropping his signet and seal overboard lest " they should be used wrongfully against him." Sitting solitary in the stern he turned upon Gerald, shouting at him loudly.

* Wm. Malmesbury, 278.　　† Freeman, Will. Ruf., i. 428.
‡ Green, i. 136.　　§ *Ibid.*, i. 334.

RANULF FLAMBARD
BISHOP OF DURHAM

To face page 42

" What are you plotting against me, Gerald ?" he cried.
" You are my man; you owe me allegiance; to break it
will never prosper you."* The skipper's mate supported
him; the mariners scented a bribe, and Gerald's courage
began to fail. Suddenly the wind veered to the south
and the ship was forced to put back to England. The
crew changed their minds; Flambard's promises saved
him, and after three days' absence he was set on shore.
Posting off to London, he appeared that evening at court,
surrounded by a larger and more boisterous train than
before. Such an uncanny escape proved his luck and
increased his influence.

He was now sent in command of the King's forces against
the Welsh, and there he acquitted himself with his usual
success, for, like many early ecclesiastics, he was something
of a soldier. In 1094 a levy of troops was ordered for
the King's service in Normandy. The drafts arrived at
Dover, each man bringing ten shillings from his shire for
his expenses overseas. Flambard took the money and
sent the men back home. Three years later the King
again crossed to Normandy, and this time Flambard was
left as joint Regent of England with the Bishop of Winchester. His colleague died almost at once, and he was
thus able to give the fullest rein to his exactions. " The
misery of the people," says the chronicle, " was so great
that the devil frequently appeared in the woods in a
horrible form to many Normans and spoke with them
much concerning the King and Ranulf."† " Many
districts were excessively oppressed by reason of the wall
which they built about the Tower, and of the bridge which
had nearly all been carried away by the river, and of the
working of the King's Hall at Westminster; and many
men perished by reason of these."‡

At Whitsuntide 1099 the King was back in England
and held his court at Westminster. There, in his newly
built hall, which he said was only to be " his bed-chamber,"

* Simeon of Durham, i. 137; Freeman, Will. Ruf., ii. 561.
† F. Worcester, 322; Ingulf. Cont., 110.
‡ Anglo-Saxon Chronicle, 143.

he appointed Flambard to the bishopric of Durham, his single recorded act within those historic walls. The see had lain empty for three years and Flambard had paid heavily for it. He was now consecrated at Canterbury, refusing to do obeisance to the Archbishop of York, and as Chancellor he sat in Westminster Hall during the ensuing Trinity term.* Then he went north to take possession of his palatinate. His enthronement at Durham was a scene of much scandal, for he gave a huge banquet to the monks, forcing them to eat forbidden food and to be served by forbidden females—"*puellas speciocissimas procacioris formae et faciei . . . strictis ad corpus vestibus, solutis in terga crinibus.*"† It was the kind of joke that appealed to Flambard and his master.

In August, 1100, William met his death in the New Forest.

> " Under the arm in a secret part
> The iron fled through the Kinge's heart;
> The turf it squelched where the Red King fell,
> And the fiends they carried his soul to hell."

His brother Henry at once seized the throne, and the initial act of his reign was to throw Flambard into the Tower—the first occasion on which that fortress is mentioned as a royal prison. Perhaps it was a concession to popular outcry, perhaps only an attempt to extort money, for the bishop was not treated badly. He was allowed two shillings a day for his keep, and as he had many friends and plenty of money he did not remain in durance for long. A rope was conveyed to him in a wine jar. His gaolers and the knights who guarded him were made drunk and " he escaped through a window, taking his pastoral staff with him, but rasping his hands, for he had forgotten his gloves; he fell heavily in his descent, for he was getting fat." He was hurried off to the river, and in company with his mother, the witch, " who had lost an eye from her frequent conversation with the devil," he fled to France. His own ship arrived safely, but that of his parent was

* Campbell, Chanc., i. 17.
† Freeman, Will. Ruf., ii. 273, note.

taken by pirates, and she was thrown ashore, " moaning and naked," on the Norman coast.*

Flambard now offered his services to Robert of Normandy, Henry's eldest brother. He became " Lord of the Pirates," and quickly made himself the directing spirit of the duchy, harrying the English fleet and trying to bribe the sailors. But in 1106 the battle of Tenchebrai brought Robert's career to an end, and Henry thought it best to keep such a dangerous enemy as Flambard under his own eye, rather than have him fomenting rebellion abroad. So Flambard came back to Durham. He had not neglected his own interests while in Normandy: he had procured the see of Lisieux for his son, aged twelve, and had undertaken to look after the revenues himself; but on his return to England he agreed to forgo this plurality and devoted himself to his own diocese.

He now kept out of politics and for the last third of his life is less heard of, being content to enjoy the goods he had got. Henry put him in charge of the Scottish border, and occasionally he appeared at councils. In 1119 he was sent as envoy to Rheims. He officiated at the reception of St. Cuthbert's body in Durham Cathedral, and at that ceremony " preached a very long sermon." His activity did not diminish with age and he took to building on a large scale. Much of Durham Cathedral, St. Cuthbert's Abbey, Norham Castle, and Christchurch in Hampshire are attributed to him. Besides fortifying his city he led several expeditions against rebellious northern barons, for he was always a fervent defender of the temporalities of his see. But as a political force he had ceased to count; Henry knew too much of him.

He lived to be an old man, benevolent, charitable and penitent, increasing his almsgiving and even paying his debts as his age advanced. In the summer of 1128 he fell ill, and feeling that his end was near he had himself carried into his cathedral; there, to atone for his past misdeeds, he placed his pastoral ring upon the high altar, and lying before it, he died. His last words were: " I wished

* Ord. Vit., 786, 787.

to do more harm than I could—*Plus volui nocere quam potui.*"*

Like many prelates and priests of those days Flambard had a mistress and a family, for whom he provided most extensively out of the possessions of the bishopric "†—his son Ranulf, and his grandson, being endowed with seven manors and a rectory. Nothing is known of their posterity.

A man of low origin and loose life, Flambard was un- lettered, unscrupulous and cruel. But he knew how to make his way. Good-looking, courageous, active and amusing, he had plenty of attractive qualities. When he had money he was openhanded; when he had not, he was marvellous at procuring it. He devoted himself to his master, pandered to the royal needs and pleasures, and quickly made his value recognized. The first William could rule his own kingdom, but the second needed a minister. Flambard became that minister, rising to power, like others after him, " by service in the King's chapel and chancery."‡ But his views were limited by his ignorance. His ideas never went beyond the needs of the prince—he ignored those of the people. He neither mitigated the wretchedness of the poor nor augmented the prosperity of the rich. Thus the years of his ministry were regarded as a time of misery, corruption and rapine. Fuller styles him the " extorting publican "; Malmesbury calls him " a sink of iniquity."§ Even at Durham he seems to have been much the same, oppressing his monks and caring for little but the material interests of his see.

Intense, restless activity was his dominant trait. A menial and a spy under the Conqueror, a clerk to the Bishop of London, a chaplain, courtier, treasurer, judge and viceroy to William Rufus, a subtle counsellor to Duke Robert, and at last in his old age a builder and a bishop— his name of Flambard was singularly well chosen. Yet his character was not all bad. His cheery courage, his fierce efficiency and his loyalty redeem it, and despite his

* Freeman, Will. Ruf., ii. 273, note.   † Surtees, i. 20.
‡ Freeman, Will. Ruf., i. 329.   § Wm. Malmesbury, 344

faults, he at least succeeded in impressing his personality upon history.   A bold, unflinching minister, a resourceful financier, "the patriarch of the long line of judges who have sat in Westminster Hall," his dexterity and self-confidence were never those of a mountebank or a poltroon, but of a strong though ruffianly master of men.

II.—ROGER OF SALISBURY

Roger, sometimes called "the Great," "the Black," or "the Rich," was born between 1070 and 1080 in Normandy.   History does not record the names of his parents, but he was of humble origin and little education.   He became a priest, and is first heard of in the reign of William Rufus.   The latter's brother Henry, then much limited in means, was living in a modest style in Normandy.   His court consisted of one knight, one clerk, and three servants. One day, when riding with them near Caen, he turned into the small chapel which Roger served and asked for mass to be said.   Roger performed the office so expeditiously that all called him just the priest for soldiers, and Henry bade him follow the little band.   The invitation was not refused; Roger was given the place of chaplain, and his zeal and industry soon commended him to a prince with no money to spare and a great liking for it; people called their association "the blind leading the blind."*

But Roger's abilities expanded with the calls upon them, and in a short time he became Henry's confidential steward. Accuracy and despatch were his leading traits, and when Henry succeeded to the throne of England he made his careful clerk Chancellor, and two years later appointed him Bishop of Salisbury.   A long dispute as to the investiture of English prelates was then being debated between Church and King.   Henry insisted that they were his liegemen and must hold their temporalities from him: Anselm, the archbishop, took the opposite view.

* Wm. of Newbridge, i. 6.

In consequence Roger's consecration was delayed until
the compromise of 1107, for he was careful to offend
neither his spiritual nor his temporal lord.

Once a bishop he resigned the chancellorship, and was
then appointed to the great post of Justiciar—" *secundus
a rege* " he is styled—which he held for the remainder
of Henry's reign. For nearly thirty years he governed
the kingdom with firmness and discretion. Henry's
frequent absences in Normandy left his Justiciar practically absolute, and Roger was able to institute a science
of government, much of which has descended to the present
day. He built up an administrative system, reorganized
the exchequer, and laid the basis of the chancery and
common law jurisdiction. In the " *Dialogus de Scaccario*,"
written by his great-nephew, many of the details of this
comprehensive scheme are given. It was a constructive
work of the very first importance, and could only have
been accomplished by a statesman of unchallenged power
and broad vision. His executive rule was equally
sagacious and under it the country enjoyed a long period
of peace and prosperity, for justice was respected and
the treasury was full.

Nor did Roger limit his activities to secular affairs.
For several years he administered the vacant primacy
and dispensed its patronage. " He did not neglect his
ecclesiastical duties, but daily diligently transacted them
in the morning, that he might then be more ready and
undisturbed for other business."*

A bishop's ambition in those days was to strengthen
and enlarge his diocese, to beautify and enrich his
cathedral. In both directions Roger was consistently
industrious. The King was generous to him, and he had
many opportunities of increasing his wealth. Abbeys and
monasteries were added to his see, manors and chases to
his property, and while he rebuilt the minster at Old
Sarum he also fortified and embellished his castles in
Wiltshire and the adjoining counties. Sherborne, Salisbury, Malmesbury and Devizes were his principal strong-

* Wm. Malmesbury, 355.

holds, and within their ambit he was secure and supreme. There he lived the life of a lay noble, and like a lay noble he wished to transmit his possessions to his posterity. He was of an amorous complexion, and by a beautiful mistress, Matilda of Ramsbury, he had several children, whom he educated well, promoting them in the public service. Early in the next reign his son, Roger le Poer, became Chancellor, while one nephew, Nigel, was Treasurer and Bishop of Ely, and another, Alexander, was Bishop of Lincoln.* The younger generation pursued Roger's policy, building castles and amassing riches, so that the connection became the most important in England. Their administration was efficient, and the nation generally was contented with their rule. So much did Henry trust Bishop Roger that he made him guardian of the captured Robert of Normandy, his elder brother and former rival; and at Devizes Castle Robert passed many years, a prisoner at large.

In 1120 came the loss of the *White Ship* and the death of the young Prince Henry. The King's second marriage brought him no issue, and in 1˙26 he pressed the barons and prelates to swear fealty to his daughter Maud, widow of the Emperor Henry. In this ceremony Roger was one of the foremost, though he added a rider to his oath that Maud should not " marry abroad " without the consent of the Council. Her subsequent union with Geoffrey of Anjou he held not to fulfil this condition.

To the end of Henry's reign, Bishop Roger's influence and power remained undiminished, and when early in December 1135 the King died, it lay largely with him to determine who should have the crown.

The Empress Maud was the right heir, but Count Stephen of Blois, Henry's nephew and the Conqueror's grandson, was the stronger and more popular claimant. He at once hurried over to England, seized the royal treasure and enlisted the support of the Londoners. Without much demur Roger took his side, for the Empress

* Dugdale, Orig. Jurid., 2, says that the Bishop of Salisbury was Treasurer under Stephen.

was identified with her husband, and the Angevins were
anathema to the Normans. To Stephen, Roger's support
meant everything, and for some years he was maintained in power. Stephen used to say, " I would give
him half England if he asked for it; till the time be ripe
he shall tire of asking, ere I tire of giving."*

Stephen, however, was of very different mettle to Henry.
Throughout his life the latter had consistently advanced
to office new men bound to himself by interest and gratitude, while he relegated the Norman barons to minor
places in the government. But the new King, uncertain
of his claim, inexperienced in rule, shiftless in character,
was compelled to let the barons share his power. They
had long viewed with jealous dismay the policy and
ministers of Henry. Their chance now returned. Gradually they were able to infect Stephen's mind with a
suspicion of Bishop Roger's good faith. He had sworn
fealty to the daughter of his old master, they said, and he
was surely intending to bring her back to England. They
pointed to his castles and his riches, to the monopoly of
the principal offices of State which his family enjoyed, to
the absolute dependence of the King upon his support and
countenance. Stephen was not indisposed to listen to
suggestions that had some colour in them, and Roger now
ceased to be Justiciar, though his son and nephews still
held their places. He had not latterly seen eye to eye
with the King, whose dilatory methods did not appeal to
him, and who took advice less readily than the bishop
perhaps expected. But in appearance their friendship
remained as before. At last, however, the barons induced
Stephen to take action.

A meeting of the Council was to be held at Oxford in
June 1139. To this the Bishop of Salisbury with his
nephews was summoned in the ordinary course. He set
out with reluctance. William of Malmesbury heard
him say: " By our Lady St. Mary, I know not why,
but my heart revolts at this journey; this I am sure
of, that I shall be of much the same service at court as

* Wm. Malmesbury, 401.

a foal is in battle."* Immediately on his arrival a quarrel was picked with his retainers by those of Count Alan of Brittany. The Count's men were put to flight, and a knight was killed. Alan complained to the King, and early next morning the Bishops of Sarum and Lincoln were seized, brought before Stephen, and directed to surrender the keys of their castles. As they demurred to this, Stephen confined Bishop Roger and his son, the Chancellor, and then taking them in his train, marched on Devizes, whither the Bishop of Ely, Roger's other nephew, "a man of greater subtlety and more activity," had already fled. On arriving before Devizes the King shut up the old bishop in a cowhouse, and kept him without food (one account says that Roger imposed on himself a penance of fasting). Matilda of Ramsbury, his mistress, was holding the castle, and Stephen swore "that he would hang her son, the Chancellor, before the very gate,"† if she would not surrender. His threats succeeded, and the vast fortress, "the most magnificent in Europe, with its treasure in gold and plate of 40,000 marks, its arms and garrison, passed into the King's possession." The bishops were grievously afflicted at the "loss of their strongholds, in which they took the greatest delight."‡

This act cost Stephen dear, for he alienated the support of the Church and showed the barons how easily they could move him. In August a second Council was held at Winchester, and there the Papal Legate, who was Stephen's brother, called the King to account for his treatment of Roger. The case was argued by the Archbishop of Rouen and Alberic de Vere on the King's part, and by Bishop Roger on his own. He took a bold, high-spirited line, denying that he had ever been Stephen's minister or received his wages.§ Nothing, however, resulted. Stephen did a nominal penance but he retained the castles, while Roger returned to his see, shattered and broken by his treatment: it is said that he even went out of his mind—*in amentiam versus.*|| He was an old

* Wm. Malmesbury, 395.   † Gesta Stephani, 75.   ‡ *Ibid.*
§ Wm. Malmesbury, 398. || Wm. of Newbridge, i. 36.

man, not strong, and the shock overthrew him.* He soon fell ill of a quartan ague, and on December 4, 1139, he died before his own high altar. His last remaining treasures, which he had dedicated to his church, were seized by the King's servants before the breath was out of his body.

Little regret, it is said, was felt at his death, " so much envy and hatred had his excessive power drawn upon him, and undeservedly too, from some of those very persons whom he had advanced to honour."† His son, the Chancellor, Roger the Poor or Le Poer, was eventually released from prison, and left England. His nephew, the Bishop of Ely, became the father of Richard Fitznigel, afterwards Treasurer. The latter did not die until 1198, so that the family continued their administrative work for a century. The noble races of Le Poer and Power may perhaps include the Norman Bishop of Sarum among their ancestors.

There is an effigy of Bishop Roger on his tomb in the nave of Salisbury Cathedral, brought from the ancient church at Old Sarum. One of the earliest examples of its kind, it shows a thin figure elaborately dressed, much more firm and nervous than his heavily built son who lies hard by.

Of Roger's private life little is known. He kept up elaborate state, feasting, hunting and visiting his manors: but the tale that he was worn out and enervated by luxurious habits, and the accounts of his unchastity, seem exaggerated. Clerical concubinage was then still the rule in England.‡ Contemporary chroniclers all call him a loyal minister to King Henry, equitable in his judgments, active and industrious in his administration; but " he ever pursued riches. If there was anything contiguous to his property which might be advantageous to him, he would directly extort it either by entreaty or purchase; or, if that failed, by force. With unrivalled magnificence . . he erected splendid mansions on all his estates; in merely maintaining which, the labour of his successors shall toil in vain."§ Yet he turned his wealth to noble

* Wm. Malmesbury, 402.   † Ibid.   ‡ Froude, " Short Studies," iv. 42.
§ Wm. Malmesbury, 401.

uses, making Salisbury the finest cathedral in England, Devizes the most splendid castle in Europe. Under his auspices was introduced that lighter and more ornamented Norman architecture which eventually gave place to the Gothic style; his buildings were beautifully finished, the stone courses being so accurately laid that the joins were invisible.

Stephen's advent to power was the turning-point of Roger's life. Up to that time he had been a model of loyalty, but his apparent violation of his oath to Henry damaged his prestige. The castles that he had built, the train that he maintained, the power that he engrossed, might have braved criticism. But the Bishops of Ely and Lincoln were less known men, and their efforts to copy him were ill-received. Nor is it certain that he acted honestly by Stephen. The author of the "*Gesta Stephani*" says: "Although he was very dear to the King, although he was more especially set at the head of the affairs of State and had the control of the King's Court, yet he sympathized nevertheless with and had greater feelings of friendship and attachment for the children of King Henry, and promised that he would keep faith with them and use every endeavour to afford them succour; but he did this secretly, lest he should give offence to Stephen. His castles he filled with very strong garrisons and an abundant supply of provisions, prudently assiduous in furthering the King's interests, but watching for a fit opportunity to assist the others on their arrival in England."* Even Roger's particular apologist remarks that "it was in every person's mouth that as soon as the Empress should arrive, he would join her party with his nephews and his castles."†

Thus there was some excuse for Stephen's mistrust. Bold, generous and affable, that prince had long been the most popular nobleman in England,‡ but he lacked political insight and tenacity, and was no match for a clever man. Not realizing how vital to his security was the goodwill of the prelates and of the officials, he gave his confidence

---

* Gesta Stephani, 73.   † Wm. Malmesbury, 398.
‡ Lingard, ii. 66.

to his own friends, who were consumed with jealousy, with
the hope of plunder and with the desire for their old
independence. By them the Bishop of Sarum and his
family were dispossessed, and in so doing they "shattered
the whole system of government. The King's court and
the exchequer ceased to work at a moment when the
landing of Earl Robert and the Empress set Stephen
face to face with a danger greater than any he had yet
encountered, while the clergy, alienated by the arrest of
the bishops and the disregard ^f their protests, stood
angrily aloof."*

Few careers so well illustrate the characteristics of the
Middle Ages as that of Roger the Great. Raised by a
discerning prince from nothing to everything, he quickly
justified his fortune. For despatch of business he was
unequalled. A strong ruler, a constructive organizer, a
judge, a financier and a pastor, "he surpassed all the
great men in the realm, both in wealth and sagacity of
intellect."† For close on forty years he was Chief Minister
—a length of time only surpassed by Burghley. Serving
the interests of his master and his country, he did
not neglect his own. Riches and power, to which he had
not been born, acquired an exaggerated value in his eyes.
He became careless, perhaps arrogant, and he began to
play fast and loose. The new King then resented the
advice and suspected the motives of his predecessor's
favourite, and determined to rid himself of the old servant.
He soon regretted the change. The fourteen years that
elapsed between Roger's fall and Stephen's death were
years of turmoil, distress and anarchy. "Adulterine
castles" sprang up all over the land, and men pined for the
firm hand of the Justiciar. But the framework of Roger's
organization had been solidly put together, and when at
last Henry II. succeeded he was able to restore it to more
than its pristine vigour and to develop a system that was
to become permanent.

Roger of Salisbury was a prototype of those great
architects who were rather statesmen than prelates, who

* Green, i. 154.   † Gesta Stephani, 83.

ROGER THE GREAT
BISHOP OF SALISBURY

To face page 54

saw that strength and order were as necessary as faith
to the development of a country, and who understood that
the peaceful prosperity of the people was the simplest
means for ensuring the safety of their souls. His temperament had made power, money, beauty and well-being
necessities to him, and in his old age he was ready to risk
principles and duty to retain them. So he kept a foot in
either camp, and fell a victim to disloyalty or indecision.
His fall was the measure of his greatness, for the value
of his work was best seen after he had gone.

III.—BECKET

Thomas Becket was born on December 21, 1118, at a
house in Cheapside, London, still marked by the Mercers
Chapel. His father, Gilbert, came from Thierceville near
Bec; his mother, Matilda or Rohesia, from Caen. His
family was thus purely Norman, some say of knightly
rank, but probably *roturier;* Becket described it as " not
base," and Henry II. (in anger) called him *plebeius clericus.*
The name Becket had perhaps a local derivation, though
its owner always styled himself Thomas of London.

Gilbert Becket had been a Rouen merchant who had
come to London, where he was at one time portreeve.
Later on he retired from business and lived on his own
means. His wife came also of a trading stock, but the tale
of her being a wandering Saracen is now regarded as a
mere legend. She was a religious and loving mother who
brought her son up "in the fear of God and the Blessed
Virgin ":* she used to weigh him on his birthday against
money, food and clothes, which she then gave to the
poor.†

When quite a boy Becket was sent to Merton Priory in
Surrey, and afterwards to school in London. He was no
special scholar, but intelligent, industrious and brave;
he once flung himself into a mill race to save a favourite
hawk. As a youth he went to study in Paris, but his

* Becket, Mem., ii. 302.   † Green, i. 158.

5

father having lost money he came home at the age of
twenty-one. After staying for some little time at Pevensey
Castle, the home of a school friend, Richard de l'Aigle,
he was employed as a clerk for three years in the Sheriff
of London's office. Then came his first chance. By some
friends of his father's he was brought to the notice of
Theobald, Archbishop of Canterbury, a countryman of
his own. The primate took Becket into his household
at Harrow, where there were a number of active and
clever men, young priests and nobles. Their learning and
abilities spurred Becket to emulation. He was conscious
of ambition and talents, he had seen the height to which
the great Bishop of Salisbury had risen, his patron was
powerful and well-disposed, and he lived in stirring times.

At first he devoted himself to two objects: to improving
his own education, and to making himself indispensable to
the archbishop. He went for a year to Bologna and
Auxerre to learn the language and to study the canon law;
on his return he became an intimate counsellor to Theobald,
by whom he was sent on several missions abroad. On
each occasion his business became more confidential and
his success more marked. In the primate's household he
had enemies—men who envied his capacity or despised
his origin. Of these Roger de Pont l'Évêque, Archdeacon
of Canterbury, was the chief, and at times Becket had to
keep away. But gradually he became Theobald's right-
hand man. In 1143 he took minor orders, and was presented to the livings of St. Mary-le-Strand and Otford.
In that year he accompanied the archbishop to Rome,
and in 1148 to the Council at Rheims. His master then
collated him to prebendal stalls in London and Lincoln.
Becket was a shrewd and useful servant, and when his
next chance came he was ready to seize it.

At this time King Stephen was striving hard to secure the
crown to his own posterity, to the exclusion of the Empress
Maud and her son Henry of Anjou. In 1152, with this
object in view, he called a Council for the coronation of
his son Eustace. Theobald, a firm partisan of Henry's,
refused to officiate and went over to Flanders. Largely

owing to his courage and to Becket's diplomacy the papal
sanction was refused and the King's project defeated.
Eventually the archbishop was recalled, and when Stephen
died two years later Henry succeeded peacefully to the
throne.

In this business Becket had deserved well both of the
archbishop and the new King, and both repaid him
lavishly. On Roger de Pont l'Évêque's elevation to the
see of York, Becket was appointed Archdeacon of Canterbury, the best paid benefice in England under the rank
of an abbey, and was made Provost of Beverley. But
Theobald was determined to do still more for him. He
was old himself, but he trusted Becket, who understood
and would follow his policy. Accordingly he recommended
him strongly to the King, and early in 1155 Becket was
made Chancellor.

The Chancellor was the head of the royal secretaries, the
keeper of the seal and the purse, and as such in constant
touch with the Sovereign. Becket had always possessed
a peculiar art of ingratiating himself where he wished to
do so. He was " a pleasant and amusing talker, with
excellent manners."[*] Able to accommodate himself to
any society, he soon gained Henry's heart. He rode,
hawked, and played games with him, entertained him at
dinner, and yet was always ready and well informed in
business. The chancellorship did not appeal to him
much—at least so he said. " The snares that were laid
for him, the work that had to be done, sickened him of
life."[†] But he did his work well, setting a good example
to all—taking no presents, presiding at Westminster,
riding circuit (the courts were not yet divided), repairing
the Tower, attending the Council, directing a large household—and gradually he became a figure in the land.

Like later churchmen and Chancellors, he maintained a
vast establishment and dispensed wide hospitality. " He
never dined without earls and barons,"[‡] says Fitzstephen,
and " so elegant was his housekeeping that clean straw was

* Becket, Mem., ii. 302.   † Ibid., ii. 305.
‡ Ibid., iii. 20.

laid daily in his hall lest the company should soil their clothes when sitting on the floor." The education of the King's eldest son was committed to his charge, and in 1158 he was sent as ambassador to the court at Paris to arrange for the prince's marriage with the French King's daughter. His train on this journey was magnificent. The chroniclers detail the names of the knights, the numbers of the escort, the richness of the liveries, the abundance of provisions, the procession of sumpter mules and waggons, the hawks, hounds and hunters, the gold and silver plate, the singers and falconers, the apes and mastiffs, that accompanied his entry to the towns along his route. " What must the King be like," said the French, ". who has such a Chancellor?"*

The results of this embassy were not satisfactory, and a war soon began. Henry was determined to recover the southern possessions of his wife Eleanor, and in the further-ance of his military projects Becket was able to shine as a soldier. The English King's expedition to Toulouse gave the keeper of his conscience an opportunity for appearing in mail at the head of his own troop of knights, and he acquitted himself as creditably in the field as he had done in the Council. After the campaign he remained with the High Constable in control of the conquered territory, and coming north again for several months he kept the French at bay in Normandy. His personal gallantry was no less remarkable than his generalship, and on one occasion he unhorsed a French knight in single combat. His advice was responsible for the introduction of scutage, by which each knight paid a fixed sum for his fee instead of serving in person. By this means mercenaries could be raised for foreign wars in place of the royal vassals, and the King became more independent of his feudal tenants.

At last in 1160 peace was made, and Becket was able to return to his duties at home. Henry had bestowed on him numerous castles and manors, and had allowed him to profit from the revenue of vacant abbeys and benefices, and Becket by now had become Chief Minister. He

* Lingard, ii. 111.

was rich and luxurious, but active and popular. From
women he kept apart, but in every other worldly pursuit
he rivalled the proudest nobles in England or France.
He was soon to fill a very different rôle.

In April 1161 Archbishop Theobald died. For a year
Henry kept the income of Canterbury in his own hands
and then he offered the see to the Chancellor. Becket
hesitated to accept. He was happy and fortunate where
he was; he liked the ways of the world; he felt that his
own nature was as masterful as the King's. Hitherto
their policies had marched together; who could say what
might befall if they should clash? But he knew that it
had been Theobald's prayer that he should succeed to the
primacy, and to the King's solicitations were now joined
those of his own friends and of the Papal Legate. The
prospect was alluring, and perhaps he looked still higher.
The only English Pope, Adrian IV., had just died; why
should not another subject of King Henry's sit in St.
Peter's chair? At last he gave his consent, and within
ten days he was ordained, elected, consecrated and enthroned in his own cathedral. At the same time he
became the Pope's legate, a privilege that he had himself
obtained in earlier days for his predecessor.

Immediately the whole tenor of his life, all his outlook
on affairs, underwent a radical change. He turned
his mind to spiritual matters, he reduced his expenses,
he took to fasting and penance, he wore a hair shirt next
his skin, he surrounded himself with poor clerks and
loathsome beggars. On his election as archbishop he
had obtained an indemnity from all his obligations as
Chancellor, and he now resigned the Great Seal. But
though quit of secular bonds he was far from neglecting
the temporal interests of his new order. He began at once
to reclaim all the alienated fiefs and benefices that had
ever belonged to the see of Canterbury, and he soon fell
foul of King and nobles. He also maintained his right
to interpose in lay questions, and took up a new line by
combating a project of Henry's for transferring to the
treasury certain " aids " hitherto retained by the sheriffs.

This was standing out as a champion of democracy, and it is the first recorded instance " of opposition to the royal will in the matter of taxation."*

Henry was at this time by far the greatest prince in Europe. He was a strong and successful ruler, who knew his own mind and was accustomed to pursue his own policy without contradiction. To be flouted openly by his friend, his Chancellor, his archbishop, the man " who had first come to court riding on a lame mule," whom he had raised to the highest place in the realm, was an unexpected check. He remarked sarcastically to Becket that it was clear that England was not large enough to hold them both, and he set about making matters even. He had long wished to equalize the position of the layman and the priest, to challenge the control of the ecclesiastical courts over offending clerks. As the common law then stood a priest, whatever crime he committed, could only be summoned before the archdeacon or the bishop, and deprivation or degradation was the worst punishment he had to fear. Even the fines of priests did not find their way into the exchequer. The question, indeed, was a hard one to resolve; it was the growth of ages; it had certain merits in its favour; it had force behind it; and it was not until the nineteenth century that benefit of clergy finally disappeared.

Henry, however, was determined to enforce an equal justice for all, cleric and layman alike, and at a Council at Westminster in October 1163 he requested the bishops to subscribe to the " ancient customs of England " and to submit all spiritual persons to the royal jurisdiction. They accepted, but " saving their order," and Becket in particular declined to surrender the privileges of the Church. The King was angry, refused to see the archbishop at Woodstock, and deprived him of several castles which he had held as Chancellor. He also withdrew the young Prince Henry from his care. Eventually Becket was induced to promise his agreement verbally, but when in January 1164 the King's proposals were

* D.N.B., lvi. 166.

formally brought before another Council at Clarendon, the primate went back on his word and refused to subscribe to the so-called Constitutions. Matters thus became serious, and Becket twice tried to leave the country, but was prevented by accidents which he regarded as the will of Providence.

Meanwhile Henry pressed on his policy, for he was sure that his project was reasonable, and he was not the man to tolerate a master. Various claims were brought against the archbishop for the recovery of manors and monies which, it was said, he had wrongfully retained. At last, in October 1164, he was cited to appear at a council at Northampton. There he was condemned for contempt of court in not appearing on a previous suit brought against him by the King's Marshal. Successive sums of £300, £500, and eventually of £30,000, were demanded of him, and it was clear that unless he was willing to compromise about the Constitutions it would go hard with him. Becket had an admission or a reply ready for each of the charges, but on the main point he was adamant. He would never forgo the rights of his order.

The position was fast becoming impossible, and the bishops now besought him to be more conciliatory, but he forbade them to oppose him. A dramatic scene ensued at Northampton. Becket was ill—an illness brought on by excitement—he was obstinate and aflame with enthusiasm. He came straight from celebrating Mass to the gates of the castle. He was surrounded by a rabble of his own followers and of townspeople. Taking his archiepiscopal cross in his hand he entered the hall—to beard the lion in his den. He made his way to the council-chamber of the bishops, but after an argument there he was left waiting, while the King and his barons debated in another room. " A fool he is," said the Bishop of London, " and a fool he always will be." At last the humpbacked Earl of Leicester, the first of the nobles and an old friend of Becket's, came out and gently bade him hear the sentence of the court. Becket ordered him to be silent, challenged the barons' jurisdiction, and taking up his cross stalked down the hall. He stumbled as he went through the excited throng, and some of the pages threw mud and straw at him and called him a traitor. He turned on them, trenchantly rebuking the King's bastard brother. The gates were opened, he mounted his mule and returned to the monastery where he lodged. Then he sent to ask for leave to depart, but as the answer was deferred, he set off secretly that night for the Continent, travelling as Brother Christian. Three weeks later he arrived in France.

This was the real end of Becket's career as an English minister or an English prelate. The remaining six years of his life were spent in tedious, intemperate, almost sordid battling with his Sovereign and his suffragans. At first there was sympathy for him, but his wrongs were soon turned to political ends. A dispute was in progress about the Papal succession. Alexander III. was living in exile at Sens; he was anxious to maintain his influence and not averse from acting as arbiter between the King of England and his primate. Louis VII. in Paris was equally glad of the chance of weighing down the scales against a rival who had married his divorced wife and who ruled half his kingdom. Thus a long contest of words began, little calculated to enhance the credit of King or archbishop, of Church or State.

Henry's first move was to send an embassy to the Pope. It had little success. The Latin of the English bishops was not brilliant, and Becket's most malevolent opponent, Hilary of Chichester, distinguished himself by coining the interesting word " oportuebat "—Ita, says the chronicler, grammatazibat episcopus Cicestrencis.* The earls were wiser and spoke in French; their modesty was applauded, but their arguments fell flat. The Pope declined to approve of the Constitutions, and at the same time refused to accept Becket's resignation of his see.

Becket now went to live at the Cistercian monastery of Pontigny, putting the abbot there to considerable expense,

* Becket, Mem., ii. 338.

for despite his penances he insisted on an excellent table. At Christmas Henry confiscated all the revenues of Canterbury and expelled all Becket's relatives and friends from England. Before leaving the kingdom they were compelled to swear that they would each visit the archbishop, who was thus continually assailed by a stream of aggrieved and penniless suitors. In 1166 he retorted from the high hill of Vezelay by a series of excommunications launched against Henry's principal counsellors. Money also began to play a part, "for the odour of bribes had infected the nostrils of the cardinals."*

Henry next announced that all Cistercians would be banished from his dominions unless Becket left Pontigny. This was a terrible blow to the monks, and the archbishop was soon obliged to move to Sens. Negotiations for a compromise were started, but neither the Pope nor the French King was a very honest peacemaker, while Becket and Henry were both dour combatants. Papal commissioners were sent to arrange the dispute, but Henry was now thoroughly enraged, while Becket was in a state of exaltation. He prayed, he communed with himself, he pored over canon law and martyrologies. Nor did he restrain his words; "archidiabolus noster," he styles the Bishop of London, who was his own archdeacon,† and he writes to King Henry as a sovereign to a subject. For several years this sort of correspondence went on, varied by interviews between Henry and the archbishop, but the latter's condition of "saving his order" was never eliminated, and this the King would not concede. The complication became a European scandal. Many views were taken of it. William of Newbridge, one of the least prejudiced of contemporary writers, says of Becket: "I cannot deem his acts worthy of praise, although they arose from a praiseworthy zeal, since no good could come of them, while the King's rage was more inflamed."‡ The world indeed had begun to tire of the quarrel.

Early in 1170 Henry determined to have his eldest

* Becket, Mem., ii. 341. † Foss., 77.
‡ Wm. Newbridge, i. 161.

son crowned. He had long wished to do this, but had been restrained by the exile of the primate, whose duty and right it was to officiate. He now availed himself of an old Papal dispensation for allowing the Archbishop of York to act, and in June the ceremony was performed. Becket had already issued his prohibition against it, as had the Pope, and he at once suspended Archbishop Roger, his old enemy, and all the other prelates who had taken part.

In the interval, however, he had had another meeting 'with the King, where an apparent reconciliation was at last effected. Henry still withheld the " kiss of peace," but he allowed Becket to return to England. Becket's final letter to him is couched in a more moderate tone. " It was my wish," he writes, " to have waited on you once more, but necessity compels me, in the lowly state to which I am reduced, to revisit my afflicted church. I go, Sir, with your permission, perhaps to perish for its security, unless you protect me."*

On December 1, 1170, after six years' absence, the archbishop landed at his own port of Sandwich. He was heralded by further suspensory briefs which he had despatched to the offending prelates. He feared that he was beaten, and he was oppressed with a sense of impending calamity, for he had no real trust in Henry's promises. " May God protect you," he wrote to a friend, " from the King's snares, which hardly anyone of all those that have had dealings with him has been able to escape."†

At Canterbury he was warmly welcomed by his own people, but during his long absence his neighbours, the de Brocs, had enjoyed his lands, and he found his palace unfurnished, his barns empty, and his coffers rifled. He determined to go to Winchester to visit the prince, his former pupil, and to take London on his way. But the Council heard of his intention, and at Southwark, where a vast concourse of people had come out to meet him, he was turned back by the sheriff.

He went home to Canterbury for Christmas, angry and

* Lingard, ii. 157.   † Hook, ii. 472.

From an MS.

THOMAS BECKET
ARCHBISHOP OF CANTERBURY
WITH HENRY II. AND LOUIS VII.

To face page 64

depressed, but firm in his resolve to maintain the privileges of his Church at the cost of any sacrifice. In the meanwhile, however, trouble was brewing oversea. The Archbishop of York, with his brothers of London and Salisbury, whom Becket had banned, had gone to Henry's court at Bayeux, and had laid their complaints before him. Besides their own suspensions, Becket had threatened to excommunicate everyone who had had a hand in the recent coronation. This meant that Henry himself was to be put under the ban of the Church, and that the cherished scheme to confirm his dynasty was to be rendered void. His fierce temper burst out and, looking round, he cried: "Of all the caitiffs that I nourish, is there none that will rid me of this low-born priest ?"*

Four knights, three of them former liegemen of Becket's, heard the words and settled to take the law into their own hands. They crossed over separately to England, met at Saltwood, a castle of de Broc's, and in the afternoon of December 29 came to the palace at Canterbury. Making their way to the room where Becket was sitting, they summoned him to absolve the bishops or to leave the country. Becket refused to make any conditions. There was a dispute, and then the knights went out and armed themselves under a tree in the courtyard. Vespers were just beginning, and the archbishop was hurried by his attendants through the cloisters into the cathedral. There they tried to bolt the doors, but Becket bade them desist. "The House of God," he said, "must be closed to no man." As he was making his way from the northern transept to one of the chapels by the choir his pursuers broke in. "Where is the traitor, Thomas Becket ?" cried one. Becket made no reply. "Where is the archbishop ?" they cried again. "Here am I," he answered, "no traitor, but archbishop and priest of God." They rushed to him and tried to drag him outside. His attendants had all fled save one, Edward Grim, who was carrying his cross. Becket, a strong man, threw down the first knight as the others struck at him. "Slay me here,"

* Froude, Short Studies, i. 155.

he said, "if you will. I am ready to die. May the
Church through my blood obtain peace and liberty, but
I charge you in the name of God that you hurt none but
me."* There was no delay. In a few moments he was
beaten down and killed, his brains scattered on the pave-
ment. As he fell a storm burst over the cathedral. The
murderers hurried out, plundered the palace, and that
night fled back to France.

The terrible crime re-echoed throughout Christendom.
The martyr was buried where he fell; miracles were soon
wrought at his tomb, and within a few years, in deference
to a universal demand, he was canonized. The four
knights took the cross and were lost or killed in the East.
The King himself was absolved from the murder, but he
did heavy penance, walked barefoot to Canterbury, wept,
and was scourged at Becket's shrine, and made ample
restitution to his kin. The troubles that pursued Henry
for the rest of his life—the hatred of his Queen, the murder
of his mistress, the death of two sons, the rebellion of all—
were ascribed to the vengeance of God. Becket became a
European character, and his path at Clarendon, his field
at Freteval, his shadow in the crypt of his cathedral, still
attest his memory. St. Thomas of Canterbury soon displaced St. Dunstan in popular esteem, and for four centuries pilgrims travelled from all over the Western world
to the holy site which he had sanctified with his blood.
Two hundred and seventy miracles were placed to his
credit, and at the Reformation it was stated that in a single
year £640 had been collected at his altar, £4 at that of the
Blessed Virgin, and one penny at the altar of God. It
was reserved for another Henry, the last of that name,
to denounce his miracles and disperse his bones.

Of Becket's personal appearance there are several
reliable accounts. He was tall, muscular, good-looking,
with a prominent nose. His pleasures were few. He
did some hawking, "but perfunctorily"† says Fitzstephen: yet when he was on the ship fleeing to France
there is a tale of his gazing fixedly on a falcon held by a

* Froude, S.S., i. 174.   † Becket, Mem., iii. 20.

groom—" And seeing the bird he remembered his former
state and forgot his exile."* His chastity was unim-
peached, though the King often tempted him, but women
never appealed to him. The Empress Maud disliked him,
and warned Henry not to make him archbishop, but the
tale that the Lady Rosamund was his friend and Queen
Eleanor his enemy has no authority. To the table he
was devoted. " White pheasants' meat and strong red
wine " were among his weaknesses, and though in later life
he strove to restrain his appetite, his robust constitution
and earlier habits probably called for generous nourishment.

His natural abilities were remarkable. Though never
a great scholar he had a prodigious memory, and once
he had read a passage or seen a face he could recall it
without effort. He was pious, keen and openhanded,
but proud, vain, dramatic, a hunter after popularity,
" ultra modum captator popularis auræ."† Henry used
to laugh at his taste for finery—he once threw Becket's
fur cloak to a beggar—though he delighted in his
companionship. Archbishop Theobald said that " the
two had but one heart and mind."‡ Yet it is doubtful whether Becket when Chancellor influenced Henry
very much. Henry was a statesman of the first order,
untiring, deep, acute, cautious; and this Becket never
realized. At the time of his flight he had already
ceased to be practical. He had become exalted, proud,
unrestrained, almost vindictive, and his later obstinacy
had the worst effect on the worst elements in Henry's
nature.§ The evil heritage of the Plantagenets, duplicity,
recklessness, rage, gradually dominated the King, and it
may well be that when he spoke the fatal words he meant
them. His knights probably acted in good faith. They
thought the deed—

"being done unknown
He would have found it afterwards well done."

A curiously compound character, Becket in his life met
with hard measure. Capable, arrogant and ambitious,

* Becket, Mem., ii. 335.   † Ibid., ii. 303.
‡ Green, i. 163.   § Stubbs, Select Charters, 148.

the wheel of fortune had cast him against a man more
capable, more arrogant and more ambitious than himself.
Loyalty had been one of his virtues. Loyal to Theobald
as his clerk, to the King as his Chancellor, he felt that
as primate the Church alone claimed his obedience.
Asceticism, opposition and misfortune hardened his heart.
If he could not be Dunstan the ruler, he would be Dunstan
the saint. His old friends, his old pursuits, were all
forgotten; gallantry, magnificence, royal favour, he set
aside: for his companions he chose monks and beggars,
for his virtues humility and patience. With a perse-
verance worthy of a saner cause he fought his losing fight
to the end, and at last with a great heart he gave his life
for his beliefs.

" Sanguis martyrum semen ecclesiæ."

The careers of the three Norman priests who had thus
ruled England at a most crucial period in her history
are not dissimilar in the main. Each was raised from an
obscure birth to the highest place in the State. Each
served his master well, and as a layman rather than as a
prelate; each had so versatile a genius as to be able on
occasion to play the part of a judge, a soldier, a statesman,
or a bishop; each was hated as an upstart by the older
nobles; each in his latter days lost the favour of his
Sovereign; each died before the high altar of his own
cathedral. All alike were men of exceptional abilities,
all were ennobled by the virtues of courage and constancy,
all were marred by the vices of luxury and pride. But
though Becket was canonized as a saint and Flambard
was cursed as a devil, it is probable that Roger, the least
known of the three, was the most practical man, the finest
character, and did the most lasting work for his country.

CHAPTER III

THE EARLY NOBLES

MARSHALL, DE BURGH AND DE MONTFORT

THE early Angevin Kings maintained the tradition of the Norman princes who had preceded them. They were the strongest, the hardest, the keenest men of their times. Better born, better bred, with better brains than the majority of their beef-eating barons, they ruled their wide dominions by force of character, by an unscrupulous policy, by a debonair daring and devilry that seemed to confirm the tale of their Satanic origin.

In the days of Fulk the Black it had been foretold that nine generations of his race should reign and that in each the father should fight the son. The gloomy prediction had left its seal on each prince of the house. All were subject to fits of ungovernable passion, in which the demon would blaze from their eyes and they would lose all thought of restraint. Then they were ready to slay their own kin or anyone else, and seemed to court the dark fate to which they believed themselves doomed. Of the fourteen Plantagenets who wore the English crown six died a violent and six a miserable or untimely death: only two can be said to have had a peaceful end.

Henry II., called Henry Fitz Empress, the founder of the dynasty in England, was a man of real mark. Ruddy, square and stalwart, always on his feet, he was as abstemious as he was untiring. Business or sport claimed all his hours, justice and order he enforced, to reason and religion he bowed, but when his temper rose he would roll on the floor in a convulsion of rage, biting the very straw. Yet he was a man of inscrutable counsel, and beneath his

69

moods lurked the wisdom of the serpent that could wait
for years to strike its prey. After the fall of Becket he
trusted to no single minister again—not even Glanvill—
but led the government himself, as he well knew how.
Through a long reign he had to deal with proud barons,
with jealous prelates, with rebellious children; but despite
all his difficulties he was able to control and maintain
intact his vast empire, to restore order to its administration and finance, and to leave it comparatively secure for
his successors.

His two sons, Richard and John, in turn sat on the
throne of England. They may be reckoned among the
worst Kings that the country ever had. The absence of
the first, the presence of the second, were equally disastrous to the State, and only the personal exploits of the
elder brother have somewhat redeemed his defects as a
ruler. Richard was indeed courageous—as were nearly
all his race. He was handsome, he was gallant, he could
be generous. But he was savage, merciless, and entirely
reckless of his people. He never learnt a word of English;
in a reign of ten years he only spent a few months in
England; and his continual and useless campaigns saddled
his English subjects with a load of debt.

His brother John, on the admission of all his contemporaries, was bereft of nearly every public and private
virtue. Cruelty, lust, greed and deceit, branded him
from his earliest years. Morose in company, forbidding
in pleasure, livid in anger, he disdained both God and man.
" Foul as it is," says the chronicler, " hell itself is defiled
by the still fouler presence of John." Well named
" Sansterre," he contributed nothing and lost all he could.
He called down the Pope's curse on his country and yielded
him up his crown; he made the land ring with his vice and
his shame, and the charter that was torn from him at the
end of his life augments rather than lessens his evil fame.

In Henry III. the bad blood of his father was not yet
burnt out. Educated among sound statesmen, with
every chance of success, the hereditary taint of treachery
was still strong within him. Threats could deter, but

loyalty could not persuade him. Credulous, wayward, reckless and obstinate, he ever preferred a foreign favourite and an exotic Church to the people and the customs which he should have cherished. A man of great desires but short sight, he strove to depress the nobles and dispense with the ministers who should have helped him. His piety alone redeemed him, for, as St. Louis said of him, " Whatever his sins, his prayers will save his soul."* In a reign of nearly sixty years he is best remembered, like his father, for a concession which was wrenched by force from his weak and unwilling hands—the first complete Parliament.

These four Kings were all foreigners at heart, speaking and thinking in French, more at home in France than in England. Their alien sympathies were largely responsible for the growth of that new nobility, blended from Saxon and Norman, which was in time to lead the native English back into their inheritance. The loss of Normandy, the interdicts of Rome, the ignominy of invasion, were themselves the bonds that bound baron and burgher into an alliance of sentiment and interest for the land in which they were born. That sentiment, that interest, were expressed in their revolt against foreign control, in their insistence on traditional rights, in their enforcement of a representative system of rule. The lord, the knight, the peasant and the priest were forced together for the common weal, and their combination at last forced the King of England to become an Englishman.

As the Kings waxed weaker, their servants had grown stronger, and the thirteenth century is marked by a succession of ministers who were soldiers before they were statesmen. By fearless policy these men taught their sovereigns a painful lesson and showed their fellow-subjects a needed example. In their days the idea of nationality was born again, by their endeavours the blessings of liberty were gained for all, and as their legacy constitutional government was first achieved. Their time is distant, their records are few, their motives are often

* Prothero, 125.

6

obscure, but from what survives their characters can still be discerned. Living in the very flower of the age of chivalry, they have left behind them an unsullied name for knightly courage, for truth, loyalty and honour, which stands out brilliantly against the dark background of their era and the gloomy figures of their Kings.

I.—MARSHALL

William Marshall, or Mareschal, afterwards Earl Marshal and Earl of Pembroke, was born, probably in Wiltshire, about 1145. His father was John, the son of Gilbert, who was master of the King's Marshalsea in the reign of Henry I.; his mother was the Lady Sybil, daughter of Patrick Devereux, Earl of Salisbury.

John Marshall, who had been a soldier and man of some position in his county, was a close adherent of the Empress Maud. During Stephen's reign he was continually fighting for her in the neighbourhood of Winchester, Marlborough, Devizes and Oxford. At Newbury he was besieged by the King in 1152, and on this occasion he had to give up his second son, William, as a hostage for the surrender of the fortress. He refused to abide by the truce, and the boy would have paid the penalty had not Stephen been delighted by his spirited and engaging manners. But his ransom cost another castle.

" William Marschalle o chance was taken at þat turne
He gaf for his delyverance þe castelle of Schirburne." *

When Henry II. came to the throne the elder Marshall received some crown lands and a place at the exchequer. He was summoned to several Great Councils, and is mentioned in 1164 as bringing a suit for a Sussex manor against Archbishop Becket. A year later he died a fairly rich man, leaving several children.

Some time before this the young William had been sent to Tancarville in Normandy to be trained as a knight. For ten years he remained in France, acquiring the

* Langtoft, i. 121.

accomplishments of the age. He accompanied his uncle, the Earl of Salisbury, to Poitou in 1163, and after the latter's death in a foray, was taken prisoner by Geoffrey de Lusignan, and kept in close captivity for several months. Ransomed at last by Queen Eleanor's good offices, he was fitted out afresh with arms and a horse at her expense, and came back to England in 1170 with the reputation of a gallant soldier. His prowess, the record of his family, and the interest of the Queen recommended him to Henry, who attached him to the person of his eldest son as a governor and companion. In 1173 he was knighted and again won distinction in the Norman campaign against the Flemings. His royal pupil held him in the highest favour and honoured him by receiving the accolade from his hands. From this time until the younger Henry's death, ten years later, Marshall was his constant adviser and friend. His bravery in battle, his dexterity in the lists, his noble appearance and manner, made him one of the most striking figures at the court. Occasional rivals were able to disturb him, but his simple, straightforward character always triumphed over them in the end.

The death of his young master in 1183 was a serious blow to his prospects. Henry's last request to him had been to carry his cross to the Holy Land, and some time in 1184 Marshall set out on that long pilgrimage, encouraged and provisioned by the old King. Marshall had already been something of a traveller in France and Germany; but an expedition to Palestine in the twelfth century was a serious adventure. He acquitted himself, however, with his usual good fortune. He was two years away, and when he came back to England he had made a name which the Knights of the Temple and the Knights of St. John spread over Europe. To the lustre of the preux chevalier he had added that of the crusader; his knowledge had been widened by his experiences in the East, and Henry II. was glad to add such a wise head to his Council.

Marshall was accordingly taken into the royal favour, sent as envoy to the French court, and chosen to act as

commander at Chinon, the Anjou home of the Plantagenets. During Henry's final struggles with his family,
he did his best to recall the King's second son, Richard,
to his duty. Henry had been compelled to retreat across
the Sarthe, when Richard, advancing on Mans, came up
with Marshall who was in command of the rearguard.
" By God's feet, Marshall," he cried, " slay me not."
" The devil slay you," said Marshall, " for I will not,"
and he contented himself with spearing Richard's horse.*
A few weeks later the old King died. His bastard son,
Geoffrey, the Chancellor, joined with Marshall in taking
his body to Fontevrault, and then the two made their
submission to Richard, who was sufficiently generous to
recognize their loyalty.

Before his death Henry had promised Marshall the hand
of Isabella de Clare, daughter and heiress of Richard,
Earl of Pembroke, and grand-daughter to the celebrated
Strongbow. This grant the new King confirmed, and in
August 1189 Marshall married his young wife—she was
only sixteen, about a third of his age. For him it was a
great alliance. Hitherto he had been " a landless man,
with naught but his knighthood."† Now he acquired
broad estates in England and Ireland, an earldom, *jure
uxoris*, and a definite position in the Council. At Richard's
coronation he shared with his elder brother, John, the
hereditary office of Marshal. He was named as one of the
King's sureties for accompanying Philip Augustus to the
Holy Land,‡ where Richard was to be burdened " with
the King of the French like a cat with a hammer hanging
to its tail ";§ and on Richard's departure for the East,
Marshall was appointed a Justiciar under Archbishop
Longchamp. With the latter's policy, however, he did not
agree, and for the next few years he was constantly
struggling to maintain his absent Sovereign's rights against
the uncertain rule of a series of rival ministers, and more
particularly against the usurping attempts of Earl John.

Early in 1194, by the death of his elder brother, he

* D.N.B., xxxvi. 226.   † *Ibid.*, xxxvi. 227.
‡ Foss, 432.   § R. Devizes, 258.

WILLIAM MARSHALL
EARL OF PEMBROKE

To face page 74

succeeded to the place of Marshal of England, and in his hands that office first acquired the power and dignity that afterwards distinguished it.

After Richard returned from his captivity Marshall again joined him in France, and for the next five years he was with him in all his fights and forays, a ready counsellor and dashing leader. When the King met his death in April 1199 it was to Marshall that he confided the care of the royal treasure, and it was mainly due to Marshall's support and that of Archbishop Fitzwalter that John's easy succession was due.

> " Ce li dist li Mar . . . Sire
> De cui nos devom faire rei
> Il respondi : ' Je entent a vei
> Le devom nos faire de Artur.'
> ' Ha ! Sire ' dist li Mar
> ' Il m'est vist que ce serreit mals. . . .
> Mes veez le conte Johan.' "*

Marshall was despatched to England, where he secured John's claim. In return he was invested with the full name and place of the earldom of Pembroke. Hitherto he had only enjoyed its revenues, now he received the title and dignity as well. Henceforward he signs in charters as *Comes Marescallus et Pembrociæ*.

Marshall was now well over fifty, but for six years he continued his steady career as a soldier, fighting for the King in Normandy, leading his armies, defending his castles. Twice he was sent as envoy to France or Scotland, and in 1206 he was left in command of the troops in England.

A year later he went over to pay his first visit to his wife's estates in Ireland. There for six years more he occupied himself in the management of her inheritance, reducing Leinster to order, making expeditions into Connaught and Ulster, and bringing the whole kingdom under some control. It was probably during these years that the best constructive work of his life was done, for he continued the policy of the Strongbows though with a

* Guill. le Mar., 11878-84.

less drastic hand. During this period John was in frequent disagreement with him, for Marshall had little sympathy with the heartless exactions by which the King was rapidly ruining England. John resented this outspoken attitude, and on his own expedition to Ireland he insisted on taking hostages from Marshall; but he recognized and respected loyalty to his dynasty, and in 1209 left him behind as Lord Deputy.

By this time John's position was becoming desperate. He had lost nearly all his continental dominions, Normandy, Anjou, Maine and Aquitaine having been successively conquered by the French. He now raised up a fresh enemy in the person of the Pope, over a dispute as to the election to the see of Canterbury. As a result the whole of England was laid under an interdict and the King himself excommunicated. His extortions had set every man against him, his lust every woman; his blasphemy was to add to his enemies every priest. But he cared for none of these things, and drove on his mad and sullen career.

Early in 1213 Marshall, now nearing seventy, came over to England. His name, his power and his prestige, no less than John's miserable situation, forced him into the place of Chief Minister. In that capacity he approved the Dover Treaty with the Papal legate, took charge of the young Prince Henry, and was left as viceroy on John's departure for Poitou.

In 1215, during the final struggle with the barons, he acted as the King's principal surety and envoy, and at Runnymede, "in the green water-meadow between Staines and Windsor,"* he witnessed the signing of Magna Carta, on which his name appears as one of the royal councillors sworn to observe its provisions. Throughout the invasion of Prince Louis and all the disasters of the next twelve months he remained loyal to John, a firm pillar to his tottering throne; and on the latter's death in October 1216 he was named one of the executors of the King's will. If anyone could save some-

* M. Paris, 255.

thing from the wreck it was he—such ⁻⁻ₛ the dying King's hope.

> " *Vos pri qu'il ait mon fitz en garde*
> *Kar james terres par nulli*
> *Ne maintendra se n'est par lui.*"*

The country was in dire straits and time was pressing. Marshall called together a few earls and barons at Gloucester, and placed the young Henry, only nine years old, before them. " Here," he said, " is your King. Rightly did we oppose his father for his many evils, but this child is innocent."†

Marshall's great age, his undisputed position, his experience, his unsullied character, marked him out as the man best fitted to hold the reins of government, and at a Council at Bristol in November he was chosen to act as Regent—*Rector regis et regni.*‡ His seal was used. in place of the Great Seal, and he witnessed the State documents at Westminster in place of the King. He did not covet this new responsibility, for he was old, and he had nothing to gain. But his life had been devoted to the service of the Plantagenets, and he was not the man to desert them at their need.

His Fabian sagacity at once showed itself. He made concessions and gained time. He republished the Great Charter, consoled the commons, and recalled many nobles to their allegiance. In May 1217 he attacked the French at Lincoln, killed their leader, the Comte de Perche—some say with his own hand—and then marched south to blockade London. Matters began to look badly for the invaders and in August, after de Burgh's naval victory off Dover, Louis came to terms. A month later he agreed to the treaty of Lambeth, and withdrew with his troops to France.

During the next year Marshall continued his work of restoring liberty and order. The Charter was reissued, and was followed by the Forest Charter, which

---

* Guill. le Mar., 15188-90.   † M. Paris, 292.
‡ W. Hemingburg, i. 257.

meant so much to the peasants. But the old soldier was
beginning to fail in health: the exertions of the last few
years had overtaxed his strength. Feeling that his end
was near, he had himself admitted a Knight Templar, and
on his birthday, May 14, 1219, he died at his manor of
Caversham. He was buried in the Temple Church in
London, where his effigy still remains—a venerable monu-
ment of his day. An epitaph styles him *Hybernicorum
nocivus edomitor: Anglis honor et gloria: Normannis
negotiator; Gallicis bellicosus; et miles invincibilis.**

By his wife, who survived him only a year, he left five
sons, who all succeeded in turn to the earldom of Pembroke and the marshalship of England; but none left
any issue—a failure due, it was said, to the curse of an
Irish bishop from whom their father had seized some
lands. The place of Marshal of England thus devolved
in 1245 on his eldest daughter Matilda, who had married
Hugh Bigod, Earl of Norfolk. Through that line it
descended to the Mowbrays and Howards, who hold it
to-day.

William Marshall was "tall, strong, good-looking and
well made, with brown hair." Valiant, wise and honest,
he was a perfect knight of the Middle Ages, a pattern of
chivalry.

As a boy he had known Stephen, and had perhaps
heard from him tales of his grandsire the Conqueror, and
his uncles William Rufus and Henry I. As a young man
he had formed one of the splendid court of the first
Plantagenet, had seen the rise and fall of Becket, had
wandered across Europe, had fought with the Saracens
in Syria. His middle life had been passed by the side
of Richard the Lion Heart, in the godless Councils of
John, and among the wild chiefs in Ireland. As an old
man he had quelled a rebellion, vanquished an invader,
and saved a dynasty: such were the tales he could tell
to his little King.

A soldier by profession, a statesman by necessity, his
sympathy and training were conservative; but he never

* M. Paris, 304.

allowed his devotion to the four Sovereigns whom he served to compromise his honour or obscure his country's rights. He saw one royal brother do homage for his realm to the Emperor, another receive it as a fief from the Pope; he saw a native prince wreak such wrongs on England that a foreigner had to come to set them right; but nothing ever shook his courage or tarnished his fame. As Richard said of him—

*" Ne fue unques malveis ne fals."**

His prowess was celebrated over Christendom, his fidelity appealed even to the faithless sons of Henry II., his sagacity secured them their inheritance. As Regent it was open to him, and by temper he may well have been inclined to recede from the promises which John had been forced to give. But Marshall's principle through life had been to keep his word, and to his personal honesty the earliest confirmation of the Charter is probably due. His sons were the firmest support of de Burgh in his troubles, and his daughter-in-law became de Montfort's wife. Thus the ideas and traditions of the old earl were handed on to the ministers who followed him.

A fine type of the mediæval hero, William Marshall was at once a warrior, a counsellor and a ruler. He stands high in that long line of English nobles who have devoted their lives and their services to the State, never swerving from loyalty to their prince, yet always safe-guarding the rights of the people. Perhaps unwittingly one of the founders of English liberty, he left a conception of patriotism, an example of statesmanship that led in less than a lifetime to a still fuller development of freedom.

HUBERT DE BURGH

Hubert de Burgh, afterwards Earl of Kent, was born about 1175, the son of Sir Reyner de Burgh of North Tudenham in Norfolk. His father's brother, William

* Guill. le Mar., 9857.

Fitzaldelm, had been Steward to Henry II., and succeeded
the famous Strongbow as Lord Deputy of Ireland in
1177. His family, however, was not of the greater
nobility (though Foss credits it with a descent from
Charlemagne), but was one of those that Henry II. had
raised to office as a balance against the engrossing power
of the Norman barons.

As a young man Hubert de Burgh was first attached
to the household of King Richard, " to whom he was a
faithful servant."* In 1200 he was sent by John on an
embassy to Lisbon to ask in marriage the King of
Portugal's daughter. Nothing came of the mission, as
John, during the absence of his envoys, chose another
wife, Isabella of Angoulême. De Burgh, however, kept
the King's favour, and on his return he was made
Chamberlain of the Household. In that year he married
Joan, daughter of William de Vernon, Earl of Devon,
and widow of William Brewer. He had already acquired
the name of a good soldier, and he now received a series
of military posts. In 1201 he was sent to guard the
Welsh border; in 1202 he was made Governor of Falaise;
in 1203 Constable of Dover Castle; and in 1204 commander
of Chinon.

It was while he was at Falaise that he appears to have
been the custodian of Arthur of Brittany, the son of
John's elder brother Geoffrey and the rightful heir to
the crowns of Normandy and England. John is said to
have ordered de Burgh to blind or kill Arthur, but de
Burgh managed to avoid doing this and also to escape
John's displeasure. The tale is doubtful, though Shakespeare's only known authority, Ralph of Coggeshall, was
a contemporary and usually an accurate writer. Whatever
the truth, de Burgh seems to have come out of the affair
with some credit both to his head and heart. His diplomacy evidently appealed to John, for he was again sent
as an ambassador, on this occasion to the King of France.
His mission was to refute the various charges against
John for defrauding Arthur of his inheritance—a matter

* M. Paris, 381.

in which he was probably well informed. King Philip, however, attached less importance to the excuses than to the opportunity they afforded, and he proceeded to attack the English dominions in France. Gradually he conquered most of them, and de Burgh himself, after a gallant but unavailing defence of Chinon, was captured in 1205. He was then kept a prisoner in France, and during several years there is hardly any mention of his name.

On his return to England John again made use of him. He was appointed sheriff of Berks, Devon, Somerset and Cornwall, and was allowed to fortify his castle of Dunster. In 1209 he married his second wife, Beatrix, daughter of William de Warrenne and widow of Lord Bardolf. When three years later she died, she left him considerable property.

In 1214 he was appointed seneschal of Poitou, one of the last remaining English possessions on the Continent. By now he had become one of John's most trusted advisers, and in the French treaty of September of that year his name stands next after that of Ranulf, Earl of Chester.* He supported the King in the Runnymede negotiations, and is cited in the preamble to Magna Carta as a royal councillor. At the signing of that document he was made Justiciar of England, his salary being fixed at £300 a year.† Many years later he said that " the lord King John committed to him the office of Justiciar at Runnengemede in presence of the Lord Stephen, Archbishop of Canterbury, Earl of Warren, Earl de Ferrars, and other great men of the nation."‡

His new duties did not make de Burgh any the less a soldier. In 1216 he was back again at Dover, where, with 140 knights, he held the castle for three months against Prince Louis of France. The latest devices of battering rams, catapults and mangonels were vainly directed against the fortress; its commander was approached with offers of bribes and honours; and finally

* Rymer, i. 191.   † Foss, 139.   ‡ State Trials, i. 14.

a strict blockade was enforced. But despite the French successes in other parts of England, despite the flight of the King, despite the defections of many of the barons, de Burgh still held out. All the southern provinces had fallen into the power of Louis, " *praeter sola castella de Dovera et Windleshores.*"*

John's death in 1216 found him still unbeaten, and the prompt action of the old Earl Marshal soon lessened the confidence of the French and restored that of the English. The young Henry was crowned, the Great Charter renewed, the invader attacked. Louis was expecting reinforcements, and to prevent their arrival was de Burgh's principal object. On August 24, 1217, a French fleet of eighty large and many smaller vessels set sail from Calais, under the command of Eustace the Monk. De Burgh had less than half this number of ships, mostly collected from the Cinque Ports. The French made for the North Foreland, intending to sail up the Thames, but de Burgh steered a course to windward of them, came up with their rear and, neglecting the transports, attacked the fighting fleet in detachments.

> " *A quelque feu ien a tore*
> *La nef sire Hubert de Bure*
> *Vint devant les autres siglant.*"†

The English had just been encouraged by the auspicious news of the relief of Lincoln. Their ships were armed with iron prows, and they threw quicklime into the air, which blew into the eyes of the French. They were adepts at manœuvring, and by shooting, boarding and ramming they were able eventually to secure a victory of the first order. Only sixteen French ships escaped, the rest were all taken or sunk. Eustace the Monk was beheaded, the convoy was captured, and the hopes of the invaders fell.‡

King Philip seems to have expected some such a result

---

* M. Paris, 282.   † Guill. le Mar., 17353-5.

‡ Stubbs (ii. 301) says that Philip of Albini and John Marshall were the responsible commanders.

to his son's adventures. In the contemporary song of the Marshal he says—

> " Certes je n'en dotoe rien
> Quant Willelmes li Mar
> S'entremeteit de ceste chose
> Que il metreit a la forsclose
> Loeis & tot sun afaire."*

In September a truce was made, and shortly afterwards Louis finally retired to France. By cutting the enemy's communications and striking at his fighting fleet England had maintained her command of the sea, and had won her first naval victory.

This success vastly improved de Burgh's position. He was continued in his place as Justiciar, and on the death of the Earl Marshal two years later he succeeded to the principal authority in the kingdom. His reputation as the guardian of the Channel and the preserver of Dover, the key of England, had made his name a household word. But he had many difficulties to contend with. The barons were powerful and dissatisfied, and there was a strong foreign party ready to play into the hands of France or of the Pope, as occasion might offer. Pandulf, the Roman legate, Peter des Roches, the Poictevin bishop of Winchester, and Ranulf, the Norman earl of Chester, led the malcontents. Their first object was to fill the chief places in the kingdom with their own friends, most of whom were aliens, to the exclusion of the English. De Burgh, however, supported by Archbishop Langton, insisted that Englishmen should be employed, and by stern measures he was able to enforce his policy.

In 1222 his opponents started a riot in London under a foreigner named Constantine, who led a rabble through the streets shouting " Montjoie," the cri de guerre of the French. The Justiciar had him hanged, cut off the hands of the ringleaders, and so suppressed the rising; but the Londoners did not forget his severity. All over the country the nobles still held garrisons in royal castles

---

* Guill. le Mar., 17610-5.

which they had seized in the time of King John. De
Burgh compelled their surrender, and so enabled the
central administration to function again. But his action
angered the barons. Pandulf, des Roches and Ranulf
tried more than once to dislodge him, but he succeeded
in defeating them all. At last the legate resigned, the
bishop went on a crusade, and even the great northern
earl made some show of submission. By 1224 de Burgh
had become predominant, and he ruled England without
hindrance.

Since he had begun to rise in the world de Burgh had
not neglected his own interests. From John and his son
he had received large grants of lands, while the profits
of his office had increased his wealth. He had also continued his system of making good marriages, each wife
being of higher rank and greater fortune than the last.
After the death of his second wife in 1212 he had led to
the altar the Lady Isabel, a daughter and co-heiress of
William, Earl of Gloucester, and widow of Geoffrey
Mandeville, Earl of Essex.* She had once been affianced
to King John, and her family was one of the first in
England. Within a few years she also was dead, and
in 1221 de Burgh flew after still loftier game. At the
wedding of Alexander, King of Scots, with the Lady Joan,
King John's daughter, de Burgh, then nearly fifty years
of age, himself married the Lady Margaret, a sister of
the Scottish King. He thus became the brother-in-law
of his own Sovereign. This alliance annoyed the English
nobles, for the importance that de Burgh now attained
brought him more honours and possessions. He became
guardian of the young heirs of the Earls of Arundel and
Norfolk; his brother was made Bishop of Ely; one nephew
received the see of Norwich, and another was given the
hand of the Countess of Essex; while Brïto, his closest
friend, was made Treasurer. He acquired or built numerous castles—" Hubert's Folly " on the Welsh border was
one; Hatfield, Dunster and Whitehall were among his

* G. E. C. disallows Lady Isabel, makes Margaret de Arsick the first
wife, and somewhat advances the dates. Cokayne, iv. 350.

houses. Thus he was pursuing the policy of the prelates who had preceded him as Justiciar, and was laying up for himself a somewhat similar lot. The same forces were at work against him; he was hampered by the same faults; and he was to fall by as sudden a fate as Flambard, though not to so deep a ruin as Roger.

In 1227, at a Great Council held at Oxford, de Burgh was created Earl of Kent, and on the same occasion Henry, now twenty years old, declared himself, on his ministers' advice, of age to assume the government. This announcement was the knell of de Burgh's control. The King was determined to be a military leader, while de Burgh knew that he was incapable of such a rôle. Accordingly he opposed his master's policy and reaped the usual reward. An unsuccessful Welsh war in 1228 and an abortive expedition against France a year later shook his influence. The death of Archbishop Langton lost him a potent ally, and his star began to pale. Henry, still anxious to earn glory in the field, insisted on another campaign against the French; but when the troops were ready at Portsmouth it was found that there were not sufficient transports. Henry lost his temper, called the Justiciar "an old traitor, who had taken 5,000 marks from the French Queen to cause this failure, as he had done before," and drew his sword on him.* The Earl of Chester interposed, de Burgh was able to withdraw, and soon afterwards he made his peace with the King. But the rift once started was carefully widened by his enemies. The nobles were already fretting at his power, his riches and his pride. The religious houses, oppressed by taxes, now added their complaints.

In 1230 the expedition to Poitou at last took place. It was unfortunate from start to finish. Nothing useful was done, for " the Justiciar Hubert would allow no attacks on the enemy, and the earls and barons spent their time feasting, . . . so that on their return an infinity of money had been spent, and numbers of nobles had died of sickness or famine, or were reduced to extreme poverty."†

* M. Paris 363. † *Ibid.*, 367.

But from these disasters de Burgh profited again, for
the deaths of several magnates gave him the custody of
their heirs and lands.

In the meanwhile his policy of taxing the Church had
roused up potent foes. He had made the great abbeys
pay fines for the confirmation and renewal of their privileges, much as Flambard had done before him, and this
was a sin not easily forgiven. He had also deeply offended
the new archbishop by suing him for some lands in Kent.
There was at this time a strong feeling against the Papal
exactions, particularly against the way in which money
was collected for Rome; and in 1232 an organized pillage
took place of the Pope's stores all over England. The
bishops accused de Burgh of connivance in this, and the
nobles supported them. Peter des Roches had just
returned to England; he was still eyed askance, and the
King was warned to avoid "*petræ et rupes*,"* but he
had considerable influence. He used it to help in the
overthrow of his old enemy, and against this combination
the waning fortune of de Burgh rapidly sank. The
treasurership was taken from Brito, his other friends were
turned out of office, and on July 29, 1232, after seventeen
years of power, he was dismissed from the place of Justiciar.

He instantly fell from everything to nothing, and for
the next eighteen months he led a hectic life. A series
of charges was at once brought against him by the King.
He was required to render a full account of all fines,
revenues, wardships and escheats that he had received
since he first took office. He answered that King John
had given him a perpetual release from such a claim.
Des Roches replied that the release had lapsed with the
new reign. De Burgh was next accused of impeding the
King's marriage, of betraying his troops to the French,
of improperly taking to wife the Princess of Scotland, and
finally, of " having stolen from the treasury a certain
precious stone that had the property of rendering its
wearer invincible in war, and of having sold it to Llewellyn
of Wales."† His friends deserted him, and only Luke,

* Campbell, Chief Justices, i. 52.   † M. Paris, 377.

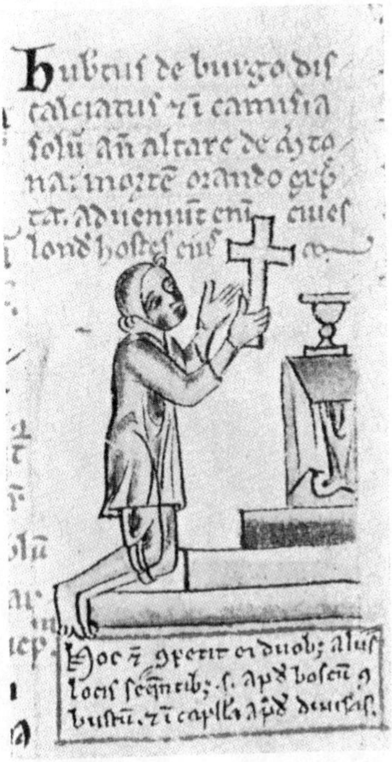

From an MS.

HUBERT DE BURGH

EARL OF KENT

To face page 86

the Archbishop of Dublin, begged the King to allow him
a reasonable time to prepare his defence. Still graver
accusations followed. De Burgh was said to have sold
prisoners for his own benefit and put rioters to death
unjustly, to have poisoned the Earls of Pembroke and
Salisbury, as well as his friend Archbishop Langton, and
to have acquired the King's favour by sorcery.

Henry, indeed, was ready to go to any extremes.
He made public proclamation that all having anything
against the late Justiciar should at once file their complaints. De Burgh saw that there was no time to lose,
and fled to Merton Priory for sanctuary. The Mayor
of London was ordered to arrest him by force; and
accordingly the citizens were mustered and set out, 20,000
strong, to give effect to the royal commands. The Bishop
of Winchester refused to protest against this violation of
the Church's privileges, and it was left to de Burgh's old
adversary, Ranulf of Chester, to warn the King that
such a tumult might lead to worse troubles. Messengers
were then despatched to recall the citizens on their march:
" one rode quickly and succeeded in bringing them back;
the other, an enemy of de Burgh's, purposely delayed,
but on his way his horse, though only ambling, stumbled
and threw him, so that he broke his neck and died."*

De Burgh was now allowed to start for his home, but
before he had got there Henry again changed his mind
and sent 300 horse after him to Brentwood. De Burgh
was aroused just in time to flee naked to the neighbouring
church. There, holding the sacrament in one hand and
a cross in the other, he faced his pursuers. Despite the
sacrilege, they seized him, and a blacksmith was fetched
to fetter his ankles. The smith asked for whom the
fetters were wanted, and on hearing, refused to work
against " the man who had so often saved the country
from foreigners, who had restored England, who had
served the King so well in France, eating even horse-
flesh; who had preserved Dover, the key of the realm."†
But his protests were of no avail. De Burgh, with his

* M. Paris, 378. † *Ibid.*, 379.

7

feet bound, was put on a horse, hurried to the Tower, and
lodged in a dungeon. This last outrage, however, was
too much for the Bishop of London. He went to the King
and threatened to excommunicate everyone concerned
unless the victim was restored to sanctuary. Again
Henry submitted, and de Burgh was sent back to his
chapel, but the sheriffs of Hertford and Essex were
directed to starve him out. This they proceeded to do,
digging a ditch and closing every entrance to the church.
For two months the blockade continued. Then, all
supplies failing, de Burgh was forced to capitulate, and
he was again taken to the Tower.

By this time, however, Henry was in a calmer frame
of mind and more willing to compromise. De Burgh
was rich: much of his treasure was kept in the Temple,
but the Templars refused to give it up without his permission: he now professed himself willing to resign it
to the King. The Archbishop of Dublin again pleaded
for him; the Earl of Chester was dead; and at last an
accommodation was come to. A hoard of gold and jewels
was handed over to the royal officers and de Burgh's
imprisonment was relaxed. The King remarked that he
would rather be thought " easy-going and a fool (*fatuus
et remissus*) than a tyrant and a man of blood; that he
had heard that Hubert had served well his uncle Richard
and his father John, and that his known good deeds should
outweigh evils that were not proven."*

In February 1233 de Burgh was sent to Devizes Castle
under the custody of Richard of Cornwall, the King's
brother, Earl Warrenne, and the Earl of Pembroke.
" There is little doubt that the sympathies of his guardians
were wholly on his side,'† as were those of the townsmen.
But the Bishop of Winchester was not yet satisfied: he
tried to get Devizes transferred to himself, and for the
third time de Burgh took sanctuary, " jumping from the
castle wall on the back of a friend into the brambles by
the moat,"‡ and then fleeing to the parish church. Henry
had not learnt wisdom, and by his orders the warders

* M. Paris, 381.   † Bodington, 19.   ‡ *Ibid.*, 20.

drove their prisoner back to the castle. The Bishop of
Salisbury protested, but no heed was paid to him, and
he had to go to London and see the King before he gained
his point. But again the sheriff was told to starve
de Burgh out, and the latter, fearing death, now determined to escape. In October, 1233, some friends seized
him and he got away to Chepstow Castle, which belonged
to his friends the Marshalls. Here for some months he
remained an outlaw and in hiding. But early in 1234 there
came a reaction against Henry's foreign favourites, and
des Roches fell. The country had begun to regret de Burgh,
and soon after Easter the King received him, embraced
him, and restored him to his earldom and possessions:
throughout his troubles the Earl of Pembroke and the
Marshall family had stood by him, and it was largely due
to their influence and to that of the clergy that he was
released.*

De Burgh was now readmitted to the Council, though
he held no office. He stuck to his old methods and
managed to marry his daughter Margaret to the Earl of
Gloucester, who was a minor and a royal ward. In 1237
he was at last reconciled to des Roches, and in the later
struggles with the barons he stood by the King. But
Henry still coveted his property, and in 1239 brought a
further suit against him. It was ill-contrived and made
up of antiquated and improbable charges. One count
alleged that he had called the King leprous, foolish,
squinting and impotent;† another that he had tried to
murder him with a knife. He was given time, however,
to present a defence, and was easily able to prove his
innocence. Nevertheless, he found it best to resign four
of his favourite castles, Blanch, Grosmund, Skenefrith
and Hatfield, which were appropriated by the King; but
in a short time he was again reconciled to Henry, and his
castles were then restored.

For the remaining years of his life he kept clear of
politics, and retired to the country. Since his confinement he had been in poor health and had intended to

---

* R. Gloucester, 180-264.   † State Trials, i. 22.

join the religious order of his old friends the Templars. But he was not able to take the vows, for on May 12, 1243, he died at Banstead. He was buried in the church of the Black Friars in London, to which foundation he had devised his house near Westminster. This was subsequently bought by the Archbishop of York, and it passed eventually to the Crown, when it became the Palace of Whitehall.

De Burgh left two sons, Hubert and John, who inherited his estates, though they did not succeed to his earldom, which had been limited to his issue by the Lady Margaret. His male line is believed to be extinct, though the families of Clanricarde and Mayo deduce their descent from his brother William.

Of his private character not much is known. He was brave, religious, saving, anxious to build up by wealth and connection a family that could withstand the assaults of the greater nobles. Avarice and ambition, perhaps intolerance and pride, were his faults, but no bribe and no threat could ever shake him. As a minister he maintained the traditions of his predecessor, William Marshall, doing his best to protect the King against the counsel of aliens and his own weak will. For twelve years he kept the country tranquil, allowing it time to recover its strength after the dismal days of Richard and John; the value of his rule is best shown by the troubles that followed when his guiding hand was removed.

His policy was purely national. He upheld the rights of the English to fill the principal offices in their own land, resisting the assumptions of Norman nobles and Poitevin priests. His opponents were at times too strong for him, but with the country at large he was popular and he had the mass of the people behind him; but their opinion was hardly yet articulate, and the protest of the Brentwood blacksmith is one of the earliest expressions of national feeling.

De Burgh's training had been sound. He had spent his early days as an active, wary captain, and his later rule was fearless and politic. Perched on an unstable

eminence, well in advance of his time, he set an example
to the English barons of what statesmanship should be.
He could remember a King whose empire extended from
the borders of Scotland to those of Spain: he had seen
much of it lost, and had learnt what evils could result
from continental policies and foreign wars. When in
middle life he came to power, he determined that England
should be the centre of her own system and not " a satellite
in an Angevin constellation." He tried to make the King
as proud of St. Edward's crown as of Rollo's coronet or
Fulk's ermine cap. Thus he strove to restore England to
the English, and the measure of his success is the name he
earned of " the last great Justiciar." Largely as a result
of his work that potent office was to be no more needed.

The exploits of de Burgh in his youth, his misfortunes
in old age, have tended to obscure the value of his long
administration. But those exploits, those misfortunes,
illustrate and embody his policy. The defence of Dover,
the defeat of the French fleet, meant that England was
to be a sea-power: the struggles with the Roman legate,
the French bishop and the Plantagenet King, taught her
that she must look to herself for leaders. Firm and
faithful, dexterous and daring, de Burgh was a soldier
that even the reckless John would regard; a statesman
that even the wretched Henry could regret; and he prepared the way for the master mind that was soon to
succeed him and to crown his work.

SIMON DE MONTFORT

Simon de Montfort, afterwards Earl of Leicester, was
born in the year 1208, probably at Evreux. He was the
third son of Count Simon IV. de Montfort and of Alix
de Montmorenci. His family, noble but not rich, took
their name from a hill castle near Chartres, where they
had been settled for several generations. They had
inherited the lordship of Evreux, and Simon's grandfather had married Amicia de Beaumont, sister and

co-heiress of Robert, fourth Earl of Leicester. At the latter's death in 1204 his earldom, which carried with it the hereditary office of High Steward of England, devolved on the elder Simon, but he was never invested with the dignity, and his English possessions were confiscated almost at once by King John, in payment for a debt.

Count Simon IV., seeing little chance of recovering his mother's property, devoted himself to the service of the King of France, who was then engaged in suppressing the heretics of Albi and in attacking their protector, Count Raymond of Toulouse. Pope Innocent III., the instigator of this Western crusade, was John's principal enemy in Europe, while Raymond of Toulouse was John's brother-in-law. Count Simon thus hoped to satisfy his orthodoxy and perhaps retrieve his estates at the same time. He was a man of remarkable character, fanatical in his faith, ruthless in war, but a brilliant and skilful soldier. He rose to be leader of the French armies, and in a series of bloody victories he was able to extirpate the reforming " atheists " of Albi and the free-thinking troubadours of Toulouse. His wife, almost as virile as her husband, used to follow him in his campaigns, and their sons were reared in a constant atmosphere of battles, sieges and interdicts. The count became a noted figure in Western Christendom, the most powerful man in the South of France, and the English barons, struggling under the tyranny of their own King, regarded him from a distance with wonder and respect. But his career came to an untimely end. He was killed by a stone at the siege of Toulouse in 1218, and his widow died three years later. He had been granted various lands in Languedoc by the King of France, and to these his eldest son Amaury now succeeded, though he had hard work to retain them. But the English property was a very speculative asset and needed individual attention. It had been given in wardship to a cousin, Ranulf, Earl of Chester, and Amaury de Montfort saw little chance of recovering it for himself. He therefore determined to make over all his claims on the earldom of Leicester to his younger brother, the latter, in exchange, ceding his rights in the French patrimony.

Accordingly in 1229 the young Count Simon came to England to win back his heritage. He had a difficult quest before him, for he was poor, a foreigner, and only just of age; but he had had a good fighting education, he held an exceptionally honoured name, and he was connected with some of the noblest families in the country.

At first Henry III. put him off, but eventually he was persuaded to promise him 400 marks a year for his military service.* Simon had enlisted the help of his cousin, the Earl of Chester, who was the guardian of his lands. " *Le Comte me mena-il,*" he says, " *avec li en Engleterre, et pria le Rai qu'il me receust a home de l'eritage mon pere, a quien j'avaie greingneur drait qe li, si comme li disait. . . . Einssinc mi sires li Rais prist mon homage e me fut ma terre rendue.*"† He now received some of his English estates, but he found them damaged and reduced in revenue, so that he still remained a poor man. Nor was he yet allowed to assume his title of Earl of Leicester, though he began to take part in the meetings of the Council. His undoubted abilities, however, his foreign blood, and his comparative detachment from English politics, recommended him to Henry's notice, and at the Queen's coronation in January 1236 he was allowed to officiate as High Steward of England.

During these years de Montfort had endeavoured to advance his fortunes by a good match—" *dans le mariage il voyait surtout une affaire* "‡—and had offered his hand to the Countess of Flanders and the Countess of Boulogne, both widows considerably older than himself. But there was strong opposition from the French court to such alliances, and Simon had to turn his attention to English ladies. There his looks, his courage, perhaps his forlorn state, helped him, and the King's sister Eleanor, the young widow of William Marshall, Earl of Pembroke, suddenly consented to marry him.

* Hen. III., i. 362.   † Bémont, 333.   ‡ *Ibid.*, 7.

In January 1238 the wedding was secretly celebrated in the royal chapel—in the corner of St. Edward's chamber. The King was privy to it, though he afterwards alleged that he had only consented to the union to hide his sister's shame. But the poor value of Henry's word, the known chastity of de Montfort, and the fact that his eldest child was not born until eleven months later, lent little colour to this excuse. Henry was essentially weak, headstrong and inclined to new counsels. The handsome and gallant foreigner probably appealed to him as much as to his sister, and it was only when the barons began to exclaim against the marriage that he regretted his decision: his dislike of Eleanor and of her husband began later on.

Objections, however, were taken to the alliance by the Church, for Eleanor had vowed never to remarry after her late husband's death. De Montfort with his wife hurried off to Rome to secure a papal dispensation for this lapse. He was aided by letters from the King and from the Emperor Frederic, who had married Isabella, Eleanor's sister. By spending money among the cardinals he managed to get what he wanted, and on his return to England he appeased by similar gifts the King's brother Richard, Earl of Cornwall.

In December 1238 his eldest son was born, and a month later his brother Amaury came over to London and finally resigned all his English rights. Simon de Montfort was then formally invested with the earldom of Leicester, and in June 1239 was chosen as a godfather to the young Prince Edward. But he was not to enjoy the royal favour for long. In the following August, at the Queen's churching at Westminster, the King suddenly accused him before all the court of seduction, bribery and debts. "*E me dit,*" writes de Montfort, "*assez de ledes paroles et honteuses que sont dures a recordeir, e la nuit maimes que nos fumes veniez a la feste de Relevailles de ma dame la Raine, il comanda qe je fuisse pris e mene a la Tour de Londres.*"*

* Bémont, 334.

Richard of Cornwall saved him for the moment, but de Montfort thought it best to fly the country with his wife. Money seems to have been at the bottom of this quarrel, and money quarrels with the King pursued de Montfort for the rest of his life. The revenues of his shattered earldom never sufficed to keep up the state of his equals; he had no patrimony of his own; he was hampered by old-standing debts; his wife's dowry was never paid; and for the next five-and-twenty years his existence was a continual financial struggle. "*La splendeur de sa fortune*," says Bémont, "*cachait bien des miseres.*"*

While de Montfort was abroad news was received of a serious defeat of the French at Gaza in Palestine. Many of his friends had been killed, and his brother Amaury, who was now Constable of France, had been taken prisoner. Throughout Western Europe there rose a wave of emotion, a resolve to retrieve this defeat, and Simon was one of the first to take the cross. Under its protection he returned to England, and with some difficulty raised sufficient funds for his journey. He sold a forest to the canons of Leicester for £1,000, and engaged himself for other sums. Then, under the leadership of the Earl of Cornwall, the expedition started. His wife accompanied Simon to Brindisi, where she remained and where her second son was born, and by October 1240 the English crusaders were assembled at Acre. But little of value was done, though Amaury de Montfort was ransomed and Ascalon was fortified, mostly at the expense of Earl Richard, who was reputed the wealthiest subject in Christendom. Of Simon's exploits there are no details, but there is a petition extant " of the barons, knights, and citizens of the Kingdom of Jerusalem" begging the Emperor "to leave him as their governor during the minority of the young Conrad."†

The offer came to nothing, and early in 1242 de Montfort was back again in Burgundy, and soon afterwards joined King Henry in his disastrous campaign in Poitou. To de Montfort the venture was also unfortunate, though

† Bémont, 10. † *Ibid.*, 15.

it should have been the reverse. He was at home in this part of France; he was just back from the Crusades; he was a practised and valiant leader, equally prominent in the Council and the field. But a single incident marred his success. Henry had wished to fight in front of the town of Saintes, and was nearly captured in so doing: de Montfort saw that such tactics were vain, and compelled him to retreat, saying that he ought to be shut up like Charles the Fool, and "*ke les maisons barrees de fer a Windesore seraient bones a son eos a garder-le seurement dedanz.*"* This insult Henry never forgot, and twenty years later he brought it against the earl.

After the winter, peace was made with the French, and the English army returned home. De Montfort had somewhat improved his position, for he had renewed his old friendships in the south and had shown Henry how useful he could be. He was now taken back into favour, and for the next five years he lived in England. When he came up to Westminster he took a leading part in the Council, where his hereditary office placed him high, and occasionally he was sent on missions to France; but for the most part he passed his time at Kenilworth, his principal castle, engaged in the education of his numerous family, and associating with some of the most famous literary men of his day. Robert Grosseteste, Bishop of Lincoln, and Adam de Marisco, the Oxford lecturer, were among his closest friends. Through them he got into touch with the teaching of the friars which was so much to influence him. About 1220 the two great orders of Franciscans and Dominicans, the Grey and the Black Friars, had first established themselves in England. They had set up schools at Oxford, and begun to teach a new religious theory of government. "The King," they said, "was responsible to God, his duty was to rule for the good of his people, and to listen to their advice." These tenets were to influence all the constitutional struggle under Henry III., and they gave the religious sympathies of de Montfort a democratic trend.†

* Bémont, 343.　　　　　　　　† Low, 481, 2

The earl lived in the generous style that his position involved, though his own tastes were simple and even severe. Money always remained a difficulty, and his wife seems never to have been an economical manager or a particularly agreeable companion. In the meanwhile Henry's government was going from bad to worse. Since de Burgh's dismissal his wild impulses had had full rein, and foreign favourites, extravagance and injustice were as rife as ever. De Montfort had as yet shown no sign of moving into definite opposition, though he acted with the other lords and prelates in several attempts to reduce Henry to reason.

In 1248 Louis IX. announced his crusade. De Montfort again took the cross, and on this occasion was selected as the leader of the English. But just at this moment bad news had come from Gascony. The most distant and unsettled of Henry's possessions, its affairs always called for a firm hand. The matter was urgent, and at Henry's request de Montfort agreed to go out there as seneschal or governor for a period of seven years. The terms on which the appointment was made included an aid of fifty knights and 2,000 marks on his arrival in the country, with all the revenues during his viceroyalty.

Gascony was a difficult land to control. It was inhabited by robber barons and factious burghers, who lived in moated castles or walled towns, and were imbued with traditions of licence and privilege which no prince had yet been able to subdue. But de Montfort knew with what he had to deal, and he had the example of his father before him. He attacked the barons and razed their castles; he besieged the towns, taking the leading malcontents prisoner; he built a chain of forts right across the country, and within twelve months he had introduced some form of order. "He so reduced the more prominent men, and bore himself so bravely and faithfully, that he obtained the praise and favour of all the King's friends, and was acknowledged to have served his country well in everything."*

* M. Paris, 767.

But although his exploits at first satisfied Henry, serious complaints from Gascony soon began to arrive at Westminster. The King of Navarre, Gaston de Bearn, the city of Bordeaux, were all powerful factors in Southern France, and de Montfort's stern rule had aroused resentment throughout the land. Continual risings of the barons kept him always at work; his troops, his supplies, and his treasure were soon dispersed, and he was forced to come to England to get fresh help from the King and to justify his actions. He writes to Henry: " *Por ce que je sui si mauvoleu de les grauntz genz de la terre, por ce que je sostien voz dreitures et de la poure genz contre aus, peril et hounte me serait.*"*

On his first visit to England he received some funds, and he returned to his government to pursue still more vigorous measures. By the middle of the year 1251 he was able to report again that the province was quiet. But on the question of his expenses disputes began, and though they were temporarily settled, another revolt in Gascony gave the King the excuse of saying that matters had been ill-managed. Further Gascon envoys with more complaints appeared, and at last the earl had to come over and stand his trial for misgovernment.

Henry had now veered round to the Gascon side and was quite ready to desert his deputy. The business was debated before the Council and high words passed. The original issue, that of ill-treating the Gascons, was soon obscured. De Montfort accused the King of not repaying the vast expenses he had incurred abroad. Henry replied that " with a supplanter and a traitor no promises need be kept." The earl leapt to his feet, saying that had not the King been protected by his name and royal dignity, " he had spoken in an evil hour."† Henry, beside himself with rage, would have ordered him to be seized then and there, but the lords present " would in no-wise consent." A bitter feud thus arose between the two. The earl returned to Gascony, with or without the King's leave, and in a few months agreed to resign his place for an

* Hen. III., ii. 53.   † M. Paris, 837.

indemnity of 7,000 marks. He was immediately offered by the French nobles the great place of Seneschal of France, with the chief seat in the Council of Regency during the absence of Louis in the East. But de Montfort refused—" he did not wish to seem a deserter."

A fresh rebellion had recently started in Gascony, and in 1253 Henry himself went there. He was soon compelled to summon de Montfort to his aid, and by him the revolt was quickly quelled. A year later the earl was back again in England, in apparent favour, and employed as before on missions to France and Scotland and sitting in the Council. He had now risen to a very high place in the estimation of his fellow-barons. His campaigns, his years of rule in Gascony, his long experience of his royal brother-in-law, had taught him much. But his hot temper, his intolerance of deceit or abuses, his continual financial troubles, had made him a hard man to deal with. As a leader he was rarely at a loss, as a subject or a counsellor he was often overbearing and obstinate. Although born a foreigner, he had come to regard himself, and generally to be regarded, as an Englishman—and he strongly resented the King's continual subjection to Frenchmen and Italians, who got money from the exchequer which more rightly should have gone into English pockets.

Henry had just accepted the barren crown of Sicily for his son; the price was a large subsidy from England. To this the Council objected, and the King threatened their leader, the Bishop of London, with deprivation. "*Tollis mitram, galea remanet,*" the fierce prelate replied. It was the spirit of the times.* The bishops were as surly and stubborn subjects as the barons; the principle of self-taxation underlay the whole struggle.

At a Council held in 1258 de Montfort had an argument with William of Valence, the King's half-brother and the chief of the foreign favourites. De Valence accused the Earls of Gloucester and Leicester of being traitors. They " turned red," and Leicester sprang up and said: " No, no, William, I am no traitor nor traitor's son; our fathers

* Prothero, 118.

were not alike."*　　This quarrel was the real beginning of the Barons' war. Immediately afterwards the two earls joined in a private alliance with several other nobles, promising a mutual support. The document that bound them is still in the Bibliothèque Nationale:

Nos Richars de Clare, cuens de Gloucestre et de Herteford ; Rogiers Bigoz, cuens mareschaux et cuens de Norfouke ; Symons de Monford, cuens de Leycestre ; Pierre de Savoe ; Hues li Vigoz ; Johans li fiz Gefroy ; et Pierre de Monford, faisun savoir a totes genz ke nos avans jure sor sainz Evangiles, et sumes tenu ensemble par celi seirement, et prometons a bone foi ke chascuns de nos e tuit ensemble nos entre aiderons e nos e les nos contre totes genz, droit feisant et prenant kanke nos porrons, senz meffeire, sauve la foi nostre segnour le roy d'Engleterre e de la corone.

En tesmoing de lakel chose nos avans feit ces letres schelees de nos sehex.

E ce fu fait a Londres, le Vendredi apres la quinzeine de Pake, l'ant de Nostre Segnour mil deus cenz et cinkante et wit.†

This meant that the die was cast. De Montfort was not a man to enter into frivolous undertakings or to consort with men of straw. He held a high place in the State, he had a close experience of government, he knew of many public wrongs to right, and he was conscious of private injuries that might well tempt him to action; while "the counsels which he received from his wife cannot have been counsels of conciliation."‡

Besides de Clare, Earl of Gloucester, he had as allies Bohun, Earl of Hereford, and Bigod, Earl of Norfolk, the holders of the great hereditary places of Constable and Marshal of England. He himself filled the principal of all those dignities, that of High Steward, and it is probable that about this time he first began to be influenced by ideas of the rights and duties that pertained to that office. Norman in origin, it had once been a

* M. Paris, 964.　　† Bémont, 327-8.　　‡ Creighton, 92.

mere court employment, but in the process of time it had assumed or been endued with far wider powers, and though their exercise had latterly fallen into desuetude— in face of the wide functions of the Justiciar—there was no reason why they should not be revived.

The High Steward (*Senescallus totius Angliæ*) was styled the "Prime Officer under the King."* Alone among his colleagues did he precede the primates, alone was he qualified with the title of "grace," alone did he have control over no special department but a general supervision of all. In the days of the early Plantagenets the office was already traditional, but its magnitude was not diminished by its mystery. An account not later than the early fourteenth century ascribes to it the most autocratic powers. Its holder could in certain cases override the decisions of the Chancellor, the Treasurer and the justices; he could act temporarily for the Great Council when it was not in session; and "if the King was being guided by evil counsellors," then after certain warnings, and acting in conjunction with the High Constable, "he could raise the royal banner in the name of the King and the kingdom, and attack and seize such counsellors as public enemies of the State."†

To a man of de Montfort's temperament, burning with patriotic zeal, acerbated by years of strife, strengthened by the knowledge of his own abilities and of his friends' support, such a plenary charge acted as a spur to force matters to a conclusion. That he attached importance to it, and that he expected others to do the same, is clear —"he paraded and emphasized his stewardship."‡ In the writs and precepts issued during Henry's captivity after the battle of Lewes the Earl of Leicester is styled "*Senescallus noster*"; and there is a royal letter addressed to the "Recluse of Hakinton" asking for details as to the duties and privileges of the office.§ What was a right was also a duty, and the opportunity lay to hand. "*Ce sont les evenements qui preparent les revolutions, ce sont*

* Haydn, 99. † Bémont, 326.
‡ Tout., Med. Engl., i. 202. § Bémont, 101, note.

*les hommes qui les executent. Simon de Montfort allait
devenir un chef de parti : il etait prêt au rôle que la fortune
lui destinait.*"*

De Montfort's pact with the leaders of the discontented
party was made in April 1258. At a Great Council held
a month later the barons all arrived armed. The King
asked if he was to be coerced. They answered " No," but
that " they must have reforms." Twenty-four commissioners were selected, who drew up a scheme, and in June
the " Provisions of Oxford " were ratified and published
in the vernacular. In the original "Sim̄. of Muntford,
eorl on Leychester," signs first of the lay lords.† A
Parliament was to be called and a permanent Council
of fifteen, of whom de Montfort was one, was to control
the King's actions. Among other conditions all foreigners
were to resign their castles. De Montfort set the first
example by giving up Kenilworth and Odiham. He pressed
de Valence to follow it, saying, " Your castles or your
head," and de Valence made the easier choice.

The King was angry and frightened at these doings.
One summer evening, at Westminster, he had gone out
to dine on the Thames. A thunderstorm surprised him,
and his galley was hastily rowed to the Bishop of Durham's
palace, where de Montfort was lodging. The earl came
down to welcome him at the river steps and bade him not
fear the weather. " I fear you," said the King severely,
and not laughing, " more than any thunder."‡ Nevertheless, de Montfort was again sent to Scotland and to France
to continue the treaty with Louis. The English people
were distressed at his absence. He returned for the
meeting of the Council early in 1259, and then again
went back to Paris. There was a hitch in the negotiations
over the question of Henry's debts to the Leicester family,
and Gloucester, de Montfort's colleague in the embassy,
blamed him for the delay. De Montfort burst out at
him, saying, " I do not care to live among men so change-
able and deceitful."§ The taunt annoyed the proud and

* Bémont, 152.   † Ingram, iii. 6.
‡ M. Paris, 974   § Creighton, 109.

SIMON DE MONTFORT
EARL OF LEICESTER

To face page 102

powerful Gloucester, and thenceforward he espoused the advanced ideas of de Montfort less warmly. The King's son Edward, however, took the reformers' side with London and the south, while the west and north were for Henry. In the autumn the French treaty was at last ratified, though de Montfort in umbrage still stayed abroad. January 1260 came, but Henry deferred the promised Parliament. De Montfort then hurried back to England. No sooner had he arrived than he was assailed with fresh charges alleging treason, with the old question of debts in the background. For the moment they hung fire, for a campaign against the Welsh took up the summer, and it was not until the winter that he was again in London. He then made an agreement with Henry to refer all their money disputes to the arbitration of the Queen of France. But the government remained the same. De Montfort appealed to Louis to urge Henry to keep his word about the Parliament. Henry replied by producing a papal bull releasing him from his promises, and he formally repudiated the Provisions of Oxford.

De Montfort and Gloucester now took the law into their own hands. They summoned " three knights from every shire south of Trent to meet them at St. Albans to treat of the common affairs of the realm."* Henry then commanded the knights to assemble at Windsor, and at this Gloucester left the popular party, and de Montfort in despair went back to France. " He would rather die a landless man," he said, " than desert the cause of truth."† For a year the deadlock continued, though the King and the earl met in Paris. Then Gloucester suddenly died, and early in 1263 de Montfort finally returned to England.

At Whitsuntide a Great Council was held. The barons called upon the King to confirm the Provisions. He refused. Their leader was again among them, and they now definitely took up arms. London and Oxford declared in their favour: the western marches, Gloucester, Hereford, and soon afterwards Guildford and Dover, were taken, and in July de Montfort and his army entered the capital.

* D. N. B., xxxviii. 292.　　　　　† Creighton, 46.

8

The middle classes, the knights, burgesses and clergy, were with him. With his approval fresh ministers were appointed, and Henry was compelled to submit. For the moment an accommodation seemed in sight. But Henry held the Tower, and Edward, now again on his father's side, was strongly fortified at Windsor.

In October de Montfort was nearly ambushed at Southwark, and after an abortive Council or Parliament at Reading, it was agreed to submit all the matters in dispute to the King of France. Louis lost little time in his award. By the Mise of Amiens in January 1264 he restored to Henry all his previous powers, disallowed the Provisions of Oxford, and only reserved to the English their earlier rights. But this last clause was the barons' loophole, "for the arbitrary power of the Crown was contrary to the Charter."*

De Montfort saw that yet another appeal must be made to arms, and he now embarked on a serious campaign. Northampton was seized, London put into a state of defence, and in May 1264 the royal army was hemmed in before Lewes in Sussex. Henry defied the barons to battle, formally renouncing their homage, and on May 14 de Montfort gained a signal victory, despite the poor fight put up by the Londoners. The King and the prince were taken prisoners, and their forces dispersed, but the Earl Warrenne escaped—a dangerous loss.

> " Sire Simond de Mountford hath swore by ys chyn
> Hevede he now here the Erl of Waryn
> Shuld he never more come to is yn
> Ne with sheld ne with spere ne with other gyn
> To help of Wyndeshore."†

A new constitution was published, and de Montfort became Chief Minister and Protector of the Realm. Almost at once the barons began to fall away from him. Many had fought for their own interests, and those interests they thought were now sufficiently secured: they did not wish to go too far. The regal power was still strong in the

* Green, i. 297. † Percy, 90.

land, and the Pope now launched an excommunication against the rebels, and forbade any commerce with England. In the west the royalists were active, while several of de Montfort's sons were intriguing with the enemy and pirating along the coast. But the earl himself held on, and in December 1264 he issued writs in the King's name, summoning to Westminster the prelates, barons, and knights of the shire.

In January 1265 met what is still called the first English Parliament. There was little legislation, but de Montfort had an unfortunate quarrel with the young Gloucester, his former colleague's son, and the latter went off to join the western lords. The earl followed him with Henry in his train. But the effect of this coercion was damaging and the nobles became nervous. Defections began, and Prince Edward managed to escape and quickly collected some troops. De Montfort moved down the Severn, then returned to Hereford, crossed the river, and on August 3 marched towards Evesham, where he expected to meet his son with reinforcements. The King said that he must halt to dine, and time was lost. Edward, with a much larger force, now threw himself between the two advancing allies, and early on August 4 arrived at Evesham.

At first de Montfort had been deceived, thinking it was his son coming to his aid. But a watcher " in the clock tower of the abbey where the earl was lodged, recognizing the banners of the King's son and of Gloucester and Mortimer, called down to him: ' We are all dead.' The earl replied: ' By the arm of St. James they come on well. They did not learn that fashion from themselves, but from me. Let God take mercy on our souls, for our bodies are theirs.' "* From the very first the fight was unequal, for the royalists were in great strength. De Montfort was soon unhorsed, but he then fought on foot, wielding his great two-handed sword. He bade his friends save themselves, but none would do so. Many were killed, and at last he was himself surrounded, and

* Hemmingburgh, i. 324.

in the mêlée was stabbed from behind. His opponents closed in on him, and there, in the water meadows under the evening sun, he met his end, crying only "*Dieu merci.*" "And so," says Matthew Paris, "he finished his labours, that magnificent man the Earl Simon, constant in word, severe in face, most faithful of all."*

As he fell a storm burst over the fields and "the heavens turned black." Henry and Guy, two of his sons, Despenser the Justiciar, Basset, Mandeville, and other bannerets were slain with him. He was horribly mutilated by his foes, his head and limbs being sent to different towns; only his body was recovered and buried by the Evesham monks. He was soon made a martyr, and his friends the friars spread his fame all over the land.

> "*Ore est occis la fleur de pris*
> *Que tant savoit de guere*
> *Ly quens Montfort sa dure mort*
> *Molt emplora la terre.*" †

The victory was crushing. All the de Montforts were exiled, their estates and dignities forfeited, and within a generation their name was extinct. For the moment the barons were subdued and Henry resumed his power, but his eldest son had learnt a lesson that was to bear fruit, and Edward's motto, "Keep troth," recalled the example of his uncle and godfather the great earl.

Few of de Montfort's relics remain. His shield of arms is on the walls of Westminster Abbey, his seal in the British Museum, and there is a painting of him or his brother in one of the windows of Chartres Cathedral —perhaps something of a portrait, with a prominent nose, a hawk's eye, and a firm chin. All else has disappeared.

He had all the traits of an ascetic. At his death a hair shirt was found next his skin. "In eating and drinking he was singularly abstemious. In prayer he was regular and frequent. All the ordinary offices of the Church he could say by heart. He affected the company of learned

* M. Paris, 998.   † Creighton, 199.

and religious men. Only in his fierce temper and want of compromise did he go amiss."*

Such was Simon de Montfort, Earl of Leicester, born of the best blood in France and England, a pious man, a brave soldier, a wise statesman, a faithful friend, punctilious to the point of honour, a preserver of the poor. Ambitious, wrangling, perhaps limited in views, he was yet animated by true patriotism and honesty of purpose, and it was largely due to his efforts that representative government in England took the exact form it did. Dr. Stubbs calls "the merit of his statesmanship adaptive rather than originative,"† and modern criticism has queried the Parliament of 1264-5 as an enlarged copy of an earlier or an incomplete sketch of a later assembly; but in the opinion of the world it still holds its own: in that year the writ of the senior barony was first issued, and in that year the sheriffs first made a complete return of knights, burgesses and citizens.

But whether or not de Montfort called Parliament into existence he certainly instilled into the common folk of England the ideas of liberty and of self-sacrifice. To them he was a hero, a champion of right, who kept to his word and who fell fighting as a martyr for the good cause. Free from the avarice and ostentation which had so often disfigured the *roturier* priests, he stood a figure apart, an aristocrat in birth, breeding and aspirations.

To the English barons he was always something of an alien, envied, admired, but never quite understood. His southern blood, his fanatical father, had given him an energy, an intensity, a skill that the slower northern breed hardly approved. Up to a point they would go with him, but their aims were often material, while his were altruistic, and at times incomprehensible.

Most of his days were spent in difficulty and distress, and at the very end he may well have thought that his life's work was wrecked. But it was not so. The seed he had sown was to blossom into a growth more vigorous and lasting than he had ever thought of, and his own

* M. Paris, 998. † Stubbs, i. 311.

stern and unwavering faith was to strike a new note in
England that still rings down the ages.

From the battle of Hastings to the battle of Evesham
two centuries had passed. In that long period England had
known but three good Kings—the Conqueror and the first
two Henries—while she had suffered under the yoke of
five bad ones; the balance was thus against the monarchy.
But Nature could assert herself; first the nobles struck, and
then, as their blows were not hard enough, they called
in the arms of the commons. The fresh help was effective,
and thenceforward only a strong master could rule: a
weakling must pay the penalty of his faults. The new
ally was as yet untried and its growth was slow, but the
day was to come when it would far outstrip its fellows and
wield nearly all the power in the State.

CHAPTER IV

THE EARLY PRELATES

BURNELL AND STRATFORD

THE fourteenth century is an exceptionally important era in the evolution of England and of the English constitution. During the hundred and twenty-seven years that elapsed from the accession of Edward I. in 1272 to the deposition of his great-great-grandson, Richard II., in 1399, the stride was made which brought the archaic life of mediæval feudalism on to the threshold of modern progress. Such a change did not take place without internal convulsions in the body politic, and the whole history of the age is marked by a series of struggles between Crown and Parliament, between Crown and Church, between Parliament and People. Lords Ordainers and Lords Appellant, Provisors and Præmunire, Labourers and Lollards, succeed each other on the statute books, and in these contests a principal part is nearly always played by the King himself. The personal equation of the Sovereign remained of the utmost importance; the minister was as yet of only secondary weight. The chief engine of government was still the Royal Council or *perpetuum concilium*, an offshoot of the *Curia Regis*. Sitting in the palace at Westminster, it directed policy, administration and finance. It was always in session, and the King was constantly present at its meetings. Thus the character of the four princes who ruled England in the fourteenth century had a capital influence on public affairs and on domestic progress.

The defeat of Simon de Montfort had established

Henry III. on the throne of his ancestors. Weak as he was, disastrous as his long reign had been, his position now became so secure that his son could leave him safely seated in England and could depart to the confines of Asia for nearly four years. When in 1272 the old man died, the absent Edward succeeded to the crown peaceably and without opposition, and on his return to England he at once began that progressive policy that has earned for him the title of the greatest of the Plantagenets.

Edward's earlier experiences had not been forgotten. He had taken to heart the words of the "Song of Lewes":

> "*O Edwarde fieri vis rex sine lege*
> *Vere forent miseri recti tali rege,*"*

and he knew that to rule his people rightly he must rule them by law. Warriors and nobles were in their proper place on the battlefield: for the Council, bishops and lawyers were better suited. This tradition was transmitted to his descendants for the next four generations, and during a hundred and eighty years the government of England remained under the control of churchmen. When, in the days of another child King, it fell back into the hands of the barons, the sun of the proud house of Anjou sank in blood to its final setting.

The first Edward was a formidable and masterful man. Long, lean and limber, he spent his life in active warfare, mainly within the confines of his realm. While his campaigns in Wales and Scotland consolidated his dominions, the destinies of his people were developed under his own eyes. Although he was *Malleus Scotorum* he was also the founder of a national trade policy; his sense and strength enabled him to meet danger without disaster, for he understood compromise. When he told fierce lords like Bohun and Bigod that they should either "go to the wars or hang," they answered that "they would neither go nor hang."† Edward had to submit, and had, in addition, to grant that confirmation of the charters which sealed the freedom of his subjects. After

---

* Kingsford, 451-2.   † Ransome, 103.

he had expelled his bankers, the Jews, he was forced to rely more and more upon the supplies granted by Parliament, and Parliament thus became a regular and recognized institution. But these concessions did not damage him in the general view; rather did they raise his reputation and prove his power; and when, after a life of seventy and a reign of thirty-five years, he died on the Scottish border, fighting and working to the end, he left behind him an honoured name, a prosperous people and a stable State.

His son, Edward II., handsome, accomplished, and with more engaging manners than his father, was of far tamer mettle. Amusement appealed to him before all things; he ate and drank immoderately, he dressed, he acted, he played " cross and pile," and he was always under the influence of his friends. His reign started with the shattering defeat of Bannockburn and the sordid suppression of the Knights Templars, a sop to the avarice of his father-in-law, the King of France. His earliest favourite, Gaveston, was a Gascon with a talent for mimicry which did not endear him to the English nobles. Lancaster he called " the old hog," Pembroke " Joseph the Jew," Gloucester " the cuckold's bird," Warwick " the black dog."* The first of these, Thomas Plantagenet, the son of Edward Crouchback or Crossback, the crusader, was Earl of Lancaster, Leicester, Lincoln, Salisbury and Derby, the King's first cousin, and the most powerful and richest subject in the land. He was the first of those political princes of his branch of the royal house who for nearly two centuries were to hold the scales between King and Parliament until at last they were to get the crown for themselves. He was not a man to annoy with impunity, and after a chequered career of five years, Gaveston was scotched and killed by the " hog," the " dog " and the " Jew."

For a few years matters then went more smoothly, until the two Despencers came on to the scene and engrossed Edward's favour. Englishmen of good family, the

* Lingard, iii. 8, note.

descendants of de Montfort's old Justiciar, they were
capable of ruling well. But an inordinate greed for land
and money blinded them to reason, and they also set the
magnates against them. The weight of such territorial
influence was immense:

> " Great Lancaster was lord of all the north
> The Mortimers were masters of the west."

The whole force of the nobility was banded against the
favourites. Edward succeeded in executing Lancaster,
but his Queen, the lovely and lustful Isabella, was capti-
vated by the arts of the young Mortimer. She fled with
her son to France, conspired against her husband, and
returning in 1326 raised an army, slew the Despencers,
and captured the unfortunate King. A few months later
Edward himself was murdered in Berkeley Castle at the
cryptic order of Bishop Orlton:

> " *Edwardum occidere nolite timere bonum est.*"

For three years the Queen and her paramour then ruled
as despots, until in 1330 they in turn met their fate—the
one a lifelong prison, the other a gallows at Tyburn.

The young Edward, third of his name, was just of
legal age to rule. Ambitious, popular and magnificent,
he had nearly everything in his favour. For four and
twenty years there had not been a real minister or a
real policy in England. Edward determined to have
both, and for the earlier portion of his reign his affairs
prospered exceedingly. Then a succession of calamities
altered the temper of the King, the face of the country,
and the balance of political power. But before those
great events occurred the last ministers of the Middle
Ages had passed across the stage, dim, unrecorded figures,
but none the less makers of English history. Their
business was to weld together Crown and Parliament,
French and English, Church and State. Deftly, quietly,
almost unconsciously, they did so, and posterity's ignorance of them is the hallmark of their success.

I.—ROBERT BURNELL

Robert Burnell, afterwards Bishop of Bath and Wells, was born at Acton Burnell in Shropshire, probably about 1235. He was a younger son of another Robert Burnell, a gentleman of some position and property in his county, and of good descent and connection: one of his brothers married a daughter of Fitzalan, Earl of Arundel. Of his education nothing is known—perhaps he was at Oxford*—but as quite a young man he went up to London, became an ecclesiastical clerk, and practised in the courts at Westminster. There he was "the most dexterous of chancery lawyers,"† a profession then rising into repute. About 1260 he met the young Prince Edward, and he had sufficient ability to make the most of his opportunity. He became his chaplain and household clerk, and eventually his close friend, accompanying him on a visit to France in that year. His ideas of policy harmonized with those of Edward, and during the Barons' war his knowledge of the Welsh border was of considerable value. He was employed on various missions in the West of England, and was probably present at the battle of Evesham. The death of an elder brother had put him into possession of his family lands, and from his patron he received considerable additions to them, being allowed to empark some of the royal forest near his home. He now established himself as a country gentleman, and apparently got married, though it is not known to whom. He received several further places from his master, being made a prebendary of London and Hereford and Archdeacon of York— benefices that could be held by a layman. But the life he lived seems to have been licentious, and he was not held by the Church in any special regard.

In 1270 he took the cross with Prince Edward, more as a secretary than a soldier. In the summer of that year, when the fleet was at Portsmouth almost ready to start,

* See Gutch, ii. 746-7. † Tout, Edw. I., 80.

Archbishop Boniface suddenly died. Edward, " anxious
to promote his clerk, Sir Robert Burnell, whom he loved
very sincerely,"* determined to raise him to the primacy.
He left the squadron and posted off to Canterbury to
press his suit. But his journey was of no avail, " for
monks prefer monks to a simple clerk,"* and he had to
return and sail unsatisfied. Whether Burnell accompanied him to Syria is doubtful; if he did so he was soon
back again, for a year later he is named as one of the
managers of the Prince's affairs, and shortly afterwards
he was made an executor of his will. In February 1272
he was present at Westminster when Henry III. took
delivery of some of the Crown jewels which had been
lodged for safe custody with the Queen of France and
had then been pawned. These, including " a great crown
of inappreciable value, 76 golden girdles, and two gold
peacocks,"† were now restored to their owner. In the
memorandum Burnell's name, as a witness, follows immediately those of the Archbishop of York and the Chancellor.
In November of that year Henry III. died, and Burnell,
by virtue of his patent as one of Edward's representatives,
became a principal member of the regency. For eighteen
months he carried on his duties, managing the exchequer
with such success that on Edward's return, in 1274, he
was appointed Chancellor, an office which he was to hold
for the rest of his life.

Four months later, in January 1275, he was, by the
King's order, elected Bishop of Bath and Wells. Such
a promotion was the usual method of rewarding a royal
servant and providing him with an income. But the see
was neither specially dignified nor well endowed, and it
was only meant as a stepping-stone.

In that year was passed the first statute of Westminster,
which summarized earlier legislation, regulated the freedom
of elections, and fixed the rates of reliefs and aids. Though
largely a codifying measure, it was the earliest constructive
work of the new King and his Chancellor, and it responded
to the clearly expressed feeling of the nation. At the same

* Wikes, 92.   † Rymer, i. 882.

time the King obtained the earliest Parliamentary grants on merchandise, the foundation of the Customs' revenue.

The first war with Wales now began. Since the struggles of de Montfort and the Marcher lords, Welsh allegiance had become nominal, and this independence was a constant danger to England. Burnell's local knowledge was again of use. In the Council his advice carried weight, on the borders his influence was important. He was continually employed on missions to Wales, on one occasion being required as a hostage during the visit of Prince Llewellyn to London. As a reward Edward determined to promote him further, and when in 1278 the archbishopric of Canterbury again fell vacant, he made a second attempt to prefer him to it. On this occasion the election by the chapter was successfully engineered, but the later stages failed, though Edward himself wrote to the Pope, mentioning the special love that he had for Burnell, whom he describes as a man *circumspectus, mitis, affabilis, benignus, misericordiæ, mansuetudinis, caritatis et pacis, fidelitatis constantia nullo tempore, nubulo vel sereno, flecti.** But Nicholas made "further enquiries" which decided him against the request, and the envoys sent by the King could not move his Holiness *nec prece nec pretio.*†

Two years later the Bishop of Winchester died. A similar process was repeated. Burnell was elected by the chapter, and then a solemn embassy, from both King and Queen, was sent to request the papal ratification. Again it was denied, and this time the electors were reprimanded for having chosen a man " already refused by the Apostolic see and sufficiently well endowed."‡ It is difficult now to gauge the exact meaning of these rejections. Burnell was both a practical and a generous man. Parsimony in the way of bribes is unlikely to have deterred his success, and his morals can hardly have been sufficiently bad to impede the Papal Court, then the most ill-famed in Europe, from a simple translation. The truth remains

---

* Rymer, ii. 118.   † Ann. Wav., Gale, ii. 233
‡ *Ibid.*, ii. 235.

hid. But the disappointment, and indeed the slur, was considerable. Burnell, however, went on with his work. He had by now become Chief Minister, a great administrator and a great judge; and he could afford to stand upon his lay offices and dispense with the Church's support.

In 1278 he had been sent on a mission to Gascony, and had been able to do some good in that distracted country. Two years later he was again at home, and in 1280 he made a signal advance in the administration of the law, by fixing the Court of Chancery at Westminster and excusing it from following the King in his progresses. This was an immense benefit to the suitor and to the exchequer— a practical proof of Burnell's consideration and foresight. From this time also dates the division of the Curia Regis into the three main tribunals of King's Bench, Common Pleas, and Exchequer, which gave to the Courts of Justice the form they held for six centuries. The effect of these modifications, among others, was to exalt immensely the position of the Chancellor, who, while maintaining his place as president in the Royal Council, became also the permanent chief of the whole legal system.

Finance was another avenue in which Burnell's activity was displayed. The ancient tenure of land was carefully tested by writs of *Quo Warranto*, and though Earl Warrenne flung a rusty sword on to the judges' table and told them that " that was his title," the great body of landowners had to submit to revised taxation.

Another Welsh campaign had now begun, and until it was finished by the defeat and death of Llewellyn, the King was frequently in the West of England. In 1283 he paid a visit to his Chancellor at Acton Burnell, and there the Parliament, adjourned from Shrewsbury, held a session to pass the Statute of Merchants. It met in the hall of Burnell's castle, which, in Leland's time, was " a greate Barne."* Few subjects have aspired to lodge and entertain an entire legislature in their own house, and it is a circumstance of interest that the Chief Minister who did so presided in it both as host and Chancellor.

* Leland, vii. 21.

In two subsequent laws—the second Statute of Westminster dealing with the foundation of entails, and the Statute of Winchester regulating the militia—Burnell took an equally prominent part, and these for the moment marked the term of his legislation.

As soon as the struggle with Wales was finally settled Edward turned his attention to Gascony. The Chancellor, taking the Great Seal with him, accompanied him on his journey to France, where they were absent for three years. But their stay abroad was not beneficial to England, and on their return a number of the judges had to be removed for taking bribes—the presence of their chief being apparently necessary to ensure their incorruptibility.

Edward's absence had depleted the exchequer, and to obtain the supplies which he needed from Parliament he had now to make a concession to popular clamour. In 1290 he was forced to banish the Jews, for many years the source from which public loans had been drawn. The act appears to have been as unjust as it was impolitic, for their expulsion threw the court into the hands of foreign bankers or of Parliament, and in the result the power of the latter was vastly increased. Burnell's part in this business is unknown, but his family received some grants of the Jews' lands. In the same year, in the third Statute of Westminster, designed to prevent the excessive subinfeudation of land and to facilitate its transfer, he had a leading hand.

The Scottish succession question next engrossed Edward's attention. The rival claims of Baliol, Bruce and other candidates for the northern crown, took him to Norham and Berwick. Through the earlier phases of the long dispute Burnell was with him, advising, negotiating and giving judgment—the principal figure after the King. He was the chief of the twelve " most perfect and wisest clerkes "* that adjudged the crown to Baliol. Suddenly, in October 1292, he was taken ill, and a week later he was dead. His body, " solemnly brought many miles," was buried magnificently in his own cathedral at Wells.

* Holinshed, Scotland, 299.

Leland, writing about 1530, says: " He lay not many yeres sins in a high Tumbe with an Image of Brasse. Now undre a plain marble."*

Of Burnell's personal appearance, of his private life, little is known. It is suggested that he was a sensualist or a votary of the table, but his brisk, flexible character hardly bears this out. His ambition had been to found a family. To that end he had acquired land in nineteen counties, including no less than eighty manors, a quarter of which were in Shropshire. South of London his estates extended in a semicircle from Woolwich to Sheen. To his daughters and his nephew these vast possessions descended, with a barony by tenure, which he had purchased, and numerous church preferments. But his brothers had fallen in the Welsh wars, his nephew died early, and in less than a century his posterity was extinct and his property dissipated.

His generosity was on a par with his riches, though at the Papal Court " his wonderful munificence never made him popular;" † his private habits failed to " satisfy the low standard of ecclesiastical decorum."‡ Among other edifices he built a great hall at Wells, which Fuller calls " the biggest room of any Bishop's Palace in England."§ It was afterwards destroyed, as was the turreted castle that he had erected at Acton. Burnell's Inn at Oxford was perhaps his foundation.

But although Burnell's personal history is unknown, although his buildings have disappeared, his national work remained, and from his days the modern forms of government and political economy largely date. " An active and wise minister, serving the Crown with zeal, energy and prudence, no Chancellor before him had ever held the Seal so long or retained so uninterruptedly his Sovereign's confidence."|| His death marked the end of Edward's successful government. A few years later Gascony had been lost, and the Crown had undergone a series of political rebuffs from both nobles and commons.

* Leland, iii. 122.   † Tout, Edw., i. 80.   ‡ D. N. B., iii. 388.
§ Fuller, Worthies, Shrap., 4. || Foss, 143.

ROBERT BURNELL

BISHOP OF BATH AND WELLS

To face page 118

The absence of Burnell's composing influence had probably much to do with these defeats. He had been, as the monk of Worcester calls him, " as useful to the King as he was pleasant to the people: beloved by all: none in our time was found like him."*

Neither Hume, Lingard, Stubbs nor Green mentions his name, though Ransome calls him " the first great Chancellor," and Tout styles him " a sort of prime minister."† His history must be culled from chance references, his influence imagined by inference. But as to his ability and importance there can be no question. He made his office, and under him " the Chancellor bade fair to become a successor to the Norman and Angevin justiciar."‡

Burnell was the first lawyer, properly so called, who rose to rule the State. He acquired the riches and enjoyed the tranquillity which are the rewards of most successful men of his cloth; he shared the posthumous obscurity into which so many of them sink. He died in his middle age, the bishop of a minor see, the minister of the English Justinian. To Edward has thus been ascribed much of the work which Burnell advised and executed, and the King has monopolized the credit which the Chancellor might have shared. But Burnell was a sagacious man. He knew how to excel in secret without rivalling his master. Hence, perhaps, his freedom from the odium which so often followed success, hence his escape from that ruin to which so many fell.

Recognizing the needs of justice and liberty, he possessed the arts of compromise and management, and he was politic enough to command both the favour of his Sovereign and the approval of his country. By these qualities he rose; by these qualities he retained power throughout his active life; by these qualities he deserves a fame which history has hitherto denied him.

* Foss, 143. † Tout, Edw. I., 130. ‡ *Ibid.*

II.—JOHN DE STRATFORD

John de Stratford, afterwards Archbishop of Canterbury, was born probably about 1280, at the town on the
Warwickshire Avon from which he took his name. His
parents were Robert and Isabella, his younger brother
another Robert. Of his family very little is known, but
his father seems to have been a burgher of moderate
means, the owner of some land, and probably the founder
of the guild chapel and almshouses in his native town.

John de Stratford was sent to Merton College, Oxford,
where he took his degrees as a doctor of civil and canon
law, and became a fellow. He devoted himself to the
Bar, which was then closely connected with the Church,
and soon obtained the reputation of being a sound con-
sultant and advocate. At the age of thirty he was sufficiently well thought of to be sent to the Papal Court as
proctor for his University, in a suit against the Dominicans.
He advanced *pari passu* in either learned profession.
Parson of Stratford and a clerk in chancery by 1319, he
was next made a prebendary and Archdeacon of Lincoln,
then a canon of York, until eventually he became Dean of
the Court of Arches, a position of considerable importance
and independence. During the four years from 1317
onwards he was also summoned to Parliament " to advise,"
not as a member, but much as the judges now receive
their writs of attendance in the House of Lords.

In December 1321 he was again sent to Avignon, this
time on Scottish affairs and on the more serious business
of asking for financial help from the Pope for Edward II.,
who was in financial straits: " *nec non pro subsidiis ali-
quibus pro statu nostro et Regni nostri conservando, a
vestra Sanctitate impetrandis.*"* In this commission he
was joined with the Bishop of Winchester and several
others. The embassy was absent for over a year, and
in April 1323 the bishop died at Avignon. Edward at
once wrote to the Pope and the Cardinals recommending

* Hook, iv. 6.

that his secretary, Robert Baldock, should be appointed to the see—" one of the most noble in our kingdom." But the death of a prelate *in curia* gave the Pope an absolute right of nomination.* Stratford was on the spot; he knew the men with whom he had to deal, and the risk was well worth running.   He enlisted the support of the Archbishop of Canterbury, he probably suborned the Cardinals in the usual manner, and within two months he had obtained the bishopric for himself.   The papal brief announcing this news to Edward describes him as " skilled in letters, elegant in manners, chaste in his life, respectable in his conversation, provident in spiritual and circumspect in worldly affairs."†

Edward was extremely angry.   He wrote back accusing Stratford of acting contrary to his duty in accepting the see, of being a " *pseudo-nuntius*," of having grievously increased " his previous faults which had been forgiven "; and he begged the Pope that the appointment might be revoked.   In the same sense he circularized no less than five-and-twenty members of the College of Cardinals, as well as several of the Pope's own family.   Stratford, however, stuck to his prize, and though, on his return to England, he was kept out of the temporalities of his see for over a year, by dint of a promise to pay the King a fine of £10,000 he got back into favour, and the fine was not exacted.

Edward's disastrous reign was now drawing to a close. He was in constant difficulties and glad to find friends where he could.   Stratford was loyal to him, and in 1324, in company with the Bishop of Norwich and the Earl of Richmond, he was sent as special envoy to the King of France for concluding a treaty of peace.   He remained abroad for some months, though he did not sign the agreement (in which Queen Isabella was largely concerned) with his other colleagues.   Later on he was employed on an even more delicate mission—that of recalling the Queen to England.   With her lover Mortimer she had taken her young son to Paris, alleging her fear of the

* Hook, iv. 6.   † Rymer, iii. 1033.

evil counsels of the Despencers.   Edward, in his letter
to his wife of December 1, says: " *Kar a ceo que le dit
Evesque nous ad reporte, nostre dit Frere, le Roi de France,
vous ad faite dire, en sa presence, que contre la forme de
vestre conduyt, vous ne seriez destorbee & pur reen ne tardez
que vous ne veniez.*"*   But Stratford's efforts were in vain,
and the Queen stayed abroad until she landed as her
husband's declared enemy in the following summer.   In
the short campaign of 1326 Stratford, who was acting
as Treasurer, adhered to the King as long as there seemed
any hope for him.   Then, when Edward's cause was lost,
he acquiesced in the *fait accompli*.

After the capture of Bristol by the Queen and Mortimer,
the name of the Bishop of Winchester stands second in the
list of prelates and barons who elected the King's son as
governor of the realm.   He had thus definitely thrown in
his lot with the new régime, and his abilities were at once
made use of by its leaders.   He preached at St. Paul's
in favour of the change of government, he was employed
to draft the document for Edward II.'s deposition, and he
was one of the three bishops sent to obtain his formal
abdication.   He was also retained as a member of the
Royal Council.   But he could not reconcile his conscience
or his reason with the immoral tyranny of Mortimer, and
in 1328 he allied himself politically with Lancaster's party.
Two years later he thought it wise to absent himself from
Parliament, and for some time he remained in hiding to
avoid the vengeance of the Queen and her favourite.   At
this time he was obliged to conceal himself in the woods
and marshes of his Hampshire diocese, living on the game
his attendants could kill, and holding his services in the
open air.

On November 29, 1330, Mortimer at last met the death
that he had meted out to so many others, and the next
day Edward III., then just eighteen years old, appointed
Stratford his Chancellor.   The bishop was experienced and
able, and he already had the name of a faithful minister;
he rapidly acquired considerable influence with the young

* Rymer, iv. 181.

King, and "came to be regarded as his political father and the second person in the realm."*

Ambitious and adventurous, Edward was determined to retrieve the errors of his predecessor. As a boy he had seen and envied the splendours of Paris, when early in his reign he had gone to do homage for his duchy of Guienne to the French King. On that occasion, before all the foreign court in the chancel of the cathedral of Amiens, he had been compelled to put off his crown, his sceptre, and his golden spurs, and to kneel down before his liege lord. Froissart indeed says, "*me semble que le Roy Edouard fit adonc homage de bouche & de parolle tant seulement (sans les mains mettre entre les mains du Roy de France).*"† But the young King never forgot the scene, and when the deaths of his maternal uncles without male heirs gave him an excuse to claim the throne of France for himself, he seized his opportunity. To pursue such a prize with any prospect of success he must have strong allies on the Continent, and his marriage with Philippa of Hainault—love match though it was—caused him to turn first to Flanders, the country with which English commerce was so closely bound. The Emperor also might be brought over to his side, and perhaps the German princes. Thus foreign affairs became his chief interest, and in these Stratford was a past master.

In April 1331 the young King and his Chancellor made a secret journey to the Continent to spy out the land, travelling in the disguise of merchants, like another Haroun al Raschid and Jaafar. Later on in the year Stratford was again sent to Flanders, this time in the open character of an ambassador, to arrange a marriage between Edward's sister and the Count of Gueldres.

During these absences abroad his younger brother Robert, who had followed in his footsteps as a canon and a clerk, and had become Chancellor of the Exchequer, was left as Keeper of the Great Seal. The Great Seal was now regarded as the chief ensign of power in the realm, the *clavis regni :* continual mentions are made in

* Hemmingburgh, ii. 381.   † Froissart, xxv.

the rolls of its delivery, its transfer, its custody "*in quadam baga de scarlato velveto*," the engaging Latin of the period.*

Stratford by his office, his ability, and the favour he enjoyed was now the Chief Minister, and when in 1333 the Archbishop of Canterbury died, both King and Pope agreed in translating him to the primacy. A year later he resigned the chancellorship, but resumed it again in 1335, presiding in the Council and directing foreign affairs. Hitherto his diplomatic work had been mainly concerned with France and Flanders. Now he had to turn his attention to the north, and for the next two years he was chiefly occupied with Scotland, where the claims of Baliol and Bruce had brought on a war. His business multiplied, and in March 1337, to ease him somewhat, the seal was again transferred to his brother.

By this time Edward had matured his military projects, secured his internal position, and formed his alliances abroad. He now submitted his claims to Parliament and the Pope, and assumed the title of King of France. For two years attempts were made, both from Avignon and Paris, to compose the quarrels between the rival princes. But they were fruitless, and active hostilities at last began. Stratford had been constantly on the Continent, occupied in numerous negotiations. He had crossed the Channel, he said, thirty-two times.† He was himself in favour of peace, but Edward wanted war, and it was at this period that differences first arose between the King and his minister.

In April 1340 Stratford became Chancellor for the third time, but on June 20 he again resigned the seal to his brother, probably because the King had refused to defer his proposed naval expedition. Four days later, on June 24, Edward won his naval victory at Sluys. It was the single success of an expensive and protracted campaign, but it was a success of the first order. When the news arrived in Paris only the King's fool was bold

---

* The rolls were only kept in "*bundellis et pokettis de canevace.*"

† Foss, 638.

enough to impart it to his master. " Ah," he said, "what cowards those English sailors are not to dare to jump into the sea like our brave Frenchmen."*

During Edward's absence in France Stratford had been left as President of the Council, though his influence with the King was diminishing. He knew well that peace was better than war, and that heavy taxation meant trouble; " he did but say what thousands thought." His prophecies were only too correct, and soon the sinews of war, which it was his task to supply, were no longer forthcoming. To remedy this deficit Edward had embarked on a comprehensive system of loans from Flemish and English merchants, increased customs, monopolies of wool, and interference with the staple system, which upset and irritated the trading community. He had received generous grants from Parliament, but by gifts to German princes and less reputable expenses of his own these were now all dissipated; and there was little, except a longer legend on the coinage and a newly quartered shield of arms, to show for them.

Military failures followed, and of these also the archbishop had to bear the brunt. He had already a sufficiency of enemies. They were led by Orlton, who had succeeded him as Bishop of Winchester and was the head of the so-called court party, while Stratford, who was inclined to be a reformer of manners, belonged to the constitutional or Lancastrian school of politics. There was now an opportunity of displacing him. His opponents combined to vilipend him, and the King was told that public funds had gone into the private treasury of his Chancellor, and that home defence was being neglected.

Late in the autumn of 1340 Edward came over secretly to England, landing at the Tower at midnight on St. Andrew's Day. He found the fortress insufficiently guarded. The excuse was enough. Instantly he visited his displeasure upon his ministers. Stratford was the chief of the offenders, but the smaller fry were dealt with

* Baker, 130.

first.   His brother Robert, now Bishop of Chichester, was relieved of the chancellorship, and the Treasurer, the Constable of the Tower, the Chief Justice of the King's Bench, the Mayor of London, and several of the chancery and exchequer clerks were at once dismissed—the opposition party taking their places.

The archbishop had early news of the crisis, and fled from his villa at Charing to Canterbury.   He was immediately summoned to appear before the Court of Exchequer to answer for his administration.   He refused, entrenching himself behind his sacred character, and he preached from his cathedral pulpit on the country's wrongs and his own innocence.   He next published a long justification of his conduct of the government, to which the King wrote, or had written for him, a severe and abusive reply—the *Libellus Famosus.*   For several weeks a series of royal and archiepiscopal rescripts succeeded each other.   In Latin and French they recapitulated the delinquencies of prince and primate, covering many pages and not tending to edification.   But the prelate had behind him his knowledge of affairs, the support of the Church, and the privilege of Parliament.   Relying on his position, invoking St. Thomas the Martyr, and appealing to the Great Charter, he denounced any trial save by his peers.   The competence of other tribunals he denied, but he came up to Westminster and took a copy of the charges against him before proceeding to the Painted Chamber where the lords and bishops were in session.   The Chamberlain of the Household barred his way, but the archbishop, with his sainted predecessor before his eyes, insisted upon his rights and laid his case before the House.   A committee of twelve was appointed to report, and they speedily concurred in sustaining his objections.

Again the archbishop came up to Parliament.   This time he was forbidden to enter by the captain of the guard.   "Whereupon he spake thus to the people that flocked about him: ' My friends, the King by his writ of summons hath called me to this Parliament, and I, who am the chief peer of the realm and who next the King have the first voice in Parliament, claim the rights of my church of Canterbury, and therefore require entrance into Parliament.' " Then, taking his cross in his hands, he swore that he would not stir from the place until he had leave to enter. While he stood there some began to revile him and call him traitor, saying that he had deceived the King and betrayed the kingdom. " To which the archbishop replied: ' The curse of Almighty God and of His blessed Mother, and of St. Thomas, and mine also, be upon the heads of them that so inform the King. Amen. Amen.' "*

By the intercession of certain lords he was eventually allowed within, when he again offered to plead before his peers. It was clear that public opinion was with him, and at last, on April 19, 1341, the King admitted him to his place in Parliament, and, after due submission, pardoned him. This act was followed a year later by a more complete reconciliation, and in 1343 all the proceedings against him were formally annulled.

But Stratford's days were drawing to a close. Already, in 1340, he had asked to be relieved of his lay office owing to his increasing infirmities, and now, late in life, he began to turn his attention more closely to his religious duties, preaching regularly and visiting the dioceses of his province. He conducted the negotiations with the Papal legates as to the Roman authority in England, firmly upholding the national privilege. During 1345 and 1346 he was again left as President of the Council, and in the latter year he received and announced officially the news of the battle of Crécy. He was then nearing seventy, and it was one of his last recorded acts.

In the summer of 1348 he fell ill at Maidstone. He was moved thence to Mayfield, one of his favourite manors in Sussex, and there on August 23 he died. He was buried in his cathedral under a magnificent tomb of alabaster near the high altar, leaving " a perfumed memory behind him for his Bounty to his servants, Charity to the poor, Meekness and Moderation to all persons."†

* State Trials, i. 64.　　　　† Fuller, Worthies, Warw., 121.

There is a fine effigy of him at Canterbury, and contemporary accounts credit him with a tall figure and an elegant gait, but beyond this nothing is known of his appearance.

Although most of his life was passed in lay rather than ecclesiastical matters, Stratford was a benefactor of several religious foundations and a generous patron to his own town, where he built and endowed a college and considerably enlarged the parish church. A sound lawyer, an experienced diplomat, a wise counsellor, an industrious administrator, he was much more than a mere official. His letters to Edward show how well he understood the advantages of peace, of economy, of stability, of respect for law. They show also that he had the courage to speak his mind. Writing during the controversy of 1341, he says: " Our late lord, the King your father, on whom may God have mercy, against the laws of the land and the Great Charter, seized on great persons and others, condemned them to death, dispersed their property, vexed them with heavy fines—and what ensued from that, you know full well."*

Edward, in one of his angry answers, had called him " *semper tumidus in prosperis, timidus in adversis . . . notorie mercenarius & vulpinæ calliditatis.*"† But these strictures are not borne out by other evidence, and the letter in question bears the stamp of clerks' drafting, and was probably the work of political enemies. The real cause of Stratford's fall was that he had opposed the King's war policy, and had exempted the clergy to the best of his ability from the loans and taxes levied for it. Edward found himself short of money and deeply in debt— " *pecunia vacuus, mole aeris alieni pressus.*" He was told by the court party that Stratford's remissness was the cause, and he visited his wrath on Stratford's head. Later on, when he saw his mistake and his injustice, he repaired them so far as he was able.

In his dispute with the King, as in his previous administration, Stratford comes out well. For nearly ten years he had been in effect supreme at the chancery, at

* Hemmingburgh, ii. 364.   † *Ibid.,* 385, 386.

JOHN DE STRATFORD
ARCHBISHOP OF CANTERBURY

To face page 128

the treasury, and in the Council; he was the first officer of the law and of the Church, and the chief director of foreign affairs. Suddenly he was attacked by his master as a dishonourable traitor, the measures directed against him being exceptionally severe. Stratford met them with dignity and courage. He was not contumacious: " *Nous esteroms en toutz pointz a jugement des nos peeres,*" he writes, " *salve toutz fois l'estat de seint eglise, de nous et de nostre ordre.*"* But he used all the weapons of his double defence. He wrote, he preached, he argued, he fulminated. With a strong case, and knowing his law, he easily won his cause, and in so doing confirmed one of the principal liberties of the subject—that an Englishman has the right to be tried by his equals. Henceforward " it was impossible for the royal power to crush . . . a minister who possessed the confidence of the nation."†

During the ten years of Stratford's ministry three striking advances were made in government, finance and law. The Commons first sat together in a separate chamber, so becoming an integral and independent part of the Legislature; the collection of tallage on the royal demesnes was finally abandoned, taxation being thereby acknowledged as a matter not for the Crown but for Parliament; and the equitable jurisdiction of chancery was established. In his days also the first definite move was made to divorce the law from the Church, the rule of England from that of Rome.

Stratford died at a fortunate moment for himself, in the plenitude of his functions, while Edward was still victorious and popular, before the Black Death had come to ravage the land. Like his predecessor Burnell, he is a little known character in popular history, for he was neither a genius nor a hero; but he was a fine type of the honest, courageous and able public servant who could deal with business in nearly all its forms, and whose capacity for detail did not forfeit his claim to be a statesman and, when need arose, a patriot.

* Stubbs, ii. 419.   † *Ibid.*, ii. 425.

Burnell and Stratford were the first of a series of six magnate Chancellors who were also Chief Ministers. In two hundred and fifty years that idea was only twice discarded, and only then for very short periods. The possession of the Great Seal had become the surest road to supremacy in the Council, and the bishopric that accompanied it was often a mere adjunct of dignity or income. Until the Reformation the wisdom of the law and the authority of the Church, working together, were to keep in the shade the former strength of the sword and the future power of the purse.

CHAPTER V

THE LATER PRELATES

WYKEHAM AND BEAUFORT

THE victories of Crécy and Poitiers had made Edward III.'s name famous throughout Christendom, but their effect was soon turned to ashes by the terrible visitation of the Black Death. Rising in the East this epidemic had swept across Europe, and in 1349 it appeared in England, where it rapidly devastated the land. Sanitation and prophylactics were unknown: there were no hospitals or nurses; medicine relied largely on magic or astrology. Half the population, or some two millions of people, is said to have perished, and under the wave of destruction the whole face of the country, the whole system of society, was changed.* The old conditions of capital and labour, of feudalism and commerce, of policy and belief, were so modified that by the end of the fourteenth century an entirely new England had emerged. Villenage had disappeared, religious reform was rife, banking and trade were adopting their modern aspect, and the English language was at last coming into its own. In the early days of Edward III., says Higden, " chylderen that goon scole, ben compelled to constrewe theyr lessons in Frensshe, syn the Normans come into Englonde. Also gentylmen's chylderen ben taught to speke Frensshe and uplondsshe men wyll lyken themself unto gentylmen to speke Frensshe for to be more sette by." " This maner," adds a note towards the end of the

* More than a quarter of the lay peers died in a few months. Moberly, 23; Traill. Soc. Eng. ii. 188.

131

century, " was moche used before the grete deth (1349)
but syth it is somdele changed, and nowe, in ye ix year
of kynge Richard ye seconde they leve all Frensshe in
scoles and use all construccyon in Englysshe."*

In 1362 the vernacular was ordered to be used in the
courts of law " because the French tongue is much unknown," and in the following year Wykeham, the Chancellor, first employed it in reading the King's speech.
But for some time longer both noble and parvenu stuck
to the French of Stratforde-atte-Bowe, and to this day
the town-crier still calls " *Oyez, Oyez*," the prisoner pleads
" *Autrefois acquit*," and law is made in Parliament with
the words " *Le roy le veult.*"

Another result of the Black Death was that the great
landlords, unable to find regular husbandmen, had converted their arable land into pasture. Many of the agri-
cultural population were thus thrown out of work, and by
the dislocation of labour a new class of political agitators
arose who spread their complaints over the country.

These radical changes had all taken place in the long
reign of the third Edward, and the King himself had also
changed. He became cruel and treacherous, careless and
immoral, languid and remote. When at last he died,
almost in his dotage, deserted by his mistress, detested
by his subjects, the lion of other days had indeed become
a lamb.

His eldest son, the Black Prince, harsh and implacable,
but a statesman and a soldier, had died a year before him,
stricken by a fell disease. The crown thus descended to
Richard II., in whom the elder line of the Plantagenets
was to end. Golden-haired, gallant and ingenuous, but
luxurious and vain, he was at first the darling of his people.
At the age of fifteen he rode forward alone into the ranks
of the Kentish rebels and bade them follow him; a few
months later he hung every man of them he could catch,
saying: " Villeins you are and villeins you shall always
be." Pleasure and art appealed to his impetuous nature
more than business or economy, and his punishment was

* Higden, lv.

heavy. A new graft of the stock was needed, and it stood ready in the House of Lancaster.

The first two Lancastrian Kings were neither of them men to be swayed by any subject's will. Henry IV. had fought for and won a mighty stake, and he was not going to lose it. With only a Parliamentary title and limited means, he had to make as many friends as he could. Orthodox and devout, always genuinely anxious to take the cross, he allied himself closely with the Church. To the principal nobles he was equally affable; many of them were his relatives, and it was he who first styled all but the barons his "trusty and well-beloved cousins." To the Commons he kept the promises that had helped him to the throne, and he allowed the Council a far more important voice in the government than it had hitherto held. But the chivalrous, sanguine and popular character that had marked him in his young days was altered for the worse after his accession. "Always in debt, kept on the alert by the Scots and Welsh, continually alarmed by attempts on his life, disappointed in his second marriage, dreading to be supplanted by his own son,"* he became suspicious, embittered, vindictive. Ever something of a casuist, "*sage et imaginitif*," his conscience irked him. The horrible leprosy to which he fell a victim was thought by many to be a judgment for usurping Richard's crown, perhaps for causing Richard's death. When in 1413 he died at Westminster, "lying in the abbot's chamber called Jerusalem," he may have felt that the wish of his life, perhaps the expiation of his sins, was at last fulfilled.

His eldest son Henry V. had begun his career young. At fifteen he was commanding on the Welsh border, at sixteen he took part in his first battle. This early association with soldiers led to a certain looseness of morals and light pursuit of pleasure; "he delighted in music, he cared a good deal for hunting and fighting and for those other things that military licence affords."† His father was ailing and left him comparatively uncontrolled, and for a time he was dissolute, extravagant and selfish.

* Stubbs, iii. 9.   † Gest. Hen., v. xvi. xvii.

But the moment that the crown which he had so coveted was his by right, his manners changed. He became repentant, serious, religious, devoted to duty. " How many days," he said, " how much of my life, do I feel to have been covered by the black smoke of Misconduct."

He quickly redeemed his youth. Just, firm, temperate and hardy, he set himself to building up the power of England, creating a navy, suppressing piracy, leading his small but confident army to victory at Agincourt. An active, mettlesome man, tall and dark-haired, slender and high-featured, he was the idol of his men. " Lads," he said to them at Harfleur, " be a good cher, and ablowe you and rekele you well and comyth up all wfth your ease, for with the love of Gode we schull have good tydyngs."* It was the heyday of the archer—

" England were but a fling,
But for the crooked stick and the greygoose wing,"

and the world began to see that knights in armour were not invincible. St. Crispin's Day, 1415, was followed by five years of successes that made Henry the virtual ruler of France. Living a healthy, active life, hunting and fighting, he did not neglect his own land. He continued the progressive policy of his father, according the Commons equal legislative rights with the Lords, interesting himself in the details of government. Avaricious, cruel at times, he was yet a true Englishman, and in the eyes of his people " he stood forth as the typical mediæval hero."† His untimely death at thirty-four was a blow to his House, a calamity to his country.

Henry VI., a child of twelve months old, succeeded. On either side he had an unpromising parentage. His mother Catherine was the daughter of Charles VI. of France, who was a lunatic, and of Isabeau of Bavaria, who was little better than a harlot, while the epilepsy of his grandfather Henry IV. was in his system. Under the tutelage of Beauchamp, Earl of Warwick, and of his great-uncle Cardinal Beaufort, he became studious and

* Gest. Hen., v. xvi. 19.   † Stubbs, iii. 81.

pious. But "his simplesse and innocence" were soon patent, and the strain of overwork that was put on him as a lad left him weak in body and mind. He grew up precocious, pale, thin and contemplative, "immersed in chronicles or scriptures," anxious to apply the dictates of the Gospels to the politics of an evil world. At the age of twenty he founded Eton and King's College, Cambridge, supervising much of the work himself. "Be good boys," he used to say to the scholars, "learn your books."* At twenty-five he was married to a hard and intrepid Frenchwoman, whose ambition was to be his ruin. At thirty he first became insane, and at forty, after being tossed about among the hardest spirits of a fierce and greedy age, he lost his throne. For ten years he lived on, a wandering fugitive or a neglected prisoner, and then, after another brief spell of phantom royalty, he lost his only son and his own life at the hands of his cousin, Richard of Gloucester. A gentleman, a student, a Christian and a martyr, he was, perhaps, the most unfortunate King that ever reigned in England.

WILLIAM OF WYKEHAM

William of Wykeham was born in the summer of 1324, at the village in Hampshire after which he was named. His father was John Ace or Long, his mother Sybil Bowade. They were of the yeoman class and poor, though perhaps some noble blood ran in his mother's veins.

Their son was tall and promising, and he found an early benefactor in Sir John Scures, who was lord of the manor and sheriff of the county. By him the boy was put to school at the priory of St. Swithin in Winchester, then known as the Great Grammar School, and famous for its ancient and deserved reputation. He made the most of his opportunities. Grammar, geometry and French he acquired, and he learnt to write a good hand—*Nemo illa ætate scripsit limatius.*† He worked hard and cured

---

* Blacman, 12.   † Moberly, 9.

himself of the *pigritudo somni* by attending an early Mass every day in the cathedral. It was called Pekismasse, from the priest who used to celebrate it, and it was held by a pillar in the nave. Years afterwards Wykeham erected on the selfsame spot his own beautiful chantry.

When he was about fifteen his patron engaged him as secretary, and passed him on to his successor in the shrievalty. Wykeham "lodged in a high turret of the castle,"* and in six or seven years he acquired some knowledge of land management, of book-keeping and of architectural repairs. When in 1346 Edington, the King's Treasurer, was consecrated Bishop of Winchester, he heard of young Wykeham's aptitude and took him into his own employment. A year later, in October 1347, Edward III., coming back from his victory at Crécy, stayed a few days with the bishop, who presented Wykeham to him. The King was pleased by his manners and appearance, received a good report of his capacity, and took him on to Windsor.

At this time Edward was in the zenith of his glory and magnificence, the cynosure of Christendom. He had just founded the Order of the Garter, and was engaged in enlarging and beautifying his castle on the Thames. Its mighty keep was to typify King Arthur's Round Table and to renew his chivalry. To help in this work he needed capable men, with some experience of labour, building and finance. Wykeham possessed just these qualifications. During his years of training at Winchester the fortifications had been renewed and he had learnt something of county business, while he was an expert at figures. At first he acted only as a clerk, but the King soon saw what a good servant he had got, and determined to promote him.

Wykeham had already received the first tonsure; he was now made one of the royal chaplains, and in 1349, the year of the Black Death, Edward presented him to the living of Irstead in Norfolk, and twelve months later entrusted him with the guardianship of an estate. During

* Campbell, Chanc., i. 225.

the next five years considerable alterations went on at
Windsor, and in the multifarious work of specifications,
estimates, materials and accounts, Wykeham had always
a hand. Nothing was too big and nothing too small for
him. He planned the King's palaces, he managed the
King's manors, he even kept the King's kennels, " receiving
a farthing a day for the food of each of the eight dogs
in them."*

In May 1356 he was appointed clerk of the works at
Henley and Easthampstead, and in the following October
he was made a surveyor at Windsor. Twelve months
later he was granted, in addition to his ordinary pay, a
shilling a day until he should receive " some competent
ecclesiastical benefice." His merits were equal to his trust,
and after three years in this position he was advanced
to be chief warden of the castles of Windsor, Leeds, Dover
and Hadleigh, and of all the parks and manors pertaining
to them. The letters patent gave him power to appoint
workmen, buy material, hold courts leet, and generally
to act as the King's bailiff in these demesnes. The royal
apartments to the east of the Round Tower at Windsor
were now designed and erected under Wykeham's supervision. He was in constant touch with the King, who
had come to repose complete trust in him. When the
new construction was completed, Wykeham is said to have
had engraved on one of the walls, " *Hoc fecit Wykeham.*"
Edward took exception to what seemed an assumption,
but Wykeham salved his conscience by explaining that
it was the castle that had made the architect. His connection with Windsor and the Garter was to be continued,
and ever since his day the Bishop of Winchester has been
prelate of that Order.

In the meanwhile other duties had fallen to his lot.
The constant association at Windsor had made him the
King's close friend. He was with him at Calais in October
1360, at the ratification of the Treaty of Bretigny—by
which most of the fruits of Edward's victories were lost.
His advice was now of real value, and the King rewarded

* Moberly, 20.

him well, loading him with places.   He was made ranger
of the forests south of Trent, dean of St. Martin's-le-
Grand, archdeacon of Lincoln, was presented to over a
dozen prebends in different dioceses of the kingdom, and
given the wardship of various manors.   His church
benefices alone were worth nearly £1,000 a year—a large
income in those days.   He was honest and generous, but
he knew how to manage his money, and gradually he
became a wealthy man.

He was next made Secretary to the King, and in May
1364, when about forty years of age, he was appointed
Keeper of the Privy Seal.   The influence of this office was
wide, though its dignity was not yet as eminent as it
subsequently became.   There is, however, no doubt of
Wykeham's position.   In his pardon of 1 Rich. II. he is
spoken of as having been at this time "*Capitalis Secreti
Concilii ac Gubernator Magni Concilii.**   He was rapidly
rising to be the first person in Edward's confidential
counsels.   In March 1365 an additional 20 shillings a
day was conferred on him, " in consideration of divers
offices touching on private businesses, with which we have
specially burdened him, and in the execution and expedition of which he has borne excessive labours and expenses,
and will be bound to bear more each day . . . not-
withstanding that he is dwelling in our actual household."†

In this year he was employed as a commissioner to
settle the terms of the treaty with Scotland, and was thus
fairly embarked in the affairs of State.   But although his
material advancement had been satisfactory, his spiritual
position was much less so.   Edward III. had identified
himself as the leader of a national Church in opposition
to the oppressive policy of the Roman court.   For
centuries the Pope had collected taxes and provided to
benefices in England without much regard for the wishes
of the King or the interests of the people.   A moment
had now arrived when his pretensions might be resisted
with some prospect of success.   Edward's victories had
raised him to an exceptional height of power among the

* Rymer, vii. 164.   † Moberly, 29.

WILLIAM OF WYKEHAM
BISHOP OF WINCHESTER

To face page 138

European princes; Urban V., born an English subject, was still an exile at Avignon. The combination was propitious. The King began to take active measures for upholding his rights, and Wykeham supported him. The various statutes which strove to combat the rule of Rome were more sharply enforced. The Pope replied by bulls and briefs, by questions, examinations, exceptions and delays. Particularly did he inveigh against pluralists— and there were few more glaring examples than Wykeham. At Wykeham, therefore, the papal attacks were aimed: by striking at the Secretary he would hit the King. "*Or en ce temps,*" says Froissart, "*regnoit un Prestre, qu'on apeloit messire Guillaume de Wican. Iceluy messire Guillaume de Wican estoit si bien en la grace du Roy d'Angleterre, que par luy estoit tout fait, ne sans luy on ne faisoit riens.*"* But Wykeham was alert. He put himself in order, made an exact return of the benefices that he held, and resigned such as were incompatible with the canons of the Church. There for the moment matters rested.

In April 1366 died Simon Islip, Archbishop of Canterbury. There is little doubt that, had Wykeham wished it, he could have had the place. But he was a very wise man. He remembered that the Primate of England was also the Papal Legate, he knew the history of Becket, and he felt that in such a position it would be difficult to serve loyally both King and Pope. There was also every prospect of the diocese of Winchester, his own home, shortly becoming vacant, and "though Canterbury was the higher rack, Winchester was the deeper manger." He determined, therefore, to wait, and he had not to wait for long. In six months Bishop Edington died. A *congé d'élire* was at once sent to the Prior of St. Swithin's, and without delay Wykeham was elected Bishop of Winchester. He was given the administration of the temporalities, and a royal letter was sent to the Pope requesting his approval. The Pope replied that the appointment lay in his own hands, and by various shifts he delayed the matter for nearly a year. Then the

* Froissart, i. 249.

Duc de Bourbon, a prisoner of Edward's, was sent to him, several large sums of money changed hands,* and eventually, by a compromise over the question of election or provision, Wykeham's nomination was ratified.

In July 1367 Urban issued his bull from Viterbo—he was on his way back to Rome. On its receipt in England Wykeham was raised a step higher, and in September was appointed Chancellor. He had already been ordained a priest. He was now duly consecrated and enthroned, and took possession of the great see that he was to administer for the next thirty-seven years.

His first act was to obtain from the King letters patent acquitting him of all faults in respect of any offices he had previously held. He could remember as a boy the government of Archbishop Stratford, and he had no wish to repeat his experiences. His own political prospects were not very promising. Edward's lucky days had gone by; his Flemish creditors and his French foes were pressing him, while his own people were by no means contented. Almost at once another war began. The campaign was disastrous and expensive. The taxes were heavy, the country disturbed. When Parliament opened in 1370 there were numerous complaints, backed by requests for a ministry not composed of churchmen. The King was annoyed, but he was obliged to submit, and on March 14, 1371, Wykeham resigned the Great Seal " at Westminster in a private room of the King's, on the Queen's bridge by the river, called the Bedchamber."† He was well satisfied to do so: his government had not been a success, though less from the failure of its leader than the difficulties of the times.

He was replaced by an undistinguished and inexperienced council of lawyers, behind whom loomed the luckless figure of John of Gaunt, Duke of Lancaster, one of the King's younger sons. But the war went on just as badly as before, and Wykeham, who was now occupied with the affairs of his diocese and the abuses in religious houses, soon came to be regarded as the most reliable member of the

* 20,000 francs according to Stow, 267.   † Rymer, vi. 683.

Opposition. In several conferences held by the Good Parliament his advice and approval were sought by both Lords
and Commons, and he began to resume his former position.
But in 1375 John of Gaunt returned from a continental
campaign where he had been singularly unfortunate, and
endeavoured to redeem his credit by further political
activity at home. The King, though little over sixty, was
now sunk in luxury and dotage; Queen Philippa was
dead; and he was largely governed by a low-born mistress,
Alice Perrers, the wife of Sir William Windsor. His
eldest son, the Black Prince, a close friend of Wykeham's,
lay sick, hidden away in a country retreat, his career of
conquest almost forgotten. The other members of the
royal house were of little weight; and Lancaster was
thus able to engross the chief power without much com-
petition from his own family. For several reasons he had
taken a strong dislike to Wykeham. There had been
some questions about his birth, and Wykeham had been
associated with these rumours. Wycliff, the reformer,
was among Lancaster's friends, and the extreme zeal of
Wycliff was much too advanced for the practical views of
Wykeham. Finally, in the debates that had followed on the
conduct of the war, Wykeham had held a principal voice,
and had strongly criticized several of Lancaster's party.

In June 1376 the Black Prince died; in July the Good
Parliament broke up; Lancaster was left in practical control
of affairs, and he determined to avenge himself. A number
of charges of the usual nature were brought against
Wykeham—malversation of money, illegal release of
prisoners, remission of fines, lack of economy in the
treasury. All related to transactions that had taken
place at least five years before, and the bishop had good
answers to all. But the Council was under the influence
of the duke, and did not hesitate to give the judgment
that he desired. Edward's consent was obtained, and
Wykeham was condemned to forfeit the temporalities of
his see and was forbidden to approach within twenty
miles of the court. This was a tremendous sentence, and
matters looked very black for him. He left London and

moved slowly from manor to manor, as they were successively taken from him.

Lancaster, however, was preparing to pursue him
further. Early in 1377 Parliament met again. Wykeham
had not received his writ, but the bishops, enraged at his
treatment, insisted on his attending Convocation. At
the same time Wycliff, who had been cited to answer for
his doctrines, appeared at St. Paul's, accompanied by
Lancaster. High words passed between the duke and
the Bishop of London, who was Wykeham's principal
friend. The citizens resented the insult to their bishop
and began to riot, abusing Lancaster and demanding
justice for Wykeham and de la Mare, the Speaker of the
Commons, who had been imprisoned. The riot grew:
Lancaster had to flee from his palace of the Savoy, and
Wykeham became the hero of the hour. But the duke
was powerful and determined. He persuaded the King
to settle all the temporalities of the see of Winchester
on the young Prince Richard, the heir to the crown, and
thus placed Wykeham in a very invidious position. On
June 18, however, this decree was commuted for a payment equal to the maintenance of three galleys for three
months, and the bishop received back his revenues. It
was said that a gift to Lady Windsor had smoothed the
way, and Baker remarks that Wykeham escaped " by his
full purse."* Yet it was hardly needed, for three days
later the old King died.

At once the whole face of politics changed. The young
Richard, mindful of his father's friend, immediately
cancelled all the judgments against Wykeham and remitted his fines. The writ of Privy Seal says: " Perceiving the welcome, useful and praiseworthy services
rendered to our grandfather by the Bishop of Winchester,
and the high place which he held with our dearest lord
and father . . . we wholly disburthen, acquit, and utterly
absolve him of all crimes and offences whatsoever . . . yet we
do not think the said bishop to be in anywise blameworthy
. . . but do hold him wholly innocent and guiltless."†

* Baker, 180.   † Moberly, 149.

A reconciliation was arranged with Lancaster, and Wykeham was at last able to retire quietly to his diocese. The whole business, however, had cost him over 10,000 marks, and had taught him how slippery is the game of government.

He now turned his mind to matters for which he cared far more than for politics: to the restoration of his cathedral, and the foundation of the two noble institutions with which his name is associated—Winchester and New College, Oxford. For some time he had prepared these projects, and he was financially " so deep a manager " that he was able to resume his plans without delay. The charter of New College was issued in 1379, and the first stone laid in 1380; that for Winchester was signed two years later, and its buildings, near the site of Wykeham's old school, were begun in 1387. When these were opened, in 1394, he proceeded with the reconstruction of his cathedral nave. For the expenses of these immense undertakings he provided out of his own pocket, endowing the new corporations with equal munificence.

Thus for ten years Wykeham was occupied with labours which were more congenial to him, perhaps more beneficial to others, than the conduct of affairs at Westminster. But he did not absent himself from his duties in Parliament. He was chosen as a principal member of various commissions. Twice he was appointed to help in the reform of the royal household, once to examine into the state of the exchequer: in all he was invaluable.

Richard had now taken the government into his own hands, and had surrounded himself with an army of favourites; De la Pole, Tresilian and de Vere were the chief. Their influence was particularly harmful at a time when the country was indigent and disaffected, and when the recent revolts of Wat Tyler and the peasants had shown to what results evil counsels might lead. Wykeham, attached as he was to the person of the young King, saw only too clearly the dangers of his policy and the risks that he was running. At last, in 1385, matters came to a crisis. De la Pole, now Earl of Suffolk, was

impeached, and the Commons insisted on a regency.
Eleven lords and prelates were named, of whom Wykeham
was one. Richard prepared to resist. His favourites took
up arms and were defeated by the five Lords Appellant—
Gloucester, the King's uncle; Derby (Henry of Bolingbroke), Lancaster's eldest son; Warwick; Arundel; and
Nottingham. In 1388 the Merciless Parliament met and,
supported by the Commission of Regency, gave the rebels
short shrift. The leaders were hanged, the King had to
submit, and for the moment there seemed a prospect of
peace.

Richard, however, was only biding his time. By
promises and prayers he succeeded in detaching his cousin
Derby from the ranks of his enemies. Lancaster was
away in Guienne, fighting for his paper kingdom of Castile.
York, another uncle, was of little account. There remained Gloucester, who now held the chief control
in the ministry. On May 3, 1389, the King entered the
Council chamber and asked how old he was. He was
told twenty-three. " Then," he said, " I must certainly
be of age; I will no longer submit to restraint, but will
govern the kingdom for myself."* He demanded the
Great Seal from Archbishop Arundel, left the room for
a moment, and returning, gave it to the Bishop of Winchester. Wykeham was not at all anxious to take it.
Politics were never his forte: his last experience had been
unfortunate, and he knew that Richard was headstrong
and unstable. But Richard was the son of his old patron,
foreign affairs were quieter than they had been, and he
felt that he could perhaps do some good towards composing the State. At last " *quamvis plurimus renitens* "
he accepted. On May 4 he became Chancellor for the
second time, with his friend Brantingham, Bishop of
Exeter, as Treasurer. Alone of the Lords Appellant
Derby remained in the Council.

Wykeham's second ministry began well. In August a
three years' truce was made with France; a reconciliation
was effected between Richard and his uncle Gloucester;

* Moberly, 213.

while a further Statute of Provisors, to check the Pope's meddling with English benefices, was passed. In addition to these public acts, Wykeham organized the business of the Privy Council, keeping minutes of their meetings and laying down rules for their guidance. " The lords of the Council shall meet between nine and ten in the morning at latest. The business of the King and Kingdom shall take precedence of all other,"* and so on, the distribution of affairs being methodically arranged.

By 1391 some semblance of order had been introduced into the government, and Wykeham felt again able to resign the seal. He handed it over at Windsor on September 27 " *in camera vocata le Parlour,*"† and returned to his bishopric and his building. He was sixty-seven years of age, and he looked forward to spending the rest of his life in comparative repose.

Richard, freed from all control, now renewed his arbitrary rule. In 1394 he lost his beautiful wife, Anne of Bohemia; she had exercised a moderating influence on him, and her death was a severe blow. Two years later he married Isabella of France, and peace seeming secure, he determined to repay his recent foes. In 1397 three of the Lords Appellant—Gloucester, Arundel and Warwick— were seized and imprisoned. Gloucester soon died—murdered, it was said—in prison at Calais. Derby for the moment remained in favour, and was even made Duke of Hereford, but he was extremely uneasy, and Wykeham, who had been a member of the regency, was hardly less disturbed. The King, however, issued a pardon to him, borrowing £1,000 at the same time.

In September 1398, as the result of a quarrel with Nottingham (now Duke of Norfolk), Derby was suddenly banished. Six months later his father died, and the King then seized all his estates and deprived him of both his dukedoms. The injustice of these actions enraged the Lancaster party and enlisted popular sympathy for their leader. His friends flocked to him in Paris and urged him to try his fortune at revenging his own wrongs and

* Proceedings of Privy Council, i. 18.   † Rymer, vii. 707.

righting those of his country. Although aware of what was happening, Richard chose this inauspicious moment for an expedition to Ireland, leaving England to look after itself.

During these months Wykeham remained at his house in Southwark, possibly expectant of Lancaster's plans, certainly nervous of Richard's intentions. He was one of the few who had withstood the King and had not yet been punished. But as at the end of the last reign, so now again matters turned to his advantage. In July 1399 Henry of Lancaster landed at Ravenspur; in August Richard was captured on his return from Ireland; and on September 30 he was deposed, Henry taking the crown for himself.

His position being again secure, Wykeham came up to attend the new Parliament and the Council. But he was eighty years of age, and his health was breaking down. He had obtained a dispensation allowing a coadjutor to act for him in his diocese, and he now retired definitely to his house at South Waltham, near his former home. He had still plenty of work to distract him. He repaired the roads and bridges between London and Winchester; he continued to decorate his cathedral; he revised the statutes of his colleges, so that they afterwards served as the models for those of later foundations; he provided for all whom he had employed and continued to dispense a princely hospitality, his daily dinner for twenty-four poor people being never omitted.

Gradually he grew weaker in body, though preserving his mental faculties, and on September 27, 1404, he closed his life. He was buried in a chantry of his cathedral, built near the pillar by which he used to hear Mass as a boy, within sight and sound of his old school and of the greater one that he had founded. His tomb was surmounted by his effigy and ensigned by the canting arms that had been granted him, "two carpenters' squares between three roses." His estates and wealth were immense, and despite the lavish gifts that he had made in his lifetime and had left in his will, he was able to bequeath a considerable fortune to his nephew and heir, Sir Thomas Wykeham. His property in money alone was over £10,000, "all of which had been obtained by honest means," for it was truly said "that he only received the revenues of the Church with one hand to expend them in her service with the other."*

Of Wykeham's appearance his statue, portrait and bust at Winchester give some idea. He was tall, thin, with a firm profile, a broad brow, and a thoughtful countenance. " Well advised in doubtful questions, prompt in reply, alert and affable, his conversation was neither empty nor tiresome." " To find a fault in him was like looking for a knot in a rush."†

Living across the dividing line of mediæval and modern England, he had used his experience well. Yet, despite his many merits, he was never an impressive figure as a Chief Minister. His heart was not in such work, and it was only his affection for the princes whom he served and his high ideas of public duty that made him undertake posts for which he knew he was ill-suited. Moderation and humility were not qualities to attract or control the later Plantagenets.

Before all things Wykeham was a practical man. Not a great scholar, a great architect, nor a great politician, he was level-headed, hard-working and straightforward. Careful of his own and of other people's money, aware of the advantages of sound education and good government, he did his best to promote both. By a sensible use of his natural capacities he was able to deal with the most varied duties; by a wise distribution of his wealth he could afford always to be hospitable, often munificent. Conservative by temperament, he could yet look ahead, and his moderation to Richard, to Lancaster and to Wycliff, with none of whose views he agreed, showed that he understood that practical politics are founded on compromise. From the riches, the arts and the learning that he had acquired he was able to provide fortunes for his family, monuments to his memory, and lasting legacies for posterity. He

* Foss, 771. † Moberly, 301.

founded the first of those great public schools of England that " have carried all over the earth a standard of conduct and character which has been a national and imperial asset of the first order."*

His life was simple, his heart humble, his spirit charitable, and he enjoys to this day a well-deserved fame, due to his own energy, honesty and forethought. Conduct, in his view, came before everything, and to the highest level of conduct he adhered through all the eighty years of his life, well maintaining his motto of " *Manare makyth man.*"

II.—BEAUFORT

Henry Beaufort was born in 1377 at the Château de Beaufort in Anjou. He was the second natural son of John of Gaunt, Duke of Lancaster and Aquitaine, and titular King of Castile, by his mistress Catherine, daughter of Sir Payne Roet, king-at-arms of Guienne.

His father was a younger son of Edward III.; his mother was the widow of Sir Hugh de Swinford, and had been governess to Lancaster's daughters, bearing him several children during the lifetime of his second wife, Constance of Castile. But in 1394 the Duchess Constance died, and eighteen months later Lancaster married Catherine, to the considerable annoyance of his family. A year later, however, his natural children were legitimatized by Act of Parliament, though they were subsequently excluded from the succession to the Crown. By his three wives he had had a numerous issue, and Beaufort was thus brother or half-brother to Henry IV. of England, Queen Philippa of Portugal and Queen Catherine of Castile, and was also a nephew of the poet Chaucer, who had married Philippa Roet, his mother's sister.

His early life was spent in France, and he was afterwards educated at Aix-la-Chapelle and perhaps for a short time at Oxford. At this period of his career he fell in love with the Lady Alice Fitzalan, daughter of Richard,

* *Sunday Times*, 16 vii. 1922.

Earl of Arundel and sister of the Archbishop of Canterbury. By her he had an illegitimate daughter Joan, who subsequently married Sir Edward Stradling of Glamorgan. Although this amour did not impede his promotion in the Church, it failed to endear him to the Arundel family, who were for many years his bitter political opponents.

While still a youth he had been presented to three prebends; he was made Dean of Wells and Chancellor of Oxford when he was twenty; and on coming of age he was appointed Bishop of Lincoln. Early in the next year his father died, leaving him some property, and seven months later his half-brother Henry of Lancaster mounted the throne. For a time Beaufort then acted as tutor and governor to his young nephew, Henry Prince of Wales. By his connections he was in the very front rank of society, and his abilities and temperament disposed him to an active political life. With his younger brother of the full blood, Thomas Beaufort, afterwards Duke of Exeter, he adhered closely to the King. In 1403, when only twenty-six years old, he was made Lord Chancellor, and a year later, on the death of William of Wykeham, he was translated to the rich see of Winchester. He then resigned the Great Seal, though he remained a principal member of the Council. But soon a rift began between Beaufort and the King. The latter had become nervous, ailing and superstitious, and was much under the influence of the Church, especially of Archbishop Arundel, who was extremely orthodox. Beaufort, although a churchman himself, was young, healthy and worldly; he regarded the heretics with disdain; and his gallantries did not diminish the affection and esteem in which his nephew held him. His employment was therefore continued, and in 1406 he was sent as ambassador to France to conclude a treaty of peace and also to arrange for the marriage of the Prince of Wales "*cum aliqua de filiabus Adversarii nostri de Francia.*"* In that year he lent £600 to the King; for his wealth was already notable, and Henry IV. was always short of money.

* Rymer, viii. 435.

The influence of the prince was still augmenting, and in 1410 Thomas Beaufort, the bishop's brother, was made Chancellor. For the next two years, during the increasing illness of the King, the government was mainly in the hands of the younger Henry and of his Beaufort uncles. Thomas Chaucer, the poet's son and Beaufort's first cousin, was Speaker of the House of Commons, and this connection helped the bishop with the popular party. Their policy comprised a certain toleration of the Lollards and a warm support of the Burgundian alliance. But in 1412 the prince fell out of favour, and his friends were displaced by the Arundel faction, who represented the High Church view and were in strong sympathy with France.

A year later, however, Henry IV. died, and on the accession of his son Bishop Beaufort was again given the Great Seal and became Chief Minister. An active campaign against France was begun, and to supplement the public revenue Beaufort repeatedly lent the King large sums of money from his private fortune. In the Lollard risings he took a firmer line than hitherto, though he was not oppressive. The link between Henry V. and his uncle was thus even closer than it had been, and Beaufort soon became the principal factor in English politics.

In July 1415 Henry prepared to start on his expedition to France. In his will, written at Southampton just before his departure, he appoints Beaufort his chief executor, and leaves him a " *Blodinum vestimentum de velveto, embraudatum de stellis* " and a " *pulchrum portophorium in duobus voluminibus per Johannem Frampton.*"*

Beaufort remained at home, and to him fell the memorable duty of announcing to Parliament the victory of Agincourt, which he followed up by a request for further supplies; and as these were not forthcoming in sufficient amount, he lent the King £14,000 privately, accepting the crown itself in pawn.

In 1416 he was in France with Henry for six weeks, the Great Seal being left with a keeper. As a rule, however,

* Rymer, ix. 291.

HENRY BEAUFORT
CARDINAL BISHOP OF WINCHESTER

To face page 150

Beaufort's duties kept him in England, for besides the control of the executive government and of his bishopric, he had his legal work, to which he paid considerable attention, extending the jurisdiction of the Court of Chancery. He also carefully superintended his property and became the greatest " woolmaster " in the realm.*

At this time the Council of Constance was sitting. It was divided between the Emperor's party, chiefly from the Northern nations, who pressed for reforms in the Roman Church, and the party of the Cardinals, including the French, Spaniards and Italians, who wished first to elect a new Pope. The English Parliament was much concerned with " this damnable schism in Holy Church," and Henry V., having seen sufficient of his own heretics, was not now so anxious to encourage reform. He determined, therefore, to let Beaufort visit the Council as his secret representative, in order to promote a compromise. Some money disputes between the King and his uncle had left a coolness, and the journey was a relief to both.

Beaufort accordingly resigned the Great Seal and set out as a pilgrim for the East, taking Constance on the way. There, by judicious management, he was able to secure the Emperor's assent to the election of Cardinal Colonna as Pope. Beaufort's own name had been freely canvassed as a candidate, and the new Pope, Martin V., showed his gratitude by naming him as a Cardinal and proposing to confer on him legatine powers in England. But as soon as they heard of this, both Chichele, the Archbishop of Canterbury, and Henry himself, strongly objected, the latter saying that " he had as lief sette his coroune besyde hym as to see hym were a cardinal's hatte."†

Beaufort was obliged therefore to forgo his ambition for the moment, and he continued his pilgrimage, making what Fuller calls a " dangerous journey to Palestine." He had met the Emperor Manuel Palæologus in England in former days, and had many friends at Constantinople, while foreign politics always attracted him. Thus

* Traill. Soc. Eng., ii. 418.   † Stubbs, iii. 116, note.

for the next few years there are hardly any details of his
doings, and he seems to have been abroad most of the
time. In 1421, however, he was back again in England.
and, despite his disappointment about his red hat, he lent
another £14,000 to the King. The quarrel, if there had
been one, was thus made up, and when a year later Henry
died in Paris, he left Beaufort as godfather and guardian
of his infant son. He knew that he could rely upon his
uncle's wisdom and loyalty: " to a house in the position
of the Beauforts, the first object was the preservation of
the dynasty."*

John, Duke of Bedford, Henry's brother, was made
Regent of France, with another brother, Humphrey,
Duke of Gloucester, to act as his deputy in England.
Between Gloucester and Beaufort a fierce feud was to
arise, lasting beyond the end of their lives and leading to
many public and private troubles. Its cause was partly
the anomalous position which Gloucester held in England,
where he was not allowed to assume as full power as he
desired; partly from the prominent place which Beaufort's
age, wealth and experience gave him in the Council, but
chiefly from Gloucester's own jealous and hectoring spirit.
His first act was to claim the protectorate of the kingdom
for himself, but Beaufort countered him effectually:

> " The bishop of Wynchester it withstode,
> With all the lordes there hole of his assent,
> Then would he been, as for ye next of bloode,
> Leuetenaunt then of England and regent,
> The bishop aye withstode all his entent,
> That Chaunceler was, by fifth Kyng Henry made
> And so furth stode; and in the office bade."†

Defeated at home, Gloucester turned to military adventure, and insisted on taking an expensive and unfortunate
expedition into the Low Countries.

In 1424, both royal dukes being abroad, Beaufort
became Chancellor for the third time, and soon had the
administration of England entirely in his hands. He
was as influential in the Council as he was in Parliament,

* Stubbs, iii. 101.   † Hardyng, 391.

and he ruled with discretion. In the city of London, however, he was unpopular, owing chiefly to some orders he had given the merchants, which the mayor and aldermen thought an infringement of their rights. To guard against possible trouble Beaufort had garrisoned the Tower with Lancashire troops loyal to himself, and by them, on his return from the Continent, Gloucester was refused admission to the fortress. He was extremely angry, and persuaded the mayor to close London Bridge against the bishop when he came over from his house in Southwark. The result was a rising of the citizens, and only with difficulty was a serious riot averted. Fearing that Gloucester might be too strong for him, Beaufort wrote to Bedford in France begging him to come over: " As ye desire the welfare of the Kyng our sovereigne Lorde and of his realmes of England and of France, and your owne weal with all yours, hast you hither: for, by my truth, an ye tarry long, we shall put the lande in a jupardy, with a Felde, suche a brother you have here: God make hym a good man."*

Bedford hurried across to London and managed to compose the quarrel for the moment. At Leicester the Parliament of Bats was summoned—so-called because arms being forbidden, clubs were carried instead. Here various charges were brought against Beaufort. He was said to have conspired against Henry IV., Henry V. and Henry VI., to have tried to murder Gloucester, and to have stirred up revolt.† Little weight was attached by the Council to these accusations, Beaufort was acquitted, and a formal reconciliation was ordered. But his prestige was damaged; he thought that he had been badly treated, and he felt it best to resign the Great Seal. A few months later he was consoled by receiving his Cardinal's hat, the price being that he should help the Pope in a campaign against the Bohemian Hussites.

In 1427 he accordingly started for Germany, but his career as a soldier was not fortunate. He raised a corps of troops and organized them with care, but before he

* Ellis, 2nd series, i. 101.   † State Trials, i. 270.

could himself lead them into action they fled at their first
encounter. Piccolomini describes how " the Cardinal
met the fugitives and marvelled at the ignoble panic
and flight of so many leaders and brave men, beseeching
them with many prayers to return against the enemy, who
was at all points the weaker party. But when he had
striven in vain, he himself was forced to share in their
disgraceful rout."* Beaufort seems on this occasion to
have behaved with great gallantry, taking his cross in
his hands and urging his men to halt, but the reverse was
damaging, and when next year he returned to England
he had not added much credit to his name.

At home there was plenty for him to do, for by the
death of his brother Exeter the effective representation
of his family had devolved more than ever upon him.
But his new dignity was not popular in England,
where the double allegiance of princes of the Church was
viewed with distrust. Gloucester was only too ready to
pick a new quarrel. He at once opposed the legatine
character which Beaufort assumed, and refused him
admission to a chapter of the Garter. The Cardinal kept
quiet and did not press his rights, devoting himself to
collecting men for another Hussite crusade. But events
in France changed his intentions. In May 1429 Joan of
Arc had relieved Orleans, and a month later Lord Talbot,
the English commander, was taken prisoner at Patay.
Beaufort's fresh troops were sorely needed as reinforcements, and at the Council's request he agreed to let them
serve in France. Thither he accompanied them himself,
and during the next two years he was continuously
employed at the seat of war. Possibly he took part at
the trial of Joan of Arc,† treating it as a political incident,
for diplomacy and administration meant much more
to him than religion. " Largely through his industry,"
says the Monk of Croyland, " the French princes were
pacified,"‡ and in December 1431 he crowned the young
Henry VI. in Paris. It was felt that he well deserved that

* Aen. Sylv. Hist. Bohem., cxlviii.   † Hanotaux, 278.
‡ Hist. Croy. Cont., 516.

honour, for he had paid for the expenses of the coronation himself.

Gloucester in the meanwhile had continued to intrigue against him, striving to dispossess him of the bishopric of Winchester under a writ of *præmunire*, and seizing his baggage and jewels at Dover. To protect his interests Beaufort was forced to return to England. There he again pleaded his cause before the Parliament, and again obtained their support, a special statute being passed to safeguard him; the large loans that he had recently made to the Crown no doubt counted in his favour. Bedford, who was always his friend, came over to England for several months, and helped to restore some peace in the Council, while the Cardinal did his best to make the exchequer solvent.

In France affairs were going badly, and the conquests of Henry V. were rapidly disappearing. In the summer of 1435 Beaufort attended a conference at Arras with a view to a truce; but no treaty was signed, and soon afterwards Bedford died. His death was a disaster. For twelve years he had been Regent of France, the most capable adviser that the King possessed in that country; he alone had been able to pacify the struggles at home; and on him the hopes of the House of Lancaster were centred, for Gloucester's jealousy of Beaufort had led him to ally himself with the rising and rival branch of York.

The Cardinal was now left as the only living English statesman, and he determined to pursue a policy of peace. It was the only possible policy for England, though it took him ten years to achieve. But his reputation and his riches made him a powerful advocate. In February 1436 a writ of Privy Seal acknowledges a further loan of £20,000 from " *magnus avunculus noster, Henricus Cardinalis Angliæ, in magna necessitate nostra.*"* In that year Paris was lost and the conquests of Henry V. shrank to Normandy and a few fortresses. Beaufort devoted himself more strenuously than ever to an accommodation with France, while Gloucester, with equal energy, headed the

* Rymer, x. 632.

war party. The Cardinal still had his eye on the papal tiara, and in 1437 he proposed paying a visit to Rome. Obstacles, however, were put in his way by the Council, for his success was regarded as more likely to damage England than to help her: indeed, his acceptance of the cardinalate had been the error of his life. But gradually his political labours began to bear fruit, despite Gloucester's constant opposition. The latter had recently charged him with being responsible for the losses in France, but the Council again defended him, and the attack was a signal failure. Gloucester had latterly lost credit. In 1441 his second wife and former mistress, Eleanor Cobham, was accused of endeavouring to bewitch the King. She had to perform a public penance, and was then imprisoned. The sorry part her husband played in this affair seriously diminished his influence.

In 1442 the King came of age, and by him Beaufort was continued as Chief Minister: the value of the Cardinal's wise rule was now universally recognized. Two years later a truce was at last concluded with France, and in 1445 Henry's marriage with Margaret of Anjou crowned Beaufort's policy with success. It was the victory of his life, though he was not to enjoy it for long. He was now nearly seventy, and he began to retire from active work, leaving the administration in the hands of his follower, Lord Suffolk. The moment seemed propitious for scotching the war faction, and in February 1447 Gloucester was suddenly arrested at Bury St. Edmunds: a few days later he died in a mysterious way. It is said that some suspicion attached to Beaufort, though the tale has no evidence to support it. The Cardinal had nothing to gain; he was in a dominant position, and he had never been revengeful. But the rumour was confirmed in the popular view by what seemed a judgment. Less than two months later, on April 11, he himself died in his palace at Winchester. His end, according to contemporary accounts, was edifying and composed, though tradition has made it dramatic. His last words are said to have been " that if England would preserve his life, he was able by his purse to purchase or by his policy to procure it."* Two centuries later another prince of the Church, Cardinal Mazarin, expressed an equally worldly view. "*Quelle domage,*" he said, the day before he died, "*de laisser tant de belles choses.*"

Beaufort's will was as munificent as his life had promised. To his friends and relatives, to the Church and to charity, he bequeathed large sums of money. King Henry, hearing that £2,000 had been left to him, said to the executors: "My uncle was very kind and generous to me when he was alive: the Lord reward him. Do what you should with his goods: we do not wish to take them."†

Of Beaufort's appearance there are some reliable records. The tapestry in St. Mary's Hall at Coventry probably represents him, and his effigy at Winchester is well preserved. He was buried in his cathedral, to the restoration of which, and to the endowment of the neighbouring hospital of St. Cross, he had largely contributed. His only issue was his daughter Joan, and the greater part of his property went to his Beaufort nephews and his niece Margaret, the ancestress of the House of Tudor. The history of his wealth is not far to seek. He had inherited considerable property from his father, and he held in succession two of the richest sees in England for nearly fifty years—his revenues at Winchester were at least £5,000 *per annum*, for Wykeham's careful management had left the lands in the best of order. He had also considerable emoluments as Chancellor, and as a member of the Council—when he was with the King in France he was paid £4,000 per annum.‡ But the chief source of his fortune was that wise economy of money which had so distinguished his predecessor at Winchester. Careful investment, judicious loans, profitable purchases, had raised him to a financial level with the Hanse or the Florentine bankers. "His loans to the Crown," says Green, "reached the sum of half a million."§ He is one

* Fuller, W. Hants. 16.   † Blacman, 10.
‡ Rymer, x. 472.   § Green, ii. 556.

of the earliest examples of the power of the purse in English politics: he used it with generosity and patriotism.

The chroniclers temper his praises: "For honesty and wisdom, riches and glory, he was pre-eminent among all the princes of England;"* "of high descent, high spirit and high preferments; hardly to be equalled by Cardinal Wolsey (a pigmy to him in birth) for wealth and magnificence;"† "more noble in blodd than notable in learning, haut in stomacke and hygh in countenance, covetous and ambitious," yet "a great stay to the Kyng and the realme."‡

Of his worldly spirit there is no doubt, of his imperious temper, of his secular ambitions. It was said that "he fought in Bohemia more boldly than befitted a bishop," and he used to style himself by the "insolent title of Cardinal of England." But he was "the mainstay of the House of Lancaster; for fifty years he had held the strings of English policy, and had done his best to maintain the welfare and honour of the nation. Merciful in his enmities, enlightened in his foreign policy, devotedly faithful, he was ready to sacrifice his wealth and labour to the King."§ He had in an exceptional degree the faculty of foresight. In his earliest days of office he had allied himself with the Commons, whose growing influence he perceived. Usually lenient in the matter of heresy, when danger threatened he was quick to repress it. He had seen his own family rise to its height and begin its downward course. Such a prince as Henry V. would not soon come again, and only by a policy of peace could his simple son hope to survive. To peace therefore, to economy, and to loyal service to the Crown, Beaufort devoted his days, running any risk to repair dissensions at home or disasters abroad, though often despairing of both.

His life was singularly packed with incident. Born close to the throne, though barred from it by his birth, he had mixed with most of the magnates of his day. He had known Chaucer, Talbot, Martin V. and Joan of Arc.

---

* Hist. Croy. Cont., 521.   † Fuller, iv. 185.
‡ Hall, 210, 211.   § Stubbs, iii. 149.

He had accompanied John of Gaunt in his Spanish campaigns and Richard on his Irish journey. He had been a pilgrim, a soldier, a diplomat, a financier, a judge, a bishop and a statesman. To three Kings he had been a minister, a comrade or a guardian. He had seen the rise of the Reformers and composed the contests of the Church. Wykeham, his predecessor at Winchester, could recall Edward II.; Waynflete, his successor, lived to see Henry VII. His descent, his riches and his influence entitled him to hope for the keys of St. Peter, but that prize he was not to win. Circumstance compelled him to subordinate ambition to duty, and after a long life of much good fortune and many rebuffs his reward was to know that he had served the State well by a lavish use of those gifts of character, sagacity and wealth with which Providence had endowed him.

Wykeham and Beaufort had been the only two Chief Ministers of England in the space of a hundred years. Their points of contrast are as striking as those of resemblance. Both were Bishops of Winchester, ruling that see between them for over eighty years; both held the Great Seal more than once; both were successful financiers, as saving as they were generous; both had to serve a weak King and support a distracted country. But the dissimilarity in their temperament made them meet their difficulties in quite different fashions. Wykeham, the yeoman's son, of a quiet nature, cared far more for his building, his colleges and his diocese than for any political struggles; his birth and breeding hampered him in his contact with great affairs, and he shrank from taking too decided a line in matters of moment. Beaufort, the King's son, suffered no such checks. Fierce, forward, forcible, " pleased with the danger when the waves went high," he relished no rival and feared no fight. Like the later Cardinals, Ximenes, Wolsey and Richelieu, he was a statesman of the widest views, and though his continental activities were circumscribed by fate, he was able at home to play a man's part in the storms of his day.

The names of Wykeham and Beaufort have survived five hundred years; but their statecraft is not their chief memorial. Scholars recall in one a type of mild beneficence; the imperious figure of the other is immortalized in the sombre lines of Shakespeare.

CHAPTER VI

THE LATER NOBLES

SUFFOLK AND WARWICK

THE House of Lancaster before its accession to the throne
had been identified with a reforming policy; and the
bold stroke of Henry IV., the successes of his warlike
son, at first promised popularity to its rule. But their
reigns together lasted little more than twenty years, and
were followed by the long minority of Henry VI., during
which the conquests abroad were lost, the people at home
misgoverned, and angry feuds maintained between factious
ministers and aspiring princes. The hereditary possessions of the Crown had been largely dissipated by the
extravagance of Richard II., while the revenues of
Lancaster, sufficient for a duke, were quite inadequate
to support a King. As long as matters went well these
revenues were supplemented by the Legislature, but when
the directing hand was removed and the victories had
become defeats, the Commons would not grant, nor the
country pay, further taxes. As the Crown grew poorer
and less powerful, a few noble families concentrated in
their hands an appreciable part of the lands of England.
The merchants had vastly expanded their staple industry
of the wool trade and were amassing wealth. The Church
was occupied with its own troubles, for the Lollards and
the New Learning had become definite dangers. Parliament was collectively strong, but the interests of its
component parts were still so much divided that it rarely
acted with energy or decision. Thus the way was open
for an ambitious or adroit leader to turn the situation
as he wished, and to make or mar the fortunes of his

country as patriotism or profit might suggest. The age was an age of individual interests rather than of popular movements, for the neap tide of democracy had ebbed, while the full flow of the Reformation had not yet set in.

In 1461 the House of Lancaster was ousted by that of York, another branch of the Plantagenets with an equally good if not a better title to the Crown. Edward IV., who now came to the throne, was as dissimilar a prince to his immediate predecessor as could well be imagined. Tall, young, ardent, admittedly the handsomest man in his dominions, he was devoted to pleasure. He had plenty of talents and some accomplishments: " *Il parlait en assez bon Francois,*" says Commines.* Essentially a politician, he was equally opportunist, and it was not long before the mild virtues of the hapless Henry were forgotten. In his early days he was close with his money, for good reason: the net revenue of the Crown had sunk to less than £40,000 a year, while the expenditure was half as much again; in addition, the late King's debts amounted to nearly £400,000. There was thus cause for economy. But in the course of ten years the proscriptions and attainders of defeated Lancastrians poured a flood of gold into the royal coffers, and by the time that he was firmly established Edward had become so rich that he could administer the government from his own income. The Commons had voted him a tonnage and poundage grant for life, and this he did not hesitate to supplement by benevolences. Nor did he let his surplus wealth lie idle. He became an active trader on his own account, competing at advantage with other merchants, and adding considerably to his capital. By these means he grew independent of Parliament and was able to initiate that system of direct rule which was so much developed by his successors, the Tudors. " His personal fitness adapted him to be the exponent of despotic theory."†

But there was another and less pleasing side to his character. From his earliest days he had been accustomed

---

* Commines. iv. 10   † Stubbs, iii. 208.

to battle, murder and sudden death, though loving his ease and determined to enjoy it. In imitation of his contemporary, Louis XI., he employed an army of spies all over the country who kept him informed of what went on. He rarely showed mercy except to those who could not hurt him. It was he who introduced the practice of torture, hitherto unknown in England, and his cry of " Spare the commons " on the field of battle was only a synonym for " Slay the lords." " *Encore m'a conté le roi Edouard*," says Commines, " *que dès quil venait au dessus il montoit a cheval et crioit qu'on sauvast le peuple et qu'on tuast les seigneurs.*"* Neither his cousin, Henry VI., nor his brother Clarence had any claim on his conscience, and he did not hesitate to allow his other brother Gloucester to kill them both. Relieved of danger he then gave himself up to food, clothes and women. He grew extremely fat, became the slave of his Italian tailor, and spent his days amid banquets, pageants and mistresses. Of these last he used to say that he had three " of whom one was the merriest, another the wiliest, and the thirde the holiest harlot in his realme, whom no man could get out of Churche except it wer to his bed."† He was, says Stubbs, " vicious far beyond any King that England had seen since the days of John, and more cruel and blood-thirsty than any King she had ever known."‡ With exceptional gifts of person, mind and fortune, his calculating nature, his unrestrained appetites, perhaps his recollection of the hardships of his youth, made him sacrifice justice to expediency, and patriotism to pleasure. At the age of forty he died, genial but insincere, successful but undistinguished, a victim to his own intemperance.

He left a numerous and hopeful family, but he left also a brother, Richard, Duke of Gloucester, the last male of the Plantagenet race to sit on the throne of England. Some writers have painted this prince, if not as a model of all the virtues, at any rate as much maligned and misunderstood—" a capable Renaissance ' *real politiker* ' rather than a crippled monster of malignity." It is true

---

* Commines, iii. 5.　　† More, Rich. III. 84-85.　　‡ Stubbs, iii.

that most accounts of Richard were composed in the days of his successor, but there is little doubt that the generally received version of his character is substantially correct. " Little of stature, ill-fetured of limmes, croke backed, his left shoulder much higher than his right, hard favoured of visage,"* with a withered arm and a lowering brow, his outward appearance was not engaging. But it was well suited to his mind. Courage and ability, like most of his family, he possessed, but to balance them he was envious, vindictive and grasping beyond measure, unscrupulous and treacherous in his plans, dark and tyrannical in their execution. He was a lover of music, a patron of letters, an early free-trader; he was responsible for one or two good laws, to which he paid no heed; to further his unjust claims upon the Crown he accused his mother's chastity, strove to marry his niece, and was almost certainly guilty of the murder of his King, his brother, his nephews and his wife.† In a reign of two years he alienated all the Yorkist and most of the Lancastrian nobles, by his ambition he destroyed a famous dynasty, and under his black auspices the House of Anjou, after governing England for over three centuries, sank to a sinister end.

The forty years from the marriage of Henry VI. to the death of Richard III. cover the Wars of the Roses. It is a period of struggle and disaster, of greed and deceit, and the rare ministers who rule are fighting men, with the virtues, the faults and the frequent fate of their calling.

I.—SUFFOLK

William de la Pole, afterwards Earl and Duke of Suffolk, was born at Cotton in that county on October 16, 1396. He was the second son of Michael, second Earl of Suffolk, and of the Lady Catherine, daughter of Hugh, Earl of Stafford.

* More, Rich. III. 8.
† Walpole explains away these mischances, and even makes them redound to Richard's credit (Hist. Doubts, vi.).

In a hundred years his family had enjoyed a remarkable and rapid rise. In the thirteenth century his ancestor, William atte Pole, as he was then called, was a prosperous wool and wine merchant at Kingston-upon-Hull, trading with France and the Low Countries. By 1296 he had become a knight. His son, another Sir William, followed and enlarged his father's business, grew immensely rich, and was continually lending large sums of money to Edward III. during his Continental wars. In return he received grants of the customs, manors in Yorkshire, and houses in the city: his London mansion stood in Pope's Head Alley, "extending from Lombard Street to Cornhill."* He sat as member of Parliament for Hull, and in his native town he often entertained the King, who used to call him "his beloved merchant,"† and who made him first a banneret, and eventually a baron of the exchequer.

Sir Michael, his son, served as a soldier under the Black Prince and John of Gaunt, and became Captain of Calais and Admiral of the Northern Fleet. Summoned to Parliament as a baron in 1366, he was employed on various negotiations in Italy and Bohemia. He endeared himself to Richard II., in 1383 was made Chancellor, and two years later was created Earl of Suffolk. But his wealth and his advancement excited envy, his government was unfortunate, and in a few years he lost his place and had to flee to France, where he died in poverty. His son, the second earl, was also a soldier, "a knight of the most excellent and kindly reputation."‡ A firm adherent of the House of Lancaster, he fought in several battles and accompanied Henry V. in his French expedition; but he died of dysentery at Harfleur in September 1415, his eldest son being killed a month later at Agincourt. William, his second son, who had also taken part in the campaign, but had been sent home sick, then succeeded to the earldom at the age of nineteen.

Of William de la Pole's secular education nothing is

* *Times Lit. Supplt.*, ii. v. 1922.
† Burke, "Vicissitudes," iii. 107.   ‡ Gesta Hen. V., 31.

known, but his military training went on apace, and
in 1417 he was back again in France " with thirty lances
and fourscore and ten archers."* In that country
he served continuously and with distinction until the
death of Henry V. His prowess and ability were remarkable. While still young he filled several important
commands, and in 1421 he was chosen a Knight of the
Garter. For the next ten years he was actively engaged
in the French war. He was largely concerned in the
victory of Verneuil, was sent by the Duke of Bedford on
a mission to Brabant, and in 1423 was advanced to be
second in command to Montacute, Earl of Salisbury.
He became military governor of the Cotentin and of
Chartres, and eventually Lieutenant-General of Normandy
and Constable of the Army. This latter office had the
supervision of the supply services, and corresponded in
some degree to the modern post of Quartermaster-
General.

In 1426 he received the Norman dignity of Count of
Dreux, and in that year he executed some brilliant raids
into Brittany; but shortly afterwards he was displaced
by Beauchamp, Earl of Warwick, " *le dit Comte de Suffolk
fut deporte du gouvernement de la basse Normandie &
y fut commis & institué le comte de Warwick.*"† He
continued, however, in active military employment up
to the siege of Orleans, and on Salisbury's death in 1428
he succeeded to the chief command of the English forces.
Joan of Arc's appearance, however, frustrated the English
plans, and in May Suffolk had to retire on Jargeau, where
on June 12 he was forced to surrender. There are various
versions of his capture. Some say that he yielded himself
to the Maid herself; others to the Comte Dunois, others
again to Regnault, an esquire whom he insisted on knight-
ing before he gave up his sword. "*Guillaume Regnault
atteignit sur le pont le comte de Suffolk et le prit. Etes-vous
gentilhomme? demanda Suffolk. Oui. Etes-vous chevalier?
Non. Le comte de Suffolk le fit chevalier et se rendit a lui.*"‡

---

* Holinshed, 559. † Monstrelet, ii. 36.
‡ A. France, Jeanne d'Arc, i. 414.

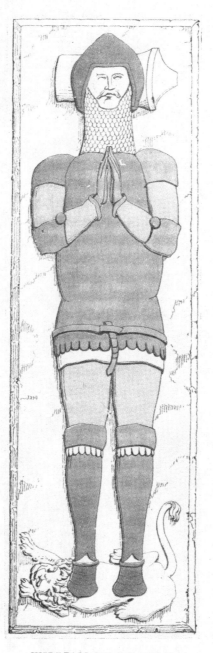

WILLIAM DE LA POLE
DUKE OF SUFFOLK

To face page 166

Suffolk's captivity was short but expensive, for his ransom cost him £20,000. In March 1430 he was back again in Normandy, and in that year he took the castle of Aumale, his final exploit in the war. After this he was seized by the plague and laid up in England for some time, being broken down in health by a service which had lasted nearly seventeen years.

He was just thirty-five years of age. His military duties had given him a wide experience in diplomacy, administration and politics; his knowledge of France and of the French language was exceptional; and he came of a family that had proved itself brave, active and loyal.

He now turned his thoughts to more peaceable pursuits, and in 1431 he married Alice, daughter of Thomas Chaucer, the Speaker, and widow of the Earl of Salisbury, his old commander. This alliance connected him with Cardinal Beaufort, who had been and was again to be Chief Minister. By him Suffolk was made a member of the Council, and in 1432 was given the custody of the Duc d'Orleans, who had been a prisoner of war in England since the battle of Agincourt. His long years in France, his friendship with the Cardinal, perhaps his association with the captive prince, inclined him to peace, and from this time he began to work in that direction. He was next appointed Steward of the Household, and gradually became an important figure at court. In 1435 he was joined with the Cardinal as one of the plenipotentiaries at the Conference of Arras, whither he went in considerable state, having a licence to take with him " gold, silver, plate and jewels, to the value of £2,000."* He was with Bedford at his death in the following September, and two months later " he delivered to the Treasurer of the Chamber the Regent's great seal of silver."† In the next year he was again back in Normandy, serving under Richard, Duke of York, who had succeeded to Bedford's place. The English position in France was becoming desperate, and in the efforts that were made for a treaty, Suffolk and Richard Neville, the new Earl of Salisbury, took a principal part. No success,

* Rymer, x. 613. † Napier, 53.

however, was attained, and after sharing in the defence of
Calais, Suffolk returned to his duties in England.

At home his reputation was good. His religious foundations at Ewelme and elsewhere had endeared him to the
young King, while the Council were only too glad to have
a soldier of distinction to withstand the bellicose projects
of the Duke of Gloucester. He was appointed steward
of the duchy of Lancaster, and Chief Justice of Wales, and
rose rapidly in favour.

In 1441 Gloucester's party fell. Suffolk had been one of
the duke's bitterest enemies, and he was named a commissioner " to enquire of all manner of treasons, sorcery
and all other things that might in any way touch or
concern harmfully the King's person. Before whom
Master Richard Bolingbroke, that was a great and a
cunning man in astronomy . . . and Dame Eleanor
Cobham, Duchess of Gloucester . . . were indicted of
treason in the Guildhall of London."* After the trial
Suffolk was granted the reversion of Gloucester's earldom
of Pembroke, with the guardianship of the Lady Margaret,
the infant daughter of John Beaufort, Duke of Somerset.
This latter charge was of the first importance, as, after
Gloucester himself, Margaret was the nearest Lancastrian
heir to the crown—but in the event it damaged Suffolk
not a little.

King Henry had now come of age. It was high time
that he should have an heir, and both the Cardinal
and Suffolk were deeply interested in his marriage. By
it they hoped to achieve a lasting peace with France
and to defeat the schemes of Gloucester. The lady of
their choice was Margaret of Anjou, daughter of Réné,
King of Sicily, and a niece of the French Queen. She was
a penniless princess, but the match had the concurrence
of the Duc d'Orleans and promised to satisfy the French
court. Suffolk was thought the best man to negotiate it,
and he was accordingly chosen as ambassador to Paris. He
had professed himself disinclined to be concerned closely
in the business, as his known friendship with Orleans, his

* Napier, 56.

connection with the French, and his activity in promoting peace had exposed him to criticism. His objections, however, were overruled by the Council, though he obtained a patent exonerating him from any blame as regards either treaty or marriage.

Early in 1444 he crossed to France. An armistice was arranged, and in May Margaret was betrothed to Henry. A month later a truce for two years was agreed on, and Suffolk returned in triumph. He was at once rewarded with the thanks of Parliament and a marquisate.

The news of the French alliance was at first only too welcome in England, for the people were pining for peace, and in the autumn Suffolk was again sent over to fetch back the youthful bride—she was just fifteen years old. He was forced to remain some months in France, and during that time the concessions he had already made were considerably enlarged, and the English were compelled to cede Maine and Anjou. It is probable that he was not as firm or as wary as he had been, and that the French traded upon his anxiety for peace.

Eventually, in April 1445, Margaret arrived at Portsmouth. She was so much indisposed from the voyage that Suffolk carried her to the shore in his arms. Immediately afterwards she fell a temporary victim to the smallpox,* but on her recovery the marriage was celebrated with great pomp, and Suffolk was again commended by Parliament for the work he had done. In the summer a French embassy arrived in London, and the peace discussions were renewed. Suffolk again took the chief part, for he was well disposed to the French envoys and popular with them. On one occasion he remarked to them "that he had seen so much of the honour and excellence of the King of France that he was very anxious that all should know that he would serve him in the presence of all men and against all men, excepting the person of his master."†

The importance of Suffolk in these deliberations

---

* Her doctor's fees were only £3 9s. 2d. Strickland, ii. 181, 182.

† Henry VI., Chron., i. 117.

gradually made him the principal figure in the Council.
The Cardinal was old, in retirement, and in " accord with
him."* Gloucester was angry but impotent; the King
civil and happy, usually limiting himself at audiences to
taking off his hat and saying " *St. Jehan grant merci.*"
The Queen, young as she was, was already an active
personality, closely interested in the peace, and a strong
supporter of Suffolk. Thus by the end of the year Suffolk
had become in effect Chief Minister, with only Gloucester
to oppose him—a foe who was soon to disappear.

Early in 1447 a Parliament was summoned at Bury
St. Edmunds, near Suffolk's home. There, on February 18,
Gloucester was suddenly arrested, and five days later he
was found dead in his bed. He had, it is true, wretched
health, and it is probable that the shock and annoyance
to which he had been subjected hastened his end, but
rumour was alive and " the grudge and murmure of the
people ceased not against the Marques of Suffolk for the
death of the good duke of Gloucester, of whose murder
he was specially suspected."† Two months later the
old Cardinal also died, and Suffolk became supreme.

He was now appointed Chamberlain of the Household,
Lord Warden of the Cinque Ports, and Lord High Admiral
of England, Ireland and Aquitaine. In the ensuing
year he was made Governor of Calais, and advanced to a
dukedom. He had thus attained the summit of political
power at little more than fifty years of age, and the favour
he enjoyed seemed to promise him a prosperous career.
But his antagonists were many, he had not sought to
conciliate them, and his French sympathies laid him open
to very damaging attacks.

On the death of Gloucester the leadership of the war
party had devolved on Richard, Duke of York, the heir
to the throne if the claim of the Beauforts were disallowed. York was commanding in France, but Suffolk
now replaced him by Edmund Beaufort, Duke of Somerset,
and sent him into comparative exile as Lord Deputy of
Ireland. Somerset's strategy was unfortunate: fresh

* Henry VI., Chron., i. 112, 123.   † Fabian, ii. 444

hostilities were begun in France, further defeats ensued, and Lord Talbot had to be left as a hostage. The capture of Rouen in October 1449 reduced the English continental possessions to Calais and its immediate neighbourhood. Thus within a generation all the glories of Agincourt had faded away, and only a burden of debt remained.

In England the French alliance and the French marriage were soon identified with these surrenders and losses, while Suffolk, the francophile minister, was blamed for the faults of his general. The followers of the Duke of York took up the cry, and a large section of the country began to attack Suffolk and his policy. He was called Jack Napes, and most of the songs of the day were directed against him.

> " Suffolke Normandy hath swolde,
>   To gete hyt agayne he is bolde."
> " The White Lion "[1] is leyde to slepe
> " Thorough the envy of the Ape Clogge[2]
>   And he is bounden that our dore should kepe
>   That is Talbot, oure goode dogge."[3]*

The King still supported his favourite, but Henry was a cypher, already under the sway of his spirited consort, while calumny now began to question the relations of the minister with the Queen.

In the winter session of 1449 Bishop Moleyns and Lumley, two of Suffolk's principal supporters, were forced to resign the Privy Seal and the Treasury, and shortly afterwards the former was murdered at Portsmouth by some sailors who were dissatisfied with their pay. The Yorkists continued stirring up public feeling against Suffolk, and early in 1450 definite charges were formulated against him. The Speaker attended before the Lords and declared that " The Duke of Suffolk, as it was said, had sold this realm to the French."† Suffolk had previously asked for a specific indictment, but he was now committed to the Tower. The accusations against him

* Wright, Pol. Songs, ii. 230, 222. [1] Norfolk. [2] Suffolk. [3] Shrewsbury.
† State Trials, i. 274.

quickly increased. It was said that he had tried to marry his son to the Lady Margaret Beaufort, intending to secure for his own family the succession to the Crown; that he had betrayed the King's counsel to the French; and that he was guilty of malversation in his various offices.

Henry and the Queen were both anxious to stand by him, but seeing the strength of his opponents, the duke determined to avoid a trial by putting himself upon the King's grace. "On the 9th March he was brought from the Tower of London . . . into the Parliament Chamber at Westminster, and . . . was committed to custody in the tower within the King's palace."* He denied all the charges, referring himself to his letters patent and the orders of the Council for a justification of his acts. On March 17 he again appeared before the King and certain lords, and then, probably by arrangement and to save him from a worse sentence, he was banished from England for five years. Two days later he left London for his own home, "journeying secretly," for there was a large concourse of people at St. Giles waiting to waylay him.

In Suffolk he stayed quietly for six weeks, bidding farewell to his friends and arranging his affairs. On May 1, 1450, he left Ipswich by sea, but off Dover one of the royal ships, the *Nicholas of the Tower*, boarded his vessel, and he was taken off by the captain, who hailed him with the ominous words, "Welcome, traitor." He was allowed a day to confess himself, and was then put down into a small boat, and roughly beheaded by an Irish knave, who told him "he should be fair ferd wyth, and dye on a swerd; and toke a rusty swerd and smote of his hedde with halfe a doseyn strokes."†

> "And when no more they could the Duke deride,
> They cut his head off on the cockboat side."

For two days his body was left on the Kentish shore, guarded by the sheriff. It was then returned to his wife and was buried at his church of Wingfield in Suffolk, where his splendid effigy still remains.

* State Trials, i. 274.　　　　　† Paston ii., 147.

He left a son, John, the second duke, who subsequently married Elizabeth of York, sister of Edward IV., but by the third generation his male issue had become extinct. His wife, who survived him twenty-five years, lies in a beautiful tomb at Ewelme, " one of the most perfect fifteenth-century monuments in England," and a noble memorial of the glories and misfortune of her husband's race.

" Few houses had served the Crown more faithfully than that of de la Pole."* Two had given fortunes to Edward III. and Richard II.; three had sacrificed their lives to Henry V. and his son ; two more were to perish on the battlefield and the block. Whatever rewards their merit may have earned they paid for them in full.

The character of Suffolk is not obscure. He was a capable soldier, an honest diplomat, but he lacked decision and resource, and he had no party. Devoted to the House of Lancaster, he followed the peace policy which had been bequeathed him by the old Cardinal. It was the only course then open, but it was ill-applied and soon became unpopular, for its director was not strong enough to be able to ignore the arts of compromise. " The Duke of Suffolk," says Piccolomini, "crushed those he hated and raised up again those he loved."† Clearly foreseeing the dangers to which he was exposed, he did not guard against them enough. With a weak master and a foreign Queen as his allies, a powerful combination of Lords and Commons against him, his chances were slight. Once the tide of his favour turned, he had no support to cling to, for neither his name, his wealth nor his accomplishments were sufficient to uphold him.

Essentially a good man, generous, pious and kind, he wanted strength. But if his management was weak, his precepts at any rate were sound. Writing to his son before leaving England, he bids him " flee the company and counsel of proud men, of covetous men, of flattering men . . . and draw to you . . . good and virtuous men and such as be of good conversation and of truth. . . .

* Green, i. 561.　　　　† Æn. Syl. Hist. Eur., xlv.

Never follow your own wit in no wise, but in all your works . . . ask advice and counsel."* Perhaps these words recalled his own faults. Most of his campaigns had been fought on the losing side; his diplomacy had always been placatory; his administration could only count on weak and alien friends, while it had to combat well-established and potent foes. Thus distrust of his own position, hesitation to enforce his programme, sapped his courage and curtailed his power, and he fell an easy victim to fierce opponents and a common cry. The general view regarded him as responsible for the murder of Gloucester, the loss of France, the penury of the King and the people. In a few months all his popularity vanished, and " he was held in horror, and was extremely odious to the whole nation."†

Like his grandfather the Chancellor, or his grandson the erstwhile heir to the throne, Suffolk was sacrificed to appease an unjust demand and excuse a luckless policy. As he said in his defence, " twenty-four years he had served in France, seventeen without returning home, thirty years he had been of the Order of the Garter, fifteen of the Council." But when a scapegoat was required such services were to count for naught, and Suffolk met a felon's death and left a traitor's name. It has been reserved for posterity to do him some scant justice and for history to moralize on his fall.

II.—WARWICK

Richard Neville, afterwards Earl of Warwick, was born on November 22, 1428—probably in Yorkshire. He was the eldest son of Richard Neville, who had become Earl of Salisbury in right of his wife, Lady Alice Montacute, daughter and heiress of the last earl of that name.

The Nevilles of Raby and Brancepeth were among the oldest and richest families in the North of England, where they had been established since the twelfth century. They had enormously increased their possessions by a series of

* Napier, 88.   † Rapin, i. 572.

fortunate marriages, and their connections and relations included most of the blue blood in the kingdom. Richard, Earl of Salisbury, was a son of Ralph, Earl of Westmoreland, the head of the Neville clan, by Lady Joan Beaufort, daughter of John of Gaunt, Duke of Lancaster; while his sister Cecily, "the rose of Raby," was married to Richard, Duke of York. Thus his son, the future Earl of Warwick, had for great-uncles Henry IV. and Cardinal Beaufort, and for cousins in the first or second degree Henry V. and VI., Edward IV. and V. and Richard III.

Nothing appears to be known of his early life or education, but when quite a boy he was contracted in marriage to Lady Anne Beauchamp, daughter of Richard, Earl of Warwick, and of Isabel, the heiress of the Despencers. The Beauchamps were the most ancient and wealthy nobles in the land, and the deaths of the old earl, of his son and his granddaughter within ten years, left the young Richard Neville owner through his wife of an enormous property in the centre and West of England. In 1449, before he was yet of age, he received, *jure uxoris*, the earldoms of Warwick, Newburgh and Aumerle, and became the premier peer of his rank. As a lord and a landowner he was thus already of more consideration than his own father, and his potential influence as heir to the Neville and Montacute estates, his family connection with either branch of the Plantagenets, made him prospectively the first subject in the kingdom.

The year of Warwick's coming of age was a critical one for England. The French dominions had been finally lost, the Duke of York had just been exiled to Ireland, and Suffolk, the Chief Minister, was rapidly nearing his fall. Warwick and his father Salisbury were closely bound by blood and friendship to York; they had for some time been at variance with Suffolk as to the wardship of the Beauchamp estates; they were alienated from the senior branch of their own family, the Westmorelands, who were, and had always been, strong supporters of the Lancaster succession; and they looked askance at the hapless rule of Henry.

In May 1450 Suffolk was murdered, and two months
later Jack Cade, a pseudo-Yorkist, led a Kentish revolt
against the court party. Throughout the more settled
and richer parts of England there was already considerable sympathy for the Duke of York, for he was
held to have been unfairly treated by the King, and public
opinion was impatient of the new Beaufort ministry under
the Duke of Somerset. Thus the moment was ripe for
a change.

Cade's rebellion was easily crushed by the royal troops,
but York seized the opportunity and, coming over to
London, definitely assumed the post of leader of the
Opposition. This the King's party had to tolerate, and
for the next three years York and Somerset carried on
a war of words, while the government went from bad
to worse. In 1453 the King became insane—" he fell
into a melancholy madness."* York was then able to
displace and imprison Somerset and to get himself made
Lieutenant of the Kingdom. Two months later, however,
the Queen bore a son—an heir to the throne—which
altered the entire position. York saw that he would have
to take more active measures, not only to further his
cause but to ensure his safety, and in the ensuing Parliament he obtained the appointment of Protector. His
Neville relations declared themselves openly for him;
Salisbury was made Chancellor, and the young Warwick
was admitted to the Council. " The Erles of Warwyk,
Richemond and Pembroke comen with the Duke of Yorke,
as it is seide, everych of them with a godely feliship.
And natheless th' erle of Warwyk wole have M.I. men
awaiting on hym."† Force prevailed and the new government went on until the winter of 1454, when the King
recovered his senses. York had then to resign his office,
Somerset was released and restored, to power and the
old system was renewed.

In May 1455 Somerset called a Council " to deal with
the King's enemies," and it became clear to York and his
friends that they must act at once or submit. They chose

* Oman, 47.   † Paston, ii. 298.

the bolder course. In the north the duke and Salisbury had a considerable following—their own retainers alone made an array of 4,000 men. They moved south towards London, and at St. Albans met the King's forces on May 22. While York and Salisbury engaged them in the streets, Warwick took them in flank from the gardens and decided the day. Somerset and Northumberland were killed; Henry himself was wounded, and the royalists were completely routed, though only 120 men lost their lives.

The power now fell to York again; and Warwick, as a reward for his prowess, was made Captain of Calais, a post which Commines calls " *la plus belle capitainerie do monde*."* It comprised the only regular troops which the King of England then possessed, a small fleet of its own and the customs control of most of the continental trade. Warwick took up his new appointment in the following year, and began that practice of diplomacy in which he was to excel. His main objects were to bring over the Duke of Burgundy to the Yorkist side, to organize an opposition to the Queen, and to keep the French power in check. He remained in Calais for nearly eighteen months, and before he returned to England he had obtained the further post of " captain of the sea," which in effect displaced the Duke of Exeter, the Lord High Admiral. In this position, by a series of dashing ventures of a more or less freebooting character, he harried the French and Spanish ships, gaining several victories. As a sailor he showed remarkable initiative, and his name became well known at home. In his visits to England he was always escorted by large bands of retainers, dressed in the red and white colours of his livery with the Beauchamp badge of the ragged staff, and at his palace he kept open house for all. When he was away from England, says Hall, " the common people judged that the sun was taken from the world."† But he lived mostly in Calais, which had become the recognized centre of Yorkist and Burgundian plots, while his father maintained the cause at home.

For four years no further fighting had taken place in

* Commines, iii. 4. † Hall, 278.

England. The King had again been out of his mind, and for a few months York had resumed his place as Protector. But after Henry's second recovery the Queen herself came forward as the champion of the royalist party, and the duke prepared for another resort to arms. In September 1459 matters came to a head. Warwick, while on a visit to Westminster, was nearly assassinated, so it was said. He went back to Calais, and shortly afterwards Salisbury, when moving from Middleham, his northern castle, to the Duke of York's headquarters at Ludlow, was attacked by Lord Audley, who had been sent by the Queen to arrest him. There was a battle at Bloreheath, where Audley was killed, and Salisbury completed his march in safety. But he had sent off word to Calais, and Warwick now arrived with six hundred men of the garrison, and marched from Sandwich to join his father. The duke and the two earls then increased their forces, while the Queen mustered an army against them. By superior strategy she was able to get between York and his own county, and when the royalists advanced their enemies melted away. On October 14 Trollope, the captain of the Calais garrison, deserted with his troops, and a panic spread among the Yorkists. The duke fled to Ireland, while the two earls, with Edward of March, York's eldest son, escaped to France, Warwick himself steering the fishing smack in which they sailed. For the moment their cause seemed lost.

A Parliament was now summoned at Coventry, and York and his principal supporters were attainted. An attempt was made to dispossess Warwick of his command at Calais; but when the Duke of Somerset " thought surely to have entered into the Haven, the artillarie shot so fiersely that he was fain to land at Whitsandbay."* Lord Rivers was next sent against him, but he was captured and soundly rated by Warwick as " a made lord and the son of a squire,"† and also by the young March, who was afterwards to be his son-in-law. For the time being, however, Warwick and his friends lay low. A letter written

* Hall, 242. † Paston, i. 184.

from Calais at this time says: " My lady Werwyk comys botte lyttell abrode but kepys her allway yn the Castell."*

In England the southern counties and London remained in sympathy with the Yorkists, while " the lordes lyeng at Caleys wer daily asserteyned of what was done in the Kynges privie chamber."† Warwick was in touch with York in Ireland, and as soon as their plans were ready a fresh venture was launched. Salisbury, Warwick and Edward, accompanied by the Papal Legate, and with their best men-at-arms, landed at Sandwich on June 27, 1460. They were met by Bourchier, the Archbishop of Canterbury, and with him they marched on London. There they were joined by George Neville, Bishop of Exeter, Warwick's brother, with 20,000 men. The city received them with joy, only the Tower holding out for the King, who was still at Coventry. With all their troops they proceeded to St. Paul's, where Warwick explained to a well-disposed audience the causes of their coming—the heavy taxes, the bad government, the exclusion of the King's blood from his counsels, the attaint-ing of their friends. The Yorkist lords flocked in to join them, and they soon had an army 30,000 strong. With these Warwick and Edward set out to attack the King, Salisbury being left in London to reduce the Tower. Arriving outside Northampton on July 10, Warwick sent his envoys to Henry, but Buckingham, who was com-manding, refused to receive them, and at two o'clock the battle was joined. Owing to the desertion of some Lancastrians it was over in half an hour. The principal leaders on the King's side were killed, " the commons being spared," and Henry was captured; but the Queen and her young son escaped to Wales. Warwick marched back to London, bringing along his prisoners " with grete solempnitie and small comfort."‡ In the King's name he reconstructed the government: George Neville became Chancellor, Salisbury Lieutenant of the northern countries, while Warwick himself was confirmed in his captaincy of Calais.

* Eng. Hist. Rev., 148, 545.   † Hall, 243.   ‡ *Ibid.*, 245.

York now arrived from Ireland, after the fighting was over. He came up to London, carrying himself as if the kingdom was already his own. Ignoring Henry, he established himself in his apartments at Westminster, assumed the royal arms without any difference, and in a long speech to Parliament " challenged the crown." But he met with little response: " The Lordes sat like Images graven in the wall, or dome gods, neither whispering nor speaking, as though their mouthes had been sowed up."* He even began to make arrangements for his coronation; but this was too much for Warwick: " the Earl stayed not and went straight to the Duke's chamber and found him standing there, leaning against a sideboard. And there were hard words between them, for the Earl told him that neither the lords nor the people would suffer him to strip the King of his crown."† At last the Duke deferred to reason and moderated his conduct. A compromise was come to, Henry remaining King and York being recognized as Protector and next heir. This agreement was confirmed, and " on All Saints' Day at St. Paul's the people shouted, ' Long live King Henry and the Earl of Warwick ! ' "‡

The Queen, however, was still at large, raising troops in Wales and the north, and seeking alliance with the Scots. York and Salisbury marched to meet her. At Wakefield, on December 30, 1460, they were attacked by superior forces and heavily defeated. The duke himself and his second son were killed, while Salisbury was taken prisoner and executed. Their heads were set up on the gates of York, that of the duke in a paper crown: " *Caput quoque ducis Eboraci in despectu coronaverunt carta.*"§

But with fortune in her grasp Margaret lost time. After her victory she delayed in the north, ravaging the Yorkist estates, and then moved slowly south, her followers pillaging as they went. Warwick had been left in London, where he had kept Christmas with King Henry in the Bishop of London's palace. On his father's death he had had himself appointed Lord Great

* Hall, 245.   † *Ibid.*, 248.   ‡ *Ibid.*, 101.   § W. Worcester, 775.

Chamberlain of England and a Knight of the Garter. He now took over the direction of affairs, and collected another army. With Henry in his train he marched out to St. Albans, and there, on February 17, 1461, he met the Queen. There was a defection on his right wing, and the Lancastrians broke through and captured the King " as he sat under a great oak watching the battle." Again the Yorkists were panic-stricken and fled, while Warwick, who had not distinguished himself by good generalship, retired westwards with only 4,000 men to join Edward of York in Wales.

Edward, though only nineteen years old, was more alert than Warwick. Gathering in all the men he could, he defeated Pembroke and Owen Tudor at Mortimer's Cross, and then hastened to reinforce the earl at Chipping Norton. The Queen, irresolute or persuaded by Henry to spare London from pillage, had not yet occupied the capital. Edward and Warwick did not hesitate, but marched rapidly south, and by the night of February 27 had arrived in London. There they were rapturously welcomed by the nervous citizens. The young prince, as his father's successor, formally claimed the throne; and within the week he was crowned and proclaimed as Edward IV.

The next day Warwick started off in pursuit of Henry and the Queen. They had moved northwards at the news of the Yorkists' coup, and their line of retreat was marked by blazing villages and angry peasants. Warwick followed them cautiously, and was caught up in Yorkshire by Edward. On Palm Sunday, May 29, 1461, at the field of Towton, the Lancastrians were again brought to bay. They were twice as strong in numbers as the forces against them, and they occupied a better position on the upper slopes of a plateau. But under cover of a snowstorm Lord Falconbridge, one of Warwick's uncles, enticed them forward until they found themselves in the hollow ground, and while they were engaged in trying to mount the opposite hill their arrows gave out. After fighting had gone on for seven hours, the Duke of Norfolk appeared and attacked their left wing. This threw them into

confusion and a retreat began, which rapidly developed
into a rout. In crossing the stream that lay behind them
many more were slain, and by the time that the flight
was over 20,000 had fallen, the Yorkists losing nearly
half that number. Henry fled to the Scottish border,
while Edward entered York and confirmed his victory
by the usual amnesty to yeomen and execution of nobles —
his regular policy. Then he returned to London, leaving
Warwick to complete the victory.

In the north the earl had to fight some of his own
kindred, the Westmoreland Nevilles, who followed the Red
Rose. This he did with little compunction, and when he
came back to Westminster he was regarded as the saviour
of the kingdom, the champion of the new dynasty. He had
now inherited his father's estates in Yorkshire and the
west, and was by far the most famous man in England.
His rewards were great. In addition to his former offices,
he was created High Steward* and Admiral of England,
Warden of the Cinque Ports, Seneschal of Lancaster,
and Governor of the Western and Northern Marches.
His relatives received similar promotions: his brother
John was given a peerage, Falconbridge an earldom, while
George Neville again became Chancellor. The Neville
clan thus bade fair to eclipse the royal house itself in
influence, wealth and power.

As if to emphasize still more the difference the young
King gave himself up to the pleasures of London—pageants,
feasting and the charms of ladies; while Warwick remained
diligent and severe as ever, administering the kingdom,
soldiering on the borders and reducing the country to
order. It was from this time that the King first began
to be jealous of the earl, and the earl contemptuous
of the King.

For the present, however, Edward was well content to
leave his cousin in control of his newly won realm. There was
plenty to be done, and a man of activity and experience
was needed to do it. The Lancastrians were not yet
beaten. The indefatigable Margaret, leaving Henry with

* Rymer, xi. 480.

RICHARD NEVILLE
EARL OF WARWICK

the Scots, had gone to France to enlist assistance. But with Louis XI. she had to deal with the most subtle prince in Europe, and with one who would not commit himself far. He gave her, however, a little money, a few ships and men, and a leader—de Brezé—one of his prisoners from the dungeons of Loches.* With these the Queen landed in Northumberland in 1462. Warwick and his brother sped to meet her, followed more slowly by Edward. They were able to detach Somerset and other nobles by offers of pardon, and fighting for the nonce was avoided; but in 1464 the struggle started again, and it was not until the battles of Hedgeley and Hexham had gone against them, and Henry had been captured and placed in the Tower, that the Lancastrians seemed crushed at last.

The main direction of policy was still in Warwick's hands, and he showed plenty of vigour. His first aim was to conclude a definite peace with France and to get Edward suitably married. The Yorkist throne was not yet sufficiently secure to ignore the value of a strong continental alliance, and after thoughts of a Spanish and a Scottish match had been set aside, Warwick himself was chosen as ambassador to ask for the hand of Bona of Savoy, a sister of the French Queen. The matter was proceeding well, when in October 1464, while Warwick was still in England, Edward suddenly announced that five months previously he had wedded Dame Elizabeth Grey. She was a lady seven years older than himself, with a large family, the widow of a Lancastrian knight. Her father was Richard Woodville, afterwards Earl Rivers; her mother, the old Duchess of Bedford. Ten years before Warwick had written to her commending another and much humbler suitor, praising her "great beauty and womanly demeaning," and promising her his patronage ;† the news of her marriage to Edward came as a thunderclap to him and to the country, for it had nothing to recommend it in point of blood, fortune or connection, while it was bound to anger the French. He tried to make the best

* Oman, 139. † Strickland, ii. 318.

of it, and as some amends the archbishopric of York was given to his brother George. The feast at his enthronement was typical of the magnificent scale on which the Nevilles entertained. At it the Duke of Gloucester dined separately "syttyng in the cheefe chamber " with five ladies, two of whom were " the Lorde of Warwicke's daughters."* But it was soon clear that new ideas were on foot and that Edward had resolved to advance his wife's family to the detriment of the Nevilles. By a series of half a dozen matches, all above their condition, the Queen's relatives were now wedded to the most noble names in England. Especially odious was the marriage of John Woodville, aged twenty, to the Duchess of Norfolk, aged eighty—" *juvencula ætatis fere iiii. xx.:— maritagium diabolicum,*" the monk of Worcester calls it.† Warwick foresaw for these new rivals a rise resembling that of his own race, and he could not tolerate the thought. " Property was at all times a matter of more importance than love to that selfish generation."‡

Matters soon assumed an even worse aspect. Early in 1466 the post of treasurer was taken from Mountjoy, a friend of Warwick's, and given to Rivers. Shortly afterwards the Duke of Exeter's child, who had been promised to Warwick's nephew, was given to Thomas Grey, the Queen's son by her first marriage; finally, the Duke of Clarence, Edward's next brother, was forbidden to marry the earl's daughter, Lady Isabel, who was the richest heiress in England. These, it may be said, were only private wrongs. A public outrage was to follow. In 1467 Warwick was again sent on an embassy to France, this time to conclude an alliance against Burgundy. He went in great state and high hopes. The instant he had started, a Burgundian mission was received by Edward, who proceeded to make a treaty with them behind his own envoy's back. Warwick on his return was met by the further news that the Great Seal had been taken from his brother. The French ambassadors whom he had brought

* Leland, Coll., vi. 3, 4.   † W. Worcester, 783.
‡ Paston, i. 271.

with him were ignored by Edward, and Warwick had to entertain them himself. At Christmas, thoroughly disgusted, he set off for his Yorkshire home, saying that "never would he come again to the Council while all his mortal enemies were about the King's person."*

In 1468 there was a small Lancastrian revolt. It came to nothing, but it showed that the other party was still alive. Warwick was angry; he was a master of intrigue, and he was now preparing for an entirely new move. In April 1469 his plans were ready. He crossed over to Calais, and as soon as he was safely there insurrections began to break out in different parts of England. In June Edward went north to suppress Robin of Redesdale's rising. Directly afterwards Clarence slipped over to Calais and was married to Isabel Neville. Then Warwick, with his new son-in-law and his brother the archbishop, returned to England, mustered his men in Kent, and marched on London. They were received without resistance, for the earl was more popular in the city than any man. King Henry was still safely lodged in the Tower, but King Edward was away at Northampton. Warwick and his various supporters converged on him from different points. In a series of small fights the royal troops were dispersed: several of the Woodvilles were taken and executed by Warwick's orders, and on July 27 Edward himself was captured at Olney. He was taken to Middleham as Warwick's guest or prisoner, and for a month two English Kings remained in the custody of a subject. Then Edward was allowed to return to London, after granting a general pardon to Warwick's adherents and adding to his offices the government of South Wales.

For nearly eight months there was peace, but Edward was burning for revenge. Like Warwick, he had as yet no son, and he determined to marry his eldest daughter to George Neville, the son of Warwick's brother John, now Marquess of Montagu. Such an alliance would detach the male heir of the Nevilles from his kindred and might counterbalance Clarence's connection.

* Oman, 174.

In February 1470 another insurrection started in Lincolnshire. Edward went off to deal with it, and having a large force of county arrays at his disposal, he seized the opportunity and ordered Warwick and Clarence to appear before him on a charge of being concerned in the rising. They were unprepared for such a move, and could only save themselves by flight; Edward pursued them hotly, declared them outlaws, and offered £1,000 for their capture. They were able to escape to France, but at Calais were refused admission and their ships had to lie outside. The Duchess of Clarence chose this inconvenient moment for being delivered of a son, but even this did not soften the hearts of the garrison. "*A grande peine voulurent ils consentire qu'on lui portast deux flacons de vin.*"*

Louis XI. was now at war with Edward, and he saw that he might turn the situation to his own advantage. He had always been jealous of Edward, whom he and the Duke of Burgundy used to talk of as "*le fils de l'archier*"—an allusion to the supposed vagaries of the Duchess of York before Edward's birth at Rouen. His diplomacy was successful, and at Angers an agreement was come to between Warwick and the exiled Queen Margaret. The bond was that her son, the young Prince of Wales, was to marry Warwick's second daughter Anne. But this scheme did not at all commend itself to Clarence, who saw his own chances of his brother's throne and his father-in-law's fortune diminishing. Edward in England was informed how matters stood, and sent over privately to his brother offering him a pardon if he would again change his colours ; and Clarence—"false, fleeting, perjured "—did not hesitate to accept.

Of these counterplots Warwick was ignorant. Outlawed and disgraced for the moment, he was still the first man in England: "His onely name sounded in every song in the mouthe of the common people and his persone was represented with greate reverence when publique plaies or open triumphes should bee shewed or set furthe abrode

* Commines, iii. 4.

in the streets."* He felt sure that he could succeed again as he had succeeded before, and his plans were laid on the old lines. In September 1470 a rising was started in Yorkshire. As usual the King set off himself to crush it. Warwick with Clarence and some French troops then landed in Devon—a county well affected to the Lancastrian cause. His retainers from the Beauchamp estates joined him, and he marched on London ten thousand strong. Edward up in the north relied on Montagu to oppose him. But Montagu was discontented, because the Percy lands had recently been taken from him. His brother's name and good luck appealed to him, and at the crucial moment he deserted Edward at Nottingham and made his troops shout for King Henry. Edward was just able to ride off to the coast at Lynn and sail with a few troops to Holland. On October 5 Warwick arrived in London, released Henry from the Tower, and proclaimed him King again. For the second time in ten years he had disposed of the crown of England.

But the country was comparatively apathetic to another change of princes. It had experienced the rule of the House of York, and was disillusioned as to the possible benefits of a return to that of Lancaster. The Londoners however, shouted heartily enough for King Henry " in his old blue velvet gown " as the hospitable earl directed them, while King Edward's Queen had to take sanctuary at Westminster, where soon afterwards her eldest son was born.

Warwick was now made Lieutenant of the Kingdom and reappointed High Admiral. Archbishop Neville became Chancellor, and Clarence Lord Deputy of Ireland. A Parliament was called and the succession was regulated anew, Clarence being named next heir to the crown after Henry's son. Peace was concluded with France and a pardon promised to the Yorkists. But Warwick's hold was not so strong as it had been. Edward had made many friends in London, the Yorkist cause had always been popular there, and Clarence was as usual meditating treachery. During the winter he kept up a correspondence

* Hall, 278.

with his brother in Flanders, offering to help him when the time was ripe, and plotting against Warwick.

Nor had Edward been idle. He had business connections in the Low Countries, and he strained every nerve to raise men and money. Early in March 1471 he sailed for England " with 2,000 troops, 300 German hand-gun men, and fifty thousand florins in gold," which he had borrowed from the Duke of Burgundy. He landed at Ravenspur in Yorkshire, where the first Lancastrian King had landed seventy-two years before. There he had a poor reception, but he met it by declaring, like Henry of Bolingbroke, that he only came to claim his duchy. Upon the cross of the high altar in York Minster he swore that he would be faithful to King Henry. He was allowed to proceed with his following, and was quick to profit from the chance. Evading Montagu, who tried to bar his way at Pontefract, by March 23 he was at Nottingham with a confident and continually growing army.

For some months Warwick had been expecting the arrival of Queen Margaret with troops from France, and had even gone to Dover to meet her. " But he was disappointed, for the winde was so contrary that she laye at the seaside tarying from November till Aprill."* Warwick therefore set out alone from London, taking his train of artillery, and summoning troops to join him from all over England. He was not yet strong enough to risk a battle, and made for Coventry, where he awaited Clarence, Montagu and Oxford. But Edward outflanked him by marching south, and so cut his communications with London. A few days later Clarence arrived at Banbury, and at once ordered his men to join Edward's forces. This was a tremendous blow to Warwick, as damaging as it was unexpected, but Montagu and Oxford now reinforced him, and, it is said, prevented him from treating with the enemy. Edward then began to move towards London, while Warwick followed some twenty miles behind, sending a message to his brother, the archbishop, to hold the capital at all costs.

* Fabian, ii. 502.

But there matters were not prospering for him. In the absence of the great earl London's enthusiasm for King Henry had cooled, while their loyalty for the approaching Yorkists rapidly increased; and when Edward appeared outside the walls he was at once admitted. De Commines gives the three reasons: "*La premiere, la royne sa femme, qui avoit eu un fils. La seconde, les grandes debtes qu'il devoit en la ville. La tierce, plusieurs femmes d'estat & riches bourgeoises de la ville dont il avoit eu grande privauté et accointance, luy gaignerent leurs maris & leurs parens.*"* The archbishop was perhaps privy to the surrender, seeing that a fight was hopeless; "he was doble (as men suppose to King Henry) and kept him at London when he would have been at Westminster. He had lettres of King Edward to kepe King Henry out of Sanctuary."†

On Good Friday, April 12, 1471, King Henry was again lodged in the Tower and King Edward in the Palace. Fresh levies of Yorkists had come in, and on the Saturday afternoon Edward moved out to meet Warwick, who had taken up a position at Barnet. "God lett never prynce be so hevy in his herte as Kynge Edward was that nyghte."‡ Each force amounted to some 20,000 men. On Easter Day, at dawn and in a heavy fog, the battle began. At first Warwick, commanding his own left wing, was out-flanked by Richard of Gloucester, Edward's youngest brother; but at the other end of the line the Yorkists were enveloped and driven back into Barnet town by Oxford's men. The latter, however, pursued too far and returning in the fog were mistaken for the enemy by some of War-wick's troops. A cry of "Treason" arose—such desertions were only too common—and Oxford fled. The rumour grew: some of the Lancastrians turned upon the Neville retainers, and Montagu was killed by his allies. Matters grew rapidly worse, and Warwick began to retire towards the hedges behind him. He was on foot, his heavy armour impeded him, "*il n'etoit jamais accoustumé de*

* Commines, iii. 7. † Leland, Coll., ii. 508.
‡ Wright, Pol. Poems, ii. 274.

descendre a pied,"* and as he came to the edge of Wrotham
Wood he was beaten down and slain. This ended the
battle; "the death of Warwick was of greater importance
than any victory "†—for it left Edward master of England.

Warwick's body with that of his brother was carried
to London, and exposed naked for two days at St. Paul's
"for all the people to see." They were then buried
at Bisham Abbey on the Thames, the resting-place of the
Montacutes: there is now no trace of their tomb.

Of Warwick's personal appearance nothing is known,
though there is a heraldic drawing of him in the Rous Roll.
Polydore Vergil suggests that he was tall and strong,
as is probable enough, for he came of a handsome family.
His issue was two daughters, the elder already wedded to
Clarence, the younger to marry Gloucester, afterwards
Richard III.; the greatest heiresses in England, they
brought the two brothers enormous fortunes and estates,
but the early deaths of their husbands and the unfortunate
fates of their children soon divided their broad lands
again. Thus there is no male descendant of the earl, and
the Neville family is now represented by a collateral, the
Marquess of Abergavenny.

Warwick's character has been appraised in the most
diverse fashions. Sir Thomas More calls him "a coura-
giouse warrior and of such strength, what for his landes,
his alliance and faver with al the people, that he made
kinges and put down kinges almost at his pleasure."‡
From his youth he was remarkable not only for real
virtues, but also for a certain art in displaying them. "He
had wonderful popularity with the people, who believed
that nothing was too great for him to undertake."§
Commines questions his courage: "*si la besogne alloit
bien pour luy, il se trouvoit a la meslée ; et si elle alloit mal
il se delogeoit de bonne heure.*"|| But this is not borne
out by any English writer, any more than Monstrelet's
tale that he killed his horse at Towton to make his followers
stand fast.

* Commines, iii. 7. † *Ibid.* ‡ More, Rich. III., 98.
§ P. Vergil, 503. || Commines, iii. 7.

Undoubtedly a dashing soldier both by land and sea, his abilities as a general were more doubtful. But his military reputation made him nearly as popular as his hospitality, which was prodigious. At his table, says Stow, " six oxen were sometimes eaten at a single meal. He entertained not only his regular dependents, but all chance comers, and visitors were allowed to carry off joints, so that the neighbouring taverns were often full of his meat. Such a nobleman had little difficulty in finding friends to fight for him. He maintained, in fact, a small standing army at all times. At his great house ' the Erber ' in Warwick Lane he rivalled the King at Westminster."*

Born of the best blood in England, endowed with a noble name and a vast inheritance, valour, pride and bounty were natural to him. He held the chief places in the gift of the Crown, nearly a third of the House of Lords were his near relations, an appreciable portion of the lands of England belonged to him by descent, grant or marriage. He owned no less than 150 manors in different parts of the country, and Commines estimated his official income at 80,000 écus. Such a fortune might well have brought content, but Warwick was " greedy of power, wealth and influence; jealous of all competitors and unscrupulous in his measures;"† " the subtlest of all men living, without faith or loyalty, revelling in intrigue and treachery, busy and turbulent,"‡ " his meate infected with the poyson of faction."§ Yet he had virtues no less pronounced. He had energy, character, decision, an ambition to be worthy of his position, a proud, if obstinate, belief in himself. At an early age he was already in the centre of affairs, and he learnt as a young man to fight and to lead, to rule and to negotiate. Then by the deaths of his father and his uncle he became the chief man in the State, and the attractions of power led him astray. To control the government, whether of Henry or Edward, was his ambition, though his natural

* Paston, i. 329.   † Stubbs, iii. 228.
‡ Green, ii. 25.   § Habington, 85.

interest inclined him to the latter side.   But the Woodville
marriage, the idle life, the debts and the amours of Edward
went counter to his sense of what was fit and proper, and
in an evil day he turned to Clarence and began to compete
in deceit with a past-master in that art.   A similar self-
confidence made him underrate Edward as a general, and
to this mistake was due his final defeat.

Warwick could never tolerate that the youth whom he
had placed on the throne—his inferior in age, experience
and power, no more than his equal in birth, should cast
him aside.   Pride and anger spurred him on; after ten
years of supremacy he would play second fiddle to none—
rather than that he would sacrifice all.   So he cast the die
and the hazard fell against him.

Yet whatever his demerits, Warwick " filled for many
years a place which never before or after was filled by a
subject, and his title of the Kingmaker was not given
without reason."*   Magnificent in fortune and descent,
famous in the field, sagacious in the State, he stands for
all time as a great historical figure, and romance with
some reason still recalls him as the " Last of the Barons."

Suffolk and Warwick were the product of their age—
an age of sedition and strife, of insecurity and self-seeking.
With their predecessor Beaufort they were the only
instances of men of high birth and great wealth becoming
Chief Minister.   Both were men of energy and talents,
and as long as they adhered to the traditional policy of
opposition to France their personal prestige sustained
them; but once they left it public opinion turned against
them.   Suffolk had no one but " the foreign woman " to
support him, and he soon went down; Warwick held a
stronger stake in the land, but against him the King's
skill was thrown into the scales and he also fell—and
a fall in those days of blood meant no recovery.   Such
careers did not encourage men who had much to lose
to venture unwarily upon the hazards of government.

* Stubbs, iii. 358.

CHAPTER VII
THE CARDINALS
MORTON AND WOLSEY

THE year 1471 in some sense divides two epochs. It saw the end of anarchy and the practical conclusion of the Wars of the Roses; it saw the death of Warwick and the break-up of the last great baronial estates; it saw the introduction into England of small arms, which were to revolutionize the art of war; it saw the birth of Wolsey, who was to start destroying the mediæval Church. Within a few years Caxton was to set up his printing-press at Westminster, Cabot was to sail from Bristol for America, Colet was to begin preaching at St. Paul's. The New Learning, the New World, the new religion, were soon to transform the old England into a more modern guise. In the sixty years which elapsed between the deaths of Warwick and Wolsey, feudalism and theocracy may be said to have come to an end; and on their ruins the Tudor dynasty built up anew the regal power which had languished for a century and a half and was now to increase again for a like space of time.

The English noble houses had been almost extinguished by the battles, executions and proscriptions of the Civil War. In one family alone, that of Buckingham, four successive chiefs had died a violent death in sixty years. Humphrey the first duke was killed at Northampton; his elder son Lord Stafford at St. Albans; Henry the second duke was beheaded in 1483; and his son Edward in 1521. The rival armies had ravaged the lands of the barons and destroyed their private property—pictures, plate, manu-

scripts, tapestry of the fifteenth century barely now exist.
The Church still remained rich, but it had played a sorry
part in the struggle, and had done little to promote
peace. The Commons had not yet acquired the strength
or the self-confidence to assert themselves. Thus the
Crown alone occupied a commanding position, and the
princes who wore it were of a character to profit from and
promote their good fortune.

Henry of Richmond, the first King of his family, had
by birth little title to the throne. Through his father he
derived, it was said, from the ancient princes of Wales;
his mother, the Lady Margaret Beaufort, was a great-
grand-daughter of John of Gaunt, though the legitimacy
of her race had always been questioned. But failing a
better representative, the Lancastrian party regarded him
as the champion of their cause, and there was a tale that
when, as a boy, he had been playing in the palace garden at
Westminster, the sainted Henry VI. had said: " This child
will one day enjoy what we are all striving for."

" He was of no great stature, his countenaunce chereful
and couragious, his heare yelow like the burnished golde,
his eyes grey, shynyng and quicke."* Sober, seemingly
dull, but prompt and ready in reply, he was careful,
politic and secret. His early life had been passed in
adversity, often in danger, and he was without any means
consistent with his new dignity. " From five years old,"
he used to say, " I have been a fugitive or a captive."†
But immediately after the battle of Bosworth he assumed
a royalty far more emphatic than had hitherto been
usual in England. He entered London in a closed coach,
instead of riding as his predecessors had always done; he
surrounded himself by a paid bodyguard, instead of by
the free retainers of his court; and he insisted upon
pardoning his poorer opponents of his own grace, and
not by any Parliamentary Act of Indemnity. He at once
confirmed his position by marrying the Lady Elizabeth,
the eldest daughter of Edward IV., uniting by this alliance
the rival Roses, ensuring the inheritance of the Crown,

* More, Rich. III., 223.   † Mozley, 12.

and transmitting to his offspring the true blood of the Plantagenets.

The earlier years of his reign were harassed by pretenders, genuine or false, but he was able to overcome them all. In foreign policy he avoided war, though he never failed to obtain large grants for its prosecution. He continued the illegal practice of benevolences and revived the fines on many ancient tenures and many obsolete offences. The maintenance of retainers he forbade, and when on a visit to the Earl of Oxford, who had entertained him at immense expense, and had provided an escort in his honour, he said to his host: " I may not have my laws broken in my sight," and mulcted him in the incredible sum of £10,000.* To deal with too potent offenders he extended the jurisdiction of the Court of Star Chamber, and for thirteen years he was able to dispense with a Parliament, so rich had he become. Economy was his passion, and yet there was method in his miserliness. He built the beautiful Lady Chapel at Westminster and wore a ragged gown; he paid from his Privy Purse only 40 shillings to " the spye with the berde," but £30 to " the damoysell that daunced."† Thus he secured his throne, diminishing the power of the remaining great families, and amassing an enormous treasure. When he died of the gout, after an unpopular and arbitrary reign of four-and-twenty years, he left the country at peace, the people prosperous, and the exchequer fuller than it had ever been before.

Henry VIII., his only surviving son, succeeded at the age of eighteen. He was tall and handsome, gallant and adroit, generous and magnificent, an adept at wrestling and casting the bar, " the best rider and archer in England."‡ " He was bred with more care than had usually been bestowed upon the education of princes."§ He had at his command a vast sum of money, his Parliament was subservient, his subjects contented, his ministers active and astute. For the first portion of his reign he allowed

---

* Hallam says £15,000, i. 15. † Seward, i. 37.
‡ Synge, 145. § Burnet, Hist. Ref., i. 10.

ambition and amusement to distract him. The panoply
of war, the splendour of pageants, the grandiose rôle of
arbiter of Europe, kept his attention from baser thoughts.
But the successes he gained only increased his egotism,
and by the time he was five-and-thirty he had become
obstinate, selfish and despotic. The wish for a male
heir, the passion for fresh wives, the desire to outshine
any prince that had preceded him, led him into a fatal
series of marriages, a wholesale confiscation of property,
an arrogant assumption of tyranny that revolutionized
both Church and State.

As he advanced in age he interested himself in abstruse
questions of divinity, but they did not improve his piety.
His health declined. He was " very abdominous and
unwieldy with fat. It was death to him to be dieted, so
great was his appetite; and death to him not to be dieted,
so great was his corpulency."* Gradually he became
cruel and callous, reckless of justice, a law unto himself.
Parliament he treated as he treated his other subjects.
When a Bill in which he was interested had been delayed
in the Commons he sent for Mr. Montagu, who had opposed
it. Laying his hand on Montagu's head as he knelt
before him, " Man, man," he said, " unless my Bill shall
pass to-morrow, this head of thine will be off."† He had
little compunction, less gratitude, no friends, and he was
an object of terror to his court; yet in popular esteem he
remained a national hero, for his very faults were his
strength. Convinced of his own strength and of that of
England, he was determined to rule as an independent
prince, and his tremendous will, his unconcern for others,
the majesty of his demeanour, the wide belief in his
power, carried him far. His earlier years were occupied
with secular affairs controlled by priests, his later days
by Church matters conducted by laymen. The division
between them marked the end of Roman influence, and
his father and he were the last Kings of England to
employ a prelate as their Chief Minister.

* Fuller, Hist. 5. v. 6.　　　　† Campbell, Chanc., i. 399.

I.—MORTON

John Morton was born about 1420 at Milborne St. Andrew in Dorset. His father, Richard Morton, was a squire of an old Nottinghamshire family who had settled in the former county, where he owned some property; his mother was the daughter of Richard Turberville, of Bere Regis, a cousin of the Seymours.

He was educated first at Cerne Abbey near his home, and afterwards at Balliol College, Oxford. There he distinguished himself, taking his degree both in canon and civil law, and being admitted to orders. He went up to London about 1445, and began to practise in the Court of Arches. A year later he acted as a commissary for his university, and, devoting himself to its interests and the practice of his two professions, in course of time he was made parson of Bloxworth, sub-dean of Lincoln, principal of Peckwater Inn, and head of the school of civil law at Oxford.

His ability at the bar and the knowledge of finance that he acquired recommended him to Thomas Bourchier, Bishop of Ely, who was a cousin, through his mother, both to Henry VI. and Richard, Duke of York. Bourchier was a powerful patron, and when in 1454 he was raised to the primacy and a year later given the Great Seal, he employed his friend's talents and added to his endowments. Morton was made a prebendary of Salisbury and Lincoln, chancellor of the Duchy of Cornwall, and eventually a member of the Privy Council. He was active and acute, and the various business in which he was engaged gave him a wide experience. He had been already a lawyer, a parson, a squire, head of a college and manager of large estates. He was now to be concerned with public affairs. His connection with the Prince of Wales' duchy had brought him into touch with Queen Margaret, and in the Wars of the Roses he joined the Lancastrian side. He was present at the second battle of St. Albans in 1461, and at Towton, after which he was compelled to fly with Margaret and her son. "The parson of Bloxworth," says Grafton, "fled the realm with the Queen and the prince, and never returned but to the field of Barnet."*

Dr. Morton, now a man of forty, was included in the list of attainted Lancastrians, and was deprived of all his possessions. With other refugees he escaped to Flanders and went to St. Mihiel en Bar, where he suffered, as they all did, considerable privations. He was there for nearly eight years, and during this period he showed himself eminently useful and faithful to the exiled princes. He rose to a high place in the councils of his party, and when, in 1470, Warwick and Clarence were reconciled to Queen Margaret under the auspices of Louis XI., Morton was one of the mediators. His value was recognized both by Louis and Warwick. He was with the latter on his landing at Dartmouth, and was sent on to London with Fortescue, one of the judges, to arrange for the change of régime. But after the battle of Barnet his star again sank, and he posted off to meet Margaret and her son at Weymouth. He sheltered them at his old school at Cerne, and stood by them at the fatal fight of Tewkesbury. The death of the young prince on that field, and of King Henry in the Tower a few days later, shattered the hopes of the Lancastrians, apparently for ever; their main reason for resistance was gone, for the Yorkists now ruled *de facto* and *de jure*. Morton was not a man to refuse to recognize a *fait accompli*. He sued for his pardon, which was easily granted, for Edward IV. was ready enough to conciliate enemies who were not a danger. Bourchier, now a Cardinal, had survived all the chances of the last ten years and was still his friend, and at the age of fifty Morton resumed his peaceable life in England, satisfied that he had done his duty and not anxious to go on his travels again.

In time he was taken into favour by the King, and, disinclined to re-engage in the hazards of politics, he turned his attention to more material prizes. He became a pluralist of an advanced type, adding to his prebends

* Hook, v. 391.

From a chancel screen.

JOHN MORTON

CARDINAL ARCHBISHOP OF CANTERBURY

and cures no less than five archdeaconries—those of Winchester, Chester, Huntingdon, Berkshire and Leicester. In 1472 he was made Master of the Rolls, and in that place he did a great work, collecting and arranging the mass of documents that the late troubles had left in disorder, and reorganizing the record office. Edward gradually came to trust him and treated him with some regard. Sir John Paston, writing on November 6, 1473, says: " Thys daye Doctor Morton, Master off the Rollys, rydethe to the Kynge, and berythe the Sealse with hym."*

In 1474 he was sent as envoy to the Emperor: " The Kyngs imbassators Sir Thomas Mongomere and the Master of the Rollys be comyng homewards from Nuse."† A year later he was with Edward at Pecquigny, when Louis XI. bought off the English with a large sum of money. Morton shared in the 16,000 crowns that were distributed among the principal ministers by the French King. His code of honour in finance was never puritanical.

Three years later the see of Ely became vacant, and Morton, now nearly sixty years old, was at last made a bishop. He took his spiritual promotion seriously, walking barefooted to his cathedral and washing the feet of some beggars, before he was enthroned. The regulation banquet he provided on a magnificent scale; roast swan, stewed porpoise, stork, peacock and " subtilties " were items—much of the *menu* being in French.

He now established himself in the fine house and garden in Holborn belonging to his bishopric—20 acres of land. He resigned the Mastership of the Rolls, but remained in close association with the court. Hastings, the Lord Chamberlain, was one of his intimate friends, and the bishop's conciliatory advice was continually sought by suitors: " My lord of Ely," says Sir John Paston, " woll move for trete and elles be displesid."‡ To the King he was a valuable servant, for though in other respects their tastes were not congenial, they had one bond that united

* Paston, v. 841. † *Ibid.*, v. 861. ‡ *Ibid.*, vi. 130.

them—Edward always needed money and Morton was an adept at getting it. He was probably responsible for suggesting that development of the "benevolence" system which was to press so hard on the country. "The King," says Lady Paston, "goeth so near us, both to rich and poor, that I wot not how we shall live."*

Twelve years of association had made Morton and Edward trust each other, and when in 1483 the King died, the bishop stood by his bedside. He was named one of the royal executors, and was left in some sort a tutor to the young prince. He was by now one of the most distinguished men in the country, a shining light at Oxford, while his court at Holborn was the "centre of the new civilization"† that was coming into vogue. But his strongest quality was loyalty, and directly he saw that the Duke of Gloucester meant to be more than Protector, he showed his mind clearly. Richard was quick to deal with opponents, and in More's history the bishop tells his own tale.

"On the 13th June, 1483, many Lordes assembled in the Tower and there sat in counsaile, devising the solempnite of the kings coronation. . . . These lordes so sytting togyther the Protectour came in among them fyrst about IX of the clock, saluting them curtesly. . . . And after a little talking with them he sayd unto the Bishop of Elye . . . 'My lord you have very good strawberries at your gardayne in Holberne. I require you let us have a messe of them.' 'Gladly, my lord,' quod he, 'woulde God I had some better thing as redy to your pleasure as that.' The strawberries were sent for, and at half past ten Richard came in again, but this time 'al changed, with a wonderful soure, angrye countenance, knitting the browes, frowning and frotting and knawing on hys lippes.' He soon discovered his hand, saying that a treason was plotted against him, that he had been bewitched and his arm withered, 'though no man was there present but wel knewe his harme was ever such since his birth.' Asking what penalty such traitors

* Paston, i. 283.   † Mozley, i. 8.

deserved, he 'clapped his fist upon the borde a great rappe.' At which token given, one cried 'treason' without the chambre. Therewith a dore clapped and in come there rushing men in harneys, as many as the chambre might hold. And anon the protectour sayd to the lorde Hastings: 'I arrest thee, traitor.' 'What me, my lorde,' quod he. 'Yea thee, traitor,' quod the protectour. And another let flee at the Lorde Stanley which shronke at the stroke and fel under the table, or else his hed had been cleft to the erthe."* Within an hour Hastings was beheaded, Morton committed to prison, and Richard had gone to his dinner and his strawberry mess.

But Morton's interest at Oxford was great, while the Protector was as anxious to stand well with the University. On July 6, at the intercession of the heads of houses, the bishop was released and transferred to the custody of the Duke of Buckingham, who carried him off to his castle of Brecknock, safe for the moment from Richard's passion.

Buckingham, who had thoughts of the Crown himself, regarded himself as hardly treated or insufficiently rewarded, for he had been Richard's friend and ally. He opened his heart to Morton, complaining of the Protector's usurpation and ingratitude. Morton, who " had gotten by greate experience, the verye mother and maistres of wisdom, a depe insighte in politike, worldli driftes,"† let Buckingham disclose his secrets and then introduced the idea of restoring the Lancastrian line in the person of Henry Tudor, Earl of Richmond, by marrying him to Elizabeth, Edward IV.'s daughter. Henry was the last heir of the Beauforts, and his alliance with Elizabeth of York would unite the rival Roses. The scheme appealed to Buckingham, and on it he built up a conspiracy which was to prove fatal to him. Henry, who was in Brittany, was to land in Dorset, while Buckingham himself led an insurrection in Wales. When the plan was ready Morton escaped from Brecknock to Ely, and fled thence in disguise to Flanders, where he put himself

* More, 70-73. † More, 139.

into communication with the Lancastrians in England. His flight was a blow to Richard.

> " Ely with Richmond troubles me more near
> Than Buckingham with his rash levied strength."

But owing to floods on the Severn the duke's advance was delayed and Henry found no support. He had to return to France, while Richard, now a King, marched on the rebels. Buckingham was speedily defeated and paid for his insurrection with his head, while Morton was able to warn Henry of Richard's intention to kidnap him in Brittany—a good office that Henry did not forget.

Morton's second exile did not last long, and he turned it to the best account. His knowledge of the state of affairs in England, his relations with the party opposed to Richard, his experience in raising revenue, enabled him to give Henry the best advice and to supply him with funds. In August 1485 a second attempt was made which was successful. Henry landed at Milford Haven with 5,000 Bretons, and marched to Stafford and Bosworth. There Richard was defeated and killed; Henry obtained the crown, and the next year married Elizabeth of York. Morton had remained in Flanders to prepare for a possible retreat; he was now recalled and, as the principal author of the new King's success, was taken into the highest favour. In October 1486 he was made Archbishop of Canterbury, in succession to his old friend Bourchier, and in the following March Lord Chancellor. "The King," says Bacon, " called to his council Morton and Fox, vigilant men and secret, and such as kept watch with him almost upon all men else."*

For the rest of his life Morton was Chief Minister, and though the majority of historians suggest that he merely fulfilled the King's policy, it is probable that much of that policy was put into Henry's mind by the man whom he had placed at the head of the Church and the law. Morton was an old man of wide experience; he had known and served intimately four successive

* Bacon, Hen. VII., 16.

princes; he was acquainted with foreign countries, and he had a special *flair* for taxation. Such qualities carried great weight with Henry, a man of barely thirty, with an insecure title and a constant need of money. The archbishop is credited with having been responsible for the system known as " Morton's fork " or " Morton's crutch," which Fuller called " persuading Prodigals to part with their money because they did spend it most, and the Covetous because they might spare it best."* No opportunities were lost. Morton made progresses through his province " with the cross of Canterbury carried before him," and in every diocese he levied fines or accepted grants. He developed his practice of getting " voluntary " grants from subjects, so that it became difficult to say what was a tax and what a gift. To this day the Crown agrees to a money bill with the words " *Le Roi remercie ses bons sujets, accepte leur benevolences et ainsi le veult.*"

Under Morton's ministry Parliaments were rarely called, and the royal power and the royal treasure rapidly increased, for besides heavy taxes, the recent forfeitures and attainders had immensely benefited the Crown. In his clerical administration he followed a somewhat similar plan. Conscious of the need of reform, he took care that it should be reform from above and from without. The Pope's authority was called in, and the King's power used to enforce it. Not only did the archbishop deal with the prelates and the parish priests, but he also turned his attention to the monasteries, which by a special bull he was enabled to visit.† St. Albans particularly came under his notice, and the improper relations of the monks with the neighbouring nuns, the " enormities and crimes " of the abbot himself, the disorder and lasciviousness of the dependent priories, were severely dealt with.‡ The extravagant dress of the priests, their sables and swords, their long hair and affectation of laymen's costume, were forbidden, and in consequence the primate's popularity

* Fuller, Worthies, Dorset, 279.   † Fuller, Hist., iv. 153.
‡ Williams, ii. 171-3.

with his clergy sank. But with the new Borgia Pope, Alexander VI., he was a favourite, more perhaps for his financial than his moral qualities, and in due course he was created a Cardinal.

In 1493 he announced at St. Paul's the capture of Granada—a triumph peculiarly dear to a Spanish Pope. In 1495 he was in Rome and there, during the French invasion and the temporary flight of Alexander to Orvieto, he was left as Papal Vicar, in charge of the Holy City itself.

Nor did the King's esteem ever fail. At the feast in honour of the creation of Prince Henry to be Duke of York, the Cardinal dined alone with the King at the high table, while the young prince "served of the towel."* In Parliament he kept his ecclesiastical character in the background, and, like Wykeham, he used to open the session with a speech bereft of any text of Scripture. His secular policy resembled that of Louis XI., and he encouraged Henry to depress the nobles. " He was in reality the chief author of the system for controlling the power of the great feudal barons "†—though, since the disappearance of Warwick and Buckingham, few of these remained; in Henry's first Parliament only twenty-nine lay lords took their seats.

As a lawyer his enactments were singularly sound. He enabled holders of real property to register their titles after five years' tenure‡—an immense boon to landowners after the changes and destruction of the Civil War. By another act he protected from the penalties of treason all those who assisted a King *de facto*. In public works he was an enlightened benefactor; near Ely, at his own expense he cut a great dyke, Morton's Leame, to drain the fens; in Kent and the adjoining counties he rebuilt many of the religious houses; Hatfield and Wisbech owe much to his repairs; and the central or lantern tower at Canterbury was also his work. To literature he was a no less generous patron; he became chancellor of Oxford University in 1495, and helped in the restoration of St. Mary's, while More and probably Caxton

---

* Hook, v. 469.   † Campbell, Chanc., i. 358.   ‡ *Ibid.*, i. 360.

were indebted to his charity. To the end of his life he preserved Henry's close friendship, and he was still in the possession of all his faculties, brisk, active and diligent, when he died of a quartan ague in September 1500, at the great age of eighty. He was buried at Canterbury where his broken effigy still remains; and there is a remarkable, almost grotesque carving of him on the chancel screen at Plymptree.

In his will he provided for numerous friends, among his bequests being one to the future Queen of Scotland, "the most benign Lady Margaret, his little daughter [goddaughter], a cup of gold and forty pounds in money."*

"Morton," says More, "was of a mean stature, but though stricken in age yet bare he his body upright. In his face did shine such an amiable reverence, as was pleasant to behold. Gentle in communication, yet earnest and sage, in his speech he was fine, eloquent and pithy. In the law he had profound knowledge, in wit he was incomparable; and in memory wonderfully excellent. These qualities, which in him were by nature singular, he by learning and use had made perfect. The King put much trust in his counsel, the weal public also in a manner leaned to him . . . for even in the chief of his youth he was taken from school into the court, and there passed all his time in much trouble and business . . . and so by many and great dangers, he learned the experiences of the world."† Of More, then quite young, Morton had a high opinion, and to the bounty of his patron the future Chancellor owed his education at Oxford. The boy used to act in the mystery plays at Lambeth, and one day after a performance the old archbishop said of him, "Whoever liveth to trie it, shall see this childe prove a notable and rare man."‡

Bacon calls Morton "a wiseman and an eloquent, but in his nature harsh and haughtie; much accepted by the King but envyed by the Nobilitie, and hated of the People. . . . Hee wanne the King with Secrecie and Diligence, but chiefly because he was his old servant in

* Hook, v. 498.   † More, Utopia, 173-4.   ‡ Hook, v. 491.

his lesse fortunes. . . . He was willing also to take envy from the King more than the King was willing to put upon him . . . hee deserveth a most happy memorie in that hee was the principall means of joyning the two Roses. He died of great yeares, but of strong health and powers."* Cheerful, prudent and steady, he was "one with whom King Henry was pleased to converse much and on whose judgment he greatly relied."† "Many condemned him in his life for acting and putting the King forward to be burthensome to his subjects with his Taxes; but his innocence appeared after his death, that he rather tempered the King's covetousness than otherwise."‡ "He was a learned man, magnificent in his buildings, and bountiful to poor scholars."§

Eminent for probity, diligence and moderation, Morton was able to accommodate himself to two diverse ages—to the passing of the mediæval system and to the beginning of modern government. He had lived in the days before printing was known or America discovered; when the Greeks ruled in Constantinople and the Moslems in Cordova. He had seen the virtues and misery of Henry VI., the victories and vices of Edward IV., the tyranny and murders of Richard III. He had lived through the calamitous campaigns in France and the civil strife in England. He had known Louis XI. and Alexander VI., Warwick and More, Cabot and Caxton, perhaps Wolsey and Cromwell.

Able, practical and broadminded, he saw that England needed a strong hand after her recent troubles, and he did not hesitate to follow a line of policy that for over a century kept her prosperous—a firm government, rest and no adventures. He knew the shortcomings of the Church, and applied the best means of reform that lay to hand; he modified the law so as to meet the difficulties of the times; he strengthened the Crown by filling the treasury. Under him the Chancellor's place rose almost to its highest power; that of the Primate did least harm.

* Bacon, Hen. VII., 198-9. † Hutchins, ii. 597.
‡ Fuller, Hist., v. 156. § Fuller, Worthies, Dorset, 279.

A wise statesman, prelate and lawyer, well versed in affairs, understanding the ambitions of princes and the sufferings of exiles, he served loyally two rival houses, he boldly withstood a tyrant, he twice staked his fortune at the call of duty, and more than any other minister he made the Tudor dynasty.

II.—WOLSEY

Thomas Wolsey—or Wulcy, as he used to sign himself—was born at Ipswich, probably in 1471. There are reasons for placing his birth a few years later, but the former date is the more likely, and has been always received. He was the son of Thomas Wolsey and Joan his wife. His father, " an honest poor man," is commonly held to have been a butcher, but he also owned lands, and was probably a farmer and grazier of some standing.

Thomas Wolsey was a forward boy, and was sent when about eleven years old to Magdalen College, Oxford. By fifteen he had taken his degree as B.A., being called the Boy Bachelor. In the further pursuit of his studies he became a friend of More and Erasmus, and eventually he was made a fellow and bursar of his college, and when about five-and-twenty was appointed master of the school attached to it. There he had under his charge the three sons of Thomas Grey, Marquess of Dorset, half-brother to Queen Elizabeth of York. About the year 1500 " it pleased this Lord Marquis against Christmas, to send as well for the schoolmaster as the scholars home to his house for their recreation. Their father perceiving them to be well improved in learning . . . was so well contented that he, having a benefice in his gift, at that present void, gave the schoolmaster the same in regard of his diligence."*

Wolsey accordingly resigned his fellowship and went off to be parson of Limington in Somerset. He stayed there, however, but a short time, for the local landowner, Sir Amyas Paulet, " taking an occasion of displeasure against him " for a drunken frolic, set him in the stocks. Wolsey

* Cavendish, 490.

long remembered this insult, and when he was Chancellor revenged it by confining Paulet to his house in London. Lord Dorset died the next year, and Wolsey thought himself lucky to get a secretary's place with Sir Richard Nanfan, " a very grave and ancient knight," who was deputy governor of Calais. This post he held for three years, helping his employer in the fiscal work of his office, and acquiring some idea of French conditions and English government. On Nanfan's retirement in 1506 he recommended Wolsey as a likely man to the King, and got him appointed one of the royal chaplains. Wolsey made the most of his chances, " having occasion to be daily in sight of the King in his closet, not spending the rest of the day in idleness, he would attend those men whome he thought to bear most rule in the Council and were most in favour with the King; which at that time was Dr. Fox, Bishop of Winchester and Lord Privy Seal, and also Sir Thomas Lovell, master of the wards and Constable."*

Henry VII. relied upon priests more than on nobles. Like other founders of dynasties, he preferred for his particular servants diligent men who owed everything to himself. Wolsey showed himself serviceable and acute, and Fox, recognizing his value, employed him in minor business. He was sent to Scotland in 1508, to confirm James IV. in his alliance, and on his return in the autumn of that year, was despatched to Mechlin as a private envoy to the Emperor. The object of this particular mission was to suggest a marriage between Henry and Maximilian's daughter Margaret; the proposal came to nothing, but Wolsey's manner of accomplishing his journey set him on the high road to fortune. When he had received his instructions, " he took his leave of the King at Richmond, about four o'clock in the afternoon, where he launched forth in a Gravesend barge, with a prosperous wind and tide; and he arrived at Gravesend in little more than three hours, where he tarried no longer than the posthorses were provided; and he travelled so

* Cavendish, 491.

speedily that he came to Dover the next morning, where the passengers were under sail to pass to Calais; so that, long before noon, he arrived there, and having posthorses prepared, departed from thence without tarrying, making such hasty speed that he was that night with the Emperor; who sent for him incontinently. The next day he was clearly despatched . . . took posthorses that night and rode without intermission to Calais and arrived at Dover between ten and eleven in the forenoon, and came to the court at Richmond that night. Taking his repose until morning he presented himself unto his Majesty at his first coming out of his bedchamber to his closet, to mass, whom, when he saw, he checked, for that he was not on his journey. ' Sir,' quoth he, ' if it may please your Highness, I have already been with the Emperor, and despatched your affairs, I trust to your Grace's contentation;' and thereupon presented the King with his letter of credence from the Emperor."* Such a man and such methods appealed strongly to Henry's cold, business-like temperament, and Wolsey was rewarded early next year with the deanery of Lincoln, one of the best benefices in England below the rank of a bishopric.

In April 1509 Henry died, and Wolsey again ran the risk of losing his position. But he now had as an ally the young Lord Dorset, his former pupil, who was an intimate friend of the new King's. Wolsey's talents were adaptable, and he made his demeanour suit the genial habits of the son as it had deferred to the more rigid manners of the father. He was almost at once named royal almoner and given a prebend and two livings, while shortly afterwards he was presented with a good house and garden in Fleet Street. In 1511 he was admitted a member of the Privy Council, made a doctor of divinity, canon of Windsor, and registrar of the Order of the Garter. He was then just forty years of age, twenty years older than Henry VIII., and in the full flush of his powers.

One of Henry's earliest acts on succeeding to the throne

* Cavendish, 492-3.

had been to marry the widow of his elder brother Arthur, Prince of Wales. She was the Princess Catherine of Aragon, a daughter of Ferdinand and Isabella of Spain, and sister-in-law to the Archduke Philip, the son of the Emperor Maximilian, the father of the future Emperor Charles V This connection with Spain and the Empire commended itself to Henry as establishing a counterpoise against the growing power of France, for in the last half-century the centralizing system and diplomatic talents of Louis XI. had raised the French monarchy to the principal place in Europe, and it had become a tradition of English policy to oppose this hegemony. The Princess Catherine had few looks to recommend her, and she was six years older than her husband, but Henry did not allow this to stand in his way, and in the first six years of his marriage she bore him several children, though only one, Mary, sur-vived. But the lack of a male heir in time estranged him from his wife, his relations with her father, Ferdinand, eventually became embittered, and in consequence the domestic life of the King and Queen suffered.

To pursue his anti-French policy Henry embarked on an expedition against Guienne. It was a failure, but in 1513 a second venture in Picardy was more successful, and the battle of Spurs gave him some fame and the possession of Tournai. He was also at war with Scotland, and during his absence the important victory of Flodden was gained. Wolsey, as almoner, had been largely concerned in the prepara-tions for the two campaigns, and he was first rewarded by being given a French bishopric. Then, early in 1514, he was also presented to the rich see of Lincoln, and six months later, Cardinal Bainbridge, the Archbishop of York, having died, he was further advanced to this high dignity—being allowed to hold it in addition to his other two sees. " His political genius, his quickness and his vast power of detailed work "* were alone responsible for this rapid rise.

But matters on the Continent were not going well, for Maximilian and Ferdinand, Henry's two allies, had left

* Creighton, 30.

him in the lurch by making a separate peace with France. Wolsey, whom the King now chiefly consulted in foreign affairs, suggested a method of circumventing them, by offering better terms to the French, and a marriage was privately arranged between Mary Tudor, the King's sister, and Louis XII. For the moment this coup restored England's diplomatic prestige, but on New Year's Day 1515 Louis died, and Wolsey again lost the fruits of his labours.

The Duke of Norfolk and a considerable section of the English nobility disliked the French alliance and regarded its author as an upstart. But Henry was young, ambitious, hand and glove with his minister. He had already asked the Pope to make Wolsey a Cardinal, but had been refused. Now, however, the designs of the new French King upon Italy made the Roman court only too glad to secure England's friendship, and in September 1515 Wolsey got his wish and his red hat. Three months later he succeeded Archbishop Wareham as Lord Chancellor, and so became without any question the most powerful man in England. Henry was content to devolve the tedious business of government on his favourite, who was well fitted to conduct it, and the Cardinal thus had Church, law and foreign policy all under his control. His success was remarkable. England had recently been poorly treated by her allies, and she stood in a position of some isolation; but in a very short time Wolsey, by adroit diplomacy, was able to confirm a peace with Francis I., to repay the Emperor and the King of Spain in their own coin, and to show the Pope that England had become the arbiter of Europe.

With Wolsey's dignities his wealth had also grown. Expenditure and ostentation pleased him, and when the French envoys came over to conclude the treaty he entertained them in a manner so magnificent that all the foreigners were amazed at the " splendour of the barbarians." The Venetian ambassador describes a supper which the Cardinal gave them at York Place—his palace at Westminster—" the like," he says, " was never given by Cleopatra or Caligula, the whole banqueting hall being decorated with huge vases of gold and silver."* Nor was this anything out of the ordinary for Wolsey. He lived in a glare of grandeur. " When he came out of his privy chamber," says Cavendish, " about eight of the clock, he was ready apparelled and in red like a cardinal; his upper vesture was all of scarlet or else of fine crimson taffeta, or crimson satin ingrained, his pillion scarlet, with a black velvet tippet of sables about his neck, holding in his hand an orange, the meat or substance thereof being taken out and filled again with part of a sponge, with vinegar and other confections against pestilent air, which he most commonly held to his nose when he came to the presses or when he was pestered with many suitors; and before him was borne the broad seal of England and the Cardinal's hat, by some lord or some gentleman of worship: and as soon as he was entered into his chamber of presence . . . his two great crosses of silver borne by two of the tallest priests that he could get were there attending on him ; then cry the gentlemen ushers that go before him bareheaded: ' On masters, before, and make room for my lord.' "†

His household, his kitchens—where the master cook went in damask with a gold chain about his neck—his stables, his guard of tall yeomen, were all on a par. Eight hundred persons served him daily, and in his court were " nine or ten lords, who had each of them two or three men to wait upon him, except the Earl of Derby who had five men."‡

His pomp did not always impress the people who had to pay the taxes.

> " Thus dayly he proceedeth forthe
> And men must take it at worthe
>   Whether he do right or wronge.
> A great carle is he and a fátt
> Wearing on his hed a red hatte
>   Procured with angels subsidy."§

---

* Creighton, 48-49.   † Cavendish, 500.
‡ *Ibid.*, 498.   § Campbell, Chanc., i. 395.

To meet the expense that such a style of living involved he amassed an enormous revenue. " He had in his hand the bishoprick of Durham and the abbey of St. Albans *in commendam*. He had also as it were in farm the bishopricks of Bath, Worcester and Hereford, for the incumbents of them were strangers."* In 1518 he was made the Pope's legate *de latere*, and as such took the *pas* of the primate in Parliament, Convocation and the Council. No English churchman had ever risen so rapidly to such a height, or had bulked so large in the eyes of Europe.

But a death was again to cause Wolsey trouble. In 1519 the Emperor Maximilian died. His grandson Charles, already King of Spain, Naples and Sicily, and lord of the Netherlands, aspired to the Empire, while Francis I., nearly as powerful and quite as ambitious, bid for it also. The seven electors, the Kurfursts, put up their votes to auction, and the Cardinal secretly promised both candidates his help. But without telling Wolsey, the Pope suggested to Henry that he should enter the lists himself, and Wolsey's task in escaping from the maze was not easy. He managed it, however, with no loss of favour and some profit, for he secured from Francis a promise of support for himself at the next papal election.

Charles was chosen Emperor, and Wolsey then proceeded to arrange for meetings between the three sovereigns. The Emperor came to Canterbury in May 1520, and a few weeks later Henry met Francis on the Field of the Cloth of Gold near Guisnes. Such pageants delighted Henry, and he knew that behind them lay the real power of his minister's statecraft. But they cost money. He returned to England, " safe in body but empty in purse," yet satisfied to know that he still retained a commanding position between the two rivals, each of whom was seeking his alliance, while the Pope had been ousted from his immemorial rôle of the presiding genius of Europe.

Wolsey was the man who had achieved all this: but the part he played was dangerous, his friends mistrusted

* Cavendish, 497.

him, and his foes had increased. The Emperor's ambassador writes of him: " The Cardinal of England said that he could do or undo whatever he liked, and conclude or not conclude an alliance between the King of England, the Emperor, and the King of France."* The whole of the recent negotiations had been managed by Wolsey alone, to the exclusion of Henry's other councillors, and by the success or failure of his policy he must stand or fall. He would tolerate no rival, and was largely responsible for the execution of the Duke of Buckingham, the chief of the English nobles.

By 1521 the differences between Charles and Francis had grown so acute that another conference was called at Calais, whither Wolsey went as the King of England's ambassador. Their letters illustrate the good relations between them at this time. Henry writes: " Mine own good Cardinal, I recommend me unto you with all my heart, and thank you for the great pain and labour that you daily take in my business and matters, desiring you, when you have well established them, to take some pastime and comfort, to the intent that you may the longer endure to serve us. Your loving friend Henry R." Wolsey replies: " Sir, In my most humble and lowly manner I recommend unto your Grace that I have received to my great consolation and comfort your most honourable and courteous remembrance . . . and more joy in this life cannot come to my heart than to perceive that your Highness doth in so good part accept and take my poor service which I trust God shall be so employed as may be to your exaltation and honour and the weal of all christendom. Yr most humble chapleyn, T. Cardlis Ebor."† Wolsey's diplomatic efforts on this occasion were of no avail, but he extracted another promise of prospective help at Rome, this time from the Emperor.

In 1522 Leo V. died, and Wolsey's name was put forward in the conclave of cardinals; but he only received seven votes, and Adrian VI. became Pope. This was his first real defeat. A few months later Henry, in furtherance

* Williams, ii. 316.   † Ibid., ii. 337; Hen. VIII., State Papers, 1. 14

H. Holbein, pinx.

THOMAS WOLSEY
CARDINAL ARCHBISHOP OF YORK

To face page 214

of a promise to the Emperor and of his own inclinations, declared war on France. As before, he had to fight Scotland also. Heavy taxes were levied, the troops were not paid, and the results of both campaigns were poor. For this the Cardinal, as the responsible minister, had to bear the blame. His unpopularity with the people increased, though Skelton, writing at the time, says that the King's palace was nearly empty because of the envoys and suitors crowding to Hampton Court or York Place.

> " He regardeth lordes
> No more than pot shordes
> He ruleth all at will
> Without reason or skyll."

More money was needed and the Cardinal had to get it. In April 1523 the single Parliament during his ministry was summoned. He went himself to the House of Commons and there, faintly supported by the Speaker, Sir Thomas More, he asked for a grant in no moderate terms. But the Commons were not intimidated, and he met with little success. No member would answer him directly, and he had to go away " with his maces, his pillars, his crosses, his poleaxes, his hat and Great Seal," annoyed and abashed by what he called " a marvellously obstinate silence." *
Eventually about half his demands were granted, and neither King, Parliament nor people were pleased. A few months later he was again disappointed of the papal tiara, a Medici being elected. Attempts to levy taxes resulted in riots all over the country, and it became clear that the only course was to make peace with France and break with the Emperor. To this Wolsey now made up his mind. But first of all the situation at home had to be put straight. Loans, benevolences and new assessments aroused more discontent. The King was vexed with the rebuffs, and Wolsey offered him Hampton Court as a sop; but though the gift was taken, its cause was not forgotten. Luckily for Wolsey the Emperor had just beaten Francis at the battle of Pavia, which encouraged

* Campbell, Chanc., i. 403.

him to drop the English alliance. He had promised to
marry Henry's daughter, the Lady Mary, but he now
turned to a Portuguese match which brought him a
million gold crowns. Wolsey seized the excuse and made
peace with France, getting twice that sum for his master,
and it looked as if he had scored another diplomatic
victory. But he had, in fact, begun to undermine the
foundations of his own power.

For many years Queen Catherine had borne no children,
and she was now over forty years of age. Henry had lost
his affection for her, and had begun to turn his attention
elsewhere. By Elizabeth Blunt he had had an illegitimate
son, whom he now created Duke of Richmond and Lord
High Admiral at the age of six. This insult to the Queen
and to her nephew the Emperor was not relished by either,
and abroad as well as at home a party began to form
against the Cardinal. Luther especially loathed him:
writing to Henry VIII. in 1525 he calls him " *monstrum et
publicum odium, pestis regni.**

In the meantime Wolsey drew closer to France, and at
last, in April 1527, a treaty was signed. In the summer
Wolsey went as the King's lieutenant and ambassador
to ratify the peace. His progress was gorgeous, his state
regal. Archbishop Warham called him " drunk with
prosperity." His procession marched " through all London
and over London Bridge, the gentlemen in velvet coats
with chains of gold, the yeoman in orange tawny coats
and the cardinal's hat with T.C., for Thomas Cardinal,
embroidered on them."† He took a week to get to Calais
—a very different rate of speed to his earlier journey.
At Abbeville and at Amiens his train vied with that of
the French King, and it was only in a boarhunt, which
he viewed " from the Lady Regent's chariot," that he
did not take the leading part. His visit was shortly
afterwards returned in England by the French envoys.
The entertainment accorded them by the Cardinal was
so bounteous " that many of the Frenchmen were led to
their beds."‡ On their departing " every man of honour

* Hallam, i, 60, note.　　† Cavendish, 511.　　‡ *Ibid.*, 524, 525.

and estimation had plate presented to them, some to the value of two, three or four hundred pounds," with gowns, furs, horses and other gifts.

But all these splendours and successes did not blind Wolsey to the fact that the King was less well-disposed to him than heretofore. A new influence was at work on Henry's mind, and it was antagonistic to the Cardinal. It was soon to cause his fall. Henry had at last determined to divorce his wife and to replace her by Anne Boleyn, one of her ladies-in-waiting. She was the daughter of Sir Thomas Boleyn and, through her mother, a niece of the Duke of Norfolk. Like her lover she was determined to get rid of the Queen, like her uncle to get rid of the Cardinal. She was a lady with a history. Her sister Mary had already been the King's mistress, and Anne herself had not the best of reputations at either the French or English courts. Her beauty was passable, but her manner, art and ambition, " and the King's great appetite," helped her on. Wolsey used to call her " the night crow which possessed the royal ear."

There were considerable difficulties in the way of a divorce, but with the aid of the Church they might be overcome. Much depended upon Wolsey. Latterly he had followed a rather independent policy in ecclesiastical affairs, for his position at home was so strong that he did not greatly regard Rome. He knew, for instance, that reforms were needed in the English religious houses, and reforms would not only produce efficiency, but might furnish money. " Shall we build houses for a company of bussing monks," the Bishop of Exeter had asked; " it is meet rather to provide for the increase of learning."* With such objects in view Wolsey had obtained a bull for the dissolution of several minor monasteries—a measure which " made all the forest of religious foundations in England to shake, justly fearing that the King would fell the oaks when the cardinal had begun to cut the underwood."† The first result of the confiscated revenues was Wolsey's foundation of a college at Ipswich, his old

* Creighton, 141.   † Fuller, Hist., vi. 3. 306.

home, and of Cardinal's College, now Christ Church, at
Oxford. These he meant to be centres of progressive
education, and not barren homes for doubtful ascetics.

Thus prepared to take his own line in controlling the
Church, he was not unwilling to support the King in
obtaining a divorce, but it must be in order to make
another political alliance. Henry had already discovered
his attachment for Anne Boleyn to the Cardinal, and had,
indeed, employed him to divert another suitor's affections
from her. At the time Anne had not been particularly
grateful, for she knew that a match between the King
of England and herself was unlikely to meet with the
Cardinal's approval. Wolsey had at first regarded the
amour as a passing fancy, but he now saw with dismay
that Henry was set on a marriage, and he realized that
it could not be withstood openly. Accordingly he
asked the bishops to pronounce upon the legality of
Henry's union with Catherine; he sent out commissions
of examination to the universities; he corresponded with
the jurists of the Vatican; he took the opinion of the
Christian world. But the matter made slow progress, and
Anne persuaded Henry that Wolsey did not intend it to
go faster. Wolsey's position was difficult. To repudiate
Catherine would have the most damaging effect with the
Emperor; to marry Anne was the last thing he wished the
King to do; and he went painfully about the business,
while "the great lords of the court who bore him a
grudge "* saw that by using the power of the new favourite
they might at last succeed in displacing him.

The fates, indeed, were working against him. Henry
was still a young man, not yet forty. He had had twenty
years of excitement in war and diplomacy, in pleasure
and intrigue. But love had not attacked him seriously.
It did so now, and he was not a man to deny himself any
gratification, for he had always had his own way. By
his persistence he soon made his divorce the chief question
in England and in Europe. The Cardinal was in a
dilemma; he realized that he would have to give in, and

* Cavendish, 505.

he exerted himself to the utmost. He begged Pope Clement to invest him with full powers; he asked for bulls to set aside the marriage with Catherine, and for briefs defining the canon law. At last, after months of struggling, during which Henry grew more impatient and Anne more hostile, a papal commission to hear the suit was issued to Wolsey and Cardinal Campeggio. But when the document arrived its powers were found to be incomplete. The trial, however, was begun in June 1529; but almost at once, on the petition of Queen Catherine, it was avocated to Rome. Wolsey's labour had thus been useless, and his disgrace was expected. He strove to obtain Anne's good graces, and at times she seemed to acknowledge that he had worked on her behalf. But his enemies, led by the dukes of Norfolk and Suffolk, were banded against him. " It was never merry in England since we had cardinals," the latter told him. With his political foes allied to Anne, Wolsey's future looked ominous. " Her hatred procured his final ruin."*

For a short time his fall was deferred. Henry received him in the country and showed him some kindness, but Anne took care that there should be no reconciliation. One evening at dinner she said to the King: " Sir, is it not a marvellous thing to see into what great debt and danger he hath brought you with all your subjects ?" Henry demurred. " Well, well, "quoth the King, " for that matter there was no blame in him, for I know that matter better than you or anyone else."† For the moment Anne said no more, but in the morning, fearing another interview with the Cardinal, she carried off Henry to see a new park.

In October 1529 Wolsey went up to London for Michaelmas term. On the first day of the sittings a bill of indictment was filed against him by the attorney-general. A few days later, on October 19, he was required to surrender the Great Seal, and directed to retire to his house at Esher. There he remained during the winter, depressed,

* Herbert, 286. † Cavendish, 536.

ill, deserted by most of his friends, and almost in penury. To obtain a pardon he then acknowledged that he had incurred a *præmunire* and handed over his temporal possessions to the King. At this time he writes to Thomas Cromwell, one of his principal followers, asking " yf the desspleasure of my Lady Anne be somewhat assuaged."* Many matters troubled him. He was seriously exercised as to the future of his two colleges at Ipswich and Oxford, and begged the King "to have pety and compassyon on the poore Dene and Canons of the sayd College—prostrat at your majesty's fete with wepyng terys."† The Oxford foundation was so far advanced that it was left alone, but that at Ipswich was dissolved by the King's command.

Henry still held his old friend in some regard, and hearing that he was ill sent him his own physician. He would not lose him, he said, "for twenty thousand pound." Wolsey, having naught else to give, gave the King his fool Patch. Later on, after he had yielded up the see of Winchester and the abbey of St. Albans, he was allowed to go to his archbishopric. Early in 1530 he made over York Place to the King, and in the spring he moved slowly to the north. He was now very badly off, for his revenues were greatly diminished and his creditors were besieging him. He was much changed and aged, but he spent the summer in Yorkshire, working at his diocesan duties, interesting himself in local affairs, and turning his mind to religion. On November 5 he was to be enthroned in York Minster, but the day before the ceremony the Earl of Northumberland arrived to arrest him. An information had been laid against him by one of his household, alleging that he had urged the Pope to excommunicate Henry if he married Anne. On this a charge of high treason had been founded.

The shock was fatal to Wolsey. He set off sadly for London, his health becoming worse as he proceeded. On his way he was met by the Lieutenant of the Tower, and he saw that the end had come. On November 26 he came to Leicester Abbey suffering badly

* Ellis, 2, ii. ci.   † *Ibid.*, ciii.

from dysentery, and so weak that he could barely sit upon his mule. " Father Abbot," he said, " I am come to lay my bones among you." It was soon clear that he could not survive. The day before his death he moralized upon his life and upon the King. " He is a prince," he said, " of a most royal carriage and hath a princely heart, and rather than he will miss or want any part of his will, he will endanger the one half of his kingdom. I do assure you I have often kneeled before him, sometimes three hours together, to persuade him from his will and appetite, and could not prevail: if I had but served God as diligently as I have served the King, he would not have given me over in my grey hairs."*

Early in the morning of November 29, 1530, he died, and next day was buried quietly in the Lady Chapel of the abbey. He left two children by a mistress named Lark—a son who eventually became Archdeacon of Cornwall, and a daughter who died a nun at Shaftesbury. Henry, who showed little regret for him, seized his few remaining effects.

Wolsey was a man of a fine presence, handsome, coarse, and fleshy, with a proud, masterful expression. Aubrey calls him " a short lusty man, something resembling Martin Luther."† He had a blemish in his right eye, and for this reason his portraits were usually in profile. Of a full habit of body he indulged himself quite sufficiently in its pleasures, while his general tastes were coarse and his life not particularly moral. Hallam styles him " profuse, rapacious, haughty beyond comparison, neglectful of decorum."‡ He was subject all his life to violent fits of temper and intemperate language, and at these times, to avoid saying what he might regret, he would often go straight to " his naked bed." His classical and canon learning was good, and he kept up his interest in it, but he never became fluent in French. His power for work was immense, and he would write on occasion for eight or ten hours without taking food. In his conduct of affairs he was methodical, keeping drafts

* Cavendish, 556.   † Seward, i. 87.   ‡ Hallam, i. 22.

of his despatches and dividing the business among his
different secretaries. He delighted in show, riches and
adulation; but his pride was more a pride of place than
of vanity. Quite early in his political career he controlled
England at home, directed her policy abroad, and held
the balance between the rival princes of Europe. In 1514
Louis XII. already writes to him as an intimate friend:
" *Vous prier & affectueusement que vous veuillex faire mes
bonnes et cordialles Recommandations au Roye et Royne. . . .
En vous priant tenir main a ce que ma Femme parte le
plus tost que se pourra . . . et en ce faist vous me ferez
plaisir & m'obligerez de plus en plus a vous.*"* A year
later the Venetian ambassador says of him that " he
seems to have the management of the whole of this
kingdom,"† while another foreign envoy remarks that
" he is extremely eloquent, of vast ability," and has
" seven times more consideration than the Pope."‡ In
1522 the Emperor begs him: " *Vous monstrer tel que je
vous tiens, mon bon & loyal Amy ; car je auray bonne
souvenance ; priant a tant nostre Seigneur vous donner,
monsieur le Cardinal mon bon Amy, ce que plus desirez.*"§
Wolsey's wealth was on a par with his power, for his
income was enormous, larger probably than that of
Henry himself. He was Archbishop of York, and held
two other rich sees, as well as the premier abbey of
St. Albans; he was Lord Chancellor; he had received
numerous grants of lands in England, and he enjoyed
large pensions from various foreign princes, the Duke of
Milan alone paying him 10,000 ducats a year. Thus his
ambition to become Pope was not unreasonable, and there
is little doubt that he would have held the keys of St. Peter
better than Adrian VI. or Clement VII. Had he sat in
their seat the Reformation might well have taken a
different turn, for he was diplomatic enough to have kept
Henry within the Roman fold.

His foreign policy, though based on dynastic alliances
and more given to tortuous than plain dealing, was on

* Rymer, xiii. 439.   † Foss, 753.
‡ Brewer, i. 60.   § Rymer, xiii. 777.

the whole successful. He strove to let others fight and to keep England at peace. When he was driven into war and saw that continued taxation would " make England bond and not free,"* he was wise enough to modify his programme. As a judge he was prompt, strictly upright, modest in matters beyond his ken—" he was generally commended for doing justice."† As a patron of learning and a public benefactor his ideas and his execution were on a noble scale. " Nothing mean could enter his minde, but of all things his structures were most stately."‡

Burnet says that in the earlier part of his career he only cared " to advance the King's will and pleasure, having no respect to the case," and that " he not only served the King in his secret pleasures, but was lewd and vicious himself."§ But his influence on the King was good in the main. " As long as he was retained in favour the royal passions were confined within certain bounds: the moment his influence was extinguished they burst through every restraint."‖ His unpopularity was largely due to his having been in power too long, and, like other peace ministers, he fell by a series of mischances. The sedate obstinacy of Catherine and the cunning chastity of Anne pulled him down at the end.

Wolsey started life with nothing but the determination to make a name and a place for himself. After some slight checks, each of which he overcame, he succeeded with a rapidity almost incredible. Continuing the tradition of Henry VII. and Morton, his policy was to increase the royal power, to devote himself to the Crown. For nearly twenty years he prospered, becoming the most powerful minister in Europe, while Henry, interested and satisfied, gave him full support. But at last desire and divorce put everything else out of the royal mind, and Wolsey, struggling in a net of intrigue and enmity, found Catherine and Anne, the Emperor and the Pope, the nobles and the people, all against him. Such a combination even he could not withstand.

* Hall. 696.   † Fuller, Worthies, Suffolk, 58.
‡ Fuller, Hist., v. 169.   § Burnet, Ref., i. 13.   ‖ Lingard, iv. 541.

As his rise had been marvellous, so his fall was pitiable. Proud in prosperity, he was abject in distress—a mark, perhaps, of the lack of tradition in his blood. Yet in the last few months of his life his good works and charity earned him respect.

> "Nothing in his life
> Became him like the leaving of it."

The first English minister who viewed the polity of Europe as a whole, the first English prelate who thought of an independent Church, he was the last to rule the State; and his work was no less striking than his ideas. It was he who first dissolved monasteries to build colleges. It was he who made the princes of Europe suppliants for an English alliance. It was he who invoked the law to dispense with Parliament. His plans were not always wise, their results not always fortunate, but their conception was grandiose, their execution brilliant, their author a master of statecraft.

Wolsey has been accused of vanity and arrogance. He lived in a gorgeous age, when pomp and its paraphernalia appealed to all. Henry, the heir of the Plantagenets, revelled in the riches and power that he had inherited; and the butcher's son from Ipswich may well be excused for some elation in the splendours which his own talents had earned. "Exceeding wise, fair-spoken and persuading," he worked for himself and for his King— *Ego et Rex meus*—but he never lacked patriotism, and after four hundred years England still recalls with pride the mighty name of Cardinal Wolsey.

Morton and Wolsey were the last two prelates to hold the place of Chief Minister in England, for neither Gardiner, Pole nor Laud can be said to have risen to that height. Both were cardinals, chancellors and archbishops; both were in office for fifteen years; both were men of exceptional eminence; but there the resemblance ends, for their characters were widely different. Morton came into

power as an old man after a long life of vicissitudes;
Wolsey sprang to supremacy with little training and
when comparatively young. The former was content to
counsel and to guide, the latter burned to act and to direct;
personality in the one was pitched in a minor key, in
the other it struck the dominant note. The first, pursuing
an even, economical path, kept his King's affection to the
end, and died in the enjoyment of all his honours; the
second, spending money and influence lavishly, lost the
royal favour while still in the flower of his age, and died
disconsolate, deserted and disgraced.

During fifty years of the century preceding the Reformation three Cardinals had ruled England; their day was
now done. Henceforward the Roman Church was to
need its own ministers, and for the future laymen were
to direct the English State.

CHAPTER VIII

THE REFORMERS

CROMWELL AND SOMERSET

THE halo which has always illumined the Tudor princes is not without a cause. Standing well above the horizon of history, they are near enough to glow with the colour of real life and yet sufficiently distant to have lost its cruder tones. They appeal at once to the reason and the imagination, for they were both practical and picturesque. Their reigns embrace some of the most striking events in the annals of England—the Renaissance and the Reformation; the field of the Cloth of Gold and the defeat of the Spanish Armada; Henry VIII. with his six wives and his matrimonial dialectics; Elizabeth with her mysterious lovers and her glorified virginity; Edward VI. burning the Papists, and Mary burning the Protestants, their father and sister burning both; tyranny, treason, religion and heresy, all recurring and inextricably interwoven.

The careers of their servants are hardly less dramatic: Wolsey, the butcher's son, rising to be Cardinal and Chancellor and dying in disgrace; Cromwell, the brewer's son, Vicegerent of the kingdom one day and driven to the block the next; Somerset, the soldier, seizing the Protectorate and losing his head; Burghley, the squire, just saving his own and surviving to be Chief Minister for forty years. The Tudors did not relish subjects who were too exalted: like Tarquin, they cut off the heads of the tallest poppies. They were the first who made a practice of burning bishops, and to be a duke in their days was

to court destruction. Of the seven peerages of that rank
that existed in the sixteenth century, five were terminated
by the axe; the last representatives of the other two died
before they were twenty.

But the personal qualities of the Tudors are not alone
responsible for the vivid contrasts of their epoch. Great
events in the outside world combined to set a stage on
which their characters could act. In the generation
immediately preceding the capture of the English crown
by Henry of Richmond, Europe had been stirred from
end to end. The expulsion of the Greeks from Constantinople, of the Moors from Spain, had released to
the Western nations an immense amount of hoarded
knowledge, which had been diffused by the infant art of
printing; the discovery of America and of the maritime
routes to the Indies had vastly increased the importance
of those countries which possessed an Atlantic seaboard;
new trade routes introduced new commodities, and the
expansion of banking magnified the value of money.
Cadiz, Genoa and Venice yielded to Bristol, Bordeaux
and Lisbon, while the peculiar position of London, in the
centre of the land area of the world, began to make it a
clearing-house for the world's riches.

With the growth of wealth its possibilities were more
fully perceived. The writings of the philosophers led
people to question the teachings of the Apostles, and an
agnostic hedonism pervaded the upper classes. Monks
lost that monopoly of learning, prelates that plenitude
of power which they had held for centuries. Architecture
was no longer confined to cathedrals, nor painting to their
decoration. The material as well as the mental amenities
of life expanded, and the pleasures of literature, of art
and of travel, were hardly more augmented than those
of comfort, of cooking and of clothes. In England these
changes were particularly emphasized, for an era of peace
had just begun, a strong dynasty was firmly established,
and the avenues of fortune lay open to all. The whole
level of living rose. Manors and gardens displaced castles
and chases; picture galleries and libraries became common

among the rich; convenience, well-being and social existence in the modern sense were first understood.

But there was an element in the fold of Christendom that was quite differently affected by the new ideas. The old fire of Lollardry was still alight. The indifference, the delinquencies and the oppression of the Popes supplied it with fresh fuel, which the breath of Calvin and of Luther blew into a flame. The genuine religious reformers were few in number, but they were convinced and strenuous. In a conservative country like England they would have had small hopes of success had not chance played into their hands. But the King coveted the authority of the Church, the exchequer envied its revenues, the nobles wished to enjoy its lands. This transfer of control profited the reformers. Something was done to further their views under Henry VIII., and more under his son. Then came the persecution of Mary, and beneath the blood of martyrs the seed flourished. Yet even at Elizabeth's accession the majority of the population still regarded the Protestant cause with little enthusiasm. They cared far less for it "than for the rights of property and the independence of the English crown." "Nineteen-twentieths of the nation halted between the two opinions, and were not disposed to risk a revolution for the purpose of giving to either of the extreme parties an advantage over the other."*

The central fact of the English Reformation was thus its material side. The change was effected by compromise, and the conversion was rather one of power and property than of ceremonies or creeds. The Tudor dynasty depended largely on the support of its newly created peers—Seymours, Cecils, Pagets, Paulets, Russells and the like. It had rewarded them with the spoils of the Church, and they could not easily be dispossessed. Some doctrinal modifications were countenanced, mainly to give colour to the crusade, but its essential elements were much more abbeys and acres than celibacy, confession or candles.

* Macaulay, v. 603.

The age was an age of transition, and the English people
were able to accomplish that transition with less stress and
less convulsion than were other nations. Partly this was
due to the phlegmatic temperament which mistrusts excess,
but partly also to the firmness, honesty and wisdom of
the three ministers whose lot it was to guide the State
through seventy troublous years.

> "Manners with fortunes, humours turn with climes,
> Tenets with books and principles with times."

I.—CROMWELL

Thomas Cromwell, afterwards Earl of Essex, was born
about 1485, probably at Putney, near London. He was
the son of Walter Cromwell, *alias* Smyth, a brewer and
blacksmith, who owned some acres of land; his mother
was the daughter of a yeoman named Glossop. The
Cromwells had migrated about the middle of the fifteenth
century from Nottinghamshire, where they had held a
respectable position, and had set up in Wimbledon.
Walter Cromwell, however, was always a turbulent spirit,
drinking, fighting and getting into debt, while his son
in early life seems to have been nearly as difficult.

When about nineteen Thomas quarrelled with his father,
and went—perhaps had to go—abroad. He used to
tell Cranmer afterwards " what a ruffian he had been
in his youth."[*] He made his way in the first instance
to Flanders and thence to Italy, where for a time he
served as servant to a private soldier—Bandello says,
" *stavo con un fante a piedi portandoli dietro la picca.*"[†]
He took part in some fighting, and after the French defeats
found himself at Florence. There he was helped by
one of the Frescobaldi bankers, who supplied him with
money and a horse: " *gli diede sedici ducati d'oro e un
bon ronzino.*" He then went back to Antwerp, where
he was employed as clerk to the English merchants.
Later on he made a second journey to Italy, as accountant

---

[*] Merriman, i. 9.   [†] Bandello, 2, xxxiv.

to a Venetian trader, and in Rome he was able to be of assistance to some of his own countrymen. There is a tale of his meeting Pope Julius on his return from hunting and securing certain pardons from him by means of a mountebank play, some country songs, and a present of English jellies, which he offered to his Holiness. During these years he acquired a knowledge of the Italian language and of Italian methods, which considerably influenced his mind and moulded his policy in later years. He travelled north again, and traded for a time as a merchant at Middleburgh in Zealand, and about 1512, when twenty-seven years of age, he at last returned to London and established himself in Fenchurch Street as a scrivener —half agent, half attorney.

He had amassed some little fortune abroad, and he now married Elizabeth Wykes, " a shearman's daughter," and widow of Thomas Williams, who brought him a share in her father's business. Cromwell was an acute and active man, and his continental connection helped him in the wool trade. He had relations with the household of Lord Dorset and with that of the Archbishop of Canterbury, and by this means he was brought to the notice of Cardinal Wolsey. In the next few years he flourished considerably, adding the collection of debts and probably the lending of money to his other activities. Wolsey gave him his patronage, employed him as his solicitor and bailiff, and made him steward of his London house, York Place.

About 1523, apparently through the influence of the Duke of Norfolk, Cromwell obtained a seat in Parliament for Taunton, and a year later he became a member of Gray's Inn. He then removed to a better house in Austin Friars, where he enlarged his demesne by the somewhat arbitrary process of advancing his boundary walls several yards into his neighbours' gardens, entirely eliminating a summer-house that belonged to the Stow family by " bearing it away on rowlers."*

His firmness and his secrecy recommended him strongly

* Stow, Survey, 187.

H. Holbein, pinx.

THOMAS CROMWELL
EARL OF ESSEX

To face page 230

to the Cardinal, and in January 1525 he was appointed one of the commissioners for surveying and reporting upon certain minor monasteries which it was proposed to dissolve. This business he carried through with despatch and success, though he gave some offence by his harsh manners. Wolsey, however, protected him, and Cromwell was next engaged to draw up deeds for the establishment of the Cardinal's new colleges at Oxford and Ipswich, being appointed receiver-general of the former foundation. He was now known as "councillor to my lord legate," and had a hand in Wolsey's most important legal affairs. He had thus many opportunities of making money, by obliging great people, dispensing patronage, and receiving presents. As a member of Parliament he showed himself busy on the side of the court, and his increasing work as a lawyer and estate agent gradually led him to discard commerce.

About 1528 he lost his wife, and in the autumn of that year came the disgrace of the Cardinal. For a moment Cromwell feared that he might share in Wolsey's fall. "It chanced me," says Cavendish, "upon All Hallown Day to come into the great chamber at Esher in the morning to give mine attendance, where I found Master Cromwell, leaning in the great window, with a primer in his hand, saying Our Lady's mattins, which had been since a very strange sight. He prayed not more earnestly than the tears distilled from his eyes. To whom I said, 'Why, Master Cromwell, what meaneth all this your sorrow? Is my lord in any danger for whom ye lament thus?' 'Nay, nay,' quoth he, 'it is my unhappy adventure which am like to lose all I have travailed for all the days of my life, for doing of my master true and diligent service. . . . I am in disdain with most men for my master's sake and surely without just cause. Howbeit an ill name once gotten will not be lightly put away. I never had any promotion by my lord to the increase of my living. And thus much will I say to you, that I intend, God willing, this afternoon when my lord hath dined, to ride to London, and so to the

16

court, where I will either make or mar or I come again.' "*

Cromwell, indeed, was not in good odour either for his own or his master's doings, and he knew that this was a crucial moment in his career. But he was wise enough to escape the slur of deserting a patron in distress, as did his colleague Gardiner. He spoke up for him in public, he did his best to save something from the wreck of the new colleges, he even urged the Cardinal's chaplains to contribute towards their master's household expenses, subscribing £5 himself. "Alas, Tom," Wolsey said to him, "you know that I have nothing to give you or them."† At the same time he conciliated what hostile interests he could, inducing Wolsey to grant pensions from his ecclesiastical revenues to the rising Boleyn family, and by his legal knowledge helping the new beneficiaries to secure their gains. In Parliament he defended Wolsey's administration with ability, and by advising him to resign his property to the King he was largely instrumental in procuring his pardon. In this way he brought himself to the King's notice at a moment when a new counsellor was needed, for Norfolk and his friends, who had taken over the management of affairs, had little character or power. "His gratitude and friendship to the Cardinal in misfortune raised his credit higher."‡

At this time Henry was set upon divorcing Catherine of Aragon and marrying Anne Boleyn; he was also in urgent want of money to meet his growing debts. These desires Cromwell determined to exploit. He was in touch with continental thought, and especially with that of Italy. He had just been reading the *Principe* of Macchiavelli, which was soon to be printed, and its ideas of exalting the power of the prince commended themselves to him. Henry sent for him, says Foxe, finding "none so apt for his purpose against the Pope. He was brought to the King in his garden at Westminster,"§

---

* Brewer, ii. 394-5.   † Cavendish, 539.
‡ Burnet, ii. 172. Hallam questions his honesty in this, i. 23.
§ Foxe, 1076.

and there, it is said, he promised "to make him the richest King there ever was in England." The tale is not improbable. Cromwell understood the politics of the Renaissance; he saw that a divorce would never come from Rome; and he had learnt the possibilities that lay in dissolving monasteries and annexing their revenues. To his versatile mind the chance of satisfying Henry's two keenest wishes presented a brilliant future, but to implement either policy successfully the King must be made independent of the Pontiff. This was the end that Cromwell set before him. He was already known to Henry as a capable servant of Wolsey's; to the Norfolk party, struggling incapably with the government, he was useful by his position in Parliament; and accordingly his advancement now began.

Early in 1531 he was admitted to the Privy Council, being employed at first on its legal business and as one of the King's secretaries. He rapidly grew in favour, and in the next year was made Master of the Jewels and Clerk of the Hanaper. He then began to unfold his projects: both their aim and their method appealed to the King; by attacking the Church, Cromwell proposed at once to coerce the Pope and to obtain money; divorce and dissolution were to go hand in hand. From about this time " he was the Chief Minister and had the King's confidence for ten years together, almost as entirely as Cardinal Wolsey."*

The earliest statutes that led to the Reformation now took shape. The penalties of *præmunire* were renewed. Bills were introduced to fine the clergy for having acknowledged Wolsey's legatine power, and to check the jurisdiction of the spiritual courts. Convocation was forced to petition the Crown that *annates*† should no longer be paid, and that " the King's obedience should be withdrawn from Rome." The Pope was annoyed and alarmed; but the divorce still hung fire. In August 1532, however, Archbishop Warham died; he had been its constant

* Burnet, iii. 3, 144.
† They had been first claimed by Alexander IV. in 1256.

opponent and a strenuous supporter of Rome, and his death was a godsend to Henry. Cranmer, a more pliable instrument, was put into his place, and matters soon moved more quickly.

Cromwell now advised the King to act boldly. Anne was created Marchioness of Pembroke and was taken officially on a visit to the French court—much to the disgust of the English peeresses who were ordered to attend her. In November she was secretly married to Henry; and "remembering how her predecessor lost the King's love with her over-austerity, she turned herself to a more open and debonair behaviour."* Cranmer declared the King's marriage with Catherine void, and that with Anne legal, and a few months later the Princess Elizabeth was born. But her birth was a bitter disappointment to Henry, who had hoped for a son; and from this moment his affection for his new wife began to cool.

Cromwell's ability had by now made him the recognized protagonist of the reforming policy. The Imperial Ambassador writes of him as "ruling everything." He had promoted a Bill for restraining appeals to Rome, and was very active in pursuing all agents of the Pope. He writes in July 1533, regarding two friars whom he had seized: "It is undoubted that they have intended and woude confesse sum grete matier if they might be examined as they ought to be, that is to sey by paynes [torture]."† True to the saying, "*Inglese Italianato è diabolo incarnato*,"‡ he covered the country with a network of spies, by whom every chance word might be construed into heresy or treason. No one was safe. "Men felt," says Erasmus, "that a scorpion lay under every stone."

This system strengthened Cromwell's hold on the King. In 1534 he was advanced to the post of Principal Secretary, given the Mastership of the Rolls, and made Chancellor of the Exchequer for life. The last appointment put him in effective control of the treasury, and marks the first association of that office with the place of Chief Minister.

* Fuller, Hist., 5, iv. 20.   † Merriman, i. 361.   ‡ Ascham, 243.

In the same year two further Acts were passed, one finally forbidding the payment of *annates* to the Pope, the other abolishing his authority in England. Henry then assumed complete control of all spiritual matters within his dominions, and took the title of Supreme Head of the English Church. This was the keystone of Cromwell's policy, for it gave legislative sanction to his acts.

For the present his star still shone, and he was next appointed Chancellor of Cambridge University. Other events helped him on. Early in 1536 Queen Catherine died, not without suspicion of poison. Henry was already coveting a third wife, while Cromwell's policy abroad required an alliance with the Emperor, which was contrary to the wishes of Norfolk and the Boleyns. The fall of Anne was therefore necessary both to King and minister. In May 1536 she was accused of adultery—the *Baga de Secretis* contains the details, but they explain nothing. Cromwell escorted her to the Tower, acted as counsel against her, and witnessed her execution. The day after her death Henry rode off to Savernake and married Jane Seymour, one of her maids of honour. Lord Wiltshire, Anne's father, then found it wise to resign the Privy Seal, which was given to Cromwell in July 1536, with a peerage. At the same time he was appointed Vicar-General and Vicegerent of the King in Spirituals, a new post of unknown possibilities, which gave him precedence over the primates and all the great officers of State. Shortly afterwards his son Gregory was married to Elizabeth Seymour, a sister of the new Queen. The Garter was then added to Cromwell's honours : he was the first man of low birth, other than a cleric, who had ever attained such a rank in England.

To make the reforming movement more popular he now started extensive propaganda all over the country. "He sent out letters under the King's spirituall seale, charging curates to teach the *Pater Noster*, *Ave* and *Credo*, the commandments and articles of faith, in English."* One of his preachers writes to him: " Please yt your good

* Stow, 572.

Lordshippe to be advertysed that I have syns the tyme of my lycence gyven me by your Lordshippe to preche, made thys yere upon the poynte off thre-score Sermons, not failing in every on off them to speke effectually ayenste the usurped power off the Busshoppe of Rhome, and some tyme as the mater gave me occasion, ayenste th' abomination off hym, his cardinals and hys cloystered hypocrites."* Recusants, whether clerical or lay, were dealt with severely. Sir Thomas More, the Chancellor, and Fisher, Bishop of Rochester—one the first scholar, the other the most saintly prelate in the land—were sent to the Tower for refusing to acknowledge the Acts of Supremacy and Succession; and in due course both were executed.

Cromwell next proceeded with the financial portion of his programme. After a commission of enquiry had hurriedly visited and reported upon them, the smaller monasteries and priories were dissolved and their revenues annexed by the Crown. In the conduct of this vast affair, which raised the most varied issues, Cromwell's power rose to an unexampled pitch. Petitions flowed in to him from all sides begging for delays, for remissions, for grants of land and manors, and promising valuable consideration in return. Lord Stafford, asking for the priory of Ronton, says: "Yf it woulde plese youe to speke but oone good worde to the Kynges Highnes for me. I hav twelve pore childerne on my hand and my lyving is not so good by ffourtye poundis a yere as hit hathe ben aforetyme;"† and he goes on to promise Cromwell forty pounds for himself. Sir Simon Harcourt, however, writing on the same quest, undertakes to give £150 each to the King and Cromwell.

The Vicar-General's influence in the State soon surpassed that of any other minister, while with the King it became supreme, for he met the royal wishes in every direction. On his first coming into office Sir Thomas More had said to him: "Master Cromwell, you are entered into the service of a most noble, wise, and liberal Prince. If you will follow my advice you shall in your counsell given to

* Ellis, iii. 3, 1.   † Ibid., iii. 3, 16.

his Majestie ever tell him what he ought to doe, never what he is able to doe." "But Cromwell," says the commentator, "never learnt that lesson, for he ever gave that counsell to his Prince which he thought would best please him, and not what was lawful."*

He pursued his policy with consistency. The Crown was now to resume the spiritual jurisdiction which during the Middle Ages the Popes had arrogated to themselves, and the Bishop of Rome was to be relegated to his original rank of a patriarch of the Church. Henry was thus reinstated in that independent position which the Norman Kings had always claimed, and which the later Plantagenets had endeavoured to enforce by their anti-Roman laws. Such a sweeping change could never have been accomplished had not public opinion been on the side of the reformers, and Cromwell's insight had convinced him that he could safely act as he did. The Church had few friends among the better classes; it was isolated, timid and demoralized; its wealth was coveted; and attractive inducements were offered to the other estates of the realm to acquiesce in its spoliation. Henry was a dominating character and still possessed some of his early popularity. So the Reformation, at any rate on its material side, went forward with comparative speed.

There was, however, some resistance. In 1536 took place the Pilgrimage of Grace, an armed alliance of the Catholic lords in the north and east of England. They raised a considerable following, and the Duke of Norfolk was hurriedly sent against them. At first he could only temporize, but a year later, when they rose again, Henry was ready to deal with them. They were heavily defeated, many executions followed, and a number of the greater religious houses, whose heads had taken part in the insurrection, were sequestrated. To enforce future order " the Council of the North " was instituted, a provincial government acting with almost unfettered powers. But the country was beginning to tire of too much change, and a halt was soon to be called.

* Seward, i. 87, 88.

Since the new policy of England had become clear the
Roman court had not been idle. Clement VII. had been
succeeded by Paul III., a Pope who knew his own mind.
Both the Emperor and the King of France viewed with
dismay Henry's novel proceedings, and were mobilizing
their forces. At last, after long delays, a Bull of Deposition was launched against him. Henry retaliated by
further measures against the orthodox party. Lords
Exeter and Montagu, grandsons respectively of Edward IV.
and the Duke of Clarence, were beheaded, while the old
Lady Salisbury, another Plantagenet, was committed to
the Tower. It was the end of the House of York.

In October 1537 Queen Jane died after giving birth to
a son, and the King was again free to marry. Cromwell
was anxious to make some headway against the continental
alliance, and was not averse to indulging his Sovereign's
penchant for matrimony. Within a year he suggested a
marriage with one of the Lutheran families in Germany.
His influence was not what it had been, for Henry, whose
health and temper were failing, now treated him with
less consideration than before: "the King beknaveth him
twice a week and sometimes knocks him well about the
pate."* But Cromwell had still several good cards to
play. He went on with his reforms in religion, and the
translation and setting up of the Bible in all churches was
largely his work. He induced Parliament to declare that
royal proclamations were as valid as Acts of the whole
Legislature, and in 1539 he completed the dissolution of
the greater monasteries and the grant of their property
to the King. To further the German marriage he sent
private envoys abroad, and after a series of visits, portraits
and medical reports a German princess was selected to
share the doubtful pleasures of the English throne. This
was Anne, sister to the Duke of Cleves, a lady who was
said to combine all the personal and political advantages
required, and whose influence might perhaps reaffirm the
minister's waning power.

But a new Parliament had just met, reactionary in

* Hen. VIII., State Pap., ii. 552.

religion and adverse to a German alliance. Under
Norfolk's leading it passed the Act of Six Articles, which
restored most of the old Catholic practices. This was a
set-back to Cromwell, and as the last abbeys had been
seized, all his hopes now depended on the marriage. Unfor-
tunately when Anne of Cleves arrived her Teutonic charms
did not appeal to Henry. He called her " the Flemish
mare," and was only induced to wed her with the greatest
reluctance. He at once determined to get rid of her
and of the minister who had forced her on him. Reaction
was in the air, there was no more money to be got from
the Church, and he was ready to discard an unpopular
servant who had served his turn. He had also cast his
eyes upon a fresh damsel, Catherine Howard. She was
another niece of the Duke of Norfolk, who seemed intent
upon sacrificing his female relations to his political ambition. Hume suggests with some plausibility that she was
employed to embitter Henry's mind against Cromwell.
The Howards all hated him, and at a dinner at Lambeth
in this year the duke gave him the lie about his relations
with Wolsey, and a bitter quarrel ensued.* For the
moment, however, the sky still looked comparatively
serene. In April 1540 Cromwell was created Earl of
Essex, and appointed Lord Great Chamberlain of
England—a combination of dignities that astounded the
nobility and seemed to ensure him the King's permanent
favour. But Henry had learnt something of Italian
methods from his minister, and was preparing to practise
them on him. On June 10, the new earl was suddenly
arrested at the council board on · a charge of high
treason. He dashed his bonnet on the ground, and called
on all present to witness what a true servant he had been
to the King. But he found no support. His George and
Garter were torn from him by Norfolk, and he was hurried
off to the Tower. All his friends except Cranmer deserted
him at once. He knew well what he had to expect and
begged only that his shrift might be short, but for six
weeks he was kept waiting for his doom, while Henry

* Rapin, i. 823, note.

extracted from him sufficient evidence to enable him to
have the German marriage annulled. Cromwell wrote
him the most piteous appeals. One of his last letters
ends, " Wrytyn at the Towre this Wednesday the last
of June with the hevy Hearte and trembling Hande of
yowre Highnesses most hevy and most miserable prisoner
and pore slave, Thomas Cromwell.

" Most gracious Prince I crye for mercy, mercy, mercy."*
His requests were of no avail. A bill of attainder was
introduced against him. It was a new procedure that
he had invented himself, by which the prisoner was not
heard in his own defence; he was to be the first to experience its rigours.† The Commons had long chafed
under his spies, his extortion, and his arbitrary rule,
while the Lords resented his excessive rewards. " His
aspiring to the Order of the Garter was thought inex-
cusable vanity."‡ In the bill he was styled " a man
of very base and low degree." He was accused of releasing
traitors, of issuing independent commissions, of encouraging heresy, of bribing and despising the nobility.
On July 28, 1540, he was sent to the block on Tower Hill,
and there, making no defence in order not to hurt his
son, and professing his belief in the old Catholic faith, he
was clumsily and slowly beheaded by two executioners.
On the day of his death Henry married Catherine Howard.

By his attainder all Cromwell's honours were forfeited,
but most of his property—about £24,000 and his estates
—was left in the possession of his family. As his son
Gregory was through his wife the King's brother-in-law,
he was created a baron by patent and this title continued
for several generations, until in 1709 the male heirs failed.
The peerage is now in abeyance. From Cromwell's
sister Elizabeth, who had married Morgan Williams, was
descended in the fourth degree the Protector Oliver.

Cromwell was a broad, thick-set man, with black hair
and a shaven face; his eyes were small, his upper lip

* Merriman, ii. 272.
† The attainder against Henry VI. in 1461 had been a different
process. ‡ Burnet, Ref., iii. 276.

long, his jowl fat and massive. With an alert and cunning expression he had little distinction in his manners, which were genial and amusing, or coarse and blustering, as occasion served: "his witty conversation especially pleased the King." He was an indulgent father, an affectionate friend, "a good servant to his master, a good master to his servants."* In his prosperity he maintained a large household, feeding two hundred poor twice a day. With but slight original education he was a fair linguist, and he read a good deal, Petrarch being one of his favourites; he is said to have known the New Testament by heart. He was something of a book collector, and he did a little hawking. In creed an Anglo-Catholic, in belief a Lutheran but not a Protestant,† he seems never to have been particularly religious, except during his confinement in the Tower. Probably he had seen too much of the business side of the Church to feel himself well suited to the part of a purist. He had "great wisdom and dexterity in business, and carried his greatness with wonderful temper and moderation; no bribery could be fastened on him . . . . With his fall the progress of the Reformation was quite stopt."‡

His fall was not regretted. Hall says that more rejoiced than lamented at his death; Foxe loads him with panegyrics, as he loads Wolsey with abuse. Fuller gives him a more just character: "Great scholar he was none, nor any studied lawyer, nor experienced soldier, nor courtier, till bred in the court of Cardinal Wolsey's house; yet the lawyer so helped the scholar, the soldier the lawyer, the courtier the soldier, and the traveller so perfected all the rest, that the result of all together made him for endowments eminent, not to say admirable. He was no stranger to Germany, well acquainted with Italy, most familiar with France." Thus he had in power and polity what he lacked in learning. He had plenty of common sense; when the heralds asked him if he would bear the arms of the ancient family of his own name, he answered

---

* Fuller, Hist., 5, v. 32. † Galton, 155.
‡ Burnet, Ref., iii. 284, 285.

" that he would not wear another man's coat, for fear the right owner thereof should pluck it over his ears."*

Keen, ruthless and resolute, his strength lay in his versatility and in his cold and calculating statecraft. " He is the first English minister in whom can be traced the steady working out of a great and definite aim."†

His intuition was remarkable, and from his earliest days he had been able to turn most situations to his own advantage. As a young man he had been brought under the influence of Italy, and to those political doctrines he adhered through life. By the ladder of the divorce he climbed into Henry's graces. Once securely established he opened his schemes for making money and strengthening the Crown. Both policies succeeded. The yoke of Rome was thrown off, the treasures of the Church were seized. The Lutheran religion, indeed, was not really desired by the people, while the King throughout his reign " dealt out equal justice or injustice to Papists and Protestants alike."‡ But the change in dogma followed the change in policy, and here Cromwell was an instrument of Providence. His methods were not extreme, for although his rule has been described as " a terror," the persecutions of Henry's days never equalled those of his two successors, and this restraint was due in some degree to the utilitarian temperament of his Vicar-General. Yet as a minister of destruction Thomas Cromwell is almost without a rival in history. He obliterated the ancient Church in England; he shattered the beliefs and customs of centuries; for two generations he made the Crown supreme, and left the liberty of the subject prostrate.

He might have laid the foundations of absolute monarchy: he did lay those of religious freedom. By a curious inversion of deserts his arms were obliterated from the title-page of the Great Bible within a few months of its publication, while his surname still stands as a symbol for political liberty all over the world. Unhampered by the trammels of birth or tradition, imbued with the fresh materialism of the New Learning, Cromwell came, saw

* Fuller, Hist., 5, v. 22, 32. † Green, ii. 151. ‡ Galton, 204.

and conquered. The task he had to perform called for a nature not too fervent, and when it was done he disappeared. His life has been called "the most dramatic incident in English history.* An unattractive character, rough, relentless and thorough, his memory is obscured by that of his later namesake, though his work was hardly less important, progressive and enduring.

II.—SOMERSET

Edward Seymour, afterwards Duke of Somerset, was born about 1505, probably at Wolf Hall in Wiltshire. His father, Sir John Seymour, came of an old family of squires who had been settled in the West of England for at least three hundred years, and were connected with several noble houses. His mother was Margaret, daughter of Sir Henry Wentworth, of Nettlested in Suffolk, who was descended through the Cliffords and Percies from Edward III. Sir John Seymour had led the regular life of an active country gentleman. He served against the Cornish rebels and was knighted in 1497. He became sheriff of his county, was present with Henry VIII. at the sieges of Tournai and Therouanne in 1513, and at the Field of the Cloth of Gold seven years later. Of his ten children, Edward and Thomas, Jane and Elizabeth, all played a part in the history of their country.

Edward Seymour, a second son, began his life early. At eight years old he was a page of honour to the Lady Mary, the King's sister, on her marriage to Louis XII. of France. He received some education, it is said, both at Oxford and Cambridge, and in 1520, by the death of his elder brother, he became his father's heir. In 1522 he was in attendance on the Emperor Charles V. on his visit to England, and during the following year he took part in the expedition to Calais under the Duke of Suffolk, who had married the Dowager Queen of France, Seymour's former patroness. On this occasion, when about nineteen,

* Galton, 201.

he was knighted.   His connection with the Suffolks, his
looks, manners and promise, pushed him on at court,
and he was made an esquire of the royal household and
Master of the Horse to the Duke of Richmond, Henry's
natural son.

In 1527 he was again sent to France in Wolsey's train.
In that year he married his first wife, Catherine, daughter
of Sir William Fillol, of Hoxton in Dorset.   Shortly
afterwards he was granted several manors from the
dissolved monasteries, and in 1530 he was made an
esquire of the body to the King.   The intimacy ripened,
and Henry showed him considerable favour.   More grants
of land were made him, as to one of which a long dispute
began with John Dudley, afterwards Duke of Northumberland, who was in the future to become his most deadly
enemy.

About 1533 Seymour divorced his wife—for some dubious
amours—and he then married Anne, daughter of Sir
William Stanhope, of Sudbury.   She was descended
through her mother from the Plantagenets, and was a
" woman of great pride."   Lord Surrey, one of her suitors,
says—

> " her looks were coy
> And froward eke her grace,"

but her marriage seems to have satisfied her aspirations.

In October 1535 Seymour entertained the King at
Elvetham in Hampshire, and there Henry first took a
fancy to his sister Jane.   A few months later Seymour
was made a gentleman of the privy chamber and given
rooms with his family in the palace of Greenwich.   A
secret passage led to their lodging from the royal apartments, and by it the King used to visit his future wife.
There Anne Boleyn, it is said, found Henry with Jane
upon his knee; the discovery was followed by the Queen's
miscarriage, her loss of Henry's favour, and some months
later by her trial and death.   The day after her execution,
in May 1536, Jane was married to the King, and a week
later Seymour was created Viscount Beauchamp, given

a large property in Wiltshire, and appointed governor of Jersey and chancellor of North Wales.

In December his father died, and he succeeded to his family estates. Henry continued to advance him; in May 1537 he was sworn a privy councillor, and in the following October, at the birth of Prince Edward, he was created Earl of Hertford. Immediately afterwards his sister died, and it looked as if his position might suffer an eclipse. But "though still young he was wise," he was a friend both of the King and Cromwell, he was known as an honest and serious man, and he could afford to wait.

For the next two years he was a constant attendant at the Council, where he was regarded as an authority on continental politics. Of the French King he was mistrustful. He writes to Cromwell: "I would aben more gladdar yf that his gentilnis had prosedid of love and not for his porpos."* Hertford had always maintained his interest in soldiering, and early in 1539 he was sent over to France to inspect and renew the fortifications of Calais. During the summer of that year he entertained the King and Cromwell in the country. The latter's son Gregory, who was almost a half-wit, had just married Hertford's second sister Elizabeth. In the following December the earl was sent to meet Anne of Cleves on her arrival in England, and he escorted her to London. Six months later his friend Cromwell was beheaded and the Howards came into power.

In 1541 Hertford was elected a Knight of the Garter, and in that year was again sent to France on a boundary commission in connection with the Calais defences. In the autumn, during the King's progress through the North of England, he was left in control of affairs with Archbishop Cranmer and Lord Chancellor Audley, and in the summer of 1542 he was appointed warden of the Scottish Marches. He was then for a short time Lord High Admiral, but early in 1543 he resigned and received the higher post of Lord Great Chamberlain.

* Ellis, i. 2, 120.

Hertford was now constantly with the King, who treated him as one of his own family. Since Cromwell's death he had become his most trusted adviser, and according to Sir William Paget, Henry's secretary, "neither Wolsey nor Cromwell ever had such freedom of speech with the King."* His military experience by now was considerable, and in 1544 he was put in command of an expedition against Scotland. Henry had claimed the guardianship of Mary Stuart, the young Queen of Scots, and Hertford, with a force of 15,000 men, was sent to enforce his Sovereign's rights. In May he landed at Leith and took Edinburgh, which he thoroughly pillaged. This success, though of little real value, pleased Henry, and on the latter's visit to France that summer, Hertford was left as lieutenant of the kingdom under Queen Catherine. But despite this charge he managed to get across so as to be present at the taking of Boulogne in September.

At the subsequent conference with the Emperor and the King of France, Hertford was the principal English representative, and after its failure he remained in command of the English forces. In January 1545, by a brilliant exploit and with a force of less than half their numbers, he defeated the French before Boulogne and rendered the town secure. He was then again despatched to the Scottish border, where he remained during the spring and summer, making short raids and reducing the local fortresses. He returned to London in the winter, and early in 1546 went back to France as lieutenant-general of the royal army. In June he concluded a peace with the French, and then finally returned to his duties at court.

The King had been for some time in bad health and was known to be approaching his end. The Prince of Wales, a boy of ten years old, was Hertford's nephew, and to Hertford, as to everyone in England, the control of the coming regency was of the highest moment. The last years of Henry's reign had been marked by an almost irresponsible tyranny. He had persecuted every sect at

* Pollard, 17.

EDWARD SEYMOUR
DUKE OF SOMERSET

To face page 246

once, " sending to death on the same hurdle the heretic who denied the real presence and the traitor who denied the royal supremacy."* Politics and religion were equally perilous, and under a weaker prince each side hoped for advantage. The Duke of Norfolk, with his son, Lord Surrey, represented the older nobility and the Catholic side, while Hertford was to some extent identified with the reforming ideas and the popular party. Their mutual jealousy was embittered by the fact that a marriage between the two rival families had recently been rejected by the Howards.

During the winter of 1546-7 matters came to a crisis, and in January the reformers succeeded in passing a bill of attainder against Norfolk and his son. The King was dying and speechless, and could not sign his name, but his assent was given, so it was said, to their execution, and Hertford conveyed the royal message to Parliament. Surrey was beheaded at once, but in the early morning of January 28 Henry passed away, and Norfolk thus escaped his doom though he was shorn of his honours and remained a prisoner.

Hertford was thus left supreme. He had received the custody of Henry's will, which named sixteen executors to act as a regency, and armed with this document he brought the young Edward to London, " the Erle of Hertford ryding before the King and Sir Anthonie Brown ryding after."† At a Council held in the Tower on January 31, he got himself chosen as Protector, though it was added that " he was to act only with the advice and consent of the rest of the executors."‡ He was next appointed Lord High Steward for the coronation, and Lord Treasurer and Earl Marshal in place of Norfolk, many of whose lands he also received; and on February 16 he was created Duke of Somerset. His principal opponent, Wriothesley, the Chancellor, was then dismissed, and in March the Protector obtained a new patent under the Great Seal confirming his position and empowering him to

* Macaulay, v. 596.   † Stow, 593.
‡ Acts of Privy Council, ii. 4-7.

17

act independently. He now styled himself "Edward, by the Grace of God, Duke of Somerset"; he commenced his letters with "We"; he had his name mentioned in the public prayers; and he wrote to the King of France as "brother." This rapid advance, far beyond the apparent intentions of Henry's will, had been concerted with Paget during the night of the King's death, "walking in the gallery of the palace." Its presage was ominous; within living memory another duke, uncle to another King Edward, had forced himself into the same place of Protector, with a fatal result.

The task that lay before Somerset was beset with dangers. Henry VIII. in his latter years had rendered himself unpopular in England and odious in Europe. The German Protestants mistrusted him, the Pope and the Emperor hated him; with Scotland he was at war, and with France he had only just made an insincere peace. The troops were unpaid, the treasury empty, the coinage debased, the people oppressed. In the churches the priests still officiated, but they loathed the government. A vast system of enclosing land had alienated the peasants, who grudged them to the new nobility, already enriched with the spoils of the abbeys. Treasons, heresies, tortures and burnings were of daily occurrence, and no man's speech was safe, for spies were everywhere. To deal with such a state of affairs needed no ordinary man.

To support him Somerset had few friends and plenty of enemies—among them his own brother Thomas. The latter, an ambitious and jealous man, had just been created Lord Seymour of Sudeley and High Admiral, and he now proceeded to marry Catherine Parr, the Queen-Dowager. But he still thought his merits insufficiently rewarded, and aspired to a higher place. Another opponent was Dudley, now Earl of Warwick, Somerset's former foe; while the strongest of the Catholic prelates, Bishop Gardiner of Winchester, disliked him for his reforming tendencies. The Protector had none of the prestige of a king to support him, nor, like his recent predecessors in his high office, was he of the blood royal;

further, " he was utterly ignorant of all craft and deceit,"[*] and he lacked the hard will and disregard for justice which might have strengthened a usurper. Yet, says Burnet, " the family was now so great that nothing but their mutual quarrelling could do them prejudice."[†]

In religion Somerset had been for some time what his critics called " a rank Calvinist "; whatever his public profession might be, his private sympathies were all with the Lutherans. He now entered into active correspondence with the Genevans. A new prayer book was prepared, largely under his auspices; visitations were renewed; dogmatic and ritualistic changes were enforced, with Archbishop Cranmer's active help; and a systematic attempt was made to abolish the Catholic doctrine in England. Yet in all Somerset's measures there was a true effort at improvement. He writes to Ridley: " We would be loth anything should be done by the King's Majesty's visitors otherwise than Right and Conscience might allow and approve; and visitation is to direct things better not worse; to ease consciences not to clog them."[‡]

To assist his internal reforms he embarked on a military policy. A marriage had been proposed between King Edward and the young Queen of Scotland, a daughter of the Catholic Mary of Guise. As the alliance was not immediately accepted, Somerset, an expert in border warfare, led an army to the north, as he had done three years before. He defeated the Scots heavily at the battle of Pinkie, killed several thousands of them, and burnt the town of Leith. But the victory was barren, and Mary's hand was at once given to the Dauphin of France. As Lord Huntly remarked, " he liked the marriage but not the manner of wooing."

Somerset, however, returned to England as a conqueror, and proceeded with his ecclesiastical programme. He was a man of more conviction than tact, an honest convert unaddicted to compromise, and he did not hold his hand. Gardiner and Bonner, the Bishops of Winchester and London, had already been imprisoned, and now images

* Foxe, 1248. † Burnet, Ref., ii. 1, 55. ‡ Burnet, Ref., ii. 1, 234.

and pictures were removed from the churches, the services were ordered to be read in English, and the communion was administered in both kinds. This was going rather too fast for public opinion, and it increased his opponents.

Other troubles were also brewing. Ever since the Black Death, English landowners had found grazing more profitable than tillage, for the scarcity of labour was counterbalanced by the profits on wool; only the monks had kept up the old style of husbandry. But the dissolution of the monasteries had now thrown a number of unemployed on the market. Their condition was rendered worse by the fall in value of the currency; and their discontent was soon shown by local insurrections. Somerset, as a landowner and a humane man, understood and sympathized with their complaints, and he allowed his feelings to deter him from an active repression of revolt. He introduced several Bills to check the system of enclosures, and on their rejection issued a proclamation enjoining the restoration of lands which had been so seized. The result was to exasperate the owners and to encourage the peasants further. More risings took place, and in 1549, unwilling to deal himself with men whose misfortunes he deplored, he allowed Warwick to lead an expedition against them. It was a dangerous move, for Warwick was his enemy, he had no scruples, and he took care to crush the rebels thoroughly.

In the meanwhile Somerset's brother, Lord Seymour, was plotting. Disputes, it is said, had arisen between his wife, the Queen-Dowager, and his sister-in-law, the duchess, as to precedency. Queen Catherine soon died, and Seymour, who envied his brother's success and wished to rival it, tried to seduce or to marry the Princess Elizabeth. At the same time he did his best to set the young King against Somerset, and intrigued against his agrarian reforms. But his schemes were not to succeed. In his capacity of Lord High Admiral he had connived at the piracy which was rife along the southern coast of England, and had come to terms, for money payments, with the privateers. These proceedings were well known to the Council, and he was repeatedly warned of the risks he was running. Now it became clear that he was a danger to the State. He was accused, arrested, attainted, and in March 1549 was beheaded, with the assent of his brother. Yet, however necessary was his death, it did Somerset more harm than good, for it argued a callousness which Warwick and the Catholic party were quick to exploit.

Since he had become Protector, Somerset, with all his democratic sympathies, had not scrupled to add to his own possessions by the acquisition of further lands from the sequestered chantries and colleges. To build Somerset House in the Strand, the palaces of three bishops and a church were pulled down, and he had even projected the demolition of Westminster Abbey. Many manors in Wiltshire, Hants and Somerset had fallen into his hands, and from his farms and forests he drew large rentals: " the Duke's Vaunt " in the glades of Savernake still commemorates his name. More capital was made out of this seeming inconsistency, and his popularity suffered in consequence.

In the summer of 1549 the Scots took several castles on the border, and the French declared war. Somerset's military successes and his foreign diplomacy seemed thus as barren as his internal reforms; his policy, both at home and abroad, had been unlucky. One cause of this was the multiplicity of his work. He conducted nearly the whole business of government himself, and yet found time to write religious treatises and to manage his increasing private interests. Paget warned him that he " had too many irons in the fire," but he went forward without heeding. Gradually a party began to form against him in the Council, and the opportunity to develop their plans came when some illness in his household kept him away.

In the autumn of 1549 Warwick headed a deputation of officers to him to ask for extra pay. Somerset refused, but, scenting danger, he issued pamphlets calling on the people to rally to his assistance and reminding them of his love " for the poore commynaltie of Englande."

Warwick had a strong party in the City, and Somerset thought it best to take the King to Windsor. The Council then seized the Tower and collected some 15,000 men to support them. By temporizing Somerset disclosed his weakness; some of the lords followed him to Windsor and laid their complaints before the King, and on October 19 he was arrested and sent to the Tower. " If the Duke of Somerset," the Council wrote, " would at any tyme have hard our advises, if he would have hard reason and acknowledged himself a subject, our meaning was to have quietly communed with him for redresse of all things."*

A long indictment was prepared against him. He was charged with " commanding Alchymie and Multiplication to be practised, thereby to abase the king's coin: of openly saying that the Nobility and Gentry were the only cause of dearth, whereupon the People rose to reform matters of themselves: that the Lords of the Parliament were loth to reform Inclosures and other things, therefore the People had a good cause to reform them themselves: that he would neither give Authority nor suffer Noblemen and Gentlemen to suppress Rebels in time convenient, but wrote to them to speak the Rebels fair and use them gently."†

Somerset saw that retreat was his only chance. He admitted his errors and begged for mercy; and in January 1549–50 he was relieved of the Protectorate, deprived of his offices, and fined £2,000 in lands. On these terms he was pardoned, and in April 1550 he was readmitted to the Council and had his property restored. To confirm the accommodation, his daughter Anne was married to Warwick's eldest son, and for the moment his future again looked secure. But Warwick was ambitious; he had tested his strength and tasted power, and he regarded the ruin of Somerset as necessary to his own advancement. He was himself a reformer—but a reformer of a very different type to Somerset. On one occasion the duke was censured in the Council as having been too gentle to the Lady Mary in conniving at her Mass. " The Mass," said

* Ellis, 1, 2, 167. † Burnet, Ref., ii. 189.

Warwick, " is either of God or the Devil: if it is of God
we ought all to go to it: if it is of the Devil, why should
it be connived at in any person ?"* In Warwick's case
belief was subordinated to policy, and persecution, which
under his rival had been unknown, was with him a convenient engine of government.

The burnings and hangings of Henry VIII.'s later days
now started again, and the nation soon regretted Somerset.
The latter then began to regain his position with the King,
and, acting with more moderation than hitherto, he
enlisted the people on his side. But his progress was
watched with envy, and when, in the summer of 1551, he
talked of a plan for seizing Warwick, the latter struck
hard. Rich, the Chancellor, had written a letter to
Somerset detailing what had happened at a meeting of
the Council. He addressed it simply—" To the Duke,"
and it was carried by an ignorant servant to the Duke
of Norfolk, Somerset's enemy. The chance was not to be
missed. Somerset was at once summoned before the
Council, and on October 16 he was arrested for the second
time. A fabricated accusation of plotting to make himself
King was now brought against him; his associates were
put to the torture, and in December a court of selected
peers was assembled under the Lord High Steward to
try him. He was found guilty of felony, though not of
treason, and for that reason was brought back to the
Tower "with the axe turned away." This proceeding
deceived the vast concourse of people standing in the
streets to greet him. It was believed that he would be
pardoned again, and even away at Bath the bells were
rung in joy at his supposed acquittal. But his enemies
were going to take no further risks, and on Friday,
January 22, 1551–2, before Parliament could meet again,
he was suddenly taken to execution. On the scaffold he
made his well-known profession of policy and faith, protesting his loyalty to the King and his devotion to the
reformed faith. " Masters and good fellows, I am come
hither for to die; but a true and faithful man as any was

* Burnet, Ref., iii. 209.

unto the King's Majesty, and to his realme. But I am condemned by a law whereunto I am subject, as we all are; and therefore to show obedience I am content to die; wherewith I am well content, being a thing most heartily welcome unto me; for the which I do thank God, taking it for a singular benefit, and as great a benefit as ever might come to me any otherwise. For as I am a man I have deserved at God's hands many deaths; and it hath pleased his goodness, whereas he might have taken me suddenly that I should neither have known him nor myself, thus now to visit me and call me with this present death as you do see, when I have had time to remember and knowledge him, and to know also myself; for which thing I do thank him most heartily. And, my friends, more I have to say unto you concerning religion. I have been always, being in authority, a furtherer of it to the glory of God, to the uttermost of my power, whereof I am nothing sorry, but rather have cawes and do rejoyce most gladlye that I have so done for the greatest benefit of God that ever I had, or any man might have in this world; beseching you all to take it soo and to follow it on still, for if not ther will follow and come a worse and great plage."*

For the moment Edward believed in his uncle's guilt, and in his diary tersely records that "the Duke of Somerset had his head cut off upon Tower Hill between eight and nine o'clock in the morning."† But a year later, when he was shooting at the butts, and Warwick, now Duke of Northumberland, said, "Well shot, my liege," Edward replied, "But you shot nearer the mark when you shot off my good Uncle Somerset's head."‡

By an act of attainder, passed subsequent to his execution, Somerset's possessions and dignities were forfeited; but in 1559 the son of his second wife was created Earl of Hertford, and a hundred years later his descendant in the fourth degree was restored to the dukedom. His first wife's issue had been postponed to their half-brothers in the succession, but the latter line eventually failed

* Pollard, 308, 309.　† Pollard, 308.　‡ Fuller, Hist., vii. 2, 21.

and the elder stock now represents the family in the persons of the present Duke of Somerset and Marquess of Hertford. His property, which even with his monastic acquisitions never amounted to much over £7,000 a year, was mostly seized by his opponents, and Somerset House, Covent Garden and Sion found their way into the hands of the Dudleys and Russells.

Somerset was a tall, thin man, with a pale face, long beard, and mild and pensive expression. There are many pictures of him. Quiet, chaste and studious, he had a singularly affectionate disposition. "He was free-spirited, open-hearted, humble, hard to distrust, easy to forgive. Religious himself, he was a lover of such as were so, and a great promoter of reformation. Valiant and fortunate he was generally beloved of martial men."* A soldier, a student, a ruler and reformer, he lacked the qualities of a politician, and his honesty made him unable to conceal his ambition and impatience. A democrat and a Protestant, he upheld the Tudor ideas of arbitrary power, though he tempered its enforcement by justice and humanity. He confided "in the two frailest supports a minister can have, the favour of a child and that of the lower people."†

Somerset was a type of the good man struggling with adversity. Born in a comparatively retired position, he was early brought into touch with the court of Henry VIII. As a young man he saw something of Wolsey and more of Cromwell, when the latter was in the zenith of his power. His sister's marriage fired his ambition, but for a time he stuck to his profession as a soldier. Then his association with Henry, with Cromwell and Cranmer, his reading, his experience of the woes of the countryman and of the abuses of the landed system, turned his thoughts to domestic politics and the Protestant faith. He believed that the accession of his young nephew imposed on him the duty of administering the government, and to strengthen his position he engrossed the principal offices of State—for he had no territorial backing behind him.

* Fuller, Hist., vii. 36, 40.   † Hallam, i. 39.

Social legislation and religious reform were the two planks
in his programme, but changes in those days, if they were
to be successful, had to be enforced by hard measures,
and Somerset had a soft heart and could see the rights
of both sides. By breaking up enclosures and dealing
gently with rebels he enraged the lords and excited
the commons. By confiscation of Church property and
leniency in dogma he made both Catholics and Protestants mistrust him. Thus, when misfortunes came, he
had powerful enemies and few allies. Warwick, an unscrupulous foe, a deep plotter, a swift and stern striker,
easily surpassed him in persecution and repression. In
conspiracy and intrigue Somerset could not compete with
such opponents, and he was quickly overthrown; " he was
better to perform than to plot, to do than to design."*

An enthusiast, an idealist and a reformer, a humane
and godly man, he was endeared to his friends, respected
by his rivals, and honoured by posterity. The judgment of the poor who dipped their handkerchiefs in the
blood of " the good Duke " was no unworthy tribute to
his simple and loyal spirit.

Such were the fates of the first Chief Ministers who had
attempted reforms in England for three hundred years:
one was the material, the other a moral architect of the
Anglican Church; the first was pursued to his death by
Norfolk, the second by Northumberland. Like their
forerunner Simon de Montfort, each gave his life for his
cause, just when it seemed to be lost.

But though the old faith and the old blood were still
strong, the wedge of change had been deeply driven in,
and after a few decades of force and resistance it was
to blend firmly in the body politic and to infuse it with
a new and permanent vigour.

* Fuller, Hist., vii. 1, 40.

CHAPTER IX

THE CECILS

BURGHLEY AND SALISBURY

THE three children of Henry VIII. all inherited their father's obstinacy, his ruthlessness and his pride, but only one shared his amazing vitality.

Edward VI., the son of the pious and colourless Jane Seymour, though handsome and well-grown, never possessed any real physical strength, and his constitution was sapped by the inordinate studies to which he was subjected as a child. " *Monstrificus puellus*," one writer calls him, "*jam septem linguas perdidiscerat.*"* A serious, sad figure among his sable courtiers, he was little more than a puppet, bandied about between his uncles, his tutors and his bishops. His principal diversion was theology, varied by changes of residence and a little sport. He promised to be as arbitrary a ruler and as wholehearted a persecutor as his father, for he was taught to regard himself as no less sacrosanct than his faith; but an attack of pneumonia, supervening on measles and smallpox, vanquished his weakened frame, and in 1553 he died at the age of sixteen.

His half-sister, the unfortunate Mary, daughter of the equally unfortunate Catherine, took his place. Pale, stunted, wizened, always ailing, " with piercing black eyes that seemed to search the heart," she appealed to none. Half a foreigner, stigmatized by law as illegitimate, unpopular and under the thumb of the priests, she yet burned with the fire of orthodoxy and patriotism. Dress was her one cheerful taste, charity her one patent virtue.

* Burnet, Ref., ii. 125.

Her early experiences had been sufficient to shatter the nerves of any young woman. Her mother had been divorced and probably poisoned; she had had five step-mothers; her father, brother and sister all disliked her; and for years she had never known when she might not meet the fate that was so common in her family. But when she had to act she could show all the mettle of her race, and in the earlier part of her reign she displayed decision, humanity and deference to the public. She reprieved most of the supporters of Lady Jane Grey, and in Wyatt's insurrection, when the Londoners were wavering, she rode to the Guildhall and told the common council that "were the marriage with the Prince of Spain to the hurt of my subjects I would never consent there-unto. Stand fast therefore against these rebels, your enemies and mine, and fear them not, for, I assure ye, I fear them nothing at all."*

Bishop Gardiner influenced her best, and it was only when his restraining hand was replaced by the imperial advice of Charles and the cold zeal of his son, that she sank into the mesmerism of bigotry. Deluded by vain hopes of love and children, deceived by the designs of diplomats, she strove to reconvert a moderate but stubborn nation by ultramontanism and *autodafés*. She failed, and saw that she had failed; she knew that she had alienated the affections of a loyal people, and she realized that her policy had been as illusive as her proselytizing and her pregnancy. The loss of Calais closed a blighted life and a gloomy reign, and the year of her death saw those of her uncle the Emperor and her only friend, Cardinal Pole.

Her sister and successor, Elizabeth, had led a hardly less perilous, though a happier youth. She, too, had lost her mother at her father's hand; she, too, had been declared a bastard by Parliament; she, too, had run dangerously near the block. But she rejoiced in a more resilient nature than Mary. "As variable as the weather," compromise or intrigue caused her no pain: "She never chose

* Holinshed, 1096; Foxe, iii. 25.

a straight road when a crooked one was open to her."*
Well-proportioned, active, "fair and high-nosed," her
appearance helped her. The Venetian ambassador
describes her, at the age of twenty-one, as "*piu tosto
graziosa che' bella, di persona grande e ben formata, olivastra
in complexione, belle occhi, e sopra tutto bella mano, della
quale ne fa professione.*"†

She was an ardent dancer, hunter, scholar and musician.
What her religion was it is hard to say. To Mary she
prayed "that the earth might open and swallow her
up if she were not a true Roman Catholic,"‡ though
history paints her as the protagonist of the Protestants.
Lord Macaulay calls her an adiaphorist, and under that
dialectical evasion her beliefs may perhaps best be classed.
Her parentage had bequeathed her a strong sexual instinct,
though Edward used to call her "his sister Temperance."
Adulation and amours were vital to her, and her household
was not such as to deter them. At the public investiture
of the Earl of Leicester, "he sitting on his knees with
great gravity, she could not refrain from putting her
hand in his neck and smilingly tickling him, the French
ambassador standing by."§ The Queen of Scots, herself
no purist, tells Elizabeth the gossip of Lady Shrewsbury
à propos of one of her suitors, the Duc d'Anjou—"*qui vous
avoit esté trouver une nuit à la porte de vostre chambre où
vous l'aviez rencontré auvec vostre seulle chemise et manteau
de nuit, et que peu après vous l'aviez laisse entrer, et qu'il
demeura auvecques vous près de troys heures.*"‖ When she
was nearly sixty she took Leicester's stepson, Essex,
into her closest favour. He was then twenty years of
age and chiefly notable for good looks and bad debts.
He was made master of the horse and, on the appearance
of the Armada, captain-general of the cavalry, a post
for which he demonstrated his fitness by sailing off,
without orders, to join the fleet. Raleigh, another
admirer, when in custody for debauching one of the
maids of honour, obtained his release by apostrophizing

* Froude, xii. 23.   † Lingard, v. 385, note.   ‡ *Ibid.*, v. 525.
§ *Ibid.*, vi. 101, note.   ‖ M. Stuart, vi. 50.

the Queen's "fair hair blowing about her pure cheeks like a nymph's, singing like an angel."*

But behind all the Gloriana atmosphere there burnt a clear flame of chivalry, and Elizabeth's own personality gave the tone to her court. Her wit and learning, the courage of her race, her inscrutable will, her indomitable persistency, made her a real force. She knew well how to set the scene. After the revolt of 1554, in which she was strongly suspected of complicity, she had been ordered by Mary to come up to London. Well aware of the danger she ran, she nevertheless entered the city in state, "preceded by one hundred velvet coats and followed by one hundred more in scarlet and silver."† The curtains of her litter were flung open, and she sat there, haughty and defiant, as she was carried to St. James's. A few days later she was sent to the Tower, and for several weeks the Spanish ambassador did his utmost to compass her death. But her spirit never quailed; Gardiner's wisdom won the day, and she was set free.

Once on the throne she developed all the virility of her father, though with more sagacity and talent. He had subordinated policy to passion: she played off her celibacy as a useful card. Frugal, vain, exacting, she was yet adored and venerated by her subjects, for she cared for them and never spared herself. She had a shrewd eye for good servants, and though a long line of gallants enjoyed her favour, while masques, pageants and progresses catered to her pleasure, the power lay with the Bacons and Cecils. Of gifts and dignities she was thrifty, and in a reign of forty-five years she only created as many peerages. "She honoured her honours by conferring them sparingly."‡ But though the great were not exalted unduly, the mass of the people were allowed to thrive.

Thus the era of Elizabeth raised England to the first rank in Europe and foreshadowed its hegemony of the world. Under her auspices a fearless and independent policy in religion and commerce was pursued. The

---

* Lingard, vi. 311, 312, note.   † *Ibid.*, vi. 561, note.
‡ Fuller, Holy State, 256.

thunders of Rome were braved, the domination of Spain cast down. A spirit of bold adventure and wise design animated her subjects and laid the foundations of their navy, their colonies and their trade. Contests of creeds and dynasties gradually took a secondary place, and under the forms of despotism a paternal government embodied the public will. It was this that distinguished Elizabeth from the rulers who preceded and followed her. " No prince living," says Naunton, " that was so tender of Honour, and so exactly stood for the preservation of Sovereignty, was so great a courtier of her people."* The advance made in her reign was due in the main to her firm alliance with her ministers and to their common pursuit of peace, order and progress; and the glories of the Tudors may justly be said to owe half their lustre to the wisdom of the Cecils.

I.—BURGHLEY

William Cecil, afterwards Lord Burghley, was born at Bourne, in Lincolnshire, on September 13, 1520. He was the only son of Richard Cecil, a country gentleman of Stamford in Northamptonshire, and of Jane, daughter and heiress of William Heckington, of Bourne.

The origin of the Cecil or Syssell family is traced by Camden to the Normans and by heraldic enthusiasts even to the Romans, but there is little certainty beyond David Cecil, father of Richard, who was mayor of Stamford, yeoman of the chamber to Henry VII., and sheriff of Northampton in 1535. His son Richard was made a page to Henry VIII., and subsequently Groom of the Robes— a place which gave him constant access to the King. He received several grants of abbey lands at the dissolution, bought the manors of Burghley and Essendon, became sheriff of Rutland, and enjoyed a modest share of the royal favour.

William Cecil was sent to school at Stamford and

* Naunton, 20.

Grantham, and in 1535 went on to St. John's College, Cambridge, " being so diligent and painfull as he hired the bellringer to call him up at four of the clock every morning."*

He showed remarkable industry, reading Greek, which was then an exceptional accomplishment. St. John's College was the most famous centre in either University, and there Cecil became the close friend of John Cheke and Roger Ascham, who were afterwards to be two of the foremost scholars in England. Cheke's mother was very badly off, and kept a wine-shop in Cambridge, and at her house Cecil met his friend's sister Mary. He became engaged to her before he was of age, and his father in consequence removed him from the University without a degree, and entered him at Gray's Inn. But Cecil would not desert the lady of his choice, and he returned to Cambridge and married her secretly, much to his father's annoyance.

He now betook himself to the study of the law, living in chambers and getting along as best he could on a meagre allowance. He gave early promise of the astuteness and care that helped him so much in later life. Being something of a gambler, on one occasion he had lost to his next-door neighbour all he possessed. He told his friends that he would be even with him—and at night, " with a long tronke he made a hole in the wall, near his plai fellow's beds-head, and, in a fearful voice spake thus through the tronke: ' O mortall man, repent, repent of thy horrible time consumed in plai, cousenage and such lewdness, or else thou art damned and cannot be saved.' The effect was so salutary that his neighbour ' in a sweate for feare . . . returned to Cecil all his money, beddinge and bookes.' "†

Early in 1544 Cecil's wife died, leaving him a single son, the future Lord Exeter. Three years later he married Mildred, daughter of Sir Anthony Cooke, of Gidea Hall in Essex. Her father was governor to Prince Edward, while Cheke, Cecil's brother-in-law, was his tutor. Cooke

* Peck, 4. † Ibid., 5.

M. *Gerara, pinx.*   *T. Lodge, sc.*

WILLIAM CECIL
LORD BURGHLEY

To face page 262

was a man of profound learning, and his daughter took after him. Like Lady Jane Grey and the Princess Elizabeth, she was a fair Grecian, while her sister Ann, who became the wife of Sir Nicholas Bacon and the mother of the future Chancellor, was equally accomplished. Cecil was thus in the leading literary society of the day, and he turned his opportunities to useful account. One day, when at the palace visiting his father, he fell in with two Irish priests, with whom he started a disputation in Latin. He was able to confound them, and the tale being repeated to King Henry, the latter was so pleased that he sent for Cecil, talked a long time with him, and ordered a place to be found for him.

Accordingly, in 1547 Cecil became Keeper of the Writs in the Common Pleas. His reputation for business and learning was already considerable, and his friends Ascham, Cheke and Cooke were able to help him. On the accession of Edward VI. the Duke of Somerset was glad to make him his master of requests. He accompanied the duke to the battle of Pinkie, and there his life was saved " by one that putting forthe his arme to thrust him out of the levell of the cannon, had it striken off."*

In November 1547 he was elected member of Parliament for Stamford, and soon afterwards was promoted to be secretary to the Protector, but on the latter's fall in 1549 Cecil, with others of Somerset's adherents, was committed to the Tower. Three months later, however, he was liberated, giving a bond for 1,000 marks as security, and in September 1550 he was appointed one of the Secretaries of State and sworn a Privy Councillor. His talents now had a wider scope, and his extraordinary memory and aptitude for affairs made him almost indispensable to the ministers, though the Duke of Northumberland still disliked him.

In 1551 he was knighted, and in April 1552 was made chancellor of the Order of the Garter. A month later his father died, leaving him considerable estates in Lincolnshire, Northampton and Rutland. He was thus com-

* Peck, 6.

18

paratively rich; he began to build and to live in a generous
style, and his general prospects looked promising. But
the death of Edward VI. put him in the greatest danger.
The project of Northumberland and Suffolk to place Lady
Jane Grey on the throne was contrary to all Cecil's ideas
of right and expediency. He refused to be a party to it
and offered to resign his secretaryship. But he was
compelled to sign the proclamation, though only, he
insisted, as a witness. "His hand," says Fuller, "wrote
it as Secretary of State, but his heart consented not
thereto."* The risk he ran during the reign of the nine
days' Queen and the subsequent trials and executions,
was tremendous. "He sent his money and plate out of
London, made over his estates to his son, and carried arms
about his person."† By his discretion, reputation and
the good offices of his friends, he avoided imprisonment,
though throughout Mary's reign he had to conform to the
old religion, hearing Mass, confessing himself, and taking
a priest into his house.

In recognition of this compromise and of his former
good services, Mary granted him a general pardon, and
occasionally availed herself of his services. In 1554 he
was sent to Brussels with Lord Paget and Sir William
Hastings, to bring Cardinal Pole to England as Papal
Legate—a mission which he did not hesitate to accept.
In the spring of the following year he accompanied the
Cardinal as envoy to arrange an accommodation between
the Emperor and the King of France—a fruitless journey.
He notes in his diary, "bought at Callice three hats for
the children at xx^d each."‡ (Their importation was
forbidden under a heavy tax.) In the Parliament of that
year he was returned as one of the members for Lincolnshire, and he supported the cause of the Protestant exiles
whose estates it was proposed to sequester; but for the
most part he held himself warily aloof from affairs of
State, "something humouring the times "§ in religion,
and not giving the authorities any excuse for persecution.

* Fuller, Hist., v. 255. † Macaulay, v. 590.
‡ Peck, 8, note. § Camden, 556.

Mary was ready to have included him among her advisers, had he been willing to abjure his own faith: " She used him very graciously and forebare either to heare his accusers or to disgrace himself."* But he had made his profession of loyalty by supporting her at the beginning of her reign, and beyond that he did not feel compelled to go.

During these years he had maintained a constant though careful correspondence with the Princess Elizabeth, " who made use of him in soliciting her affairs."† She was the heir to the throne, the favourite sister of his late master, and the hope of the English Protestants. When, in November 1558, Queen Mary died, a broken and disappointed woman, it was to Cecil that Elizabeth turned. She was at her house at Hatfield when the news arrived, while Cecil was waiting in London. Within an hour he drew up the proclamation which announced her accession. He changed the guard at the Tower, closed the ports, despatched couriers to Brussels, Vienna, Venice and Denmark, had the beacons lit and the garrisons warned on the southern coast and the northern border, selected a safe preacher for St. Paul's on the following Sunday, and sent Sir Thomas Gresham off to Antwerp to raise a loan.‡ He was the first to take the oath of fealty as Secretary of State. As he knelt before her, she said: " This judgment I have of you, that you will not be corrupted with any manner of gifts, and that you will be faithful to the State."§ Her intuition was sound. She had chosen a counsellor who for forty years was to serve her with a loyalty, patience and discretion that have probably never been surpassed.

In January 1559 the new Parliament was summoned, Cecil again being a member. In February he was elected chancellor of Cambridge University. His brother-in-law, Sir Nicholas Bacon, had been made Lord Keeper, and his other friends constituted an important party in the House of Commons. Cecil took a firm hold of the reins

* Peck, 8.   † Camden, 558.
‡ Froude, vii. 14.   § D. N. B., iii. 1317.

of government. Even the Spanish ambassador called him
" an able man though an accursed heretic."* The Act
of Supremacy was renewed, the Act of Uniformity passed,
peace was concluded with France, and overtures were
made to Scotland.

At Mary's death the Queen of Scots, who was the wife
of the dauphin Francis, had claimed the crown of England
for herself, on the ground of Elizabeth's illegitimacy and
her own descent from Henry VII. Six months later, on
the accession of her husband, she became Queen-Consort
of France. War was then declared on England, but its
results were unfortunate to the aggressors. The French
were beaten at sea, and in the spring of 1560 Cecil was
sent to Scotland to conclude peace. His mission was
successful, but his enemies said that he had granted too
much, and in consequence he offered to resign his place.
He writes thus to the Queen:

" It may please your most excellent Majesty—with a
sorrowful harte and watery eies, I your poore servant
and most lowlye subject, an unworthy Secretory, besech
your Majesty to pardon this my lowlye suite, that con-
sidering the proceding in this matter for removing of the
French out of Scotland doth not content your Majesty,
and that I cannot with my conscience gyve any contrary
advise, I may, with your Majestie's favor and clemency,
be spared to entermeddle therein. And this I am forced
to doo of necessitie, for I will never be a minister in any
your Majestie's service, whereunto your owne mynd shall
not be agreeable, for thereunto I am sworne, to be a
minister of your Majestie's determynations and not of
myne owne, or of others, though they be never so many.
And on the other part to serve your Majesty in any thyng
that myself cannot allow, must nedes be an unprofitable
service, and so untoward, as therein I would be loth your
Majesty should be deceyved. And as for any other
service, though it were in your Majesty's kytchen or
garden, from the bottom of my harte I am ready without
respect of estymation, welthe, or ease, to doo your Majesty's

* Froude, vii. 68.

commandment to my lyve's end. Whereof I wish with
all my poor sorrowful harte, that your Majesty would
make some proofs, for this I doo affyrme, that I have not
sence your Majesty's reigne, any one daye's joye, but in
your Majesty's honor and weale."*

Lord Robert Dudley, a son of Northumberland's and
afterwards Earl of Leicester, was at this time rising in the
favour of Elizabeth, and there were reports that the Queen
would marry him. Cecil was a bitter opponent of this
alliance, while in politics Dudley was a rival of Cecil's,
and he lost no opportunity of criticizing his work, in
which he was supported by his many friends at court.
Cecil, however, had a firm ally in Winchester, the Lord
Treasurer, and he maintained his place in the Queen's
favour. The Scottish treaty turned out better than had
been expected, and when, in December 1560, Francis II.
of France died without issue, his widow had to come
home to her northern kingdom a much less important
figure than hitherto. Yet she was to be a fruitful source
of trouble for many years.

Elizabeth now gave Cecil the lucrative office of Master
of the Court of Wards. It was a tribunal notorious for
its abuses, and hated by the nobility, but he was able
at once to reform its faults and increase its revenue. His
work at this time was prodigious. The Queen was still
a young woman—only twenty-nine—she was occupied
with favourites and amusements, and she devolved most
of the public business upon her secretary. Thus Cecil
superintended nearly everything, and his health suffered
not a little. In addition his private affairs were considerably embarrassed ; his eldest son Thomas was
embarking on a course of expensive dissipation abroad,
while his own schemes of building at Burghley and
Theobalds, which he had just bought, outran his income.

In 1563 he was elected Speaker of the House of
Commons, but the position was incompatible with his
other duties and he declined it. In the summer of the
following year he successfully organized the Queen's visit to

* Wright, i. 24, 25.

Cambridge, where a bad reception had been expected. The University as a recompense created its chancellor a master of arts. Foreign affairs, however, were his principal concern. Events on the Continent and in Scotland were full of risk. Mary Stuart's claims on the crown of England, Philip of Spain's persecutions of the Lutherans in the Netherlands, Charles IX.'s campaigns against the Huguenots in France, combined to excite both Catholics and Protestants. The Scottish tragedy came to a head first. Mary's light conduct soon alienated her subjects. In 1566 her lover Rizzio, and in 1567 her husband Darnley were murdered, probably with her connivance, and she went off with another lover, Bothwell. She was compelled to abdicate, and next year she fled to England. Seven years of her rule had been sufficient for the Scots.

Cecil went warily and dealt with his dangers one at a time. In 1566 peace was made with France, though the civil war there still continued. But the King of Spain remained unappeased. The greatest potentate in Europe, his arm stretched across half the world, and his power must either be met or acknowledged. Writing to his ambassador in England in August 1569 he says of Cecil: " I am in the highest degree dissatisfied with him. He is a confirmed heretic, and if with Lord Robert's assistance you can so influence the matter as to crush him down I shall be delighted."* Cecil knew of these threats, but, like his royal mistress, he was no believer in the sword if it could be avoided. "Warre," he used to say, " is soon kindled, but peace very hardly procured. A realme gaineth more by one year's peace than ten years' warre."† The enemies of England looked on him as their chief foe, and there were numerous plots to kill him; but though he was "strangely unmoved by the peril,"‡ they undoubtedly hardened his character. Leicester was suspected of a hand in some of these plots, though maintaining apparent friendliness: Norfolk was undoubtedly deeply concerned in all.

* Froude, viii. 90.   † Peck, 45.   ‡ Jessop, 18.

In 1569 a rebellion broke out in the northern counties. " It was planned professedly in the interest of Mary Stuart and of the Catholic party in England, but . . . it was supported by Spanish gold and French goodwill."* The rebels, however, had no success. They were easily crushed and mercilessly punished, more by Elizabeth's insistence than Cecil's counsel. The Pope then issued his famous bull " *Regnans in Excelsis,*" which deposed Elizabeth from her throne and absolved her subjects from their allegiance. The document was nailed in the night on the door of the Bishop of London's palace, and was quickly followed by more active measures. Secret emissaries from Rome were scattered broadcast over England, and Cecil, ready to run risks as regards his own life, was sedulous to secure that of the Queen. Spies were suborned, torture employed, and the harshest treatment levelled against recusants. Norfolk, the last of the dukes and the first of the Catholics, was beheaded, and heavy fines were levied on his friends. Close intelligence was kept up with the leading members of the reformed faith on the Continent, and few intrigues were hatched of which Cecil was not informed. Confidence in his administration gradually increased and the opposition diminished. He used to say " that he overcame the envy of some great lords more by Patience than by Thwarting."†

In 1571, after twelve years' service as Secretary of State, he was created a peer—the fourth baron who had been made in that space of time. " My stile," he writes, " is Lord of Burghley and if you list to wryte truly, the poorest Lord in England."‡ A year later he was elected a Knight of the Garter, and in the summer of 1572, on the death of the old Marquess of Winchester, he was appointed Lord High Treasurer. With the Queen he still had a difficult task. " The Commons," he writes in that year, " are sound throughout, and in the Lords there is no lack; but in the Highest person such slowness and stay in resolution as it seemeth God is not pleased."§

* Jessop, 18. † Camden, 558.
‡ Wright, i. 391. § Froude, x. 362, note.

On August 24, 1572, took place the massacre of
St. Bartholomew. Admiral Coligny, writing to Burghley
in May, had warned him that "*les supposts de Sathan
font tout ce qu'ils peuvent pour empescher des œuvres saints*";*
but such a crime had not been imagined. The indignation
and horror in England was unparalleled. The court went
into mourning, and the Treasurer writes: "We have great
cause in these times to doubt all fair speakers, and therefore we do presently put all the sea-coasts in defence and
mean to send her Majesty's navy to sea with speed, and
so continue until we do see further whereunto to
trust."†

His work was now considerably increased, for, in
addition to conducting the ordinary administration as
Secretary of State, he had to supervise the national
finances and the provisioning of the army and navy.
Besides these duties he also presided as a judge in the
court of Star Chamber. Here his despatch was as notable
as his integrity. Presents he invariably refused if a suit
was pending—an unusual practice at that time. He
dealt with petitions as fast as they came in: "there was
not a daie in terme when he received not threescore,
fourescore or a hundred petitions; which he comonly read
that night, and gave every man annswere himself the next
morning as he went to the hall."‡ At the treasury he
was not less fortunate. "He would never paie a penny
of the Queen's money without her warrant,"§ and under
his management the revenue so much increased that
Elizabeth used to say that "with her purse and his head
they could do anything." "Yet he never liked that the
Treasury should grow too great while the rest languished
and pined away: but he made it his endeavour that both
prince and people might grow rich."||

His public duties did not make him neglect his own
affairs. He had three houses, "one in Westminster for
necessity, one at Burghley for computency, and one at
Waltham for his younger son." The expense of enlarging

* Wright, i. 423.   † Jessop, 23, 24.   ‡ Peck, 15.
§ *Ibid.*, 32. || Camden, 558.

and beautifying these mansions swallowed up much
money. But he always kept a numerous household and
a plentiful table, and set a fine example of hospitality and
charity.

By 1572 the power of Elizabeth and the position of
Burghley were well confirmed. In the last six years the
Queen had three times forbidden Parliament to discuss
or proceed with matters " which were too high for them,"
commands to which they thought it wise to bow. On
the Continent her fame was equally high. In 1575 the
Netherlands offered her their crown, while the King of
Sweden, the son of the Emperor, and two successive heirs
to the French throne, sought her hand. But though in
Europe she figured as the champion of the reformers, at
home, like her father, she pursued a middle course. The
cabals of the Catholics were hardly more distasteful to
her than the psalm-singing of the Puritans, and severe
Acts were passed against both. In her private chapel she
still held to the old ceremonies, and she rarely failed to
mark her disapproval of married prelates.

But this policy pleased neither Spain nor Rome, and
for ten years their plots and counter-plots never ceased.
In East Anglia the country gentlemen were continually
harbouring priests, and to curb this Elizabeth, accompanied by Burghley and the Council, made progresses
through Norfolk and Suffolk, staying at the principal
houses and fining or admonishing the culprits. By
Burghley's agents the Jesuits were hunted down, and the
Babington conspiracy to assassinate the Queen discovered; and at his advice the Court of High Commission
was set up to deal with heresy and treason. From all
these dark attempts the hand of Mary Stuart was never
absent, and at last it became evident that either the Queen's
life or hers must be sacrificed. For some years she had
been a prisoner in England, and in 1586 she was at last
brought to trial, Burghley being one of the Commission.
She was sentenced to death, and early in the following
year she was beheaded at Fotheringay. Once the deed
was done Elizabeth disowned it, roundly abused Burghley,

and kept him for several weeks in apparent disgrace; but public opinion in England commended the act, and the Treasurer was soon restored to favour.

The execution of Mary Stuart was a shrewd blow to the Catholics, and Pope Sixtus now proclaimed a crusade against England, enjoining the King of Spain to undertake it. Philip had long had such an expedition in mind. His pride, his power and his pocket had all suffered from the policy of Elizabeth; she had refused his hand and spurned his religion; she had harried his troops in the Low Countries and pillaged his ships on the Spanish Main; the rivalry between the two countries had risen to a pitch that needed blood-letting. Delay was dangerous, and the moment seemed propitious. In 1588 the Great Armada set sail for the North. Burghley sat at the seat of government, stirred up the country and provided for defence. But the intrepid leadership of a few men, the courage of a volunteer navy, and the providence of the elements gained the day. Sir Francis Drake, writing to the Queen from the fleet, says: " We caste the army of Spayn to the northwardes, as they could neither recover England nor Scotland; and within three days after we were entertayned with a great storme the which hath not a little served to drive the enemy away."* The victory was complete. Much of its credit was ascribed to Burghley's policy, and within a few months his only remaining enemy, Leicester, was dead. At the same time the Catholic Henry of Valois was murdered—to be succeeded by Henry of Navarre, a discreet Protestant. The battle of Ivry and the new King's abjuration gave pause to the religious contests in France, and for the moment the continental horizon seemed comparatively clear.

Burghley was now at the zenith of his power. By the Queen he was treated with an affection and consideration that he alone enjoyed. When every other courtier knelt in the royal presence, a chair was always set for the Lord Treasurer. Nor was his gout made the excuse: " It is

* Wright, ii. 385.

for your good head not your bad legs,"* Elizabeth used
to say. She writes to him with the greatest intimacy and
freedom:

"Sir Spirit, I doubt I do nickname you, for those of
your kinde (they say) have no sense, but I have of late
seen an ' *ecce signum* ' that if an ass kicke you, you feele
it too soone. I will recant you from being my spirit,
if ever I perceive that you disdaine not such a feeling.
Serve God, feare the Kinge, and be a good fellow to the
rest. Let never care appeare in you for such a rumour,
but let them well know, that you rather desire the righting
of such wrongs, by making knowne their error, than you
be so silly a soule, as to foreslowe that you ought to do,
or not freely delyver what you thinke meetest, and pass
of no man so much, as not to regard her trust, who puts
it in you.

"God bless you, and long may you last.

"OMNINO, E.R."†

But though in public Burghley prospered, his domestic
affairs were not so happy. In a few years he had suffered
many losses in his family. His mother died in 1587,
one of his daughters in 1588, and his wife in 1589. He
was seventy years of age and had survived most of his
old friends. His eldest son Thomas was of little comfort
to him, and his hopes were centred on Robert, the child
of his second marriage.

He had need of support, for his health was failing, he
was deaf, and so gouty that he could often hardly use
his hand. A fresh party had been formed against him
by the young Lord Essex, the Queen's new favourite,
aided by Burghley's own nephew, Francis Bacon. But
isolated and invalid as he was, his faculties were still
supreme. His presence was considered vital when any
business of moment had to be done, and in September
1595 the Queen came to hold a Council in his bedroom.
In these last years his son Robert was his constant helper

---

* Fuller, Holy State, 257.   † Wright, ii. 201.

and attendant, and to him Burghley opened his heart.
In the last letter written with his own hand Burghley
counsels him to " serve God by serving of the Quene,
for all other service is indede bondage to the devil."*

In the summer of 1598 he became seriously ill, though
he went on transacting business. But early in August he
had a convulsive fit, and on the 5th he died, " lying
praieing to himself and saying the Lord's praier in Latin."†
He was almost seventy-eight, he had been Lord Treasurer
for more than a quarter of a century, and had held
the place of Chief Minister for forty consecutive years
—a term unequalled before or since. At the news of his
death Elizabeth, it is said, shed tears—a rare tribute
from her. His obsequies were carried out at Westminster
with magnificence, but his body was buried quietly in his
old home at Stamford. By his first wife he left one son
Thomas, afterwards Earl of Exeter, whose descendant,
the present marquess, is the senior representative of the
family. From his younger son Robert comes the Salisbury
line. Of his daughters one was married to Lord Oxford,
and one to a son of Lord Wentworth, but they both
predeceased their father.

Burghley's fortune, despite his many opportunities for
increasing it, was not inordinately large. He left some
£25,000 in money and plate, the best proof of his moderation. From the Court of Wards alone it was calculated
that he could have made five to six times as much profit
as he actually did. His income from his lands—he
owned 300 manors—and from the offices he filled, was
considerable, but he lived in a noble style, keeping three
houses always open, and he was continually building.
" Twelve times he entertained the Queen and her court,"
often for several weeks at a time, and each visit cost him
from £2,000 to £3,000. In 1585 he writes: " I have not
for these 26 years been benefited from Her Majesty so
much as I was within four years of King Edward. . . .
My fee for the Treasurership doth not answer to my charge
of stall."‡ Nor was he covetous of dignities. After forty

* Wright, ii. 488.   † Peck, 42.   ‡ Froude, xi. 5, note.

years of royal favour and service in the highest place in the State he was content with the lowest rank in the peerage.

Burghley, says his anonymous biographer, was "well proportioned, of the middle syze of makeing. Very straight and upright of bodye and leggs; neither fatt nor leane, but well flesht: of visage, very well favoured; and of excellent complexion. Even in his latter daies, when he was well and warme, or had newe dyned or supped, he had as good coloure in his face as most fare women. His beard of a reasonable length faire, white and comely.

"He was of a spare and temperatt diett, eating but two or three dishes: drinking very seldome wine. He seldome or never plaied at any game; for he could plaie at none. Riding in his garden and walks upon his little muile was his greatest disport. His recreation was chiefly in his books, reading in Latin, French or Italian; very seldome in Englishe. He tooke great paines and delight in pedegrees, and wrote whole bookes of them with his own hand: which greatly augmented his knowledge both abroad and at home.

"He delighted to talke and be merrie with his friends, onlie at meals. For he had no more leisure. If he coulde gette his table sett round with his young little children, he was then in his kingdome. But what busyness soever was in his head, it was never perceaved at his table; for he never made anie man of his counsell; nor did anie ever knowe his secretts. His speeche was more plaine and compendious than often or muche; seldome using a word in vaine. His eloquence was in comon wordes, without affectation, easye to be understoode and remembered. His ordinary speeches weare comonly cherefull, merrie and familiar; but witty, sharpe and pithy: without dulness or sowrnes. He hated idleness, and was ever more weary of a little idleness than of greate labor. It was said of him that he cold call to mynd anie thinge that he hade done, sene or read. His greate paines got him great knowledge; and his continuall practice deep experience. So what was to others most difficult he cold dispatch with the greatest facilitie.

" He was by nature very kind and courteous, to his friends affable and kind. Readie to do them good, when he might doe it of himself; but that not frequentlie. He was patient in hearing, ready in despatching and myld in answering suitors. But there was not any man livinge cold move him to doe anie thinge in favoure or hindrance of a cause in any court of justice before him. He was seldom seen angrie, or moved with joie in prosperitie, or sorrow in adversitie."*

His sayings epitomize his policy, " that he had gotten more by temperance than ever he did by his witt "; that " honest counsellors to the Quene, and good judges and officers in courtes of justice were the pillars of the state "; that " where there wanted a good ministery, there were ever bad people. For they that knewe not howe to serve God, wold never obey the Kinge "; that " that state could never be in safety, where there was a toleration of two religions. For there is no enmytie so greate as that for religion. And they that differ in the service of God can never agree in the service of their contrie."†

In foreign affairs he was especially apt, and there his memory had made him a well of information. " He could tell throughout Spain, every part, every port, every ship with its burden. To the counsell of captains he did not lean; but he was never remiss in his care for the poore soldier. He was the first who devised to apparell them, and procured their wekely lendings to be paid by pole. For the captaine was wont to receave the whole paie for all his soldiers."‡ In matters of trade his views were Protectionist.

Naunton calls him " of a most subtile and active spirit wholly intentive to the service of his mistris: a person of most exquisite abilities."§ Gueran, the Spanish envoy, writing in 1569, styles him " so true an Englishman that he thinks all the sovereigns of Christendom cannot conquer this island. He it is who governs all. He thinks we are none of us a match for him."||

* Peck, 29-42. See also Ascham, 187-8. † *Ibid.* ‡ *Ibid.*
§ Naunton, 31. || Froude, ix. 374.

As to his attitude in religion there is some question. Froude considers him a latitudinarian, but Macaulay blames him for persecution. " The deep stain upon his memory is that for differences of opinion for which he would risk nothing himself, he, in the day of his power, took away without scruple the lives of others."* There is no doubt that he temporized in matters of dogma. He was a Protestant under Edward VI., a Catholic under Mary, while under Elizabeth he conformed to the newly established Anglican faith, which did not differ greatly in her own case from that of Rome:—she told the Spanish ambassador, " *Que in muy poco deferia ella de nos otros : que ella pensaba salvarse tan bien como el obispo de Roma.*"†

Burghley was no zealot. He regarded Christianity as necessary to salvation, but was not much exercised as to its particular form. He would punish no Catholic for his opinions, but he refused to recognize the Pope's right to declare rebellion a religious duty. For England in those days the creed of Rome was a menace, so recognized by nearly all moderate men; " such be the humours of the Commons house, as they think nothing sharp ynough against papists."‡ The King of Spain, the Queen of Scotland and the Pope were vital dangers, and to guard against them was Burghley's business. When fair means could not avail he employed foul; he repeated the practices of Henry, Edward and Mary, and at the end he secured peace. In his own mind he had probably little need to justify his actions by the arguments of the Jesuits.

The mainspring of his policy was practical patriotism, and it was because heretics were potential traitors that he dealt with them as such. A God-fearing man enough, he was not made of the stuff that seeks the stake. He had seen the whole of the Reformation. In his early life Luther and Calvin had preached it, while Wolsey ruled England: he had lived through the days of the divorce and the dissolution, of Cromwell and Somerset, of Mary Tudor and Mary Stuart, of St. Bartholomew and Ivry:

* Macaulay, v. 591.   † Lingard, vi. 22, note.   ‡ *Ibid.*, vi. 83, note.

he died in the same year as King Philip—the chief of the Catholics. Such a career could not have succeeded without pliability, and only statesmen who possessed that quality could hope to survive under the Tudors. Like the old Lord Winchester, his predecessor at the Treasury, Burghley had in him as much of the willow as of the oak.

Moderate, cautious and versatile, " an old fox," he advised so wisely that his advice was nearly always taken. His loyalty and integrity were never questioned, his ability and judgment rarely challenged. His silent nod was proverbial; as the Queen said: " Be you ever so burly, my lord Burghley, yet you make less stir than my lord Leicester." " Of all men of genius," says Camden, " he was the most of a drudge; of all men of business the most of a genius."* His ambition was not for himself: had it been so he could have secured more material blessings than he did. His simple pleasures, his buildings, his gardens, his reading, show him a quiet man. He wished only to ensure the happiness of his country and the rule of his sovereign. To do this a firm hand was needed, and he did not hesitate to apply it. His work lived after him, and he has left a name and a posterity as illustrious as any in England.

II.—SALISBURY

Robert Cecil, afterwards Earl of Salisbury, was born on June 1, 1563, at Cannon Row in Westminster. He was a younger son of Sir William Cecil, afterwards Lord Burghley, by his second wife Mildred, daughter of Sir Anthony Cooke; she was called by Roger Ascham one of the most learned women in Europe.

At the time of his birth Cecil's father had been Secretary of State and Chief Minister to Queen Elizabeth for five years; his uncle, Sir Nicholas Bacon, was Lord Keeper; and his grandfather, Sir Anthony Cooke, had been governor to King Edward VI. His half-brother, Thomas Cecil, was twenty years older than himself, and showed little

* Jessop, 37.

SERO, SED SERIO.

M. Gerard, pinx

ROBERT CECIL
EARL OF SALISBURY

To face page 278

disposition for a political career. On Robert therefore his father's interest was centred. He was, however, a very weakly child, undersized, and somewhat deformed, and for this reason he was at first educated at home under his mother's care.

At sixteen he was entered at his father's old college, St. John's, Cambridge, where, according to the vice-chancellor, " he showed an example of godly diligence both at sermons and disputations."* He was then admitted to Gray's Inn, and apparently elected to Parliament as early as 1580—though this date is not quite certain. At the age of twenty-one he went to France to attend lectures in Paris and to travel. Three years later he became member for Westminster, and early in 1588 he was attached to Lord Derby's mission to Flanders in the peace negotiations with Spain.

His letters during these months describe the towns he visited, the people he met; the food—" an orange and half a red herring for dinner "; the fires—" of turfs which makes him envy the seacoal at home "; the ladies—" not a fair woman nor an honest."† But he looked about him to some purpose, and on his return was able to convey much useful information to his father. Then came the Armada, when Cecil, it seems, served on board one of the Queen's ships and saw the fight off Dover.

Early in 1589 his mother died, and on August 31 he married Elizabeth Brooke, daughter of William, Lord Cobham. She only survived seven years, and little is known of her beyond chance allusions. On one occasion Cecil writes that she is " not to let anybody know that she paied under £3 10s. 0d. a yard for her cloth of silver. I mervaile she is so simple as to tell anybody what she paies for everything."‡

After serving as sheriff for Hertfordshire, Cecil now became member for that county and was a regular attendant at court. His father was getting old and failing in health, and had felt severely the recent losses in his family; while Essex, the successor of Leicester in Elizabeth's

* Cecil, 14.   † *Ibid.*, 26-31.   ‡ Wright, ii. 414-15.

graces, was striving to supplant him at the head of affairs. Thomas, Lord Burghley's heir, was something of a runagate and on Robert devolved the task of maintaining the Cecil influence. He devoted himself to affairs and lived after the "ten precepts" which his father wrote for his guidance. They include much worldly wisdom and deserve record.

"Use great providence and circumspection in chusing thy wife; for from thence will spring all thy future good or evil. Enquire diligently of her disposition: let her not be poore, nor yet chuse a base and uncomely creature altogether for wealth.

"Let thy hospitalitie be moderate . . . rather plentiful than sparing, but not costly. Beware thou spend not above three of four parts of thy revennewes. That gentleman who sells an acre of land sells an ounce of credit. For gentility is nothing else but ancient riches.

"Bring up thy children in learning and obedience, yet without outward austerity. Praise them openly, reprehend them secretly.* Give them good countenance and convenient maintenance according to thy abilitie; otherwise thy life will seem their bondage. Marry thy daughters early, lest they marry themselves; and suffer not thy sons to pass the Alpes.

"Live not in the country without corn and cattle about thee. Let thy kindred and allies be welcome to thy house and table.

"Beware of suretyship for thy best friends.

"Undertake no suit against a poor man.

"Be sure to keep some rich man for thy friend, but trouble him not for trifles.

"Towards thy superiors be humble yet generous; with thy equals be familiar yet respective; towards thy inferiours show much humanity and some familiarity.

"Trust not any man with thy life, credit or estate.

"Be not scurrilous in conversation nor satyricall in jests."†

From much of this good advice Robert Cecil profited.

* He speaks of "divers scholars of Eton who be run away for fear of beating" (Ascham, 188).   † Peck, 47-49.

In May 1591 Elizabeth visited her Lord Treasurer at his great house at Theobalds—an expensive honour which cost him £100 for every day she stayed. Robert Cecil, arrayed as an anchoret, met her and delivered an address of welcome written by Peele. On the Queen's departure he was knighted, and two months later he was sworn a privy councillor. His real advancement now began. The place of one Secretary of State had been vacant ever since the dismissal of Davison by Elizabeth after the business of Mary Stuart's death-warrant. Burghley had intended to put his son into the office, and for several years Cecil had done the work without pay. But the insight that he thus got into public affairs and the training he received from constant association with his father were worth more than any salary.

Expeditions to Ireland, France and Spain were at this time occupying the government's attention; Cecil had much to do with their conduct, and gradually became his father's right-hand man. But for some years he had to be content with an unofficial position, for Essex had a candidate of his own, Sir Thomas Bodley, for the secretary-ship, and he "detracted from Cecil's reputation with odious comparison."* There was also another difficulty. Between the younger generations of the Cecil and Bacon families there was considerable rivalry. Francis Bacon, son of the Lord Keeper and Ann Cooke, and Robert Cecil, son of the Lord Treasurer and Mildred Cooke, were equally promising young men. The genius of the former had not yet developed, and the interest of the latter made him for the moment the greater man. Bacon had attached himself to the fortunes of Essex, and to Essex it was a matter of prestige to press his own follower forward. One winter morning in 1594, when Essex and Cecil were driving back from the Tower where they had been present at the "examination" of a prisoner, Essex urged Bacon's appointment as attorney-general. "Lord," replied Sir Robert, "I wonder your Lordship should go about to spend your strength in so unlikely or impossible a matter.

* Camden, 524.

If at least your Lordship had spoken of the solicitorship, that might be of easier digestion to her Majesty." " Digest me no digestions," said Essex, " the attorneyship for Francis is that I must have. I could name a younger man than Francis, of less learning and no greater experience, who is shoving and suing for a far greater place than the attorneyship."*

Nothing was done for Bacon, but at last, in 1596, when the favourite was away from England, Elizabeth appointed Cecil Secretary of State. But the prize was soon discounted, for at the end of that year he lost his wife—a sorrow he never forgot, and for the rest of his days business had to serve both as his work and his pleasure.

Cecil was soon in high credit with the Queen, " passing the most part of the day in private and secret correspondence with her."† He really admired her extraordinary energy and ability. Writing to Essex in July 1597 he describes her reception of the Polish ambassador, who had made a pugnacious oration in Latin: " I swear by the living God, her Majestie made one of the best answers, extempore, in Latin, that ever I heard, being much moved to be so challenged in publick, especially against her expectation. The wordes of her beginning were ' *Expectavi legationem, mihi vero querelam adduxisti* ' . . . I never heard her (when I knew her spirits were in a passion) speake with better moderation in my life."‡ After finishing she turned to the court and said: " God's death, my Lords, I have been enforced this day to scour up my old Latin that hath lain so long rusting."§

Cecil gradually began to take over his father's place of Chief Minister, and he became Chancellor of the Duchy of Lancaster and, according to some accounts, Lord Privy Seal.‖ In the spring of 1598 he was sent on a special embassy to France with Southampton, Brooke and Raleigh, to prevent the conclusion of an alliance with Philip of Spain. He showed himself an acute diplomatist,

---

* Birch, i. 153; Cecil, 80.   † *Ibid.*, ii. 281.
‡ Wright, ii. 479, 480.   § *Ibid.*
‖ He was Keeper of the Signet, a different duty.

but there was nothing to be done, and in May he was back in England. Three months later the old Lord Treasurer died. Throughout the last years of his life he had been in the closest correspondence with his son, and to him he left the mantle of his power.

Yet Cecil's position at his father's death was not easy. He had lost his wife, his elder brother was of little help, and he had no great connections. Nor was he rich. His father had left him such money as he could spare—some £1,600 a year—and his favourite house of Theobalds, but the one could hardly support the other. The Queen in her old age had become even more arbitrary and difficult, and as a Cabinet did not exist, the weight of government rested almost entirely on his own shoulders. But against these drawbacks Cecil had his own abilities and the advantage of being well established. The white staff of the Lord Treasurer was given indeed to the Queen's cousin, Lord Buckhurst, but the chief direction of affairs remained with the Secretary of State.

In 1599 Cecil was made Master of the Court of Wards, his father's old place, and he then resigned the duchy of Lancaster. In that year Essex, who had made a failure of his expedition to Spain, was sent as Lord Deputy to Ireland. There he plunged into worse errors, and then suddenly returned without leave to London. For this he lost the Queen's favour, and was speedily arrested and examined before a commission. Cecil was one of the members, but he treated the earl with great forbearance and discretion, and was largely responsible for his release. But Essex knew no restraint. Early in 1601 he determined to seize the government himself, and after intrigues with Scots, Catholics and Puritans, he headed a wild insurrection in London. He was then seized, tried and condemned to death. In the course of his trial he made accusations against Cecil of having questioned the Queen's right to the throne. It was a dangerous charge in those days, and might have done Cecil serious harm. But he met it in the most open manner. " For wit," he said, " I am your inferior; I am your inferior for nobility; a swordsman I am not, and herein also you go before me, yet doth my innocence protect me and I stand as an honest man before a delinquent."* The suggestions were easily refuted, and the incident added to Cecil's reputation.

The shock of Essex's death affected Elizabeth deeply, and from this time she began to fail. She was nearing seventy, and though her spirit never faltered, it was clear that she had not long to live. Everything pointed to the King of Scotland as her heir. He was her nearest cousin of the Tudor blood, and his succession would unite the two crowns of Britain and confirm the security of the reformed religion. For some time Cecil had secretly kept up a correspondence with him, and had prepared for the coming change. But he held his favour with the Queen, and as late as December 1602 she was at his house in London. " On Monday the 6th her Majestie dyned with her Secretary. He gave her ten several giftes, the most part very ritch jewells. The Queen was merrye and well pleased." At her departure " she refused helpe to enter her barge, whereby stumbling she fell and a little bruised her shyne."† Such entertainments were expensive. Cecil had already spent more than he could afford on his new house in the Strand, the site of the present Hotel Cecil. He had just " lost better than £800 at cards in a single night," and had lent £4,000 to his friend Raleigh.‡ The crisis of his life was approaching, and speculation was in the air.

Early in 1603 Elizabeth went to the palace at Richmond, suffering from a chill, which rapidly grew worse. She was a prey to fears of assassination, and kept a sword by her with which she used to thrust into the arras. Her temper became uncontrollable, she would remain for hours without speaking or eating, and no one could reason with her. As her end approached she got up and, as one of her maids of honour tells, " she sate for two dayes and three nyghts on the stole redie dressed and wold never be brought by anie to go to bed." The rest of the Council were awaiting events at Whitehall, but Egerton, the Lord Keeper, Cecil, the Secretary of State, and Howard,

* Camden, 617.   † Lingard, vi. 659, note.   ‡ Cecil, 168.

the Lord Admiral, stayed with her at Richmond. From the last-named she consented to take a cup of broth, " as he was of her own blood," but the others she treated with profound contempt. " Cicell," she said, " know that I am not madd. You must not think to make Queene Jane of me." Cecil then insisted that she must go to bed. " 'Must' ? " she said. " Is ' must ' a word to be addressed to princes ? Little man, little man, thy father, if he had been alive, durst not have used that word; but thou art grown presumptuous because thou knowest that I shall die."

During the night of March 23 the three begged her to say who should be her successor—the King of France or the King of Scots—but she made no sign. Then they mentioned Lord Beauchamp, Somerset's grandson, who through his mother, Lady Catherine Grey, was heir to the Suffolk claims. At his name the Queen's spirit was roused, and she muttered: " My seat has been the seat of Kings; I will have no rascal's son in it."* Those were her last words : at three o'clock in the morning she died. At six the Council met, and messengers posted off to Edinburgh to tell James that he was King of England. With his own voice Cecil proclaimed the new monarch at Whitehall and Charing Cross. The glories of the Tudors were over, and the troubles of the Stuarts had begun.

Cecil at once became the new King's chief support. He had " continual access to him, keeping the signet."† He retained his place as Secretary—at first not without " trouble, hurrying, feigning and suing,"‡ but soon grew in favour. In May 1603 he was created Lord Cecil of Essendon; fifteen months later he was advanced to be Viscount Cranborne, and in 1605 he was made a Knight of the Garter and Earl of Salisbury, his brother Thomas becoming at the same time Earl of Exeter. It is said that the King insisted on a heavy fee for this honour, though Thomas certainly did not want it. He writes on January 12: " I am resolved to contente myselfe with this estate I have of a baron."

* Lingard, vi. 647-8. † Goodman, i. 301. ‡ Lingard, vii. 5.

On his journey to London James had stayed at Theobalds and was so well pleased with the house that the new Earl of Salisbury had to exchange it for the royal manor of Hatfield, the house in which the fortunes of his family had begun. But he got full value over the bargain, both in cash and consideration, and started to build a new palace. *" On lui bailla,"* says Boderie, *" par ladite exchange une terre beaucoup plus noble, en beaucoup plus belle assiette, autant et plus de domaine et beaucoup meilleure, et deux cens mille francs pour batir une autre maison . . . neanmoins encore a-t-il fort obligé le roi son maitre."** But he did not relish losing his house any more than losing his mistress. When someone congratulated him on not being obliged to address the King on his knees, as he always had done to Elizabeth, " I wish to God," he said, " that I spoke still on my knees."† With Queen Ann, James' wife, he did not at first get on, but his tact gradually overcame her dislike, and eventually he became her chamberlain and close friend.

Before leaving Theobalds, Salisbury had given a grand masque in honour of a visit from the King of Denmark. It was distinguished by considerable licence. A guest describing it says: " The ladies abandon sobriety and one is seen to roll about in intoxication. One of the performers . . . overset her caskets into his Danish Majesty's lap and fell at his feet. His Majesty then got up and would dance with her, but he fell down and humbled himself before her, and was carried into an inner chamber. The entertainment went forward, and most of the presenters went backward or fell down."‡

The early years of James' reign were disturbed by a series of conspiracies against the dynasty. The attempt to place Lady Arabella Stuart on the throne, the Main Plot, the Bye Plot, the Gunpowder Treason " to blow the Scots back to Scotland,"§ all needed careful watching and swift action. Salisbury was indefatigable, prompt and astute. Some of his own Brooke connections were

* Lingard, vii. 106, note.   † Birch, ii. 216.
‡ Lingard, vii. 102, note.   § Jesse, Mem. Lond., ii. 176

concerned, but he allowed no family feelings to deter him, and Raleigh, Cobham, Catesby and Fawkes were successively caught and punished. Behind most of them was the hand of Rome. Yet Salisbury was moderate to the Catholics. Writing of the priests to James he says: " I condemn their doctrine: I detest their conversation: I foresee the peril which the exercise of their function may bring to this island: only I confess I shrink to see them die by dozens when they come so near loyalty." In another letter he ends: " By God, the priests swarm."*

Salisbury had succeeded his father as chancellor of Cambridge University and lord-lieutenant of Hertfordshire, and in 1608, on the death of Lord Dorset, he became Lord High Treasurer. " My Master," he said, " hath laid this honour upon me without suit and without merit."†

He still kept on his Secretaryship of State, and to his other duties now added that of managing the exchequer. Here he was able, to some extent, to repair the ravages inflicted on the country by James' rapacity. Despite monopolies, taxes, and gifts of all sorts, the revenue was increased. In two years it was raised by £150,000, while over a million of debt and deficit was paid off.

The policy which the minister had to advocate was at times too advanced for the Commons. They would not agree to the King's wish for the union of England and Scotland, nor to Salisbury's plan of commuting the old feudal dues in exchange for a fixed grant to the Crown. The Treasurer " was indefatigable in attempting to bring the King and the Commons to terms,"‡ but Parliament was beginning to lay claim to rights of freedom in debate, control of elections and other privileges which in Elizabeth's days they had been content to leave alone. They remonstrated against the Court of High Commission, the abuse of royal proclamations, and the practice of impositions. James' favourites from the north and his new friends in the south were all intent on furnishing their own pockets, and on Salisbury lay the onus of resisting them. At this time he was the single man capable of

* Cecil, 233, 350. † Lingard, vii. 106, note. ‡ Gardiner, ii. 83.

carrying on the government. " My Lord Treasurer Cecil growing into years, having been a good statesman, the only supporter of the Protestant faction, discloser of treasons, and the only mercury of our time, was well acquainted with the affairs of this commonwealth."*

In most matters James agreed with him, though he thought him prejudiced against Scotland and suspected him of Puritan tendencies; but the value of his financial work he always recognized. Yet Salisbury's difficulties were immense: to restrain the enormous expenditure on which the King embarked; to get supplies from the careful Commons; to reform the many abuses. " Money," he used to say, " is the only antidote for future mischief." † One of his many expedients to get it was the institution of the order of baronets, at a creation fee of £1,000 apiece (a fictitious receipt for that amount still accompanies the patent); while another and less known contribution was his resignation to the State of all the profits of his office of the Court of Wards.

His own money troubles still went on. Like his father, he could never stop building and laying out gardens. To Cecil House, Cranborne Manor and Hatfield were now added. The cost for the last-named far exceeded the estimates, and he was continually in straits, " having been busied too much with mortar."‡ Between two and three millions of bricks were needed for the walls, while the Maze garden, the Pheasant garden, the Privy garden, the Knotwork garden and the Vineyard recalled the glories and expenses of Theobalds. In the plans he was largely his own architect, though he did not live long enough to inhabit the house.

He had never been a really strong or healthy man, and in 1610 his constitution began to break up. All through the next year his suffering increased, though he still attended to business. But the failure of his financial projects, the constant struggles with self-seeking rivals, his lonely and ailing life, depressed him, and he became " melancholy and heavy-spirited." " Ease and pleasure,"

* Harl. Misc., v. 355.   † Cecil, 303.   ‡ Jessop, 63.

he said, " quake to hear of death, but my life, full of cares and miseries, seeketh to be dissolved."*

In April 1612 he went to Bath, hoping to get some benefit from the waters. He was a great eater of fruit, especially grapes, and it was thought that these made him worse. His condition did not improve, and on May 21 he started home; but he was suffering from a complication of diseases, and he only reached Marlborough. There, at St. Margaret's rectory, he died three days later, "killed by overwork." He made a most humble and affecting end, " enjoining his chaplain to preach at his funeral and not to say one word in his commendation."†

His fortune was not large, though his income is computed to have been some £10,000 a year. But his debts were considerable, and it is said that at his death he owed nearly £40,000, to liquidate which some of his lands had to be sold. He was succeeded in the title by his only son William, who had married Lady Catherine Howard. His descendant in the eleventh degree is the present marquess.

Salisbury was almost a dwarf—five feet two or three in height at the most—with a " wry neck, crooked back and splay foot." The two Sovereigns whom he served rarely spared his feelings about this; Elizabeth used to call him her " little elf "; James his " pigmy " or his " little beagle." " His face was the best part of his outside,"‡ for though white and drawn, his expression was vivacious and pleasing. Despite his defects of body, he was a man of ample courage and no little gallantry; D'Ewes, indeed, speaks of his " unparalleled lust and hunting after strange flesh,"§ a remark that has little to support it. He was a good public speaker, amusing and apposite, " always very tender for the liberty of the subject."‖ His integrity was remarkable. Although he was " the projector of baronets," he refused all the customary gifts pertaining to his office of Treasurer, and his desire to reform the Court of Wards is said to have damaged him considerably with the King. He has been accused of taking a pension

---

* Burke, 1631. † Goodman, i. 30. ‡ Naunton, 59.
§ D'Ewes, i. 50. ‖ Goodman, i. 33.

from the Spanish government for many years—and Gardiner seems to authenticate the charge. Yet that historian admits that "to the day of his death Salisbury's policy was decidedly and increasingly anti-Spanish."*

With all his father's assiduity and judgment Salisbury had a real instinct for diplomacy and counter-espionage— "the Picklock of the Cabinets of Foreign princes."† "Robert the Devil," the Spaniards used to call him. It has been said that he "died in a general hate,"‡ and it is true that his influence was on the wane: "the King did not love him, for he knew the King's disposition to an inch."§ After his death many skits appeared against him, as malignant as they were unjust:

> "Here lies, thrown for the worms to eat,
> Little bossive Robin that was so great.
> Not Robin Goodfellow nor Robin Hood,
> But Robin, the encloser of Hatfield Wood,
> Who seemed as sent from ugly fate
> To spoil the prince and rob the state,
> Owning a mind for dismal ends
> As traps for foes and tricks for friends."

His cousin Bacon hastened to mark his faults. He writes to the King: "Your Majesty hath lost a great subject and a great servant. But, if I should praise him in propriety I should say that he was a more fit man to keep things from getting worse, but no very fit man to reduce things to be much better. For he loved to have the eyes of all Israel a little too much on himself and to have all business still under the hammer, and like clay in the hands of the potter, to mould it as he thought good, so that he was more *in operatione* than *in opere*."‖ His Essay on Deformity was believed to point to Salisbury. "Deformed persons are commonly void of natural affection . . . extreme bold . . . to watch and observe the weakness of others . . . as good spials and good whisperers. They will if they be of spirit, seek to free themselves of scorn."¶

* Gardiner, i. 215. † Fuller, Holy State, 250.
‡ D'Ewes, i. 50, 51. § Goodman, i. 38, 44.
‖ Bacon, vi. 52. ¶ *Ibid.*, x. 112.

The sensitive temperament of a man so afflicted felt these arrows of malice; nor were they outbalanced by his political success, much of which he undoubtedly regarded as Dead Sea apples. " 'Tis a great task," he said, " to prove one's honesty and yet not mar one's fortune." " A court bringeth little comfort on earth, and no wise man looketh this way to heaven."* The continual strain and tension of government in hazardous times prevented him from confiding in others, or others from confiding in him. Thus he had not many friends, though those he had were devoted. Few tributes can surpass that of Dorset in his will. After speaking of Salisbury's " infinite cares, crosses, labours and travails, both of body and mind, his dexterity, sincerity and judgment incessantly employed for the service of the public," he praises his " sweet nature so full of mildness, courtesy, honest mirth, kindness, gratitude and good discourse, so easily reconciled to his foes, so true unto his friends."†

Salisbury always felt a certain degree of uncertainty under James. He once consulted the attorney-general as to what security a minister might have with a prince who did not keep his word, and in a paper that he wrote on his own office he says, " all the Secretary has to trust to is that his prince will be ' semper idem '; his place is dreadful . . . who lives at mercy."‡ But he had plenty of courage; he was " his father's own son, and a pregnant proficient in all disception of State . . . the staffe of the Queen's declining age . . . a craftsmaster in foreign intelligence."§ Cautious, able and silent, he had long been necessary to Elizabeth: before her death he had made himself necessary to James, and with immense industry and a swift facility he steered through the shoals that encompassed the new King. He guarded him from traitors; he kept him on some terms with his Parliament; he held him to the French and away from the Spanish; he pledged him to the Protestants. How far his ministry would have endured may be questioned. " James had

* Burke, 1631.　　　　　　　† Cecil, 374-5.
‡ Harl. Misc., v. 167.　　　　　§ Naunton, 59-62.

long been weary of the yoke,"* and Salisbury knew it.
He stood alone while he lived, for he was out of
sympathy with the men of his own generation. His
death was quickly followed by that of Prince Henry, a
youth of high promise, and by the rise to favour of Carr
and Villiers. Their specious qualities might soon have
wrecked the older tradition.

Salisbury's administration lasted for fourteen years,
and in that space of time much was done. The foundation of the East India Company in 1600 started the
English trading ventures in the East. The colonization
of Virginia and Bermuda in 1607 marked the beginning
of the American States and of the British Empire overseas. The Authorized Version of the Bible and the enforcement of the Commons' privileges confirmed the new
religion and the new liberties of England.

When he died, though still a young man, he had gone
far to complete the work of Burghley in strengthening
his country against her foreign foes and preparing her to
meet the coming assaults of her own rulers.

Burghley and Salisbury first raised the office of Treasurer
to its subsequent high place in the State; and as they
were the first, so they were the last great Treasurers:
after Salisbury's death the practice began of putting the
office into commission. It may be too much to call them
the first real statesmen who have ruled England; but
they were the first who founded a tradition of statecraft
and a family of statesmen. In three centuries three of
their house have already held the place of Chief Minister:
a fourth will surely follow.

* Gardiner, ii. 143-4.

CHAPTER X
KINGCRAFT

BUCKINGHAM AND STRAFFORD

A NEW century and a new dynasty marked a moment when Englishmen could put their new thoughts into action. Prosperous days at home, bold travels abroad, the spread of learning, the contests of religion, had opened their eyes and strengthened their sinews, and they began to advance along the political path. A King, they saw, was no less made for his people than a people for their King. Self-determination was in sight.

The Tudors, Welsh in origin, had been eminently English in character. Ruling under the guise of autocrats, they yet were in touch with the feeling of the nation, and despite their despotism the nation loved them. In little over a hundred years they had done a mighty work and left a famous name, and when their heritage fell to their Northern cousins it seemed goodly and secure. But the appearance was deceptive. The tradition, the temper and the tact of the old stock had forbidden any overt acts of assertion while they still filled the throne, but with other times came other manners. A calm vision and a deft hand were needed to steer the ship through the uncharted seas that lay ahead, and the Stuart race possessed neither. Anxious only to enjoy those sweets of power and plenty which they had never known in Scotland, they thought it easy to emulate Elizabeth, and they hurried south, bringing with them divine right and the sacred hunger for gold, but leaving foresight and sympathy behind.

The descent of the Scots upon England is well illustrated by the contemporary ballad of the " fine old English

293

gentleman who had a large estate," until his heir came
in and dissipated the savings of his father. Elizabeth,
with her masques and triumphs, her gowns and silk
stockings, was a true economist. Lavish spending never
appealed to her, and parsimony she reckoned as a virtue;
yet all her life she revelled in luxury. In Scotland the
Stuarts had existed on a very different plane. There
James had lived in penury, a pensioner on the Queen of
England's bounty. When he crossed the border he found
himself master of riches beyond his wildest dreams, and
his courtiers urged him to ride with a full rein. He did
not hesitate to do so. The royal households were mounted
on the most extensive scales. His two elder children had
141 attendants assigned to them, 56 above and 85 below
stairs, and within a few years Prince Henry's establishment had increased to nearly 500 persons, two-thirds of
whom were in receipt of salaries. The King loaded his
Scottish nobles with the most generous presents, paid in
good English coin. To Lord Dunbar he gave at various
times £15,000, to Lord Mar the same amount, to Lord
Haddington twice that sum. His entertainments, instead
of being provided by his loving subjects, were paid for
out of the English exchequer, and drunkenness, indelicacy
and blasphemy were amongst their principal features.
Hunting, cockfighting, golf and eating formed his recreations, varied by classical subtleties and sententious maxims
that earned for him the name of " the wisest fool in
Europe."

His appearance was uninviting. Short, fat, with rolling
eyes, a tongue too large for his mouth, and a shuffling gait,
clad in heavily quilted clothes to turn a dagger, he did
not attract beholders. But to a sycophantic court he
was the Solomon of his age. His temper was hasty,
easily aroused, and easily appeased. When angry he
would shout and scream and curse, kick his pages, and
then beg their forgiveness with tears—qualities not calculated vastly to impress his English subjects. Yet with
all his lack of dignity he had a real respect for his virgin
predecessor, and he strove to deal with Church and State

as he thought she would have done. By the aid of a capable minister he evaded the plots planned against him in the early part of his reign, and he kept a reasonably safe course between the extremists of either side. But with Parliament he struck more dangerous reefs. There the new entry had a proper pride of their own, they fancied that they could appraise Kings at their right value, and they were not for resigning their liberties, their faith or their purses to a prince who inspired them with neither love, fear nor esteem. After several unfortunate struggles with the House of Commons, James found it best to let them alone, and at his death he left them a legacy of nearly a million pounds of debts.

From such a father Charles I. had little to learn. Early brought under the influence of the handsome and exquisite Buckingham, he soon began to criticize the weakness and moderation of his parent; and despite James' moral and political axioms, he determined to set up a standard for himself, and to rule his three kingdoms at his own good pleasure. He was a small man, pale, delicate and refined, with a slight impediment in his speech. His tastes, his demeanour, his point of view, were all elegant and exclusive. He had no sympathy with the ideas of democracy or puritanism, and whatever he may have condemned in his father, he inherited from him a grand conception of the regal prerogative and a firm belief in the Anglican Church. When he came to the throne he had neither experience nor ballast, though he was obstinate, vain and self-confident. But of domestic virtues he was full; he was chaste, religious, agreeable and affectionate, and it was his misfortune that these qualities were not enough appreciated to help him as a ruler.

After the death of Buckingham he resolved to have no favourite but his wife, and her influence was for reaction. " Of the many women who have tried to take part in affairs of State, from Cleopatra downwards, nobody by character or training was worse fitted than the wife of Charles I."* Then the dark figure of Strafford loomed

* Warner and Marten, ii. 355, note.

20

on to the stage, and Charles, weak, floundering and shifty, soon felt its strength. He fell under the sway of his imperious minister, and in an evil day his minister trusted him. In the gaunt hall of Westminster, the memorial of two childless Kings, their distant successor watched his mighty servant struggle and succumb. Eight years later he was himself to stand on the same stones and to be served with the same scant justice. His friends had fallen by the axe or the knife, his subjects had shed their blood and spent their fortunes in his quarrels, and at last he had brought his own crown to the block. By a besotted policy, a complete misapprehension of the relation between his people and himself, he had dragged his country into a civil war and had scattered the traditions of centuries. Like the men who had lent him their help, he bore his share of the common punishment bravely, though their fate had failed to teach him how to keep faith or how to maintain his inheritance.

I.—BUCKINGHAM

George Villiers, afterwards Duke of Buckingham, was born at Brooksby, in Leicestershire, on August 28, 1592. He was the second son of Sir George Villiers of that place by his second wife Mary, daughter of Anthony Beaumont, Esq., of Glenfield, in the same county. She was a lady about whose history there are many tales; she had been a " serving gentlewoman " who had made her way to the front, and her beauty and talents had much to do with the fortunes of her children.

The Villiers family, owners of a moderate estate, had been established for several centuries in their county " rather without obscurity than with any great lustre."* There were no less than eight children to provide for, and George, a younger son of the second marriage, had only his good looks and abilities to rely on. At ten years old he was sent to the local school of Billisden, and on

* Wotton, 308.

his father's death, three years later, was taken " by his beautiful and provident mother to her house at Goodby . . . where he was the domestic favourite." He had learnt some slight music and literature, but as he was " by nature little studious and contemplative, she chose rather to endue him with conversative qualities and ornaments of youth, as dancing, fencing and the like."* In these arts he became so apt that his teachers had to restrain his forwardness, so that his brothers might keep pace with him. At eighteen he was sent in company with Sir John Eliot to France, where he passed another three years. " He returned," says Fuller, " one of the compleatest Courtiers in Christendom, his body and behaviour mutually gracing one another."†

In 1614 he came up to London " in an old black suit, broken out in divers places," and fell in love with a daughter of Sir Roger Ashton, the King's Master of the Robes. But his poverty was an impediment—he only possessed £50 a year—and one of the gentlemen of the bedchamber, Sir John Graham, advised him not to think of a girl who " had not enough money to buy her own pocket handkerchiefs,"‡ but to try his fortune at court. His good looks and demeanour had already been noticed by James at Newmarket, and in August 1614 he was presented to the King on a progress at Apethorpe. Villiers showed "that readiness of speech in which James delighted," and the latter then resolved " to make him a masterpiece and to mould him platonically to his own idea."§ Carr, Earl of Somerset, was for the moment the royal favourite, and he at once opposed any special notice of a possible rival. But Villiers had made an impression, and in November he was appointed a cupbearer, an office which gave him occasional access to the King.

At the court there was already a strong feeling against Somerset, who was allied with the Spanish and Catholic party. He was " growing daily more wearisome " to the King, and several of his opponents now determined to

* Wotton, 308.　　　　　　　† Fuller, Worthies, Leic., 130.
‡ Burke, Rom. Rec., ii. 295.　　§ Wotton, 309.

set up Villiers against him. Archbishop Abbot was
employed to solicit the co-operation of the Queen, who
at last agreed to help, though after many refusals. "My
lord," she said, "you know not what you desire. If
Villiers gains the royal favour we shall all be sufferers.
I shall not be spared more than the others. The King
will teach him to treat us all with pride and contempt."*

On St. George's Day 1615 the cupbearer was appointed
a gentleman of the privy chamber with a salary of £1,000,
and next morning he was knighted. That year saw the
fall of Somerset, whose hectoring manners and unpopular
sympathies few regretted. Villiers stepped into his shoes.
He had not as yet any definite political ambitions, but
he had powerful friends behind him, and a promising
share of James' affection. He was still "modest and
affable, free from bribery, and ready for instruction,"†
and for this instruction he turned to Bacon, who lavished
on him the stores of his marvellous mind. In his Letter
of Advice he says to Villiers: "You are a new risen star:
let not your own negligence make you fall like a meteor."‡
But the idea of Bacon's which Villiers laid most to heart
was that of government by the few rather than by the
many—a policy which was to ruin both Charles' ministers
and to bring about the fall of the monarchy.

The promotion of the new favourite was rapid. In
January 1616 he was made Master of the Horse, in April
a Knight of the Garter, and in August a viscount, with
a grant of £80,000 in land. Five months later he was
sworn a privy councillor and created Earl of Buckingham,
and soon afterwards was appointed lord-lieutenant of that
county, being then just twenty-four. His bearing to the
King was engaging, his appearance radiant; he was genial,
amusing and ornamental; and at first he left matters of
State to wiser heads, concerning himself rather with those
of patronage. His income rose rapidly, and he was soon
worth £15,000 a year. His mother had still great influence
with him, and his earliest business was to provide good
places and satisfactory matches for his family. "He had

* Lingard, viii. 137, note.   † Gardiner, iii. 28.   ‡ Bacon, iii. 465.

a numerous and beautiful female kindred,"* and to them he devoted himself. Within the space of three years Edward, his eldest half-brother, was knighted, made Master of the Mint and Comptroller of the Court of Wards; John, another brother, "who had more wit and honesty than all," was made groom of the bedchamber to the Prince of Wales, married to an heiress, and created a viscount; while Christopher, a third brother, became Master of the Robes, and was given several grants of money. Eligible husbands were found for the sisters, and Lady Villiers was created a countess. Nor had the favourite's own honours come to an end. In 1618 he was advanced to be a marquess, and soon afterwards was appointed Lord High Admiral, Chief Justice of the Parks and Forests south of Trent, Master of the King's Bench office and Constable of Windsor Castle. The King showed no hesitation in his largess. " I confess," he said, " that I love him more than anyone else. . . . Christ had his John and I have my George."† He used to call Buckingham " Steenie " from a supposed resemblance to a picture of St. Stephen the Martyr. On his side the favourite was all smiles and submission. To James he used to sign himself " your poor slave and dogge;"‡ and on one occasion, asking for some jewels, he adds," your dogge will want a collar."§ At times James complained. Buckingham, he said, had given him " three notable servants: a gentleman of the bedchamber who could not truss a point, for he had but one hand; a chaplain who could not say prayers, for he scrupled the use of our liturgy; and a Secretary of State who could neither read nor write (Lord Conway)."||

By now Buckingham's influence and that of his mother were supreme. " Peerages were created, offices distributed, and ecclesiastical preferments conferred at his pleasure; his influence extended into the courts of law and every department of government; and crowds of applicants for his favour—peers, prelates and commoners—

* Fuller, W., Leic., 130.   † Gardiner, iii. 98.   ‡ Seward, i. 220.
§ Jesse, Stuarts, ii. 296. || Rapin, ii. 199, note.

were all careful to purchase it by large presents of money
or the grant of an annuity on their salaries."*

Bacon, the Lord Keeper, and Coke, the Chief Justice,
had to bow before him. The former would wait several
hours in Buckingham's antechamber until he was dismissed without an apology; the latter was struck off the
Privy Council for not giving his daughter with a sub-
stantial dowry to one of the Villiers brothers.

But his rapid success had made Buckingham scorn
advice, and his dubious ventures led him into frequent
difficulties. In 1621 he was mixed up with a sale of
monopolies, in which two of his brothers had also a considerable interest, and he did not scruple to suggest their
sacrifice in order to clear himself. Directly afterwards
came the impeachment of Bacon for bribery. Here again
Buckingham narrowly escaped, for he had been constantly
interfering with suits in chancery. He made some weak
attempts to save the Chancellor, and forced him to sell
York House in return; but in the result the philosopher
went down and the favourite crested the wave, boasting
that he was " Parliament-proof."

Buckingham had recently turned his attention to his own
marriage, and in 1620 had begun to court Lady Katherine
Manners, "the Rose of the Vale "—daughter of the Earl
of Rutland, a prominent Catholic. There is a tale that
he carried her off to his lodgings in Whitehall and kept
her there for some time until the old earl intervened.†
The King, however, opposed their union, and insisted
upon a nominal conversion of the lady before he would
allow it; but her Roman influence soon made itself felt
on her husband. Since the fall of Somerset and the
Howards, Buckingham had veered round to the Spanish
side of politics. James was anxious to support his son-
in-law, the Elector-Palatine, newly chosen King of Bohemia,
and he believed that the help of Spain could be secured
by a marriage between the Prince of Wales and the Infanta
Maria. The project was not new; Gondomar and Digby,
the respective ambassadors in London and Madrid, were

* Lingard, vii. 194.   † Burke, Rom. Rec., ii. 299.

privy to it, and Buckingham supported it. Accordingly, he and Prince Charles set out incognito for France and Spain, on a mission half of business and half of pleasure. It was an opportune moment for Buckingham to leave England, for he was already becoming unpopular, and he hoped to retrieve his position by effecting a promising dynastic alliance.

The two travellers " began their motion on Tuesday, 18th February, 1623, from the Marquis' house at Newhall in Essex; setting out with disguised beards and with borrowed names of Thomas and John Smith and attended by none but Sir Richard Graham, Master of the Horse to the Marquis."* After nearly being recognized by the ferryman at Gravesend, the mayor at Canterbury, and two German gentlemen at Boulogne, they arrived safely in Paris. Here " the prince spent one whole day in viewing of a famous city and court." The two also secured admission to the gallery of the palace " and saw at the practice of a masquing dance " two ladies with whom they were to have more to do in the future—Anne of Austria and Henrietta Maria, the French King's sister. From Paris they rode post to the frontier and in ten days they were at Madrid. They were received with the highest honours, for the Spanish had been deluded with a suggestion of the Prince's possible conversion. James writes to them: " The newes of youre gloriouse reception thaire makes me afrayed that ye will both miskenne your old dade hereafter."†

For eight months they remained in Spain. The Infanta and Charles were brought together, formal arrangements were made for the marriage, a papal dispensation applied for, and oaths exchanged. But James had no intention of making any concessions to the Spaniards on the point of religion, or without a definite undertaking of their co-operation in the Palatinate, and Count Olivares, the Spanish minister, was equally obdurate. Nor did the two envoys make themselves liked. Charles showed himself heartless and Buckingham immoral. The latter

* Wotton, 310. † Lingard, viii. 243, note.

was openly dissolute in a decorous court, and further offended the grandees by his familiar manners—they did not understand a nobleman who sat on a table and talked to his prince in shirt-sleeves. Worst of all, he quarrelled with the all-powerful Olivares: and even went so far as to attempt an intrigue with the minister's wife, who substituted a *fille de joie* for herself at the rendezvous. At their final interview Buckingham said to the count: " To the King, the Queen and the Princess I shall always prove myself a humble servant: to you never." " I am honoured by the compliment," was the reply.*

Thus when Charles returned to England nothing had been done beyond irritating the Spanish court, and Buckingham was soon as bitter against the marriage as he had previously been fervent for it. During his absence he had gained another step in the peerage, for a duke's patent had followed him out; there had been none in England since the execution of Norfolk fifty years before, and the revival of the rank was not auspicious.

Buckingham now began definitely to assume the place of a Chief Minister. His earliest programme was a war with Spain, but this was negatived by the Council. He succeeded, however, in bringing the marriage negotiations to an end, and then started a fresh proposal for Charles' alliance with a French princess, while he organized an attack on Middlesex, the Lord Treasurer, who was a supporter of the Spanish match. James was much annoyed at these proceedings. He told Buckingham " that he was a fool and was making a rod for his own back," and the prince " that he would live to have his belly full of impeachments."† But Middlesex was fined £50,000, imprisoned and excluded from Parliament, while the duke was offered the Lord-Lieutenancy of Ireland with the right of non-residence, an offer which he refused. " Buckingham," said the King, " had he knew not how many devils on him since his return."‡

The Spanish war and the French marriage were both

* Lingard, vii. 251.   † Clarendon, Hist., i. 23.
‡ Lingard, viii. 268.

pushed rapidly on. Troops were despatched to the Palatinate and special envoys to Paris. Richelieu, who knew that Buckingham could not afford to make a second failure, and that his credit depended on his success, exacted a promise of toleration for English Catholics as the price of his consent; and James hoped to see some silver lining to the cloud of war in the wedding of his only son. But he was not to live for the ceremony, for on March 27, 1625, he died, leaving his successor still under the domination of the favourite.

Buckingham was now appointed Chief Commissioner of War and general of the fleet and army. But he first undertook to see the marriage through. He led the embassy that was to bring over the princess, lavishing on it the splendour that so well became him. It is said that he took " twenty-seven suits of clothes, all as rich as invention could frame or art fashion. One, of white satin cut velvet, was set all over with diamonds, the value whereof was thought to be worth fourscore thousand pounds, besides a feather made with great diamonds, with sword, girdle, hatband and spurs with diamonds."* While in France, "he lost one of these stones at a state ball, but it was strangely recovered the next morning in a court full of pages."†

Nor did he limit himself to display, for he made violent love to Anne of Austria, who had accompanied her sister-in-law as far as Amiens. It is doubtful if he advanced far in her graces, but he did not hesitate to advertise his success, for he left the princess at Abbeville and posted back to Amiens, where he burst into the Queen's bedchamber in front of her attendants. He was ordered to leave, and the insult was resented by Louis and revenged by Richelieu, the Cardinal being perhaps actuated, as Dumas suggests, by jealousy no less than policy. To the duke the result of his visit to France was as damaging as had been that of his journey to Spain.

In the meanwhile preparations for war were going on

* Lingard, viii. 311.
† Wotton, 314; Gardiner questions these tales, v. 330, note.

and supplies were required. Buckingham, as Lord High Admiral, had paid some attention to the state of the fleet and had done his best to appoint capable officers. He had further purchased for himself the wardenship of the Cinque Ports, being determined to keep the control of any naval expedition in his own hands. But he was unable to secure the assistance that he counted on from France, or the credits that he needed from Parliament. The Commons said " that they had heard much about the war but were ignorant who was the enemy," and they criticized the Lord High Admiral's lack of experience. " It is not fit," said Phelips, " to repose the safety of the Kingdom upon those who have not parts answerable to their places."*

Owing to an epidemic in London the session was adjourned to Oxford, and there, in Christ Church Hall, Buckingham summoned both Houses before him and presented a naval policy which he did not appear to understand. But although " the government was centred in his person,"† he effected nothing, the complaints against him increased, and by August the King found it best to dissolve Parliament.

During the autumn the duke went on with his scheme of a continental alliance against Spain, himself crossing to Holland and concluding treaties with Denmark and the States General. An expedition was despatched to Cadiz, but it returned without having achieved any success, and in the interim troubles had arisen with France. Richelieu complained that the English Catholics were not receiving the toleration promised them, and Buckingham accused the French navy of convoying Spanish merchant men. Parliament had not granted sufficient supplies for any large military operations, and the King, having tried to pawn the crown jewels in Holland, turned to illegal methods of raising money, levying unauthorized duties, requiring benevolences, and suspending the payment of salaries. At the coronation, early in 1626, when Buckingham officiated as Lord High Constable, considerable sulkiness was shown by the people. As the King was mounting the

* Gardiner, v. 429. † *Ibid.*, v. 418.

steps of the daïs the duke offered his arm as a support, but Charles was heard to say to him: "I have more need to help you than you have to help me."*

Buckingham now entered upon the final stage of his career, and Charles upon his first struggle with Parliament. Early in the session the duke was charged with neglect of his naval duties, with engrossing lands and offices for himself, and with subverting justice in the interest of his friends. The fact that his mother and his father-in-law were Catholics, and that British ships had been lent to France to aid in reducing the Huguenots of La Rochelle, added to the grievance. On May 8, 1626, he was impeached in the Commons, and his dismissal demanded. Charles replied by forcing the University of Cambridge to elect his favourite as their chancellor, and by threatening again to dissolve Parliament. The Lords petitioned that they should be given two days more. "Not a minute," said the King, and on June 15 the Parliament ended. As Buckingham observed: "The King would place the defence of him, the duke, before his own interest."† The Queen, however, was already jealous of his influence. On one occasion, when she had told him her mind, Buckingham boldly warned her to beware; "that there had been queens in England who had lost their heads."‡ But his position was not nearly as strong as it had been. On his leaving London some bands of unpaid sailors stopped his coach, and when he left the city the mob shouted after him, "Begone for ever."§

During the autumn the affairs of Charles' brother-in-law, the Prince Palatine, became desperate, and the Protestant allies were badly beaten on the Elbe. English relations with France had got worse, and Buckingham suggested going himself to Paris as ambassador. This proposal, however, was at once rejected by Louis XIII., and it was then resolved to send an expedition in support of the French Huguenots, whom Richelieu was attacking. To get money for this, Charles raised a forced loan through-

* D'Ewes, i. 293.　　　　† Lingard, viii. 291, note.
‡ Clarendon, Hist., i. 60.　　§ Gardiner, vi. 128, 138.

out England, and collected tonnage and poundage on merchandise without legal sanction. By various shifts Buckingham managed to get together a fleet of transports and from 6,000 to 7,000 troops. In June 1627 he sailed for La Rochelle, and on July 12 he landed on the Isle de Rhé and commenced the siege of the fort of St. Martin. But his military efforts were fruitless, disease decimated his men, and the inhabitants of Rochelle hesitated to accept foreign aid. In September a French flotilla broke through the English blockade, and late in October Buckingham, after a vain attempt to storm the fortress, was forced to retreat. He behaved with conspicuous gallantry, and was himself the last to leave the beach, but the embarkation cost nearly 4,000 casualties and twenty pairs of colours; and when in November he landed in England, " the mislike of all men against him, at his coming safe home, occasioned almost as much sorrow as the slaughter and perishing of all the rest."* The expedition had been a complete fiasco, though the charges of treachery which were afterwards brought against him were never substantiated.

He continued nevertheless to press his arbitrary advice on the King; new expeditions were devised, a standing army was advocated, and ship money was levied. The Commons became more restive, and when in June 1628 Charles returned an evasive answer to the Petition of Right, a member remarked that "The Duke of Bucks is the cause of all our miseries: till the King be informed thereof we shall never sit here with honour."† As Warwick says, "His want of experience, as having never seen the reverse of fortune, made him too great an enterpriser to succeed."‡

By now Buckingham was the most hated man in the kingdom. "His fame remained more and more in obloquy amongst the mass of the people . . . so as he saw plainly that he must go abroad again to rectify his own reputation."§ He had lost his hold on the Lords,

* D'Ewes, i. 368.   † D. N. B., lviii. 335.
‡ Warwick, 15.   § Wotton, 319.

while the Commons threatened to impeach him a second time, saying that no man could manage " so many and weighty affairs as he had undertaken," and they asked that he should be removed from all the King's counsels. But Charles was still under the control of his friend, and Buckingham was still fixed on retrieving his lost laurels. At last some subsidies were granted in exchange for Charles' assent to the Petition.   But the organization of the troops remained hopelessly deficient; on August 6 Buckingham writes: " I find nothing of more difficulty and uncertainty than the preparations for this service of Rochelle.   Every man says he has all things ready, and yet all remains as it were at a stand."*

At this juncture Charles had just secured two new counsellors, Laud, who had been made Bishop of London, and Wentworth, who had come over from the Opposition. Buckingham remembered Somerset, and saw that, to maintain his position, he needed some striking success. On August 17, 1628, he posted off to Portsmouth to hurry forward his next expedition.   The outcry against him was considerable: in the streets an attack was made on him by drunken or mutinous sailors; his physician, Lamb, fell a victim to the mob; and ominous rhymes pursued him.

> " Let Charles and George do what they can
> The Duke shall die like Dr. Lamb."†

It was said that he had presentiments of his death; but he had refused to disguise himself or to wear a coat of mail, which he called " a silly defence against any popular fray; and as for a single man's assault he took himself to be in no danger."‡   But he asked Laud to protect his wife and children with the King: " Some adventure," he said, " may kill me as well as another."

On August 22 he was somewhat indisposed, and the King came to see him at the house in which he was lodging at Portsmouth.   " At his majesty's departing the duke embraced him in a very unusual and passionate manner."§

* D.N.B., lviii. 336.   † D'Ewes, i. 378.   ‡ Wotton, 320.   § Ibid., 321.

Early the next morning, just as he had finished breakfast, he came out into the hall of his house. A half-pay naval officer, named Felton, was waiting there, and instantly struck him to the heart with a knife. The duke staggered and fell down, saying, " God's wounds, the villain hath killed me!"* In a few minutes he was dead. The duchess was dressing in an upper room, and the house was full of his attendants, but the whole business was almost instantaneous. The news was hurriedly taken to the King, who was in church. It was whispered to him by one of the lords in waiting, " but his Majesty continued unmoved and without the least change in his countenance, till prayers were ended, when he suddenly departed to his chamber and threw himself upon his bed, lamenting with much passion and abundance of tears. ' Who,' said he, ' can prevent a stroke from heaven ?' "† " He continued in this melancholic discomposure for many days . . . and from that time almost to the time of his own death he admitted very few into any degree of trust who had ever discovered themselves to be enemies to the duke, or against whom he had manifested a notable prejudice."‡ The assassin gave himself up and was quickly executed. He maintained that he had done the deed for no private enmity, " but to serve God, the King and his country," and the people hailed him as a public benefactor.

The duke was privately buried at Westminster Abbey, the King paying his debts of over £60,000, and taking his family under his especial care. In 1635 his widow married the Marquess of Antrim. Of his two sons George, who succeeded to the title, became a dissolute and dangerous politician, and died without legitimate issue, while Francis, who never married, was killed in the Civil War at the age of nineteen; his daughter Mary, though thrice a wife, left no children.

Thus perished at the early age of thirty-six George Villiers, Duke of Buckingham, who surpassed, in the

* D'Ewes, i. 368.   † Clarendon, Hist., i. 47; D'Ewes, i. 86.
    ‡ Clarendon, i. 48.

rapidity of his rise, the wealth and honours he engrossed and the royal favour he enjoyed, all favourites, and who owed most of his successes to his handsome face and fascinating manners. "He had," says Gardiner, "been even more than a modern Prime Minister is in a modern Cabinet. His word had given the impulse to the whole machinery of government. Every act had been submitted to his approval. Every office had been filled by his followers."*

He was a man of extraordinary charm, tall, slender, with a pointed beard, flashing eyes, and a wonderful complexion. D'Ewes, who had little love for him, describes him in 1620 as "full of delicacy, his hands and feet especially effeminate and curious."† Clarendon gives his character at length: "This great man was a person of noble nature and generous disposition. He understood the arts of a court and all the learning that is requisite there exactly well. By long practice under a master that discoursed excellently he had obtained a quick conception and apprehension of business, and had the habit of speaking very gracefully and pertinently. He was of a most flowing courtesy and affability to all men who made any address to him; of a courage not to be daunted . . . and at the Isle of Rhé no man was more fearless and more ready to expose himself. His single misfortune was that he never made a noble and a worthy friendship with a man so near his equal that he would frankly advise him for his honour and true interest against the current, or rather the torrent, of his impetuous passion. He was such a darling of fortune that he was at the top before he was well seen at the bottom, and he was supreme the first month he came to court. Yet he was in his nature just, candid and bountiful."‡

He was never a great dissimulator, but as vehement to his enemies as to his friends. He was, says Green, "amazingly ignorant," but this did not deter him from laying down the law; his conversation was sparkling, his cheerfulness in all circumstances unabashed. To his

* Gardiner, vi. 360.   † D'Ewes, i. 167.   ‡ Clarendon, Hist., i. 48.

gallantry he set no bridle. When he attended church it was " to wink and smile at comely young women being baptized,"* and his amours in Spain, in France and in his own country did almost as much harm as his policy. His luxury was phenomenal: houses, gardens, clothes, horses, banquets, racing and play shared his attention with politics. He is said to have been the first person who used a sedan chair in England or drove a coach-and-six. In the arts he had an extensive taste. By 1625 he already possessed pictures " worth three times more than they cost. For a collection made by Rubens he gave £10,000; Wotton bought largely for him in Venice; and Lord Arundel offered him £7,000 for Titian's ' Ecce Homo.' "† His unpopularity was latterly extreme, and " at his death he had already passed the meridian of his greatness . . . if he had escaped the knife of the assassin he would perhaps have fallen by the axe of the executioner."‡ Macaulay calls him " a weak, violent and dissolute adventurer, who, with no talents or acquirements but those of a mere courtier, had in a great crisis of foreign and domestic politics ventured on the part of Prime Minister."§ Gardiner stigmatizes him as " among the most incapable ministers of this or any other country."‖

It is difficult to dissent from these judgments, for Buckingham's abilities were quite unequal to his fortunes, and his character has little to redeem it. His opportunities were immense, his achievements dangerously evil. Not content to follow the rôle of a favourite or to limit his activities to a court, he insisted on plunging into the maelstrom of great affairs—he became a vain apostle of kingcraft and the harbinger of rebellion. Even as a hero of romance he played a sorry part, while as a minister he was a disaster. In his brief spell of power he had pitted himself in love and war against Richelieu and Olivares, the two wiliest heads in Europe, and had outraged the pride of the Kings of France and Spain, the two proudest

* D'Ewes, i. 389. † Jesse, Stuarts, ii. 280-1.
‡ Lingard, viii. 341. § Macaulay, v. 551-2.
‖ Gardiner, vi. 358.

P. Rubens *pinx.*

GEORGE VILLIERS
DUKE OF BUCKINGHAM

To face page 310

monarchs of Christendom. He had taught his master to spurn his people, to steal their money, and to sacrifice their blood. When the reckoning came it was as swift as it was complete.

II.—STRAFFORD

Thomas Wentworth, afterwards Earl of Strafford, was born in Chancery Lane, London, on April 13, 1593. He was the eldest son of Sir William Wentworth, of Wentworth Woodhouse in Yorkshire, and of Anne, daughter of Robert Atkinson, of Stowell, Gloucestershire, a bencher of Lincoln's Inn.

The Wentworths were a very ancient family, divided into several branches and settled in various parts of England. They had included a Lord Chancellor and a Bishop of London in the days of Edward III., had received a barony from Henry VIII., and were connected with the Houses of Plantagenet, Despencer, Tiptoft and Seymour. The owners of Wentworth Woodhouse, though the elder and richer division, had not achieved any special honours, but they were among the leading families in their county, and to that position they attached great importance.

Sir William Wentworth was an ordinary country squire, his wife " a wise, learned and religious lady." Their son Thomas was sent first to St. John's College, Cambridge, and having attained some distinction there he was entered at the Inner Temple. In October 1611 he was married to Lady Margaret Clifford, eldest daughter of Francis, fourth Earl of Cumberland, and a month later was knighted, his father having just been made a baronet. In 1614 he was elected one of the members for Yorkshire, and in the same year he succeeded to the baronetcy and some £6,000 a year—" a splendid fortune in those days, even though encumbered by provisions for seven brothers and four sisters."*

He did not speak in his first session of Parliament, but

* McDiarmid, 256.

21

occupied himself with the law and his family affairs. His brother-in-law, Sir George Savile, had just died, and Wentworth was left to look after two nephews. He was a zealous guardian, embarking in several chancery suits to protect their inheritance, and making "as many as thirty journeys to London" on their account. In the country he hawked a little, read much, and looked after his property. He took an active part in county business, and in 1615 was nominated *custos rotulorum* of the West Riding, in place of Sir John Savile dismissed. Savile, however, succeeded a little later in retrieving Lord Buckingham's favour, and Wentworth then received a letter from the favourite telling him that the resignation of his new office would be well received. But Wentworth, even at the age of twenty-four, was not a man to surrender anything easily, and he answered explaining that he had not sought the place, which had been freely granted him. His view was accepted. Writing in September 1617, the minister says: " I am so far from doing the least indignity to any gentleman of your worth that I would be ready upon any occasion to do you the best service I can. Your assured friend G. Buckingham."* A lifelong quarrel between Savile and Wentworth was the result.

For four years there had been no Parliament, but at the election of 1621 Wentworth defeated his former rival and was again chosen a member for his county. He now removed his family into London " at the Austin Friars." Besides his Parliamentary duties he attended regularly in the court of Star Chamber, where he acquired considerable knowledge of legal practice. His health was not good: in 1622 " he had a great fever," and in that year he lost his wife. He went back to Yorkshire for a time, " but in the next spring he had a double tertian, and after his recovery a relapse into a single tertian, and a burning fever."† Later on he suffered severely from gout, which was to pursue him all his life.

In February 1625 he was married for the second time,

* Strafford, i. 4. † *Ibid.*, ii. 430.

his wife being Lady Arabella Holles, daughter of John, first Earl of Clare. She was "a lady exceeding comely and beautiful, and yet much more lovely in the endowments of her mind;"* to her and to her memory her husband was always devoted.

A month later King Charles came to the throne. Wentworth was now beginning to take a prominent part in the House of Commons debates. He had disliked the foreign policy of the late reign, being anxious to avoid war on the Continent; "his policy was purely English and in domestic legislation he took the deepest interest."† But while firm in opposition he was also moderate, and was ready to compromise with the King's party. He was against the Puritans, and willing enough to support a strong government, though he had little respect for that of the Duke of Buckingham.

In 1625 he lost his seat to Savile, but was soon re-elected. His influence was thought worth conciliating, and Buckingham now attempted to secure him for the court. Wentworth.replied that "he was ready to serve him as an honest man and a gentleman,"‡ but he did not cease to oppose the Spanish War and to insist upon petitions being considered before supplies. The King's threats of dissolution did not help matters forward. Wentworth's independence was aroused, and he took a strong line against Buckingham's methods. In consequence, although Charles called him "an honest gentleman,"§ he was pricked as sheriff for his county, a duty which precluded him from sitting in Parliament. This did not deter him from writing to the Secretary of State and asking for the high office of President of York, the head of the Council that ruled the northern parts of the kingdom. "I am fully resolved," he says, "not to ascend one step of this kind except as a special obligation to my lord Duke, whose bounty and goodness I do acknowledge."|| The place, however, was not vacant, and the demand was thought preposterous; soon afterwards Wentworth's

---

* Strafford, ii. 430.   † Gardiner, iv. 238.   ‡ Strafford, i. 34.
§ Gardiner, vi. 33. || Traill, 14.

name was taken off the commission of the peace, and he was dismissed with some indignity from his place of *custos rotulorum*, which was again given to Savile. It is probable that the real reason was his having refused to countenance the collection of the King's " free gifts."

This slight threw Wentworth still more on to the popular side, and when in 1627 a forced loan was demanded under a writ of Privy Seal, he refused to pay his quota of £40. He was accordingly committed to the Marshalsea and there remained for six weeks, after which he was allowed to live at Dartford in a kind of open arrest. But in 1628 he was back again in the House of Commons, taking a stronger line than ever against the Minister's policy. There he seemed " to have a casting voice: for where he was pleased to dispose his Yea or Nay, there went the affirmative or the negative."*

He now spoke continually and with vehemence against benevolences, billeting and loans. He condemned the French and Spanish wars, and he inveighed against government by the Privy Council. " We must vindicate," he said, " our lawful and vital liberties, by reinforcing the ancient laws made by our ancestors. Our desires are modest and just. I speak both for the interest of the King and the people. If we enjoy not these [liberties], it will be impossible to relieve him."† When subsidies were asked for Wentworth delayed their grant, and at last it became clear to Charles and Buckingham that he was their most dangerous opponent—"the man who hath the greatest sway in Parliament." " His leadership of the Commons in this session," says Gardiner, " was the brightest, noblest period of his life."‡ There he was regarded as a champion of the people's rights; Eliot, Pym and the leaders of democracy were among his friends, and it was largely due to his efforts that the Petition of Right was forced on Charles. " He had laid the foundation "§ of this great statute, and of it the Speaker writes to him on May 28, 1628: " I pray God send us good success

* Fuller, W. Lond., 210. † Traill, 21.
‡ Gardiner, vi. 338. § Gardiner, vi. 237.

in our great Business to-morrow. No man I know can
further advance it than yourself, and I assure myself no
man is more willing to see all settled in perfect Peace
and Happiness."*

On June 7 the Petition of Right received the royal
assent, and on the 26th the Parliament was prorogued.
Eighteen days later, on July 14, it was suddenly announced that Wentworth had been created a peer. The
news was received by the popular leaders with the utmost
dismay and astonishment, for to all it seemed a political
apostasy. The death of Buckingham followed almost at
once, and three months later the new lord was advanced
to a viscounty and appointed to the office he had coveted,
Lord President of the North.

Various explanations have been given of this remarkable and apparently unexpected *volte-face*. Wentworth's
apologists maintain that he was honestly converted to
the King's views; his critics stigmatize it as simple bribery;
while some suggest that he had opposed the authorities
only to exact from them place and power. Sir Philip
Warwick says that he had " discerned the immoderate
designs of some popular leading persons."† Radcliffe, his
constant and intimate friend, records the transaction
without comment:—

" 1628. June, the Parliament ended: Reconciled to
the Duke of Buckingham. July he was made Baron
Wentworth, Newmarsh and Oversley by Patent; but the
Lord Savile was made Baron before him. In Michaelmas
Term he was made Viscount Wentworth (solemnly created)
and President of York."‡

History, indeed, has never clearly solved the problem,
but a combination of circumstances was probably responsible for the change. Wentworth saw that Buckingham
was daily losing credit; he believed that the King's
mistakes were due to evil counsellors, and that he could
replace them himself with a sounder policy; and he was
anxious to regain the pre-eminence in his own county.
His ruling idea hitherto had been to reconcile King and

* Strafford, i. 46.   † Warwick, 48.   ‡ Strafford, ii. 430.

Parliament; now that that had failed he preferred to protect the constitution. Gardiner concludes that his only real thought was "how the King's government was to be carried on. In the maintenance and elevation of the royal authority lay for him henceforth the only path of safety and wisdom."* However it may be, from this moment Wentworth, the former protagonist of liberty, became the chief promoter of autocracy. A tale is told that before he left London for the North his old colleague, Pym, said to him: "You are going to leave us; but we will never leave you while your head is on your shoulders."†

Wentworth had now obtained a great office. He had become an administrator, a financier and a judge, for the Council of York wielded all the jurisdiction of the courts of common law and chancery, as well as that of the Star Chamber. The northern counties were under a separate and more arbitrary rule than the rest of England, and the President united in himself nearly all the powers of the Council. The new incumbent was to exercise them to the full.

Early in 1629 a short and stormy session showed the Commons that their recent victories were nugatory, and in March, after another dissolution, the King began to govern alone, advised and supported by Bishop Laud.

Away in the North Wentworth applied himself seriously to his duties and showed his master that he was both a loyal and an efficient servant. In November 1629 he was admitted to the Privy Council, and there he made friends with Laud, who was as much opposed to the Presbyterians as Wentworth had become to extreme Parliamentarians. In Yorkshire his government was firm and just. He stood strictly upon the privileges and ceremony of his position, though he met with plenty of opposition among the local magnates. Mr. Bellasis, the son of Lord Fauconberg, who omitted to remove his hat when the Lord President left his seat, was summoned before the Council in London and made to apologize formally in York; Sir Thomas Layton, the county sheriff,

* Gardiner, vii. 134.   † Seward, i. 323.

was imprisoned for contempt of court for not immediately obeying the President's order to appear before him. Such methods were severe, but they were salutary; the North had always been bold, factious and independent.

Wentworth possessed a dauntless temper, and he was determined to uphold the rights of the Crown; he was not to be put aside by criticism or panic. " None of these clamours or apprehensions," he writes, " shall shake me or cause me to decline my master's honour and service, thereby to soothe these popular frantic humours. . . . I have not so learnt my master, nor am I so indulgent to my own ease as to see his affairs suffer shipwreck, whilst myself rest secure in harbour. No, let the tempest be never so great, I will much rather put forth to sea, work forth the storm, or at least be found dead with the rudder in my hands."*

This utter fearlessness, this absolute sincerity, made him a minister of far other mettle than Charles had yet known. When a matter touched him nearly he did not hesitate to employ exceptional means, writing to the judges to influence the course of justice in the direction he believed right. The King realized that he had got a master mind to serve him, and in 1632 Wentworth was appointed Lord Deputy of Ireland, though still retaining his presidency at York.

He had just lost his second and favourite wife in childbed, and he now married for the third time Elizabeth, daughter of Sir Francis Rodes. She seems to have felt that she was not quite equal to the position she was called upon to fill, perhaps with reason, for Wentworth tells her: " It is no presumption in you to write to me. You succeed in this family two of the rarest ladies of their time. Equal them in the excellent dispositions of your mind."†

In July 1633 the Lord Deputy sent forward his household to Dublin. In St. George's Channel a privateer, *The Pickpocket of Dover*, seized his goods to the value of £4,000, with £500 worth of linen—" a cold welcome," he

* Traill, 57, 58. † *Ibid.*, 78.

called it. One of his first acts on arriving was to suppress
such pirates, most of them Spaniards, and within a year
he had swept them from the seas. Ireland was in an
unruly and impecunious state. It was governed by
Englishmen who paid little attention to native needs,
but ruled on the colonial system. Wentworth set himself
to redress this, with the object of making the island
prosperous in itself and also remunerative to the
Crown. His ideas, embodied in the word " thorough,"
were to concentrate the royal power in a small but dis-
ciplined army, to place public before private interests,
to reform the Protestant Church and to expand trade.
Ability and authority were in his eyes the chief requisites
for a ruler; Gardiner questions if, like Thomas Cromwell,
he may not have been a student of Machiavelli.

He kept the King constantly informed of his doings,
and the King approved them. Writing in October 1633,
Charles says:

" WENTWORTH,
" I hope you have found by effects, or to say better
by the doing myself no hurt as yet, the answer in part
of those letters you wrote unto me: likewise my approba-
tion.
" Your loving friend,
" CHARLES R."*

Wentworth replies: " I shall always esteem it a great
honour for me to take the Envy to myself and singly to
apply the advantage to your Majesty."† And at the
New Year he adds: " With this letter I send an ingot of
silver of three hundred ounces, being the first that ever
was got in Ireland."‡

The army in Ireland was now brought into a high state
of efficiency. Trade was encouraged. By careful administration the Irish revenues were increased and they gradually
rose from an annual deficit of £20,000 to a surplus of
£60,000. In 1634 an Irish Parliament was summoned,

* Strafford, i. 140.　　† Ibid., i. 165.　　‡ Ibid.

and by a close majority six subsidies were voted for payment of the royal debts. Immediately after the prorogation Wentworth, who was always inclined to be a little in advance, asked for an earldom. Charles, however, refused, preferring to originate his favours himself. Two years later a similar request met with the same reply.

In the meanwhile perilous matters were making in England. Since 1629 no Parliament had sat, and the King's resources for carrying on the ordinary government were rapidly disappearing. But his counsellors and his own ingenuity discovered new and revived old methods. From the nobles large sums were collected for their encroachments on the royal forests; on the gentry fines were levied in distraint of knighthood; to trading companies monopolies were granted for the sole rights of selling such articles as soap, starch and beer; while the city corporations were amerced in considerable amounts on nearly any pretext. A fresh tax was now started by the introduction of " ship money," an aid dating from the days of the Danes. Its incidence on the maritime towns was at first tolerated, but when the inland counties were also called upon to pay, strong resentment was felt. Wentworth, however, went further. He had already been spoken of as likely to fill the vacant place of Lord Treasurer, for his reputation as an economist was considerable, and his counsel carried weight. He now observed that " since it was lawful for the King to impose a tax towards the equipment of the navy, it must be equally so for the levy of the army. . . . Moreover, what is law in England is law also in Scotland and Ireland."* The latter opinion was important, for the Scots, irritated by the new ritual that Laud, now Archbishop, was imposing, were promising trouble, and the King had to consider means to coerce them.

In Ireland affairs had improved. Wentworth had reformed Church, State, finance and trade, and had made the army a real weapon. He had introduced the linen manufacture into Ulster, and was reclaiming large tracts

* Strafford, ii. 61, 62.

of land for the Crown in the wilds of Connaught. But his despotic temper handicapped his success. Lord Mountnorris, the Vice-Treasurer of Ireland, had come under his displeasure for some small irregularity, and his younger brother, an officer in a foot regiment, for a breach of military discipline. A few days later one of Mountnorris's kinsmen, a gentleman usher at the vice-regal court, dropped a footstool on the Lord Deputy's gouty foot. Mountnorris alluded to this in a careless way at dinner, saying that "his brother would not take such a revenge." The words were magnified into a treasonable threat to murder the King's representative, and Mountnorris was summoned before the Council, tried by court-martial, and ordered to be shot. The sentence was of course remitted, but the offender was dismissed the army, and the tale re-echoed through Ireland to the detriment of Wentworth. Later on another unfortunate incident occurred. This time it was with Loftus, the Irish Lord Chancellor, as regards a settlement on his son's marriage. The matter was brought judicially before the Lord Deputy, and by him decided against Loftus. It was then alleged that the judgment was partial, and that Wentworth had debauched the lady concerned, the Chancellor's daughter-in-law. Loftus disputed the jurisdiction, refused to abide by the sentence, and in the result was deprived of the Great Seal. The rights of the case were never exactly known, but their effect upon Wentworth's reputation were very damaging, and he found it necessary to go over to England and justify his general administration.

His chief friend in the Council was Laud, who voiced his interests and seconded his views. The opportunity for his advance to higher office had now come, for Charles was in extreme need of a minister, of money, and of troops to deal with his northern kingdom. Wentworth could supply all three, and he acquired a new position in the royal favour. His advice began to be taken on matters outside his viceroyalty. In 1637 he writes to Laud that "Mr. Hampden and others to his likeness should be well

whipped into their right senses."* He discouraged the
King from a foreign war, and concentrated on the troubles
at home. Ireland was secure, but although it had
prospered from a material point of view, and had become
more valuable to England, Wentworth's rule had been so
arbitrary that he " had prepared the way for a terrible
reaction."† He had raised up enemies there whose
opportunity was soon to come. In the words of one
who knew him well, he was " of great observation and
piercing judgment, both in things and persons; but his
too good skill in persons made him judge the worse of
things . . . and he relied wholly upon himself. Of all
his passions his pride was the most predominant "‡: " he
endeavoured to be just to all, but resolved to be gracious
to none but to those who affected him."§

Charles had determined to lead an army against his
native Scots to coerce them into obedience. That army
lay ready in Ireland, with a commander well fitted to
carry through his policy. In 1639 Wentworth was sent
for, and in September " he went into England, passing
from the bar of Dublin to the bar of Chester in thirteen
hours."‖ He now became Charles's principal adviser, and
in fact his Chief Minister. His first business was to raise
money, but the treasury was empty, the London merchants
refused any more loans, and his attempts to obtain one
from Spain were fruitless. " About Christmas he was
made Earl of Strafforde (which is the name of the wapen-
take or hundred in which his house stands) and Lord-
Lieutenant of Ireland. He then moved the King for a
Parliament in Ireland, which was instantly summoned,
and afterwards for a Parliament in England, against the
coming of the New Year."¶

Early in 1640 the Short Parliament met. There had
been no Legislature for eleven years, and the country was
boiling with anger. Strafford took the lead in the House
of Lords, threatening a dissolution unless supplies were

---

* Strafford, ii. 136, 156. † Ransome, 238.
‡ Clarendon, Hist., 1403. § Warwick, 111.
‖ Strafford, ii. 431. ¶ *Ibid.*

voted. In Lent he returned to Ireland, whence he wrote offering the King his troops. "After a stay of about a fortnight he embarked for England on April 3, being sick of a flux and the gout." On his arrival in England he again fell ill, for being visited by the King he had taken off his gown and had caught a fresh chill. When he recovered the Parliament was dissolved. Lord Northumberland had been named to command the army for Scotland, but he was indisposed or unwilling to go, and accordingly "the Earl of Strafforde was stayed from going into Ireland and made Lieutenant-General of the English forces and sent into the North, where the English army was."* Lord Conway was already there in temporary command, and before his chief's arrival he advanced against the Covenanters. But in August he was compelled to retire; the Scots crossed the border, and the two northern counties were soon under their control. Strafford was able to keep the Yorkshiremen loyal, but he was still ailing, and well aware of the detestation in which he was held both by English and Scots: "To the popular imagination 'Black Tom Tyrant' was the embodiment of arbitrary power."† "He will not suffer a gard to attend him, knowing he hath terror enough in his bended browes to amaze the prentices."‡ The King, however, clung to him, and in September gave him the Garter, his last gift.

Charles' position was now lamentable. He was engaged in a civil war without the sanction of his people or his Parliament; he had no means of carrying it on; and the only methods by which he could obtain money were illegal and likely to lead to greater disturbance. A Great Council was held at York, but it was of no avail, and at last, in November 1640, he was forced to summon his fifth and final Parliament, which was to outlast his own life. Its first acts were to impeach Strafford, the Lord-Lieutenant of Ireland, Laud, the Archbishop of Canterbury, and Finch, the Lord Chancellor. The third-named fled the country, the second hesitated and was lost, but

* Strafford, ii. 431.　　† Warner, ii. 369.　　‡ Cokayne, vii. 264.

Strafford came straight up to London "with more dangers beset than any man ever went out of Yorkshire." "I will go," he said, "and look my accusers in the face."

On November 3 he appeared in the House of Lords, and was making his way to his seat, "with a proud glooming countenance,"* when Pym presented himself at the bar with a resolution of the Commons for his impeachment. The Lords would hardly hear Strafford; he was committed to Black Rod and sent to the Tower, "no man capping him, but all crying 'What is the matter?'" A month later he was followed there by Laud.

With their enemies safely housed Parliament then sat down to work. During the winter the Triennial Act was passed, a commission was issued to remove images and altars from churches, and a motion was introduced to exclude bishops from the Upper House. The articles of impeachment against Strafford were next prepared; they amounted to nearly a hundred. Their gist was "that he had traitorously endeavoured to subvert the fundamental laws of the realms of England and Ireland and to introduce an arbitrary and tyrannical government."† But though the greatest pains were taken to collect evidence sufficient, it hardly amounted to treason. "The law of England," says Hallam, "is silent as to conspiracies against itself." Hasty expressions that Strafford had uttered, questionable actions in his government, dubious commercial ventures, billeting of troops and the like, were all that could be found.

On January 30, 1641, he was brought up to hear them read, and on March 22 his trial began in Westminster Hall. The managers for the Commons included Pym, Hampden, Digby, St. John and most of his former friends, and for nearly three weeks they pressed their suit against him. Eloquent and convincing, he repelled the charges, " daily gaining affection with the simple sort, and especially with the ladies."‡ The most damaging count was an alleged remark to the King at a Council: "You have an army in

* Carlyle, xi. 226.   † Lords Journals, iv. 97.   ‡ Carlyle, xi. 232.

Ireland with which you may reduce this kingdom."*
Did the words "this kingdom" refer to England or to
Scotland ? The prosecutors chose the worst interpretation.
The tale was founded on a private note of Sir Henry Vane's,
one of the Secretaries of State, from whose desk it had
been taken by his son, Strafford's most inveterate opponent. Gradually, however, it became clear that there
was little chance of a conviction for treason, and Strafford's
enemies began to devise other means. "The proceeding
in a judicial way was laid aside,"† and on April 10 a bill
of attainder was introduced in the Commons. St. John,
in bringing it before the Lords, observed that "it was
never accounted cruelty or foul play to knock foxes and
wolves on the head, as they can be found, because these
be beasts of prey: the warrener sets traps for powlcats
and other vermin for preservation of the warren."‡

Against this new procedure Strafford again made a
brilliant and affecting defence—"the best of all speeches,"
says Carlyle, "that has yet been printed in the English
tongue." He observed that his counsel had been given
in honesty and secrecy, and he disputed the justice or
the wisdom of such *ex post facto* methods. "Let us not,
my Lords, be ambitious to be more learned in these killing
arts than our forefathers were before us."§ But he
spoke to deaf ears. On April 21 the bill passed the
Commons by 204 votes to 59. Two days later Charles
wrote to Strafford assuring him "on the word of a King"
that he should not "suffer in life, honour or fortune. . . .
This is but justice, and therefor but a very mean reward
from a master to so faithful and able a servant as you
have shown yourself to be. Yet it is as much as I con-
ceive the present time will permit, though none shall
hinder me from being your constant, faithful friend
Charles R."‖

Undoubtedly Charles wished to save Strafford, but he
only helped to ruin him. He went down to the House of
Lords on April 30, summoned the Commons before him,

* Carlyle, 180. † Strafford, ii. 430. ‡ Harl. Mis., v. 82.
§ Traill, 184. ‖ *Ibid.*, 193.

and told them that he could not admit Strafford's treason, but would allow his misdemeanour and dispense with his services. This speech was construed as an interference with current legislation, a breach of privilege, and it again roused the popular party. Stories of Strafford's intended escape were set about. The King was said to have sent a hundred men of his Guard to the Tower, where they were refused admittance by the Lieutenant, while a ship was waiting in the Thames to carry the prisoner off. Excitement and passion were general. The people were egged on to support the Commons, the streets were filled with placards against Strafford, the names of his supporters were posted on the walls, and the avenues to Palace Yard and Whitehall were crowded with an armed and shouting mob. At last coercion succeeded. On May 8 the bill of attainder passed the Lords by 26 to 9; out of eighty peers who had attended the trial, only half came up to vote. But the Inflexibles won the day.

The onus was now cast upon the King; his position was difficult for a strong man, pitiable for him. During Sunday the 9th he debated the matter with the Queen, the bishops and the judges. Strafford wrote to him releasing him " from all his former promises and engagements to save his life: which his lordship thought would be the best discharge of the King's conscience." The Queen, it was said, had the deciding voice; she was no friend of Strafford's; and early on the Monday morning Charles signed a commission for the royal assent to be given. That day the bill became law. One more attempt the King made to save his servant's life, sending the young Prince of Wales to the House of Lords with a letter begging for a commutation " to endeare it the more I have chosen him to carry it that of all your House is most deare to me." But nothing was of any avail, and on May 12 Strafford was beheaded. " He died," says his secretary, " like a Gentleman and a Christian; a martyr for the Church and King."* As the axe fell the silence of the great multitude was broken by a universal shout of joy. The streets

* Strafford, ii. 433.

blazed with bonfires. The bells clashed from every steeple. Many rode home, waving their hats and crying, "His head is off."*

Only Cardinal Richelieu, when he heard the news, remarked that "the English nation were so foolish that they would not let the wisest head among them stand on its shoulders."†

"*Il était justement accusé*," says Guizot, "*et injustement jugé.*"‡

Strafford was buried at Wentworth Woodhouse. His honours were all forfeited, but within the year his only son had his earldom regranted to him, and in 1662 the original attainder was repealed. In the second generation his male issue became extinct, but his estates and the representation of his family have descended through the Marquess of Rockingham to the present Earl FitzWilliam.

Lord Strafford was "of a tall stature, but stooped much in the neck."§ His features were harsh, dark, imperious and disdainful, but ennobled by their expression "into more than the majesty of an antique Jupiter; his fixed look full of severity, of mournful anxiety, of deep thought, of dauntless resolution."|| Yet "he seemed never able to shake himself free from the sense of impending failure."¶ "He was a man," says Clarendon, "of great parts and extraordinary endowments of nature; not unadorned with some addition of art and learning; for he had a readiness of conception which made his learning thought more than in truth it was. His first inclinations and addresses to the court were only to establish his greatness in the country: but they were so prosperous that he contented not himself. . . . His successes, applied to a nature too elate and haughty of itself, and a quicker progress into the greatest employments and trust, made him more transported with disdain of other men and more contemning the forms of business. . . . He was a man of too high and severe a deportment, and too great a contemner of ceremony to have many friends at court,

* Green, iii. 204.   † *Ibid.*   ‡ Guizot, i. 6.
§ Warwick, 112. || Macaulay, v. 537.   ¶ Gardiner, vii. 135.

THOMAS WENTWORTH

IEARL OF STRAFFORDI

To face page 326

and therefor could not but have enemies enough—particularly Lord Holland, of whom he had once said 'that the King should do well to cut off his head,' and Sir Henry Vane, for taking the barony of Raby with his earldom (Raby being the house of the Vanes)—which was an act of the most extraordinary provocation and I believe the chief occasion of the loss of his head—and lastly the whole Scottish nation, an enemy more terrible than all the others."*

Sir Philip Warwick speaks of his " sowre and haughty temper."† Sir George Radcliffe, his cousin, secretary and biographer, calls him " exceeding cholerick, an infirmity with which he had great Wrestlings," but lays stress on "his continual consultation of one or two of his intimate friends in all private or public affairs. He never did anything of any moment, concerning either political or domestical business, without taking advice; not so much as a letter written to any great man, but he showed it to his confidents if they were near him. He was exceedingly temperate in Meat, Drink and Recreations. Beef and Rabbits his ordinary food, or cold powdered meats, or cheese and apples. He was never drunk in his life, as I have often heard him say. He was a good Falconer and played excellently well at Primero and Mayo. After supper, if he had company suitable, he would retire into an inner room and set two or three hours telling stories."†

" He was well studied in the laws and very eloquent. This perfection he attained first by reading well penned authors in French, Latin and English, and observing their expressions; secondly by hearing eloquent men; thirdly by a very great care and industry in penning his epistles. Above all he had a natural quickness of Will and Fancy, with great clearness of Judgment and much Practice. Among all his qualities none was more eminent than his friendship—in that he never failed. He bore a particular affection for the King, and he was always a lover of monarchy . . . for he thought that regal power and popular privileges might well stand together—but the

‡ Clarendon, i. 234, 403.   † Warwick, 110.   ‡ Strafford, ii. 433.

22

longer he lived his experience taught him that it was far
safer that the King should increase in power than that
the people should gain advantages on the King."* Charles
himself wrote of him afterwards: " I looked upon my
Lord Strafford as a Gentleman whose abilities might
make a Prince rather afraid than ashamed to employ him
in the greatest affairs of State."†

Such were the views of Strafford's contemporaries: of
the King, his master; of Radcliffe, his counsellor; of
Clarendon, his future successor. A later historian has
launched a terrible invective against him. " This great,
bold, bad man, among the richest and most powerful
commoners in the kingdom, distinguished by force of
character and personal courage, unequalled in force and
brilliancy of expression . . . yielded to seduction, abandoned his associates and hated them ever after with the
deadly hatred of a renegade. He employed all his power
for the purpose of crushing those liberties of which he
had been the most distinguished champion. His counsels
were fierce and arbitrary—government without parliament
and government by the sword, was his favourite scheme.
He established vast monopolies for his private benefit;
he imposed taxes arbitrarily; and the proceedings against
him were justified by that which alone justifies capital
punishment or war—the public danger."‡

It is now two hundred years since Strafford's death,
and to some these words may seem too severe. Strafford,
whatever his faults, was brave, loyal and wise. He
could remember the glories of the last Tudor Sovereign
who had ruled by herself and by her minister; he hoped
to recall them, to mend the times that were out of joint,
and to strengthen the weak hands of the prince who sat
in her seat. He was no democrat, though he was ready
to reform, but from above rather than from below; ability
and authority were, in his view, to be the chief claims to
government; the King was to be supported, not ruled, by
Parliament. Had Charles been freer from the worst faults

* Strafford, 435.   † King Charles, Eik. Bas., 4.
‡ Macaulay, v. 557, *et seq.*

that can befall a prince, his last minister might perhaps have done more for his country and left a happier name.

In little over twelve years the two Chief Ministers of Charles I. had met with violent deaths, with the hearty approval of the public. One had enjoyed all the gifts of personality, the other all those of talent ; both had pursued an oligarchic policy; both had been faithful to the King; both had been odious to the country. The inference augured ill for their master.

As the fall of Buckingham had marked the end of parliamentary government, so the fall of Strafford marked the end of personal rule; within a few months the nation rebelled and the Civil War began. Between them they had driven the English monarchy into the arms of Cromwell.

CHAPTER XI
CHURCH AND STATE

CLARENDON AND DANBY

THE Civil War—or, as some style it, the Great Rebellion—came to an end with the battle of Worcester, and in 1651 Charles II. retired to the Continent and Cromwell sat in his seat. But in England there was no Utopia, and the Puritans were singularly disappointed. They had expected a new heaven and a new earth, but they found that they had merely exchanged a King for a Protector, who was another Rehoboam. The Cavaliers or Malignants sulked in their castles and manors, spending as little as they could, or else eking out a precarious existence abroad on such rents as were sent them. The preachers, the anabaptists, the fifth monarchy men and the tinkers ruled the roast, and made matters thoroughly unpleasant, until the Lord General came down and swept them all away. As the years went on the law became more martial and the government more direct. Foreign victories maintained its prestige in Europe, but at home people felt that life had been far more comfortable and regular under the old régime, and those who regretted it increased daily. Less than ten years of the rule of Republicans and the religion of Roundheads had disillusioned everyone, and when in 1658 the great Oliver died and the army became omnipotent it was but a short step back to the monarchy. That step was quickly taken by General Monk, and in 1660 the second Charles returned to his kingdom. " I never knew," he said as he landed in Kent, " that I had so many friends."

330

The pendulum now swung across and within a year the reaction was complete. Excepting for a few regicides, who were hanged with little interest, the magnates of the Commonwealth sank into their native obscurity. The lords and the bishops came back, and with them two new importations arrived from France—the household troops and the King's mistresses. A standing army and a royal harem became for the first time regular features of the English court. To support them additional taxes were needed, and the King's debts soon figured as a permanent item in the Budget, but beyond that Charles would not go; he had no wish, he said, to set out on his travels again.

He and his brother James were a remarkable pair. Both, like the villains of romance, were dark and dissolute; both were everlasting talkers. But whereas Charles was ugly and amusing even for a King, James was handsome and an inveterate bore. The one could understand if he would, the other would if he could. Charles was devoid of faith or principle, "a slave and often a dupe," but quick, intelligent, interested, full of tact, and always ready to say the right thing. James was a fervent Catholic, wedded to his Church and his rights, but bungling in word and deed, and safe to offend if possible. "They will never kill me," said Charles, "to make you King."

With all his moral backslidings Charles was no fool: he had considerable natural talents, and he had learnt adversity in a hard school. Only his idleness prevented him from being a successful ruler. "*Il était capable de tout dans les affaires pressantes et incapable de s'y appliquer quand elles ne l'étoient pas.*"* He sauntered through life much as he strolled down the Mall, buying virtue and selling honours, rating every man and woman at their lowest price, hating work, as he said, like the devil. Parliament and the country chafed, but endured it, remembering his ancestry, his troubles and his wit ; and when at last he made an edifying end, surrounded by five

* Grammont, i. 108.

out of his six ducal bastards, most of England felt they
had lost a friend.

" For though the whole world cannot show such another
We had better have him than his bigoted brother."

The crown devolved upon James, Duke of York. He
had already gone through some tribulation for his faith,
and had by now become so rank a Papist that he soon
cast restraint to the winds. For a moment the rebellion
of Monmouth gave him pause, but directly that was
scotched no power could hold him. Duty, inclination and
belief all pointed out the same path, and that path he
painfully pursued. Acting as his own minister in the
main, he also relied on friends who were quite as untrust-
worthy and far cleverer than himself. In three years
England saw that she would have to choose between
Rome and a revolution: she chose the latter, and their
High Mightinesses the Prince and Princess of Orange
were invited to come over from Holland and take possession of the British Crown. Again the Stuarts had been
found too much for their country to bear.

But the family connection, and to some extent the
family policy, still prevailed. William was a nephew of
Charles and a grandson of Henrietta Maria; Mary was a
daughter of James and a granddaughter of Clarendon.
The new King, like his father-in-law, managed his own
affairs, but he managed them in a much more effective
manner, and in the little, lame, ailing Dutchman the
English Parliament found that they had met a master.
For twelve years they fought him, while he fought the
French. In the end they beat him, but not before he
had committed them to a war which was to raise England
to the first place in Europe.

Throughout this evil era political morality had ebbed.
The uncertainties of the times, the wish to recoup past
losses, the example of the court, the reaction against
cant, had made men sceptics, trimmers, opportunists;
personal honour was less regarded than perhaps it had
ever been before, and the average minister thought quite

as much of himself as of his country. The older men, whose memory went back to the days before the Civil War, still strove to follow the old tradition, usually with unfortunate results; but the younger generation, who drew their ideas from Versailles and Breda, owned fewer scruples, and they gradually brought the business of government into such disrepute that to serve two Kings and take bribes from a third was not considered a departure from the normal code of honesty. Time-serving was at a premium and consistency at a discount; the good minister came to grief and the bad one flourished. The Glorious Revolution was no doubt glorious in its results, but many of the motives that inspired and most of the men who managed it owed as much to faction and self-interest as to patriotism or principle.

I.—CLARENDON

Edward Hyde, afterwards Earl of Clarendon, was born at Dinton, near Salisbury, on February 18, 1608-9. He was the third son of Henry Hyde, a squire of that place, by his wife Mary, daughter and coheiress of Edward Langford, a rich clothier of Trowbridge.* The family had come originally from Cheshire, but in the time of Queen Elizabeth, Laurence Hyde, Edward's grandfather, had acquired some property in Wiltshire and had settled there. Two of his sons had succeeded at the bar, one becoming attorney-general to Ann, Queen of James I., the other chief justice of the King's Bench. Henry Hyde, however, had preferred to travel, and after visiting Germany and Rome, and sitting for his county in Parliament, he had retired to a life of rural repose. He sent his sons to Magdalen College, Oxford, where Edward, who had been intended for the Church, took his degree as B.A., and came down " rather with the opinion of a young man of parts and pregnancy of wit, than that he had improved it much by Industry, the discipline of that time being

* She was never in London in her life (Craik, i. 5).

not so strict as it hath been since."* After leaving
Oxford he was entered at the Middle Temple, where his
uncle Nicholas was treasurer, and while a student he
mixed a good deal with the officers who surrounded
Buckingham, "though without any signal debauchery."†
Two years later Sir Nicholas became Chief Justice, and
in 1628 Edward Hyde rode circuit with him as marshal.
He had been suffering from ague, and at Cambridge, the
first assize town, he fell a victim to the smallpox, and was
so ill that his life was despaired of. He recovered, however, and after recuperating at home, went back to London,
only to lose the uncle who had been his mentor and mainstay. But this did not prevent him from sticking to his
profession, though " he could not bring himself to an
industrious pursuit of the Law, but rather loved polite
learning and history."‡

In 1629 he married his first wife, Anne, daughter of Sir
George Ayliffe, of Grettenham, in Wilts, a connection of
the Villiers family. Within six months she died of smallpox—a loss " which he bore with so great passion and
confusion of spirit that it shook all the frame of his
resolutions,"§ and he nearly left England altogether.
But being now called to the bar he turned to work with
serious energy. Three years later his father died, and
in 1634 he married again, this time Frances, daughter of
Sir Thomas Aylesbury, Bart., a master of the Court of
Requests. The alliance helped him in the law; he received
the place of Keeper of the Writs in the Common Pleas,
and began to get briefs and to distinguish himself as
an advocate.

It was about this time that Hyde first came into touch
with Archbishop Laud, then one of the commissioners of
the Treasury. The occasion was a petition which Hyde
had drafted for some London merchants as to delays
suffered at the King's wharves. Laud was much impressed with his knowledge and attention, and made use
of his help in raising monies for the rebuilding of St.

* Clarendon, Life, i. 7. † Ibid., i. 9.
‡ Ibid. § Ibid., 12.

Paul's. "He spoke well of him on all occasions, so that
Mr. Hyde was used with more countenance by the judges
in Westminster Hall and the eminent Practisers, than was
usually given to men of his years; so that he grew every
day in practise, of which he had as much as he desired . . .
yet he made not himself a slave to it, but kept both his
friends at Court and about the Town."* His intimates
included Ben Jonson, Selden, Sir Kenelm Digby and Sir
Lucius Cary, and he gradually got to know some of the
leading politicians. He was quiet and industrious, "avoid-
ing that sea of wine and women and quarrels and gaming
which almost overspread the whole kingdom . . . con-
versant with a rank of men above his quality . . . and
had ambition enough to help him from being satisfied
with his own condition."†

In this manner Hyde went steadily forward, improving
his position at the bar and in his county, increasing his
wealth, gaining knowledge and reputation, though still in
a moderate way. In 1640 he was elected member for
Wootton Bassett, and in the short Parliament of that
year he gave his support to the popular party. In the
Parliament of 1641 he sat for Saltash, serving on several
committees, but concerning himself principally with
reforms of the legal administration. He helped in preparing the impeachment of Strafford and voted, it seems,
for his attainder, but soon afterwards he began to disagree
with his friends in their treatment of Church questions.
Partly perhaps from his father's teaching, partly from
his association with Laud, he was a strong believer in
episcopacy, and he resisted all attacks on the privileges
of bishops or clergy—an attitude which brought him to
the favourable notice of the King. Since he had taken a
prominent part in Parliament Hyde had gradually withdrawn from his practice at the bar, finding himself occupied
with his business in the House. The times were momen-
tous; within a few months the courts of High Commission
and Star Chamber were abolished; the Councils of the
North and of Wales were bereft of their powers; peace

* Clarendon, Life, 27.   † Ibid., i. 68.

was made with Scotland; and the King went off to Edinburgh to regain the alliance of his former foes.

In the House of Commons Hyde was making a name. He presided over the committees dealing with the suppression of the Earl Marshal's court, with the illegalities of the Court of York, with the jurisdiction of the President of the Welsh Marches, and with the Queen's manors. In the last-named business he had occasion to reprimand Mr. Cromwell for " his indecency and rudeness, and his contrary and offensive language."* He was able so well to obstruct the passage of the Root and Branch Bill, which was to do away with episcopacy, that the King sent for him to Whitehall and told him that " he had heard from all hands how much he was beholden to him; and that when all his servants in the House of Commons either neglected his service or could not appear usefully in it, he took all occasions to do him service,"† and he congratulated Hyde on his affection for the Church.

This placed Hyde's foot on the ladder. At first he did not take any office, but he kept Charles advised as to how the Commons could best be dealt with—advice which he was well qualified to give. Adhering to strictly legal procedure, he began to form a new royalist party in the House of Commons, by which he gave great umbrage to the popular leaders. He discountenanced arbitrary acts, such as the attempted arrest of the five members, which was planned without his knowledge and " much displeased and dejected him "; and he recommended Charles to go warily, to grant what he was compelled to grant by law, to avoid appeals to force, and to adopt a passive policy. Being a master at drafting, he was responsible for the King's answer to the Grand Remonstrance, and for most of his subsequent replies to Parliament.

For some time he was able to keep his connection with the court a secret, being taken " at night to the Queen's back stairs and seeing the King and Queen privately;"‡ and with Falkland and Colepepper he used to discuss the King's business every evening at his house in Westminster

* Clarendon, Life, 80.   † Ibid., i. 82, 83.   ‡ Ibid., i. 88.

after Charles had gone to the north. He was offered the place of solicitor-general, which he declined, believing he could be of more service to the King as a private member; but his correspondence with Charles was soon known of in Parliament, and there he now became suspected and disliked.

By this time it was clear that a clash must occur, and the King wrote to Hyde to join the court at York. Hyde had, as he says in his Life, " a very particular Devotion and Passion for the Person of the King; and did believe him the most and the best Christian in the world. He had a most zealous esteem and Reverence for the Constitution of the Government . . . and was just as much troubled when the Crown exceeded its just limits as if the least branch of the Prerogative was torn off."* His loyalty to the Church was equally a matter of conviction, and his honesty so much impressed Charles that he used often to ask, when advice was submitted to him, " whether Ned Hyde were of that opinion."†

In May 1642 Hyde set out for the north, " having told the Speaker that it was very necessary, by the advice of his physician, that he should take the Air of the country for his Health."‡ His flight greatly annoyed the House of Commons, but he reached York safely. In August matters came to a head with the Parliament, and Charles raised the royal standard at Nottingham. At the battle of Edgehill he gained his first victory, and by October he was established at Oxford. Hyde had been summoned back to London by the Speaker, but he had refused to return, being now one of the King's most trusted advisers. Early in 1643 he was knighted, sworn of the Privy Council, and appointed Chancellor of the Exchequer. He had already declined the place of Secretary of State, though Charles had said " that he could trust nobody else," and he now refused it a second time.

The year 1643 was one of varying fortunes. The Commons lost Hampden and Pym, the King lost Falkland. But the rise of Cromwell as a general, and the signature

* Clarendon, Life, i. 96.　　† Ibid., 97.　　‡ Ibid., 116.

of the Solemn League and Covenant between the Scots
and Parliament, inclined the balance to the side of the
latter. Money was the King's principal need, for the
plate of the Church, the colleges and the Cavaliers did
not go far, and Hyde had his work cut out to raise funds.
With this object he obtained the calling of the Oxford
Parliament, and by it he achieved some success. He was
one of the so-called junto of five, and in the negotiations
at Oxford and Uxbridge he was the leading figure. But
his moderation damaged him with the King's other
advisers, and in 1645 he was sent off to Bristol as one of
the Prince of Wales' council. On the day he left he
had a long conference with Charles; it was the last time
he was ever to see him.

Hyde's duties in his new appointment were neither
pleasant nor easy. He was not a soldier, and the business
was mainly military; he was not well known to the Prince
or his court; and neither his demeanour, his habits nor
his religion commended him much to them. For a year
he struggled with the difficulties of a divided control;
then the battle of Naseby left the royalists in a bad
way, and the security of the Prince became of the first
importance.

Early in 1646, having moved further and further to the
West, Hyde took his royal charge across to the Scilly
Isles, and after a stay there of six weeks they went on
to Jersey. By now the King had joined the Scottish
army at Newark, but his affairs were getting worse. The
Queen, who had been in France for some time, was pressing
the Prince to join her, and to this the King at last consented. In July 1646 the move was made. It was against
all Hyde's ideas. He feared the Queen's influence, the
French government's action, and the effect of the Prince's
flight on public opinion in England. For his own part he
felt that he could do more good by keeping on British
soil, and accordingly he remained at St. Helier. There
for two years he occupied himself in supporting the King's
cause by propaganda and correspondence. In his leisure
he composed much of his " History of the Great Rebellion,"

supplementing it with State papers which he alone
possessed. At this time, he says, " he enjoyed the
greatest tranquillity of mind imaginable, spending his
day in ten hours regular work, and keeping house with
Lords Hopton and Capel. They never used to sup, but
met always upon the sands in the evening to walk."*
After his friends had left he lodged in the castle with Sir
George Carteret, the Governor; and it was in this period
of his life that the main portion of his literary work was
done.

In 1648 the second stage of the Civil War began. The
Queen and the Prince then summoned Hyde to join them,
and he set off for Paris. After an eventful journey by
Caen, Rouen, Ostend and Flushing, in which he was
robbed of his belongings by a pirate, he arrived at last
at The Hague, where he found Prince Charles just returned
after the defeat of the royalists by Fairfax. A few
months later the King was brought to trial, and on
January 30, 1649, he lost his life.

At The Hague it was now thought that Hyde's influence
would come to an end, but despite his mother's wishes
the young King retained him, and as one of the principal
members of the Council Hyde drew up Charles II.'s
proclamations and circulars to foreign princes. He then
permanently established himself in the Netherlands and
brought over his family to Antwerp; but he was short of
money and they had to live in a very modest way. As
yet he had no great influence with Charles. When there
was a proposal of the latter's going to join the Queen-
Mother in Paris, Hyde tried to dissuade him, but as other
counsels gained the day he thought it wise to accept a
mission to the Spanish court, chiefly with the hope of
raising money for his master.

Accordingly he and Lord Cottington were accredited
as Charles' ambassadors, and they set out in May 1649,
travelling via Antwerp and Brussels to St. Germain,
where Hyde to some extent made his peace with the
Queen. In September they went on to the South, and

* Clarendon, Life, i. 199.

arrived two months later in Madrid, where they were received with only moderate courtesy, the Spanish court being more inclined to cultivate a friendship with Cromwell than with Charles. Hyde remarks that " all the foreign ministers residing in Madrid, except the English and the Dane, were Italians, and all but the Venetian were subjects of the Great Duke of Florence."* While in Spain he learnt something of the language and saw what he could of the country, but in December 1650 the two envoys were made aware that their presence was distasteful, and Hyde accordingly returned to Paris. He was depressed, not in particular favour, poor and suffering badly from gout. He went on to Antwerp and stayed there with his family for some months.

In November 1651 Charles came back to France after his expedition to Scotland and his defeat at Worcester. He sent to Antwerp for Hyde, and the latter soon became his most intimate counsellor. During the absence of Sir E. Nicholas he acted as Secretary of State, managing Charles' political business, encouraging the royalists in England, keeping together their friends on the Continent, and carefully watching Cromwell. Various attempts were made to dislodge him by rivals: he was accused of corresponding with the Protector and maligning the King; but Charles knew that he had got a discreet and faithful minister. " He was very well satisfied," he said, " in the Chancellor's affection, and took nothing ill that he had said."†

In June 1654 Charles went to Spa to stay with his sister the Princess Royal. During the visit the Princess made Hyde's daughter Anne one of her maids of honour, much against her father's wish. She was a young lady of varied attractions, and when in the winter of 1656 she accompanied the princess to Paris, she there met the Duke of York, who fell in love with her, apparently at first sight.

The exiled court remained for a time at Cologne, and then went to Bruges. Hyde had now risen to be its

* Clarendon, Life, i. 228.   † Ibid., Hist., vi. 696.

mainstay, and in January 1657-8, on the death of Lord Keeper Herbert, Charles appointed him Lord Chancellor. In the following summer Cromwell died, and a prospect opened of the King's return. Throughout the secret negotiations which eventually brought this about Hyde took the leading part, and he ensured a restoration without any formal loss of regal power; but he made enemies in the process, for his attachment to the Church of England was disliked both by Catholics and Presbyterians, and at court his monopoly of influence caused jealousy. Another difficulty was in store for him. In November 1659 the Duke of York again met Anne Hyde, this time at Breda, and he then became secretly engaged to her, unknown to her father. Their alliance was to lead to complications in the future.

In May 1660 the Parliament in England at last invited Charles back to his kingdom. On May 25 he landed at Dover, and on June 1 Hyde took his seat as Chancellor in Westminster Hall, being the virtual head of the government. Three months later the Duke of York was privately married to Anne Hyde; and though her father protested his ignorance, declaimed against the marriage, and begged to have it annulled, his consideration was augmented by it. In November he was created a peer, and five months after, at the coronation, he was advanced to be Earl of Clarendon. He then received a gift of £20,000 from the King and the estate of Cornbury in Oxfordshire to support his dignity, and in the same year he was elected chancellor of Oxford University.

He was now a man of over fifty, twenty years older than the King. For fourteen years he had been away from England, and though his views were sound and his knowledge exceptional, he had little *flair* for the arts of a courtier. Ideas had changed not only in England but in Europe during his period of exile. The serious days of Charles I. and Louis XIII., of Strafford and Richelieu, were over, and a more easy-going, laughter-loving society now set the fashion. The strenuous Protector, the stern Puritans, were hardly more out of date than Clarendon's own sober industry, and although his contemporaries envied his success, he was regarded by the younger generation as antiquated and dull.

For the moment, however, his position was secure and his experience needed, while the King and the more intelligent royalists realized what a debt of gratitude they owed him. But his daughter's marriage weighed on his mind, for he knew that alliances with the royal family had rarely been fortunate for ministers. Public opinion, however, took the news calmly, though the Duke of Gloucester observed that the new duchess "smelt of her father's green bag," and her prenuptial reputation was not enhanced by the birth of a son six weeks after her wedding: but she amused Charles and "led her husband by the nose in all but his amours."* So Clarendon let the matter rest, content to see himself the possible grandfather of kings: and he modestly declined the Garter †

His domestic policy was sagacious. He kept the King to the promises made at Breda, he enlarged the Act of Indemnity, and he deprecated severity to the Puritans. His ventures into foreign affairs were less fortunate: he allowed the King to marry Catherine of Braganza and to sell the port of Dunkirk to the French. But his root idea was to get back to the old constitution of Elizabeth and to restore its former powers to the Church. At a French alliance he looked askance, distrusting the Queen-Mother, and condemning the vagaries of Versailles. This attitude gradually brought him into opposition to the tolerant Charles, and his critics took advantage of it. The new Parliament was eminently zealous and loyal, and had already passed several Acts enforcing religious tests. Charles, who had leanings to the Catholic faith, and had just married a Catholic princess, wished to mitigate this severity by a declaration of indulgence. But he was prevented from doing so, and he associated this check with Clarendon's ultra-Anglican views. Bennet, the new Secretary of State, was believed to be a papist; he agreed with his master, and in 1663, with his con-

* Burnet, Own Times, i. 291, note. † Craik, ii. 81.

EDWARD HYDE
EARL OF CLARENDON

To face page 342

nivance, Lord Bristol, the head of the Catholic party in England, brought a futile charge of high treason against the Chancellor. The peace with Holland, the sale of Dunkirk, the marriages of the King and the Duke of York, were all laid to his charge. The judges quashed the indictment and the King denied its truth, but it showed the way in which the tide was running.

Other circumstances combined to diminish Clarendon's power. " He was always pressing the King to mind his affairs, but in vain. He was high and was apt to reject those who addressed themselves to him with too much contempt . . . and with too magisterial a way."* Since his return to England he had much enlarged his scale of living, and was now building a palace facing the upper end of St. James's Street. Its cost and magnificence were equally damaging to his purse and his popularity. " The common people," says Pepys in 1664, " have already called it Dunkirke House, from their opinion of his having a good bribe for the selling thereof."† His staid manners were too much of a contrast to the loose morality of the court. The King and Bennet, he says, on one occasion, " grew very merry and reproached his overmuch severity, now he grew old and considered not the infirmities of younger men."‡ Bennet was a great mimic, " raillery being his best faculty," and one which carried much weight with Charles, and Clarendon's appearance, his gait and his habit of body lent themselves to that art. His gout had become worse, he was hampered in getting about and was often confined to his house, but on his visits to the palace he never hesitated to tell the King his opinion of the manners of Whitehall. Charles bore with his criticisms, though he did not leave them unanswered, on one occasion making the remarkable statement that " a lady of honour who dedicates herself only to please a King ought not to be branded with any Name or Mark of Infamy, but hath always been looked upon by all Persons well-bred as worthy of respect."§

* Burnet, Own Times, i. 160. † Pepys, ii. 212.
‡ Clarendon, Life, iii. 682. § Ibid., iii. 687.

Public events, however, conspired against Clarendon
even more than private intrigue.   The royal marriage was
not popular with King, court or people.   Queen Catherine
had come from Portugal attended by " *six monstres qui
se disaient filles d'honneur et d'une duenne, autre monstre,
gouvernante de ces rares beautes.*"* She had few looks and
a constant indisposition, and the union was fruitless.

> "Three sights to be seen,
>   Dunkirk, Tangier and a barren Queene."

Clarendon, it was said, had arranged it with a view to his
own grandchildren succeeding to the throne.   Another
cause of complaint against him was the persecution of the
Puritans and Dissenters.   This was ascribed to his extreme
orthodoxy, and in the towns he was especially discredited.

In 1665, contrary to his wish, war was declared against
the Dutch, the chief Protestant nation of the Continent,
and although several English victories were gained, they
were unpopular.   Immediately afterwards the Great
Plague broke out in London, to be followed a year later
by a war with the French and the Great Fire.   In London
alone " thirteen hundred houses and ninety churches were
destroyed.   The loss of merchandize and property was
beyond count.   The treasury was empty, and neither
ships nor forts were manned, when in June 1667 the Dutch
fleet appeared at the Nore, advanced unopposed up the
Thames, burned three men of war and sailed proudly along
the coast the masters of the Channel."† The public
resentment was immense, and it fell upon the devoted
head of Clarendon.   His windows were broken, his walls
placarded, his trees cut down.   The court was already
bitter against him, the King lukewarm, and Parliament,
hitherto friendly, was now enraged at his attempt to raise
troops without their leave and at his advice for a dissolution.   His chief enemies, Bristol, Buckingham and
Bennet, now Lord Arlington, persuaded the King that
the only way to save him from impeachment would be
to relieve him of office.   " The business," says Pepys,

* Grammont, i. 116.   † Green, iii. 384.

" was designed in my Lady Castlemaine's chamber."*
At first Charles treated him with some consideration, but
eventually on August 30, 1667, he had to resign the Great
Seal. Nor did this calamity come alone, for a few days
previously he had suddenly lost his wife.

Clarendon was only fifty-eight, but he was an old man.
He had led a strenuous and chequered life. For twenty-
five years he had been in the heart of affairs, the close
confidant of two Kings, the central wheel of their policy.
To lose his place at such a moment, just as comfort and
power were beginning to attract him, was a shrewd blow,
and he clung to hope as long as he could, taking his fall
hardly, " staying in his bedchamber very sad."† His
friends, he found, were few. His two sons, Lord Cornbury
and Laurence Hyde, who both had places at court and
seats in the Commons, fought manfully for him, while his
son-in-law, the Duke of York, gave a more doubtful
support. But the dice were loaded against him.

In October 1667 Parliament met. Charles announced
that he would never employ Clarendon again; but this
was not enough. The Cabal had come into power and
were determined to impeach him. The Lords, however,
refused to accept a general charge, and Clarendon wrote
to the King protesting his innocence. Charles only remarked that " he wondered he did not withdraw."
Clarendon understood that all was over. Evelyn found
him " in his garden at his new built palace, sitting in his
gowt wheel chayre, and seeing the gates set up. He
looked and spake very disconsolately."‡ A few days
later, on November 29, he left England secretly, never to
return alive.

He had been assured by the Duke of York that " he
should not be prosecuted or suffer in honour or fortune,"
but his flight was taken as a confession of guilt. He
was banished by Act of Parliament, his pardon only to
be granted by consent of both Houses. It was the end
of his political life.

He went first to Rouen and then came back to Calais,

* Pepys, iii. 230.   † Evelyn, ii. 223, 228.   ‡ *Ibid.*, ii. 228.

where he lay ill for three months, in want and distress. At Evreux he was maltreated and robbed by some mutinous English sailors. In June 1668 he travelled south to Avignon to take the waters, and there and at Montpelier he lived for nearly three years, reverting to literary work, studying Italian, and completing his history of the Rebellion. Twice he begged to be allowed to return to England, but his petitions remained unanswered. The French government at first used him ill, instigated by his enemies in England; latterly, however, more courtesy was shown him. His last years he spent in some comfort and content, occupied with his writing and seeing the society of the neighbourhood. His sons and a few old friends visited him, and as far as was possible his exile was mitigated. In May 1674 he moved back to Rouen, and there, on December 9, he died. A month later he was buried in Westminster Abbey. His money affairs were involved, for his London house, in which he had never lived, had cost three times its estimate; and his eldest son was afterwards compelled to sell his country estate.

Clarendon's daughter, the Duchess of York, the mother of Queen Mary and Queen Anne, had died in 1671. His elder son Henry became Lord Privy Seal and Lord-Lieutenant of Ireland under James II., but the difficulties of his position after his brother-in-law had abdicated made him distrusted by King William, and for some time he was imprisoned in the Tower. He died in retirement in 1709. Laurence, the younger son, was created Earl of Rochester by Charles, and under James II. was Lord Treasurer. After the Revolution he enjoyed some favour and was twice Lord-Lieutenant. He had inherited his father's literary tastes and was the publisher of his works. He died two years after his brother, and by 1753 the male line of the family was extinct.

Clarendon is described as a " fair, ruddy, fat, middle-statured, handsome man "; there are many portraits of him. Before he was forty he was a martyr to gout, and even during his first exile he had to lead a very sedentary life. Pepys, recounting a visit in 1664, writes: " The

Chancellor said: ' Come, Mr. Pepys, you and I will take a turn in the garden ' " ;* but he had to be helped downstairs. This inability to take active exercise turned his attention to indoor pursuits, and he became a collector of books and pictures, a reader and a historian. Although his account of the Rebellion and of his own life are coloured with prejudice and lack of proportion, they are among the most valuable records of the times. His conversancy with nearly everything of moment from the days of Strafford to those of the Cabal made him an authority of the highest class, and his style clothed his thoughts with dignity. To Oxford he was a beneficent head, almost a reformer, for he once proposed that the curriculum should include acting, dancing, fencing and riding. The profits of his history went to the University funds, and the Clarendon Press still perpetuates his name.

He was a placid man, but of great resource, happy in business or letters, and able to accommodate himself to varying fortunes. Nearly half his adult life was spent abroad, often with scanty means, yet he was never idle and rarely sad. At the bar he had made his mark before politics claimed him, but when he became a judge he felt that his law might be weak, and so always supported himself in his decisions by the concurrence of two colleagues. Burnet calls him " a good Chancellor, only a little too rough, but very impartial "; but adds that " he never understood foreign affairs well "† Warwick praises his cheerful and agreeable conversation, his extraordinary industry and activity, his felicity of tongue and pen, though his language and style were a little too redundant.†

The causes of his fall are patent. He was a strong Protestant, a strong constitutionalist, a serious and industrious man. The King was the reverse. The Duchess of Cleveland, Charles' principal mistress, and Arlington, his principal Secretary of State, hated Clarendon, and lost no opportunity of ridiculing him. " One gentleman of the bedchamber used to carry the bellows about the room, instead of a purse, and another before him with a shovel

* Pepys, ii., 145.   † Burnet, Own Times, i. 161.   ‡ Warwick, 196.

for a mace, and could counterfeit his voice and style very
exactly: with which the King was much pleased ";* and
Buckingham used to say to Charles: "Here comes your
schoolmaster." To the courtiers he was odious. They
could tolerate the rise of a lawyer to be Chief Minister,
but that he should marry his daughter to the King's
brother was more than they could stand.

Southampton, the Lord Treasurer, who died a few
months before Clarendon's disgrace, had been his chief
support. He was convinced of the Chancellor's integrity,
and his last words were: "While he is in place we
are secure of our laws, liberties and religion."† But
the papists knew that while Clarendon was minister their
chances of success were small, while the Presbyterians
bore him almost equal ill-will.

In an evil age Clarendon's administration had been
singularly free from self-seeking or corruption. He told
his son truly, " If my friends can but forgive me the folly
of my great house there is nothing they may not well
defend me upon."‡ As to the sale of Dunkirk, there is
no doubt that he was largely responsible—he said as much
to the Comte d'Estrades, adding that the necessity of
English affairs had imposed it on him; but the benefit
that he derived from the transaction was limited to some
books from the Louvre Press which Louis XIV. had sent
him as a compliment. The articles of his impeachment
were never heard, and he was sacrificed for his master,
his services forgotten, and his advice ignored. Charles
had come to hate him for striving to save his government
from contempt, while the people identified him with a
disastrous war and with the other calamities that had
just visited the nation. His high place, his apparent
riches, his ostentatious way of living, pointed him out as
a scapegoat, and his foes were alert to hasten his fall.
He knew the sorrows of exile only too well, and he clung
to office for a moment—but when he saw that there was
no appeal he went on his last journey with a bold heart;

* Burnet, Own Times, i., 445, note.   † Rapin, ii. 646, 647.
‡ *Ibid.*, 441, note.

nor did he ever let his treatment mar the truth of his writings. " He acted for liberty," says Horace Walpole, " but wrote for prerogative "* He created the abiding tradition of a great party in the State, which lasted for a century and a half.†

Clarendon's real misfortune was that he was out of touch with a new age. " He was a lawyer by breeding, and his theory of the State was a lawyer's theory:"‡ he was probably the last statesman who believed in Divine Right. The King wished to manage the House of Commons by bribes—to take bribes from the King of France, to be tolerant in religion; such a policy was contrary to all Clarendon's ideas of right: he could not adapt himself to what seemed a degradation of the constitution and the Church.

Yet he had many great qualities. He was conscientious, reverent, loyal and sincere. " No man wrote abler State papers. No man spoke with more weight and dignity in Council and in Parliament. No man was better acquainted with general maxims of statecraft. . . . But tact and docility made no part of his character. He had an inordinate contempt for youth . . . and his morals, as well as his politics, were those of an earlier generation. To him England was still the England of his youth. The royal prerogative was still sacred in his eyes, and . . . he was unable to perceive that the House of Commons must be supreme in the State."§ His master had a quicker eye, a more pliable hand, and a harder heart, and, like his father, he did not hesitate to discard an old servant. Few statesmen and few historians have been more honest or more steadfast than Clarendon: few have reaped less reward.

II.—DANBY

Thomas Osborne, afterwards Earl of Danby and Duke of Leeds, was born at his father's seat of Kiveton, in Yorkshire, late in 1631. He was the elder son of Sir

* Gibbs, iii. 265, note.   † Craik, i. 8.
‡ Green, iii. 359.   § Macaulay, Hist., i. 172, 173, 195, 196.

Edward Osborne, first baronet, by his second wife Anne, daughter of Thomas Walmsley, of Dunkenhalgh, in Lancashire, and widow of William Middleton. The Osbornes were a family of commercial origin derived from a sixteenth-century Lord Mayor of London, who had rescued his employer's daughter from drowning and had afterwards married her. They had become rich, and had settled in Yorkshire, where Sir Edward had been Vice-President of the Council of the North under Wentworth. He was a strong royalist, and was for some time lieutenant-general of the King's forces in that part of England. His wife was a coheiress through the female line of the Nevilles, Lords Latimer, and Danvers, Earl of Danby—titles which her son was afterwards to revive.

The early part of Thomas Osborne's life was passed at home, and at the age of seven, by the death of his elder half-brother, he became his father's heir. While he was still a boy the Civil War began, and his kinsmen being all Cavaliers, his sympathies and interests lay with the King's party.

In 1647 his cause was defeated and he lost his father. He was then sent abroad, and spent some time in France, where he was " a young traveller and tennis player "* with William Temple, and an intimate friend of John Evelyn's: " every day at my father-in-law's house and table." Writing from Paris in October 1650 Evelyn says: " Sir Thomas Osborne and Lord Stanhope shot for a wager of 5 louis to be spent on a treat: they shot so exact that it was a drawn match."† Osborne's youth enabled him to visit England without much difficulty, and when he was twenty-one he paid his addresses to a cousin, Dorothy Osborne, who was afterwards to become the wife of his friend Temple. On her refusing his hand he turned to Lady Bridget Bertie, a daughter of Montague, second Earl of Lindsey, and to her he was married in 1652. She was a lady with plenty of character and ambition, who took a prominent part in her husband's career. While in England Osborne had become a close friend of the young

* Browne, 176.   † Evelyn, ii. 19.

Duke of Buckingham, the son of Charles I.'s minister, and when at last the Restoration arrived the duke brought him to court. There he soon identified himself with the High Cavalier or country party and devoted himself to politics.

In 1665 he was elected member for York, and at once joined in the attack on Clarendon. The latter styles him " a dependant and creature of the Duke of Buckingham who had told many people that if the Chancellor were not hanged he would be hanged himself."* In Clarendon's impeachment Osborne took an active part, and a year later Buckingham rewarded him by getting him the post of Treasurer of the Navy jointly with Sir Thomas Lyttelton. The King told the two of them on their appointment " that he had long been abused in his treasurer and that he was now safe in their hands."†

Osborne made some progress in Charles' favour, and more in that of Buckingham, whose " chief friend he was above all."‡ For four years he supported the Cabal government, improving his position at court, and working assiduously in his office. At the Navy Board the Duke of York praised " his capacity and diligence,"§ while Pepys reckoned himself " fifty per cent. securer in his place after a conversation with him."‖

In 1671 Osborne succeeded in obtaining the whole of his office for himself—it was said that he played an unfriendly part in Lyttelton's dismissal—and in May 1672 he was sworn a privy councillor.

During these years Charles and his committee of five ministers had reduced England to perhaps the lowest position in Europe she had ever held. By the secret treaty of Dover he had become a pensioner of the French King, had declared himself a Roman Catholic, and had undertaken to support the Bourbons in destroying the power of Holland. A French mistress had been sent over by Louis XIV. to manage him, and French troops

---

* Clarendon, Life, iii. 847. † Pepys, iv. 47.
‡ Burnet, Own Times, i. 460. § Browne, 179.
‖ Pepys, iv. 174.

were promised, if required, to manage his country. But the secret was suspected and the policy disliked, and the government paid the penalty.

In 1672 the Duke of York, who had recently lost his wife Anne Hyde, was publicly received into the Church of Rome, and the King issued a declaration of indulgence to Catholics. Parliament rejoined by passing the Test Act, to enforce conformity upon all persons holding office under the Crown. The affair brought the Duke into great odium, which reacted on the Cabal. He was already unpopular, though he was Charles' presumptive heir, for he arrogated to himself a higher place. In 1672, on the first day that Lord Shaftesbury presided in the House of Lords, the Duke took his seat on the right of the throne. The Chancellor observed that that was the place of the heir-apparent, and that the Duke should sit upon the left. This request was refused, whereupon Shaftesbury said that the House could not proceed until it was in proper form. The Duke then submitted, but as he moved across he said in a passion: " My Lord, you are a rascal and a villain." Shaftesbury replied, with great composure: " I am much obliged to your Royal Highness for not calling me a coward and a papist."* Such were the agreeable relations between the ministers and their future King.

Shortly after this the Cabal broke up, unable to withstand the feeling against them, and early in 1673 they had to retire. To the universal surprise Osborne, on the recommendation of Buckingham, was placed at the head of affairs. He was created a viscount, appointed Lord Treasurer, and a year later advanced to be Earl of Danby, while the lieutenancy of the West Riding was also given him. These honours were supposed to be due to Buckingham's influence:

> " Clifford and Hyde before had lost the day
> One hanged himself, the other ran away.
> 'Twas want of wit or courage made them fail
> But Osborne and the Duke must needs prevail."†

---

* Browne, 187, note.   † State Poems, i. 100.

The new Lord Treasurer was enough of a courtier not to be very squeamish in pursuing his master's policy. He divided the salary of his office with Clifford, one of the late ministers, that being part of the bargain which had secured him his place. The practice of dealing financially with such positions spread to the House of Commons, and under the new administration the system of paying members for their votes definitely began. " Every man who had a vote might sell himself to Danby."* His wife, according to Reresby, " drove a private trade in good employments, not without his lordship's participation and concurrence,"† and at his London house her family were supreme.

" At Charing Cross hard by the way
Where all the Berties make their hay."‡

Whether he himself profited from the secret service funds and the other opportunities that lay in his way is not certain, but in 1669 Pepys describes him as owing £10,000 and not having an income of over £1,200 a year, while ten years later he was a very rich man.

His period of office was inglorious. Although he was the " minister primier," Parliament never trusted him; Buckingham and Shaftesbury soon began to oppose him, and the King gave him only a half confidence. But he applied himself with some talent to a difficult task. He attempted to restore stability to the national finances, and in 1674, Parliament having passed resolutions against a standing army, he was able to conclude peace with Holland. He then endeavoured to strengthen the Crown, and a year later introduced a Bill to make all placemen declare that any resistance to the King was unlawful. This was passed by the Lords but rejected by the Commons, and Charles, despairing of coercing them, then accepted an annuity of 500,000 crowns from the French King to prorogue Parliament. At the same time he closed the London coffee-houses, in order to prevent political discussion.

Such a style of government recalled the days of his

* Macaulay, Hist., i. 224.   † Reresby, 219.   ‡ State Poems, iii. 57.

father, and in 1677, when the Houses met again, Shaftesbury and Buckingham questioned the length of the
prorogation, for which they were promptly sent to the
Tower. In the interval, however, Danby had succeeded
in arranging a marriage between William, Prince of
Orange, a nephew of Charles, and the Princess Mary,
the Duke of York's eldest daughter. It was his most
popular stroke of policy, and he received the Garter for it.'
But he omitted to conciliate the Duchess of Portsmouth,
the King's principal mistress. As Sir John Reresby
delicately observes, there were only two roads to this
lady's heart, and as soon as Danby ceased to employ
that of the purse his shallow favour lapsed.

A new war was now threatening between France and
Holland, and Parliament had voted supplies to assist the
latter country. Charles, to counter this, made another
private arrangement with Louis, promising in return for
a further sum of money to dissolve Parliament, to disband
the army, and not to help the Dutch. The design was
the King's, but the draft was Danby's, and it was to cost
him his place.

In 1678 the Popish Plot was discovered. Immediately
there came a flood of accusations against the papists.
Many were brought to trial, and Parliament petitioned for
the Duke of York to be dismissed from the King's counsels.
The country was in the throes of a strong anti-Catholic
excitement, and at this opportune moment Louis XIV.,
having made peace with the Dutch, coolly allowed his
treaty with Charles to be divulged. Montagu, the British
ambassador in Paris, through whom the negotiations had
passed, had asked Danby to get him the place of Secretary
of State; but Danby, with little sense of gratitude and less
of expediency, had refused. Montagu then determined
to be revenged: he persuaded Louis that Danby was
intriguing with the Dutch, secured a seat in the Commons,
and moved for the incriminating despatches. This was
ruin to Danby, although he had, as he thought, covered
himself by getting Charles to endorse them—" This is
writ by my order C.R." But " he sat very loose with

the King," and "to complete the happy and envied state of this Chief Minister the Duchess of Portsmouth and the Earl of Sunderland were joined with the Duke of Monmouth and the Earl of Shaftesbury in the design of his ruin."*

In December he was impeached. One of the counts was that he had said: "A new proclamation was better than an old Act."† Strong speeches were made against him. "The person to whom we owe the dangers of the French King against us; the ruin of this Nation; the raising of a standing army; is now laying down his staff and making up his accounts in the Treasury to enrich himself out of the spoils of the People and so depart."‡

Lord Strafford was one of the most violent against him. This vastly amused the King, who observed to Reresby "that he wondered at it much, seeing his father came to his unfortunate end by the very same procedure."§

In February 1678-9, largely to save the Treasurer, Charles dissolved the Parliament. But a month later the new House of Commons was equally virulent against him. A dispute between Lady Danby and Mrs. Seymour, the Speaker's wife, did not improve matters, and though the King went to Westminster and spoke on his minister's behalf, the Commons only replied by substituting a bill of attainder for that of impeachment.

Danby fortified himself with a royal pardon, to which the King himself attached the Great Seal, the Chancellor demurring; but the House refused to accept it, alleging that it was antedated.‖ Thus all his supports fell away, and though he had just married his daughter to Lord Plymouth, one of the King's natural children, and had secured a marquess' patent for himself, in April 1679, before it could pass, he was committed to the Tower. For a few days he lay hid in Whitehall, but he soon surrendered and accepted his sentence. "The King,"

* Temple, ii. 478.   † Rapin, ii. 677.
‡ *Ibid.*, ii. 704.   § Reresby, 216.
‖ It was finally settled by 2 Will. III. that a pardon shall not be pleadable in bar.

says Burnet, "was weary of the vexation he had long been in and desired to be set at ease ";* and the whole Council was dismissed *en bloc*.

The Lord Treasurer was not regretted. "His stateliness and difficulty of access made him hated."† He had not been gracious or generous, and his fall was the subject of many lampoons.

> " Farewell my Tom Danby, my Pimp and my Cheat,
> 'Twas for my own ends that I made you so great,
> The Plot is discovered, our money's all spent,
> I'll leave you to hang and myself to repent.
> Our Masters the Commons begin now to war,
> And swear they will either have you or my Whore,
> Then, Danby, forgive me if I am forsworn
> And leave you to die like a traitor forlorn."‡

Brandy was an obvious rhyme to his name, and his appearance provided plenty of material.

> " He is as stiff as any stake
> And leaner too than any rake
> Envy is not so pale:
> And though by selling of us all
> He wrought himself into Whitehall,
> Looks like a bird of jail."§

His appointments had been deplorable, and his integrity more than doubtful; but though his plans had turned out badly, he had designed them with some ideas of patriotism. He had wished to unite the Cavalier party, to exalt the King's prerogative, and to keep out the Catholics, rather with a view of strengthening the government than of imposing a despotism. The marriage of the Princess Mary with William of Orange was his chief work; writing of it years later, he says that "his hope was that the French interest in this court would thereby be rooted out."||

For the moment, however, the combination against him was too strong for any defence to avail: he had against him the Duke of York, the French faction, the King's favourite son, his favourite mistress, Parliament and

---

* Burnet, ii. 199. † Evelyn, iii. 389. ‡ State Poems, iii. 129.
§ *Ibid.*, ii. 205. || Browne, 220.

public opinion, and for the nonce his only course was silence.

While he remained in the Tower further charges were brought against him in connection with the Popish Plot, but they led to nothing. North says that "he thought he could serve himself of this plot of Oates and accordingly endeavoured at it: but it is plain that he had no command of the engine; and he found himself so intrigued that it was like a wolf by the ears: he could neither hold it nor let it go; and it bit him at last. . . . He failed in thinking that a lord treasurer that had enriched himself and his family could ever be popular: and he was within an ace of being accused of Godfrey's murder."*

Danby was kept a prisoner for nearly five years, but though he suffered considerably from illness, his confinement was not too rigorous, and his friends were allowed to see him. Evelyn, writing on December 7, 1683, says: " I went to the Tower and visited the earl of Danby. I dined with him and staied till night, his lady railing at the keeping her husband so long in prison."†

At last it was felt that he had purged his crime, and early in 1684 he was released on bail, the Dukes of Somerset and Albemarle, and the Earls of Chesterfield and Oxford becoming his sureties in £20,000. A year later, on the accession of James II., he was discharged from his recognizances and his impeachment was annulled; he then resumed his seat in the House of Lords. But the policy of the new reign did not at all commend itself to his Protestant ideas, and he now maintained a consistent opposition to Catholicism and autocracy. He was thus brought into touch with the popular party, where his position as a leading Tory made him of considerable importance.

The country had at first tolerated James with dislike: but this soon deepened into aversion and fear, as he proceeded to outrage the laws and liberties of the land. The only hope of the future was that his daughter, the future Queen, was married to a Protestant. When, there-

* North, i. 340.   † Evelyn, ii. 424.

fore, in June 1688, a Prince of Wales was born, something like a panic ensued. James was enervated and diseased, and though he had had a dozen children, all the sons had died as infants. There was thus some colour in the suggestion that the new heir-apparent was supposititious. In the ominous autumn days preceding the Revolution, while William of Orange was waiting to sail for England, his chances and those of the little Prince went up and down as the weathercock turned. Lillibulero and similar songs were sung in the streets:

> " Hush-a-bye baby on the tree top,
> When the wind blows the cradle shall rock !"

> " Arrah ! why does he stay behind ?
> Hark, my soul, 'tis a Protestant wind."

Danby was deep in the Opposition secrets, and had hurried off to the north to await William's landing. He writes in October 1688 to Chesterfield:

" MY LORD,
    " The long acquaintance I have had with your lordship, and the confidence I have of your honour and worth, makes me venture to impart to your lordship the great design that is now on foot. The Prince of Orange, if the wind serves, will land in England with 12,000 men within this fortnight; Hull will be delivered to him, and the greatest part of the King's army with many of the nobility will revolt. I confess, as to my own part, I had rather lose my life in the field than live under an arbitrary power and see our laws and religion changed, which is now visibly the King's intention, but I do not know what your lordship's thoughts may be on this matter, and therefore I will stay at Leicester till you send me word. If you doe approve of our undertaking, I will come over to Bretby, aud after having acquainted you with all the particulars of our whole design, take my measure with your lordship; but if you dislike our proceedings, I will not doe you so great a prejudice."*

* Browne, 303, 304.

THOMAS OSBORNE

EARL OF DANBY, AFTERWARDS DUKE OF LEEDS

To face page 358

At last the East wind blew, the Protestant prince arrived, and the Catholic King fled. Danby, who had taken a prominent part in the invitation, seized York for William. When the Revolution was accomplished he claimed his reward, and in April 1689 he was made Marquess of Carmarthen. He also received back his lord-lieutenancy in Yorkshire, and was appointed President of the Council. But he had higher ambitions: the salary of his new office was much less than the £8,000 a year he had drawn as Lord Treasurer, and had far fewer pickings; he wished again to be Chief Minister and he grudged the power that was wielded by Halifax. But he had to deal with a cautious master who gave his confidence slowly. The "White Marquess" was equally difficult: he sulked in the country, rarely attended the Council, and quarrelled with his colleagues. Many of the Whigs distrusted him, and shortly after his appointment the Commons presented an address begging the King to dismiss all ministers "who had ever been impeached." William, however, disregarded the hint; he was beginning to know his men better, and he took his own course.

In 1690 the Tories obtained a majority: the versatile Halifax retired and a larger share of influence fell to the Lord President, who now secured rooms in St. James's Palace. But his unpopularity did not diminish, and on one occasion at Bath he was badly hustled by a mob. He was called "a thin, ill-natured ghost that haunts the King," "the Tyrant" and "King Thomas."

> "David we thought succeeded Saul
> When William rose on James's fall,
> But now King Thomas rules us all."

His old methods of bribery still stood him in good stead; he kept a number of members of Parliament dependent on him, and whenever an office was to be had he bid for it. With the King he gained favour, and he gradually re-assumed the position of Chief Minister. During William's absence in Ireland, he was left as Queen Mary's principal counsellor, though she did not care for him. Writing to

her husband, she says: "Lord Carmarthen is upon all
occasions afraid of giving me too much trouble, and
thinks, by little and little, to do all; everyone sees how
little I know of business, and therefore, I believe, all
be apt to do as much as they can. Lord Marlborough
advised me to resolve to be present as often as possible:
out of what intention I cannot judge, but I find they
meet often at the Secretary's office, and do not take much
pains to give me an account."* Again, discussing a
commission which the Council had refused to pass, she
says: "I asked Lord President what answer was to be
sent. I told him I was much surprised at the refusal:
he was very angry and talking at a great rate: but I
stopped him and told him I was angry enough and desired
he would not be too much so, for I did not believe it a
proper time. I desired he would add this—I could not
change my mind—if it were proper to say so much. He
said it was rather too little."†

The Lord President had become by now "very peevish,"
and was "continually complaining." But though he
was losing his power and his influence, he was still a
leading figure in the House of Lords, and in January
1692-3, at the trial of Lord Mohun, he acted as Lord
High Steward. At last, in May 1694, he obtained the
object of his desires, and was created Duke of Leeds. In
little over twenty years he had risen from a commoner
to the highest rank in the peerage—a feat less rare than
is generally believed.‡

But his troubles were not yet over. There had always
been a suspicion as to his sympathy with James, and it
was now suggested that he was in treasonable correspondence with the court at St. Germain. The truth was that
offers had been made to him, though he had not succumbed to them, but the tale did him harm. In 1695,
however, it was discovered that he had received 5,000
guineas from the East India Company for procuring them

* Browne, 369.   † Ibid., 324.
‡ Of the eighteen English dukes the ancestors of ten were
similarly advanced in their own lifetime.

a new charter. As to this he defended himself, saying that such gifts were the custom and recalling his past services. But he was again impeached, and though the trial was not proceeded with for want of evidence (and because the King himself had received 10,000 guineas) it cost him his place. He was directed to absent himself from the Council for a time, and when he returned his position had become nominal and his authority nugatory. For a few years he held places on one or two commissions, and in 1698 his eldest son was attached to Peter the Great during his visit to England, but in 1699 he resigned definitely and left the government. Perhaps a clearer appreciation of his talents made William prefer to be without them, and for the remainder of his life the Duke of Leeds was not employed. " His politics indeed unfitted him for advising the possessor of a revolutionary crown."

Yet he did not cease to take an interest in public affairs, and during the reign of Queen Anne his old Toryism returned in great strength, " though he was not much regarded." He questioned the prudence and right of Parliament in assigning the throne to the late King, and even deprecated his own part in the Revolution, publishing an account of his earlier ministry. But he did not hesitate to write and offer his services to the Electoral Prince of Hanover when he saw how the wind was blowing.

In 1704 he had lost his wife: " she had nearly been killed in a carriage accident some years earlier, but recovered to plague her husband, her son and many others some time longer."* He took a prominent part in the defence of Dr. Sacheverell, " having an amazing vitality," but after that he lived chiefly in retirement, and at last, on July 26, 1712, he died at Easton in his eighty-first year. " He left a princely fortune," besides a number of diaries and letters which are now in the British Museum. One son and five married daughters survived him. The present Duke of Leeds is his descendant.

* D. N. B., xiv. 1197.

In early life Danby was " a comely person," but as he grew into middle age he became thin and pallid, due perhaps to his long sojourn in the Tower. There are several portraits of him. Of his private life little is known.

He had considerable parliamentary talents. Burnet calls him " a very plausible speaker, but too copious and could not easily make an end of his discourse. He gave himself great liberties and . . . was an implacable enemy. He was a positive and undertaking man: and when his hopes failed he had always some excuse ready to put the miscarriage upon. . . . Had it not been that French and popish counsels were so visible he had very probably raised the King's power and brought things to the state they were in before King Charles I.'s time."* Macaulay gives him a worse character: " greedy of wealth and honours, corrupt himself, and a corrupter of others. Yet he was not without the feelings of an Englishman and a Protestant: nor did he, in his solicitude for his own interests, ever wholly forget the interests of his country and of his religion."† Neither Evelyn nor Pepys liked him, and he had few intimates. His methods were unpalatable to many, even in those days. Ambitious, a seeker after rank, place and fortune, Danby succeeded in getting all three. But they did not enhance his reputation. An unattractive personality, his best excuse is that he held power during the worst period of a bad age. That he used the methods of his day to serve his master may not mean that he did not try to serve the State, but it is perhaps to his advantage that his memory and his services are obscured by time.

The policy of Clarendon and Danby was similar in idea, though applied by men of very different character: support of the Church, hatred of Popery or Dissent, a high notion of the prerogative, an effort to unite King and Parliament. The former looked backward and

* Burnet, ii. 12, 90.   † Macaulay, Hist., i. 224

cherished his integrity; the latter looked forward and savoured bribery. Both were duped and deserted by their master; both fell at the fiat of France; both were execrated by the nation. Clarendon died an exile, but his name is still a household word; Danby died a duke, and his doings are wisely forgotten.

CHAPTER XII
THE NEW IDEA

GODOLPHIN AND HARLEY

THE age of Anne is a capital epoch in the political history of England, for it is the link between the days of direct rule and those of parliamentary government. Its short space is packed with events of the first importance. In the reign of Anne the Sovereign last refused her assent to a Bill of the Legislature, she last coerced the Upper House by a creation of peers, she last presided over the meetings of the Cabinet. In those twelve years the first of English generals gained his greatest victories, the first of English premiers started his political career, the arts and letters of England began a new lease of life. Even in the simple annals of the poor, Queen Anne's bounty and Queen Anne's death still strike a chord.

Yet little of the fame that adorns her era is due to her own personality. She had much, it is true, to help her; in her own lifetime her uncle, her father, her sister and her cousin had worn the English crown; she was a woman, the last of a royal race; tradition, environment and experience might well have made her a ruler of men. But nature was too strong, and female weakness triumphed. Fat, red-faced, indolent and nervous, proud yet stubborn, the mother of nineteen children none of whom survived her, the slave of flatterers and bullies, Anne spent her aimless days in quarrelling with her ministers, in galloping across Windsor Park, and in drinking tea. A kind, unstable and feckless character, divided between her duty to her brother, her duty to her Church, and her duty to her country, she struggled painfully through her reign, and closed a colourless life before she was fifty, an insubstantial foil to the magnificence of Marlborough and the domination of his wife.

This amazing couple had already filled the stage for close on a generation, and the survivor was to play a part on it for a generation more. Born mere " shrubs of gentry," they had risen to be grandees of the finest water, the principal *arrivistes* of their time. Their first fortunes had been founded on good looks and good luck. John Churchill was an exceptionally handsome and engaging ensign in the Guards, and he early found favour with the notorious Duchess of Cleveland; his sister Arabella was ugly and dull, but she succeeded in attracting the attentions of the Duke of York.* " *Tous convenoient,*" says Anthony Hamilton, " *qu'un homme qui étoit favori de la maitresse du roi et frère de celle du duc, ne pouvoit manquer de faire fortune.*"† But Churchill was much more than a mere carpet knight. In the campaigns of 1672 and 1673, under Turenne and Monmouth, he distinguished himself by a brilliant daring and resource. No venture cooled him; no danger appalled him; no scruple checked him. His sister helped him with her lover, and he devoted himself to the deception of that portentous prince.

His promotion was rapid. He became a colonel, a general, a baron and an earl. He had married a clever wife, with the face of an angel and the temper of a fiend. Together the two possessed themselves of the Princess Anne, monopolized her household, and subjugated her mind. Then came the Revolution. Marlborough deserted James, his benefactor, and sold himself, as did many others, to William. William knew his value as a soldier and employed him. Marlborough took his money and led his troops, but did not fail to tell the exiled James when and where they were to be expected. For a short time he was under a cloud, but when William died and

---

* The Duke's mistresses were not famous for beauty: King Charles used to say that the priests gave them to him for a penance.

† Grammont, i. 379.

Anne came into her own, the fortunes of the Churchills knew no bounds. All restraints were removed, and the transcendent genius of the leader blazed forth. In a few years he had become the captain of Europe and of the age. Serene, Olympian, invulnerable, unconquerable, he passed from battle to battle, from siege to siege, from victory to victory, a master of the art of war. At home his avarice, his treachery, his meanness were all forgotten, only his triumphs and his services were recalled, and every honour that his Sovereign or his country could bestow was showered upon him. His friend Godolphin directed the government while his wife dominated the Queen. For several years their rule was maintained, but at last there came an end; Anne rebelled against the tyranny of the duchess, and the duke fell. He reverted to his old tactics, and veered to the Pretender; but this time he was too late, the die was cast against him, and when he returned to England at the accession of King George he had ceased to count as a serious factor in politics. In a few years his marvellous mind sank into imbecility.

The influence he had had upon home affairs had been indirect, but his example was remembered. Walpole, his colleague in the ministry, had seen the fate of trimmers and time-servers, of Danby and Godolphin, Harley and St. John. He had learnt that an English statesman must rely on Parliament rather than on the Crown, and that the nation still appreciated the virtues of consistency, altruism and honesty. He laid the lesson to heart, and under his rule the political morality of England began slowly to take an upward trend.

I.—GODOLPHIN

Sydney Godolphin, afterwards Earl of Godolphin, was born early in June 1645, at the place of his own name, near Breage in Cornwall. His father, Sir Francis, came of an ancient family in that county; his mother, Dorothy, was a daughter of Sir Henry Berkeley, of Yarlington in

Somerset. The Godolphins had long been honourably distinguished in the West. Sir Francis had acted as governor of the Scilly Isles for the King during the Civil War, and at the Restoration he was created a Knight of the Bath. Of his six sons, William, the eldest, was made a baronet, while Henry became Provost of Eton and Dean of St. Paul's.

Sydney, the third son, was sent when a boy to Charles II.'s court in Holland. He then went to Oxford, and soon after the Restoration he was appointed a page of honour in the royal household. In March 1667 he lost his father, from whom he inherited only a very small competence. Three months later the Dutch fleet sailed up the Thames, and Godolphin, like many other young courtiers, asked for a commission in the army. He became, like Chatham, a cornet of horse, though his military services were not utilized, as he fell ill. But the next year he was elected member of Parliament for Helston in Cornwall, a borough which owned allegiance to his family.

About this time he fell in love with Miss Margaret Blagge, or Blake, a daughter of Colonel Thomas Blagge, an old Suffolk royalist. She and her sister Henrietta were maids of honour to the Duchess of York, Lord Clarendon's daughter. Henrietta, according to Anthony Hamilton, was foolish, frivolous and ugly; but Margaret was a very different character. A religious and serious student, she was a close friend of John Evelyn's, and on her early death he wrote a singularly charming account of her beauty and her piety. Godolphin's courtship was long and not very promising; he had no income, and his family looked upon the alliance as a poor one. His sister writes home from London: "These are ill times to set up with upon their foundation. I pray God send better."* Nor had Miss Blagge any desire to shine at court; she only wished to live a quiet life in the country.

In 1672, however, Godolphin was advanced to be a groom of the bedchamber, a post which gave him a salary

* Elliot, 66.

of £1,000 a year. Charles II. had some liking for him, and once said: "Sydney Godolphin is never in the way and never out of it."* This promotion made the marriage more possible. Miss Blagge forwent for the nonce her retired tastes and was induced to appear in a play at court, acting the part of Diana, Goddess of Chastity— the other rôles being filled by the Princesses Mary and Anne and Miss Sarah Jennings, afterwards Duchess of Marlborough. In May 1675 Godolphin was secretly married, and soon afterwards he and his wife established themselves in a small house near Scotland Yard. Their married life was only too short. In September 1678 their single child was born, and a week later the mother died of fever, leaving her husband distraught with grief; he was unable to attend to any business and incapable of being present at her funeral. Her loss was the greater blow as he was now really beginning to make his way. The King had recently appointed him Master of the Robes, and, perhaps because of his former residence in Holland, had sent him over as envoy to Brussels and The Hague. At Nimeguen Sir William Temple saw a good deal of him, and when, in the following year, his plan of a new Privy Council was adopted, he recommended Godolphin to the King as a suitable member.

In March 1679 Godolphin was appointed a junior lord of the treasury, and after Danby's fall he became, with Rochester and Sunderland, one of Charles' more intimate counsellors—the three being known as "the Chits." Godolphin was an opponent of the Duke of York and a friend of the Prince of Orange, but he devoted himself principally to his work at the treasury.

The time was one of intrigue. The French Duchess of Portsmouth still held Charles' favour, and with her Godolphin allied himself. He did not scruple to deceive James, whose friend he had formerly been, and to become a pronounced exclusionist. James accordingly hated him. "Nothing," he said, "will go well till Godolphin and all the rotten sheep at the end of the gallery are turned out."†

* Macaulay, Hist., i. 295.   † Elliot, 91.

But Godolphin's progress went on. In April 1684 he was appointed Secretary of State, and four months later he was created a peer and made First Lord of the Treasury in the place of his friend Rochester. At Charles' death, in February 1685, the French ambassador writes: "*Milord Sunderland, Madame de Portsmouth et Milord Godolphin possedoient seules toute l'autorité auprès du feu Roi d'Angleterre.*"*

The accession of James seemed likely to be fatal to the favourites. "The earl of Sunderland was looked on as a man lost at court: and so was lord Godolphin."† But the former "insinuated himself into the Queen's confidence," and was kept on as Secretary of State; while the latter, "who was more esteemed and trusted by her than any man in England," was made her lord chamberlain‡—he was said, indeed, to nourish a secret passion for her. It may be that James, who was for the moment on his good behaviour, thought it wise to keep round him some of his brother's counsellors, and "Godolphin's obsequiousness, industry, experience and taciturnity could ill be spared."§ His new post was not an exalted place for one who had been at the head of the treasury commission—but as a court appointment it was important, and Godolphin had passed many years as a courtier; in any event it was better than dismissal from the government; and perhaps, in James' view, it would afford opportunities of conversion, or at any rate of supervision. So Godolphin

"Beat time with politic head, and all approves,
Pleased with the charge of the Queen's muff and gloves."

With Rochester, the new Lord Treasurer, and Sunderland, the Secretary of State, Godolphin was on the best of terms. He had also a third friend, Lord Churchill, the future Duke of Marlborough. Churchill was five years his junior, and had been a page with him; they had received their first commissions in the same year, and their

* Elliot, 87.   † Burnet, O. T., iii. 8.
‡ *Ibid.*, iii. 8.   § Macaulay, Hist., i. 447.

wives had both been maids of honour to the late Duchess of York. Their politics were similar, though their principles were different; and as Churchill was at this time one of James' closest friends, his good word was invaluable to Godolphin. The latter thus regained the favour he had lost, and James soon gave him his confidence. Godolphin had little sympathy for arbitrary rule, but he bowed himself in the House of Rimmon. He took part in the secret negotiations with Louis XIV. to get James a pension for not calling Parliament, and he conformed outwardly to the new religious programme by attending Mass. He was said to be " always on the verge of becoming a professed Roman Catholic."* His colleagues, however, were less sanctimonious, though equally loyal. Reresby, writing early in 1686, says: " The lord chancellor had now like to have died of a fit of the stone, brought on by a furious debauch of wine, when he, the lord treasurer and others drank themselves into that height of frenzy, that they stripped into their shirts and, had not an accident prevented them, had got upon a signpost to drink the King's health."†

Early in 1687 Rochester had to give up his white staff, as he refused to abjure the Protestant faith. Godolphin wrote the letter directing his colleague to resign, and when the treasury was again put into commission, he became its head. He was also appointed keeper of Cranborne Chase, a post which gave him a house in Windsor Park and kept him near the King; but he was still " content to mould policies," and did not seek to create them.

James was now acting as his own Chief Minister, assisted by the Papal nuncio, the French Ambassador, and his Jesuit confessor. As his government grew more despotic and his prospects more desperate, Godolphin began to show some fight. On the declaration of the indulgence he opposed Lord Chancellor Jeffreys in the Council, and "broke loose from him to trim in some clauses."‡ But at the Revolution he stuck to his master.

* Elliot, 109.   † Reresby, 325.   ‡ Clarendon Diary, ii. 189.

He was one of the Council of five appointed to remain in London when James advanced to Salisbury, and he was subsequently one of his three commissioners deputed to treat with William. To help the King in his flight he lent him a hundred guineas which he had already refused to supply from the treasury, and he lodged £20,000 of his own with the Princess Anne for safety. In the Convention debates he voted for a regency—that is to say, against the transfer of the crown. But William was wise and magnanimous and could distinguish between opposition to a constitutional change and opposition personal to himself. " Godolphin's calm and cold way suited his temper,"* and he was kept on at the treasury, though not at its head : his connection with the late King and his known Tory sympathies made this at first impossible.

For some time Godolphin was now regarded as one of James' principal representatives, and in March 1690 he left the treasury—unwilling perhaps to serve as a sub-ordinate where he had more experience than all his colleagues. But in the following November he was reinstated as First Lord, and there he remained for the next six years. He was in a peculiar position, for during much of the time he was in correspondence with the exiled court at St. Germain, sending over to James intelligence that he obtained from his official knowledge, and even announcing the despatch of the British expedition to Brest. He often tried to resign his place, but was not allowed to do so by the King. William writes to him in 1692: " You have too much friendship for me to wish to abandon me. . . . I assure you that the wish to see you continue in my service does not so much proceed from the benefit I draw from it as the satisfaction of having near me a person for whom I have such a personal friendship and of whom I have so good an opinion."†
" William knew what manner of man he had to deal with . . . and he knew also most of the secrets of the Jacobites."‡ Godolphin's financial ability was invaluable,

* Burnet, O. T., iv. 7.   † Elliot, 152.   ‡ *Ibid.*, 153.

and despite the accusations that were brought against him, he was more useful to the King in the government than out of it. A First Lord of the Treasury was not so important as a Lord Treasurer, and Godolphin confined himself for the most part to departmental work, rarely attending the Council, and leading a retired life. But at the treasury he devoted himself to business, saving money, reducing the Budget, controlling the receipts and expenditure of the exchequer. He had a difficult task, but he did it well, and he also gave his Sovereign sound advice. He writes on one occasion: " If it pleased God to grant your Majesty an honourable peace . . . your Majesty would quickly find that the Jacobites would turn moderate churchmen and loyal subjects, and the Whigs much more obsequious courtiers and easier servants than now they are."*

In 1695 and 1696 Godolphin was one of the seven lords justices appointed to act during William's absence abroad. In the latter year came Fenwick's plot to assassinate the King. With this Godolphin's name was mixed up—the culprit alleging that he had been reconciled to James. Godolphin denied this, but the suggestion damaged him, and as he was the only Tory left in the government he thought it best to resign. It is said that he was tricked into doing so by Sunderland. William recognized his innocence and regretted his loss, but he could not withstand the hostility of the Whigs.

Godolphin was now a man of fifty, with an unrivalled experience of finance and a reputation for prudence that had enabled him to steer safely through fifteen troublous years. He was friendly with William, with Anne, and probably with James. His cautious policy was to take him still further. In 1698 his only son Francis was married to Lady Henrietta Churchill, Marlborough's eldest daughter, and the alliance between the two families was confirmed.

In December 1700 the Tories returned to power and Godolphin again became First Lord of the Treasury—the

* Elliot, 164, note.

Marlboroughs being determined that he should no longer play a passive rôle. But in the following year he again resigned, partly as a protest against the new war with France, partly because of his friendship with the Princess Anne, who was on bad terms with her brother-in-law the King. She writes to Godolphin in the winter of 1701: " It is a very great satisfaction to me to find you agree with Mrs. Morley [herself] concerning the ill-natured cruel proceedings of Caliban [William III.]."* Three months later the King was thrown from his horse. In a few days he died, and the political scene instantly changed.

The Princess Anne succeeded to the throne. Lord Marlborough was made a duke, captain-general of the army, and Master of the Ordnance; his wife was appointed Ranger of the Royal Parks, Groom of the Stole and Mistress of the Robes. Between them they soon enjoyed an official income of over £60,000 a year. Godolphin, the third of the trio, became Lord Treasurer and the ostensible head of the government. He had recently sold his lodge at Windsor and established himself at Godolphin House (afterwards Stafford, and now Lancaster House) in St. James's Park. In those days it was a simple building of red brick concave to the south. He was still a comparatively poor man, and his taste for racing did not improve his private circumstances; but he understood public economy, and he was now to hold the most lucrative place in the ministry and to dispense enormous patronage.

At first he demurred to taking office, but the Queen pressed him, while Marlborough made his acceptance a condition of assuming command of the army. The two friends thus became " the real government of the Queen. Their colleagues were ciphers."† Godolphin's honest wish seems to have been rural bliss—

" Granville shall seize the long expected chair
Godolphin to some country seat repair "—

but his friends were too strong for him, and the undivided control of his favourite treasury was an attraction hard to resist.

* Elliot, 195, note. † Paul, 45.

The war with France had just begun, and was generally popular in the country. But it was a Whig war, and the ministry was Tory, though the intrigues of the next eight years were to transform it into a government of Whigs. Marlborough, a Tory himself, was nervous of the too complete control of his own party, and was anxious that its Jacobite extremists should not prevail. He believed that a coalition would prevent this, and gradually he allowed the government to be watered down.

In 1703 Rochester was dismissed, in 1704 Nottingham; while Harley and St. John, two moderate Tories, joined the ministry. Godolphin soon began to lose command of his crew. Marlborough was away fighting in the Low Countries, but his wife was at St. James's, dominating both the Queen and the Lord Treasurer, who had a dis- piriting task.   "The life of a slave in the galleys," he said, "was a paradise in comparison with his."* Party struggles did not attract him in the least; he was compelled to find money for wars with which he had no great sympathy, and much of his time was perforce given to foreign politics rather than to the finance in which he excelled. But he was able to blend the two together. "Though not a free trader in the modern sense of the word, he was too good a man of business to neglect the vast importance of international trade,"† and the Methuen treaty with Portugal was due to his initiative. At home he was a principal promoter of the union with Scotland, and was one of the commissioners for negotiating the treaty. In the early years of his ministry matters went well : "the credit of the country was never raised so high in any age nor so sacredly maintained."‡ But although he was the Chief Minister of the Crown he was losing the confidence of his Sovereign and of Parliament, and the Revolution had made these conditions essential to the permanence of a government, though the country had not yet realized the change.

In 1705 there was a general election, and in the new Parliament the Whigs had a majority. To carry on the

* Elliot, 402.   † Paul, 33.   ‡ Burnet, O. T., v. 292.

SYDNEY GODOLPHIN
EARL OF GODOLPHIN

To face page 374

government Godolphin was compelled to seek their alliance, and in so doing he alienated many of his Tory friends. The Whig Lord Sunderland, Marlborough's other son-in-law, became a Secretary of State, while Harley began to loom large as a power in the Cabinet. At his house, early in 1706, the Whig leaders dined with Marlborough and Godolphin, and came to an apparent agreement. The pact was disliked, but Marlborough remarked that " England will not be ruined because a few men are not pleased."*

As a reward for his good work Godolphin, who had received the Garter in 1704, was now advanced to an earldom. But his hold on his followers was rapidly slackening. He found himself in the unusual predicament of having to restrain the warlike projects of the Whigs and the pacifist tendencies of the Tories. He writes to the Duchess of Marlborough: " As to what you say of the Whigs I am to learn that till they have the power in their hands they will be against everything that may be an assistance to the Queen and the government."†

The duchess's influence with the Queen was also on the wane. She was particularly distrustful of Harley, who was " climbing up the back stairs " at court, and she pressed Godolphin to get rid of him. The Whigs had Godolphin largely under their control, and as he resented the power of Harley and St. John, in 1708 he forced them to leave the ministry. Walpole then joined it, Somers was made Lord President, and its complexion became purely Whig.

The High Churchmen, formerly Godolphin's strongest supporters, now began to attack him. The Queen, a strong Tory, was irritated by his apparent pusillanimity and outraged by the tyranny of the duchess. Harley, through his cousin, Mrs. Masham, one of Anne's personal attendants, encouraged her, and various slights were put upon the duke and the Lord Treasurer. Marlborough was still abroad, and Godolphin had to meet the storm alone. He often threatened to resign, but he never

* Green, iv. 94. † Duchess of Marlborough, i. 30-1.

25

carried his threats into effect, and the Queen ceased to fear him.

In 1709 the victory of Malplaquet with its immense losses gave the Opposition an opportunity, and when Marlborough preferred a request to be made captain-general for life he was refused. Despite his victories the country was becoming tired of the war.* He concealed his chagrin; he would rather, he said, be envied than pitied; and he strove to maintain his power in the government. " His enemies saw that his chief strength lay in the credit that the lord Godolphin was in at home, so they laid their aims to attack the Lord Treasurer."† In August and November of that year Dr. Sacheverell, a High Tory, preached two sermons assailing Godolphin by the name of Volpone. He was impeached, but escaped with a light sentence, and his trial caused a great reaction against the Whigs. The Tory leaders then urged Anne to strike.

On April 6, 1710, the Duchess of Marlborough had her final quarrel with the Queen, " reproaching her in so loud and shrill a voice that the footmen at the bottom of the backstairs could hear her."‡ She was then dismissed from all her offices, and shortly afterwards other changes were made in the ministry without the knowledge or consent of Godolphin. " The Lord Treasurer submitted meekly to the affront and went on betting at Newmarket."§ He wrote, however, to the Queen, begging her not to desert those who were most loyal to her. Speaking of the Duke of Shrewsbury, whom Anne had just appointed Lord Chamberlain, he says: " I must endeavour to get your Majesty to see things as they really are; and to bring him into your service just after his being in open conjunction with the Tories and in private correspondence and caballing with Mr. Harley, what consequence can this have but to make every man that is now in your cabinet uneasy and run from it as they would do from the plague ?

---

* The rumour of the duke's death at Malplaquet originated the song of *Malbrook s'en va-t-en guerre* (Stanhope, Queen Anne, 397).
† Burnet, O. T., v. 175.   ‡ *Ibid.*, v. 440, note.   § Paul, 92.

. . . However, for my own part I must humbly beg leave to assure your Majesty I will never give the least obstruction to your measures or to any ministers you shall employ."*

Anne had struck her first blow with success. She knew that Godolphin and Marlborough were not in complete agreement, and Harley was at her elbow to advise her. She went on boldly, and in June 1710 Sunderland was removed. Then came the final act. At a Council early in August there was a quarrel between Godolphin and Shrewsbury, in which Anne took part; on the 7th Godolphin had an audience in which he complained of Anne's secret counsellors; next morning a royal footman left him a letter from the Queen in the following terms:

" The uneasiness which you have shown for some time has given me very much trouble, though I have borne it; and had your behaviour continued the same as it was for a few years after my coming to the crown I would have no dispute with myself what to do. But the many unkind returns I have received since, especially what you said to me personally before the lords, makes it impossible for me to continue you any longer in my service; but I will give you a pension of £4,000 a year, and I desire that instead of bringing the staff to me, you will break it, which I believe will be easier for both."†

Godolphin obeyed the command and replied with a dutiful letter; writing to Marlborough on the same day, he says that he had not had the least notice of what was to happen. To the Treasurer the loss of office was serious, for it meant the end of affluence; he was still a poor man, for he had been scrupulously honest in his place. Yet he took the change stoically enough. His pension, it is said, was never paid, though by the death of his elder brother his family had just inherited a moderate income. But his own work was over. His health was broken, he had long suffered from the stone, and he was nearing seventy. Two years later, on September 15, 1712, he

* Elliot, 412. † *Ibid.*, 418.

died while on a visit to the Marlboroughs at St. Albans, almost a forgotten man. He was buried in Westminster Abbey.

In his later years Godolphin had led a lonely life, for the tale of his second marriage is not substantiated. He left a single son, Francis, whose wife eventually became Duchess of Marlborough in her own right; but as she had no surviving male issue that title passed to the Sunderland family, and the earldom of Godolphin became extinct. Of her daughters one married the Prime Minister Duke of Newcastle, and the other the fourth Duke of Leeds, whose family, the Godolphin-Osbornes, are now the Lord Treasurer's heirs of line.

Godolphin was a heavily-built man, short, with beetling brows and a "very black and stern countenance":* "Baconface" he used to be called. North says that "he had mastered all the classical learning, and being naturally dark and reserved became an adept in court politics. His talent of unravelling intricate matters and exposing them to an easy view was incomparable. He was an expert gamester, and had a felicity of wit."† Cards, cockfighting and horseracing were his amusements —the Godolphin Arabian commemorates his name—but they never made him neglect his work. His personal distractions, indeed, belied his public character. Economical but poor, cautious yet a gambler, he was a contradiction in terms. His reserved temperament and his taciturnity got him few friends, and his political vagaries lost him more.

His application to the business of the treasury was rarely surpassed, and his regard for detail was meticulous; on an indent for a new silver trumpet for the Life Guards he minuted "What has become of the old one?" But in large issues he could take a broad and distant view, and his administration of the exchequer earned the respect of his contemporaries and the praise of posterity. Domestic legislation appealed to him less, and although his diplomacy was lucky his foreign policy

* Gibbs, v. 455.   † North, ii. 58.

was often timid. His critics always accused him of cowardice.

> " Whatever did he in his life perform
> But shrink at the approach of every storm ?"

His real wish was to be quit of continental entanglements, but the duke abroad and the duchess at home were usually too strong for him.

Burnet calls him " the silentest and modestest man that was perhaps ever bred in a court. He had a clear apprehension and despatched business with great method, and with so much temper that he had no personal enemies: but his silence begat a jealousy which hung long upon him. His incorrupt and sincere way of managing the concerns of the treasury created in all people a very high esteem for him. He loved gaming the most of any man of business I ever knew: and gave one reason for it, because it delivered him from the obligation to talk much: he had true principles of religion, and was free from all vanity, and never heaped up wealth: so that he was one of the worthiest and wisest men in our time."* Lord Dartmouth adds, however, that " he had a very morose, haughty behaviour and could disoblige people by his looks, more than he could have done by anything he said to them, though his answers were commonly very short and shocking." " He constantly refused everything that he was sure would be forced upon him."†

Macaulay approves his finance but questions his loyalty. " His great object was to be in favour with both the rival kings at once, and to keep, through all revolutions and counter-revolutions, his head, his estate and a place at the Board of Treasury—zealous for no government and useful to any government, he had become an almost indispensable part of the machinery of state. Like most men of cautious tempers and prosperous fortunes, he had a strong disposition to support whatever existed."‡ Mr. Paul styles him " a man of low character, low aims,

---

* Burnet, O. T., ii. 239, 240.　　　† *Ibid.*, v. 8, note.
　　　‡ Macaulay, Hist., iv. 390; iii. 21; ii. 255.

low tastes and pursuits," but adds that " in a corrupt age he was incorruptible and the finances of this country never had a more vigilant steward."*

> " Who would not praise Patricio's high desert,
> His hand unstained, his uncorrupted heart,
> His comprehensive head ! all interests weighed,
> All Europe sav'd, yet Britain not betray'd—
> He thanks you not, his pride is in picquette,
> New-Market fame, and judgement in a bett."

Godolphin is an unimpressive, nebulous figure—little known to his own or later ages. A man without passions or politics, though an honest and capable public servant, he was a fish out of water in the days through which he lived. Forced to accommodate himself to the manners of his times, he went no further than was necessary, content to do his own work and to elude as far as possible the dirty work of others. Controlled by the two stronger spirits with whom he acted, he never realized that ministerial responsibility and a ministerial majority had become a part of the British constitution, and he strove to continue the old methods by a process of compromise and coalition. His was one of the last attempts to govern England on other terms than those of party government. With all the training of a court he had few of its arts, and in old age even these seem to have failed him. But his record as an administrator is so high that it may well cover his deficiencies as a statesman.

II.—HARLEY

Robert Harley, afterwards Earl of Oxford, was born in Bow Street, Covent Garden, London, on December 5, 1661. He was the eldest son of Sir Edward Harley, K.B., of Harley and Brampton, in Herefordshire, by his second wife, Abigail, daughter of Nathaniel Stephens of Essington in Gloucestershire. His family, says Collins, was one of the most noble in England, " undoubtedly more ancient

* Paul, 21, 95.

than the Norman Conquest, and so illustrious that those in France may be descended from it."* Originally seated in Shropshire they included among their ancestors Sir William, a crusader in 1098; Sir Richard, who fought at Lewes and Evesham; Sir Bryan, a companion-in-arms of the Black Prince; Sir John, who was knighted on Tewkesbury field; his grandson, who fought at Flodden; Sir Robert, Master of the Mint to James I., and a number of collaterals hardly less distinguished. By marriage they were allied with the de Veres, Mortimers, Clares, Marshalls, Staffords, Corbets and Conways, and though only country gentlemen of a moderate estate, were of the best blood in the West of England.

Sir Edward Harley, a man of moderate views and a strong sympathizer with the Presbyterians, had fought valiantly for the Parliament in the Civil War, and had sat as member for Hereford. But in 1647 he opposed Cromwell and Fairfax, was impeached by the army, and joined the King's party. At the Restoration he was appointed Governor of Dunkirk, and was able to hand over to the King a sum of £10,000, which he had saved during his term of office. For his services he was offered a viscounty which he refused, and was then created a Knight of the Bath.

Robert Harley, his son, was educated by Dr. Birch, of Burford in Oxfordshire, at a private school which was remarkable for producing at the same time a future Lord Treasurer, Lord Chancellor and Lord Chief Justice, all contemporaries at school and in Parliament. He then went, it is believed, to Westminster, and in 1682 he was admitted a student at the Inner Temple, though he was never called. In May 1685 he married his first wife, Elizabeth, daughter of Thomas Foley, of Witley Court in Worcestershire, a strong Whig. This alliance and the vagaries of James II. modified the royalist views of the Harleys, who again became prominent Dissenters, and at the Revolution father and son raised a troop of horse at their own expense and marched on Worcester, of which

* Collins, iv. 37.

town Sir Edward was made governor for the Prince of Orange.

In March 1689 Robert Harley was appointed high sheriff of Herefordshire, and shortly afterwards was elected member of Parliament for Tregony, a seat that he exchanged a year later for Radnor. He made a rapid advance in the House, and in 1690 was chosen a commissioner for the public accounts. He was a man of industry and application; and he soon " knew the forms and records of Parliament so well that he was capable both of lengthening out and perplexing debates. Nothing could answer his aspiring temper; so he joined with the Tories to create jealousies and raise an opposition."* This was his second change of party. He was, it seems, dissatisfied with the little recognition he had received at the Revolution, and he adopted the not unusual method of advancing himself by attacking the government. With his connection Mr. Paul Foley, he was soon a constant trouble to the ministry.

In 1694 he brought in the Triennial Bill, which was passed; in 1696 he set up the National Land Bank, which was a complete failure, and in 1697 he succeeded in getting the army establishment considerably reduced. Although frequently acting with the moderate Tories, he did not lose touch with his own Whig dissenting friends, and by keeping a foot in either camp he became a power in the House.

In 1700 Harley's father died, and he succeeded to a considerable fortune. In February 1701, when he was just thirty-nine years old, he was elected Speaker by a majority of 120 over Sir Richard Onslow; at the end of the year he was re-elected, though he only defeated his predecessor Lyttelton by four votes; and in Anne's first Parliament he was for the third time chosen to fill the chair.

Godolphin and Marlborough were already beginning their difficulties with the High Tories, who were averse to carrying on the French war with vigour. Harley was

* Burnet, O. T., iv. 191.

a man from whom they hoped to get assistance as a go-between, and in April 1704 he was sworn a privy councillor, and a month later appointed a Secretary of State in place of Lord Nottingham. This office he held concurrently with the speakership for nearly a year. One of his friends, Henry St. John, also a moderate Tory and distinguished for his eloquence and scepticism, had joined the ministry at the same time, and for some years the two acted together, each supplying the other's deficiencies. Harley, though not brilliant, was learned, and it was about this time that he first began to interest himself in the collection of books and in a patronage of literature which made him popular with the political writers.

At the general election of 1705 the Whigs had a majority, and from this time the composition of the government began rapidly to change in their direction. Harley was the principal minister in the House of Commons and the chief cementer of the new alliance. At a dinner which he gave to the rival leaders in January 1706, " after the Lord Treasurer had left, he took a glass and drank to everlasting union and wished he had more Tokay to drink it in." Lord Cowper adds: " We had drank two bottles, good but thick " . . . and then remarks of his host: " If any man was ever born under a Necessity or being a knave, he was."*

Three months later Harley was named one of the commissioners for the treaty of Scotland, which was to result in the Act of Union. He now felt the ground firmer under his feet. Bishop Burnet says: " At this time he had gained great credit with the Queen, and began to set up for himself and to act no more under the direction of the Lord Treasurer: there was one of the bedchamber women nearly related to Mr. Harley, and the two entered into a close correspondence. She learned the arts of a court and observed the Queen's temper with so much application that she got far into her heart; and she employed all her credit to establish Harley in the supreme confidence of the Queen and to alienate her affections

* Cowper, 33.

from the Duchess of Marlborough."* The bedchamber
woman was Abigail Hill, Mrs. Masham, and with her aid
in the royal closet and that of St. John in Parliament,
Harley now began to work against Marlborough and
Godolphin. He gradually became such a power in the
Cabinet, so fruitful in increasing the mutual jealousy
between the parties composing it, that Godolphin determined to get rid of him. He was accordingly accused of
a treasonable correspondence with the French, and though
the charge broke down, Godolphin and Marlborough
enforced his retirement by absenting themselves from
the Council, until at last the Queen was obliged to dismiss
him. St. John went with him, and in their place some
more Whigs, including the young Robert Walpole, joined
the ministry. But Harley's bolt was not shot. "Throughout the whole summer after his dismission," says the
Duchess of Marlborough, "the Queen continued to have
secret correspondence with him. And that this might be
the better managed she stayed all the sultry season, even
when the Prince was panting for breath, in the small
house she had purchased at Windsor, as hot as an oven,
because from the park such persons as Mrs. Masham
had a mind to bring to her Majesty could be let in privately
through the garden."†

Throughout the years 1708 and 1709 Harley continued
to intrigue. His position in the Commons was more than
a match for that of Godolphin in the Lords, while the
flattery of Mrs. Masham was much preferred by the Queen
to the abuse of the duchess. Malplaquet and Sacheverell
improved his opportunities, and he went on methodically
dislodging his opponents and enticing the neutrals, until
at last he was able to strike his final blow at the ministers
and to rise upon their ruin.

In April 1710 the duchess was dismissed, and in August
Godolphin followed her. The Tories took over the government, St. John was made Secretary of State, and a new
commission was issued for the treasury, with Harley as
Chancellor of the Exchequer. "Lord Poulet was first

* Burnet, O. T., v. 326.   † Jesse, Rev., ii. 50.

in form, but Mr. Harley was the person with whom the secret was lodged; and it was visible that he was the Chief Minister."* He had started a new form of political attack, which Walpole was still further to develop. It was an organized campaign against his opponents by means of the press. For this purpose he called to his aid the services of Swift and Defoe, and by their articles in the *Examiner* and the *Review*, no less than by his own management in the House of Commons and that of his cousin at court, he confirmed his power. But it was a power without principle. St. John, his friend and ally, wrote of it later: " I am afraid that we came to court by the same disposition as all parties have done; that the principal spring of our actions was to have the government of the State in our hands; that our principal views were the conservation of this power, great employments to ourselves, and great opportunities of rewarding those who had helped to raise us, and of hurting those who stood in opposition to us."†

Shortly after the new ministry had been formed an accident gave Harley a considerable access of popularity. In March 1711 the Marquis de Guiscard, a French spy in British pay who had been in correspondence with Marlborough and Godolphin, fell out with his employers. His letters were intercepted by the government, and he was arrested and examined by the ministers at the Cockpit in Whitehall. While before them he suddenly made an attempt upon Harley's life, stabbing him with a penknife. The wound was slight, but Harley showed courage and calmness; Guiscard was speedily set upon by St. John and his colleagues, and was so hurt by their swords that he soon afterwards died in Newgate. But the affair was invaluable to Harley. He was extolled as a martyr, publicly thanked by Parliament, and his services specially commended to the Crown. The Queen seized the opportunity of further rewarding him. In May 1711 he was appointed Lord Treasurer—the real summit of his ambition—and created an earl. He was content with no

---

* Burnet, O.T., vi. 9.   † Paul, 99, 100.

common name. Aubrey de Vere, hereditary Lord Great Chamberlain of England, and twentieth Earl of Oxford in a direct line from the Conquest, had recently died without male heirs, and on the plea of his connection in blood with that family Harley revived the title for himself, adding to it the almost equally illustrious one of Mortimer. " His greatest fault," says Dartmouth, " was vanity "*—and the pompous preamble to his patent was couched in " fulsome rhetoric, being prepared by his own direction."

He was now " the chief, if not sole minister, for everything was directed by him."† He brought forward a scheme of funding the national debt, and started the unfortunate South Sea Company, of which he was shortly afterwards elected governor. At the same time he pressed on the preliminaries for the Peace of Utrecht; but owing to his careless management the Bill was defeated in the Lords by the Whigs. The Lord Treasurer replied by advising the Queen to dismiss the Duke of Marlborough from all his offices and to create twelve new peers in order to carry the vote. On their appearance in the House Lord Wharton enquired " whether they would vote singly or by their foreman."‡

The peace proposals were then passed, but they were unpopular; their terms were not thought sufficiently good, though they had been put through with a singular disregard for England's allies. Oxford probably, and St. John certainly, had been intriguing with the Pretender. The latter had just been created Viscount Bolingbroke, but he had been refused the Garter, which was given three months later to Oxford, and he grudged this difference in honours. The two ministers had other reasons for not being as friendly as before. Oxford was, at any rate in appearance, a supporter of the Hanover succession, while Bolingbroke was an almost professed adherent of the exiled House of Stuart. Well aware of his own advantages over his colleague in ability, the latter was jealous of Oxford's superior place, and he now began to cabal against him.

* Burnet, O. T., vi. 45.　　† *Ibid.*, 63.　　‡ Paul, 123.

On March 31, 1713, the Peace of Utrecht was at last signed. "My lord Oxford's peace," said Wharton, "is like the peace of God: it passeth all understanding."* For the moment, however, it did the ministry some good, and at the ensuing general election they maintained a majority. But Bolingbroke was working secretly against the Protestant succession, corresponding with St. Germain, coquetting with the High Tories, and covertly undermining his chief. Oxford was a poor speaker, and a worse financier. Management of the Lower House had been his forte, and that art he could no longer exercise. His hard drinking was damaging his health, and he had got all he wanted. He became lethargic and indolent, often "in a state of alcoholic torpor." Bolingbroke, on the other hand, was a real orator, "all accomplished," restrained by no scruple, eaten up by ambition.

The Whigs were growing stronger, and Oxford had to use all his resources to combat them. This he did in the received fashion of the times. He writes to Swift in March 1714: "I have heard that some honest men, who are very innocent, are under trouble, touching a printed pamphlet. A friend of mine, an obscure person, but charitable, puts the enclosed bill in your hands, to answer such exigencies as their case may immediately require. And I find he will do more, this being only for the present." The cover is endorsed by Swift : "Lord Treasurer Oxford's letter to me in a counterfeit hand with a bill for £100, when the printers were prosecuted by the House of Lords."†

In July 1714 the Queen began to fail. Oxford knew that his favour was on the wane: Bolingbroke was bent on succeeding him at any cost. Lady Masham, now a peeress, was still on the scene. She had quarrelled with the Lord Treasurer, and her kind offices were now enlisted by the Secretary of State. By her arts the Queen's High Church feelings were again aroused, and the fall of Oxford prepared.

The Treasurer saw what was coming and sent the Queen an account of all his administration, a history not without

---

* Paul, 141.   † Swift, xvi. 126.

dignity. He ended: "And as to myself, do with me what you please; place me either as a figure or a cypher; displace me or replace me, as that best serves your Majesty's occasions, you shall ever find me, with the utmost devotion and without any reserve, Madam, your most dutiful, most faithful, most humble, most obedient subject and unworthy servant Oxford."*

His efforts were of no avail. On July 27 there was a stormy scene between the two rivals in the royal closet. "Each accused the other of corresponding with the Pretender, and both were believed."† As the result Oxford was ordered to resign his staff. "The Queen," writes Swift on that day, " has told all the lords the reasons of her parting with him, viz. that he neglected all business; that he was seldom to be understood; that when he did explain himself, she could not depend upon the truth of what he said; that he never came to her at the time she appointed; that he often came drunk; and lastly, to crown all, that he behaved himself to her with bad manners, indecency and disrespect. The stick is yet in his hand, because they cannot agree who shall be the new commissioners."‡

But Bolingbroke's treachery defeated itself. The excitement of the struggle was too much for the Queen. She had a fit and could do no business. The Whig magnates were alert and determined to keep out the Pretender. At a Council at Kensington Palace on July 30 the Dukes of Argyll and Somerset unexpectedly appeared; they recommended that the Queen should appoint the Duke of Shrewsbury, who was already Lord Chamberlain and Lord-Lieutenant of Ireland, to the post of Lord Treasurer; and Anne put the white staff into his hands, saying with her last breath: "Use it for the good of my people." A few hours later she was dead; the Jacobite plans miscarried; George I. was safely proclaimed; and the rule of Oxford and the hopes of Bolingbroke came to an end together.

* Rapin, iv. 385.   † See also Marl. Desp., v. 617
‡ Swift, xvi. 191-2.

In the commission which the Hanoverian minister now produced from his Sovereign, neither of the two were included, and during the autumn both of them, with their principal allies, the Duke of Ormond and Bishop Atterbury, feared the worst. Oxford went to Greenwich to join in the King's reception, but was met with marked coldness—at which Bolingbroke exulted.

In March 1715 the new Parliament met. Bolingbroke then fled to France and openly took office under the Pretender. But Oxford remained in England. In June a motion to impeach him was carried in the House of Commons, and a week later he was sent to the Tower. There Ormond came to see him, before fleeing himself. " Farewell," he said, " Oxford without a head." " Farewell," replied Oxford, " duke without a duchy."*

A long indictment was prepared against him, chiefly with regard to the Treaty of Utrecht and the abuse of the royal prerogative. But the matter dragged on, nothing further was done, and for two years he remained in confinement. At last, in June 1717, his trial was begun in Westminster Hall before Lord Cowper as Lord High Steward. But he had friends to help him and money, and the two Houses failed to agree on questions of procedure. Walpole controlled the Commons, the new ministers were not vindictive, and on July 1 the impeachment was dropped, and Oxford was released. It was generally believed that " the real cause of his acquittal was a Letter or Paper signed by the Duke of Marlborough just before Queen Anne's death, which showed his connexion at that time with the abdicated family, and which letter Lord Oxford had in his possession."† The earl, however, was excepted from George I.'s Act of Grace, and though he still attended the House of Lords, he was forbidden the court. His political life was thus finished, and he now turned his mind entirely to improving the wonderful collection of books and manuscripts with which his name is associated. He was a rich man with an inherited interest in such matters, for his grandfather

* Stanhope, i. 188.   † State Trials, xv. 1179.

" had been compelled to use his manuscripts to fill a breach in his walls during a siege in the Civil War." Oxford had begun this pursuit as early as 1705, and by 1721 he possessed over 20,000 parchments, rolls and charters. He had bought the collections of Foxe, Stow, D'Ewes, and Charles, and for many years had been equally famous as a patron of authors. These pleasures engaged his declining years, his politics were forgotten, and as an old man he filled a new rôle as a beneficent Mæcenas. On May 21, 1724, he died at his house in Albemarle Street, just three years after Robert Walpole had become Prime Minister.

His fortune was very large. The Harleys had been the owners of Marylebone Park, and their names and titles remain in Harley Street, Wigmore Street, Mortimer Street, and the district north of the Oxford Road. The chapel in Vere Street was built to commemorate Lord Oxford, and " to accommodate the inhabitants of his manor."*

By his first wife he had an only son who succeeded him in his titles and literary tastes, but left no male issue; his earldom then descended by a special limitation to the children of his nephew, until in 1853 it finally became extinct. Of his two daughters one was married to the third Duke of Leeds, the other to the eighth Earl of Kinnoull. By his second wife, Sarah, daughter of Thomas Middleton, he had no children.

Oxford was a man of unprepossessing appearance, with a long nose, a fleshy jowl, and an overbearing expression. " His countenance was heavy, his figure mean and his gestures uncouth."† As a young man he had been an active politician, more inspired perhaps by the prospect of his own advancement than by any great regard for the public weal. Bolingbroke used to say of him: " Where anything was to be got he could wriggle himself in. When any misfortune threatened him, he could find a way to wriggle himself out."‡ He was personally quite

---

* Thornbury, vi., 442.   † Macaulay, Hist., iv. 463.
‡ Jesse, Rev., ii. 45.

G. *Kneller, pinx.*   *T. W. Mote, sc.*

ROBERT HARLEY
EARL OF OXFORD

To face page 390

fearless, almost without feeling, qualities for which his admirers gave him full credit:

> " A soul supreme in each hard instance tried,
> Above all pain, all anger and all pride.
> In vain to deserts thy retreat is made,
> The Muse attends thee to thy silent shade."

He was so reserved that even his intimates never knew his plans. His temper was equable, but he was, according to Swift, " the greatest procrastinator in the world."* Pope said " that he spoke in the epic way, for he always began in the middle." He fancied that he had literary talents, and he was a continual scribbler of trifling verses.

In Parliament his knowledge and experience earned him the highest place that assembly had to bestow. " Yet no man," says Macaulay, " would have listened patiently to Robert Harley anywhere but in the House of Commons. His intellect was slender and slow. To the end of his life he remained a tedious, hesitating and confused speaker. Yet he was heard with respect. For such as his mind was, it had been assiduously cultivated. He had that sort of industry and exactness which would have made him a respectable antiquary or King-at-arms."†

The doctrine of ministerial responsibility formed no part of Oxford's political creed. Speaking in his own defence in the House of Lords, he said: " If Ministers of State, acting by the immediate commands of their Sovereign, are afterwards to be made accountable for their proceedings, it may one day or other be the case of all the members of this august assembly."‡ To this, however, Lord Rochester, among the highest of High Tories, took a different view. As early as 1711 he had observed that " they were told that the Queen did everything, but they knew that the contrary was the case and that ministers were the real authors of policy."

Oxford's maxims were sententious and his jokes callous.

---

* Jesse, Rev., ii. 67.   † Macaulay, Hist., iv. 463-4.
‡ Rapin., iv. 431.

" None of us," he once remarked, " know how much the good people of England will bear." To a poor suitor for a place abroad he recommended the study of Spanish. The applicant came back several months later and said he had learnt sufficient of the language. " Then, Sir," said Oxford, " I envy you the pleasure of reading Don Quixote in the original."* Among the wits and poets he had many friends—Swift, Pope, Parnell, Gay, Prior; to them he was courteous and hospitable, and they repaid his kindness well. A contemporary writer calls him " easy and disengaged in private conversation: endowed with great learning and a great favourer and protector of it. A courteous neighbour; a firm and affectionate friend; a kind, generous and placable enemy; a despiser of money, and an uncorrupted minister."†

These eulogia may be true. But whatever praise Oxford deserves, few will accord him the name of a statesman or a patriot. Up to the time of his becoming Speaker he had been, as the times went, a comparatively honest man. But when the horizon expanded before him his character sank and ambition overmastered him. He changed his party and manœuvred to oust his chief, only to find the same fate himself a few years later. With the attainment of supreme power the incentive to energy had gone: he thought his foes were routed, and he devoted himself to his bottle and his books. But a cleverer knave than he was at his heels, and was soon to trip them up. Some relics of his old intrepidity still remained, and when danger threatened he stayed boldly to stand his trial and defended himself with spirit. But he was a man animated by no real principle, regarding Queen and Parliament as pawns to be played in a political game, and he closed the unfortunate succession of Stuart ministers as an example of what a Chief Minister should not be. By instituting the idea of government by the majority in the House of Commons he contributed to the constitution, but in public affairs he was a trifler, and for the moment the day of triflers was done.

* Jesse, Rev. ii. 71.   † Collins, iv. 79.

The Stuarts went out as they had come in, by the death of a childless woman who left her crown to a distant cousin, the ruler of a foreign land. Under the Tudors religious reformation had confirmed the Church, under the Stuarts political revolution had strengthened the State. Each dynasty had closed with striking military victories and a golden age of letters.

The ministries of Godolphin and Harley mark the transition from ministerial to party government, from the idea of rule by the Sovereign to that of rule by Parliament. The last exponent of the old system was scrupulously honest and singularly efficient as an administrator, but he failed; the first exponent of the new system was not remarkable for either quality, but as a party leader he succeeded. Neither left a notable name in political history—the one is best remembered for his horses, the other for his books: the honest man was put in the shade by the genius of Marlborough; the dull man by the brilliancy of Bolingbroke. The time had come for quicker blood, firmer beliefs, bolder policies. New men were to supply them.

CONCLUSION

COMPARISON OF CHIEF MINISTERS

FROM the tenth to the eighteenth century there were thus twenty - seven Chief Ministers of England — Dunstan, Godwin, Harold, Flambard, Roger, Becket, Marshall, de Burgh, de Montfort, Burnell, Stratford, Wykeham, Beaufort, Suffolk, Warwick, Morton, Wolsey, Cromwell, Somerset, Burghley, Salisbury, Buckingham, Strafford, Clarendon, Danby, Godolphin and Harley.

Their lives extended over eight hundred years in an unbroken chain, for each was living in the days of his predecessor, but their total tenure of office amounted to less than half that space of time, an average of some twelve years apiece. Under the Saxons and Normans their spells of rule were long, some twenty years each; under the Plantagenets this figure sank to nine years; with the Tudors it rose again to sixteen; and with the Stuarts it approached the modern term of six years.

Dunstan, Godwin, Roger and Burghley between them were Chief Ministers for 125 years; de Montfort, Suffolk, Somerset and Strafford for eight. Burghley held the place for forty years, Strafford for fifteen months. Only four—Dunstan, Wykeham, Beaufort and Danby—filled it more than once. After the Conquest no Chief Minister ever served more than two Kings, and no King ever had more than two Chief Ministers.

The Tudors used Chief Ministers most—for seventy years out of 118; the Plantagenets least—for less than a third of the 330 years of their rule. The longest periods in which there was no Chief Minister are from the fall of Dunstan to the rise of Godwin—40 years; from the flight of Becket to the return of Marshall—48 years; and from the death of Burnell to the accession of Stratford— 38 years; corresponding roughly with the reigns of Ethelred, of Richard and John and of Edward II. The longest space of time in which they were continuous was the ministries of the two Cecils—the era of Elizabeth.

As to their origin four were Frenchmen, while of the remaining twenty-three, eleven belonged to the West of England. Five came from Wiltshire, three were Yorkshiremen, three were born in London.

Of their education history is often silent: ten were mostly brought up abroad, six went to Oxford, and four to Cambridge; seven or eight were students of an Inn of Court. Nearly all had travelled on the Continent.

Ten were prelates, five being bishops and five archbishops; three of these became cardinals, and two were canonized as saints. Seventeen were nobles, of whom five inherited and twelve were granted their titles or peerages: they included four dukes, twelve earls and a baron—one of them became a king. All the laymen who lived after the institution of the Garter received it except Clarendon, and all the prelates except Morton. Twelve had been soldiers at some time of their lives; twelve had followed the law; five were interested in art or letters; fifteen were famous builders.

All the laymen married, and at the average age of twenty-seven, one having four wives, one three, and four or five two each. All but one of these left male issue, as did five of the churchmen; but the male line of only four—Somerset, Burghley, Salisbury and Danby—is still known to be extant.

Their average age for first receiving some principal office was thirty-three; for first becoming Chief Minister, forty-six; for finally leaving that place, fifty-seven. Buckingham was only twenty-five when he attained it, and Morton over eighty when he relinquished it.

Six were Chief Minister as Justiciar, eight as Chancellor, six as Treasurer, three as Admiral, one each being High Steward, Lord President, Privy Seal, Marshal and Lord Lieutenant.* Warwick, Cromwell and Somerset also held the place of Lord Great Chamberlain.

Their average length of life was sixty-one, but allowing

* Danby was once Chief Minister as Treasurer, and once as President.

for those who had their days prematurely cut short, this
figure would be sixty-five. Wykeham, Morton and Danby
all lived to eighty. Buckingham was killed at thirty-six.
Nine perished by a violent death; three by the sword,
three by the axe, three by the knife; three died in disgrace.
Ten were exiled or driven to flee abroad; ten were imprisoned in the Tower; ten were impeached or attainted.
Of the six who were definitely accused of having made a
fortune in office, four had most of it taken from them.
Nine of the nobles were near relations or connected by
marriage with the King, and of these six were slain in
battle or beheaded. In the two centuries from 1450 to
1650 only three out of ten ended their lives in prosperity.
To many the unlucky Queens from France were a bane.

Such are summaries of the scanty records that remain.
To draw deductions from so few lives spread over so
long and so diverse a space of time would be fallacious;
yet some main facts emerge.

The favour of the prince was always the road to power;
its maintenance often involved in addition the approval
and support of his household, of the Council, or of
Parliament: but from the days of Alfred to those of Anne
the Sovereign selected his servants " *mero motu* "; only
with Walpole did the choice of the nation begin. Wealth
and connection were not material; in eight hundred years
there are only three cases of rich men or near relatives
becoming Chief Ministers. Learning, industry and talents
were assets, but they were not indispensable: one dependent
on the prince alone was as likely as any other to get his
foot on the first rung of the ladder. Rarely did a great
noble rise to the top—Harold, Suffolk, Beaufort and
Warwick are the examples; nor was the man of mean
extraction more common—Flambard, Roger, Wolsey and
Cromwell are the instances, and they were all characters
of exceptional strength. The tendency was rather to
men of ordinary birth, fortune and ability. Three-
quarters of the Chief Ministers were average country
gentlemen, born and bred amid rural surroundings, with
the tastes and ideas of their class.

Innovators, whether for reaction or reform, seldom saw the success of their policies. Harold, de Montfort, Warwick, Cromwell, Somerset and Strafford all tried to change the dynasty, the constitution or the faith, and all of them fell by the sword. The country preferred moderate measures and steady men. Yet the main epochs of advance are nearly all associated with some Chief Minister—Magna Charta, the First Parliament, the Trade Laws, the Reformation, the Petition of Right, the Restoration—only the Revolution lacks a leader. In the great political contests it is much the same: the struggles between Saxon and Norman, between Crown and Church, between Crown and Barons, between Lords and Villeins, between Papists and Protestants, between Cavaliers and Roundheads, between Crown and Parliament—nearly all are associated with the name of some master statesman.

By whatever touchstone they are tried few Chief Ministers can be stigmatized as evil; a good King had good servants always, a bad King often. Avarice and pride were their most common faults, but these were as a rule patent and venial, more damaging to the sinner than the State. Beneath them lay vigorous virtues.

When their checks and handicaps are allowed for—the atmosphere of their age, the temptations which assailed them, the power they exercised, the risks they ran, the forces they had to fear, the fragile favour on which they built, their lack of means for gauging public feeling— when all these drawbacks are discounted, it is hard to deny that the vast majority of the Chief Ministers were worthy of their trust. Carrying their lives in their hands, never knowing from day to day what fate might await them, prepared to see their families and their fortunes, their policies and their lives, swept away at a single blow, they yet provided for the safety, honour and welfare of their Sovereign and his dominions. " I know," says Sir Henry Wotton, " that it is very dangerous to be employed in Princes' affairs: yet wise and discreet officers will not presently obey their hasty and unadvised commands." Few of the Chief Ministers failed to live up to this high standard of statesmanship or to withstand their King when they knew him to be wrong; and in their days that meant much. The three or four who escaped any vital danger to life or property are those of whom least is known—Burnell, Wykeham, Salisbury and Godolphin. Character and courage were of more value than compromise, and these were the distinguishing traits of nearly all.

To many these patriarchs of history are but empty names, yet they point landmarks in the annals of their country. The reputation of some rests on their victories, their finance, their policy or their law. Some are heroes of poetry, drama or romance. Some have left names that are still household words in England—St. Dunstan's Day, the Goodwin Sands, Wykehamists, Somerset House, the Clarendon Press, the Harleian Miscellanies, may well outlast the other records of those whom they recall. Some are best remembered by a single feature of their lives: to fight like Harold or de Montfort; to die like Becket or Wolsey; to dress like Buckingham or keep house like Warwick struck the imagination more than the reforms of Roger or the administration of Burghley. But all live on.

The English people were never easy to control: "*c'est le plus perilleux peuple qui soit au monde,*" says Froissart, "*le plus outrageux et orgueilleux.*" Intolerance of misrule brought salvation, and later on Commines writes: "*Entre tout les seigneuries dont j'ay connaissance, la chose publique est mieux traitée en Angleterre.*" As the country made its Kings, so it made its ministers, adding to their native pluck and strength the wiser virtues of foresight, discretion and goodwill. "It is an assured sign of a worthy and generous spirit whom honour amends." Most Chief Ministers governed themselves by such a maxim. Many were ambitious, many were execrated, some were unfortunate, some were ill-advised, but nearly all served their King, their country and their conscience with steadfast loyalty and with amazing courage.

CHRONOLOGICAL LIST OF CHIEF MINISTERS

Chief Minister.	Period in Power.	Sovereign.
		Edward the Elder, 901–925
		Athelstan, 925–940
		Edmund, 940–946
Dunstan ...	946–955	Edred, 946–955.
		Edwy, 955–959.
	959–980	Edgar, 959–975.
		Edward the Martyr, 975–979.
		Ethelred II., 979–1016.
		Edmund Ironside, 1016.
		Canute, 1017–1035.
Godwin ...	1022–1051	Harold I., 1035–1040.
		Hardicanute, 1040–1042.
Harold ...	1053–1066	Edward the Confessor, 1042–1066.
		Harold II., 1066.
		William the Conqueror, 1066–1087.
Flambard ...	1094–1100	William Rufus, 1087–1100.
Roger... ...	1100–1139	Henry I., 1100–1135.
		Stephen, 1135–1154.
Becket ...	1154–1162	Henry II., 1154–1189.
		Richard I., 1189–1199.
Marshall ...	1214–1219	John, 1199–1216.
de Burgh ...	1219–1230	Henry III., 1216–1272.
de Montfort ...	1263–1265	
Burnell ...	1274–1292	Edward I., 1272–1307.
		Edward II., 1307–1327.
Stratford ...	1330–1340	Edward III., 1327 1377.
Wykeham ...	1367–1371	
	1389–1391	Richard II., 1377–1399.
		Henry IV., 1399–1413.
Beaufort ...	1413–1417	Henry V., 1413–1422.
	1424–1427	Henry VI., 1422–1461.
	1432–1447	

Chief Minister.	Period in Power.	Sovereign.
Suffolk ...	1447–1450	
Warwick ...	1461–1471	Edward IV., 1461–1483.
		Edward V., 1483.
		Richard III., 1483–1485.
Morton ...	1486–1500	Henry VII., 1485–1509.
Wolsey	1514–1529	
Cromwell ...	1532–1540	Henry VIII., 1509–1547.
Somerset ...	1547–1550	Edward VI., 1547–1553.
		Mary, 1553–1558.
Burghley ...	1558–1598	
Salisbury ...	1598–1612	Elizabeth, 1558–1603.
Buckingham ...	1616–1628	James I., 1603–1625.
Strafford ...	1638–1640	Charles I., 1625–1649.
Clarendon ...	1660–1667	
Danby ...	1673–1678	Charles II., 1660–1685.
	1692–1695	James II., 1685–1688.
		William III., 1689–1702.
Godolphin ...	1702–1710	Mary, 1689–1696.
Harley ...	1710–1714	Anne, 1702–1714.

BIBLIOGRAPHY

OF WORKS TO WHICH REFERENCE IS MADE
IN THE TEXT

ADAMS: Lives of the Old English Worthies. By J. H. Davenport. Adams. 1877.

ÆNEAS SYLVIUS PICCOLOMINUS: Opera omnia quæ exstant. 1571.

ANGLIÆ NOTITIA. By E. Chamberlayne. Two volumes. 1671.

ANGLO-SAXON CHRONICLE. (Church Historians series.) 1853.

BACON: The Historie of the Raigne of King Henry the Seventh. 1622.

BACON: The Works of Francis Bacon. Ten volumes. 1803.

BAKER: A Chronicle of the Kings of England. By Sir Richard Baker. 1665.

BANDELLO: Le Novelle. Four volumes. 1740.

BAYEUX TAPESTRY. By F. R. Fowke. 1898.

BECKET. Materials for the History of Thomas Becket. Seven volumes. (Rolls series.) 1875–83.

BELL: Unknown London. By Walter George Bell. 1919.

BÉMONT: Simon de Montfort. Par Charles Bémont. 1884.

BIRCH: Memoirs of the Reign of Queen Elizabeth, 1581 to 1603. By Thomas Birch, D.D., Two volumes. 1754.

BLACMAN. Henry the Sixth. Edited by M. R. James, D.D. 1919.

BODINGTON: History of Devizes. By E. J. Bodington. 1903.

BREWER: The Reign of Henry the Eighth. By J. S. Brewer, M.A. Two volumes. 1884.

BROWNE: The Lives of the Earls of Clarendon and Danby. By J. H. Browne, LL.B. 1858.

BURKE: Burke's Peerage. 1917.

BURKE: Romantic Records. By J. Bernard Burke. Two volumes. 1850.

BURKE: Vicissitudes of Families. By Sir Bernard Burke. Three volumes. 1860.

BURNET: History of the Reformation of the Church of England. By Gilbert Burnet, D.D. Three volumes. 1681–1715.

BURNET: History of his own Times. By Bishop Burnet. Six volumes. 1823.

CAMDEN: Britannia. By William Camden. 1610.

CAMDEN: The History of Elizabeth, Queen of England. By William Camden. 1675.

CAMPBELL: Lives of the Lord Chancellors of England. By John, Lord Campbell. Ten volumes. 1858.

CAMPBELL: Lives of the Chief Justices of England. By John, Lord Campbell. Four volumes. 1874.

CARLYLE: Miscellanies. By Thomas Carlyle. Five volumes. N. d.

CAVENDISH: The Negotiations of Thomas Wolsey, the great Cardinal of England. By Mr. Cavendish. (In Harleian Miscellany, vol. iv.)

CECIL: A Life of Robert Cecil, first Earl of Salisbury. By Algernon Cecil. 1915.

CLARENDON: The History of the Rebellion in England. By Edward, Earl of Clarendon. Six volumes. 1819.

CLARENDON: The Life of Edward, Earl of Clarendon. By Himself. Three volumes. 1761.

COKAYNE: Complete Peerage. By G. E. C. Eight volumes. 1887–1898.

COLLINS: The Peerage of England. Nine volumes. 1812.

COMMINES: Memoires de Messire de Commines. 1649.

COWPER: Diary of Lord Cowper. 1833.

CRAIK: Life of Edward Hyde, Earl of Clarendon. By Sir Henry Craik, K.C.B. Two volumes. 1911.

CREIGHTON: Life of Simon de Montfort. By the Rt. Rev. W. Creighton. N. d.

DESIDERATA CURIOSA. By Francis Peck. Two volumes. 1779.

DEVIZES: Richard of Devizes. (Church Historians series.) 1858.

D'EWES: The Autobiography of Sir Simonds D'Ewes, Bart. Two volumes. 1845.

DICTIONARY OF NATIONAL BIOGRAPHY. Twenty-three volumes.

DITCHFIELD: The Counties of England. By F. H. Ditchfield, M.A. Two volumes. 1912.

DUCHESNE: Historiæ Normannorum Scriptores Antiqui. A. Duchesne. 1619.

DUGDALE: Monasticon Anglicanum. By William Dugdale. Six volumes. 1655-1723.

DUGDALE: Origines Juridicales. By William Dugdale. 1680.

DUNSTAN: Memorials of Saint Dunstan. Edited by Rt. Rev. W. Stubbs, D.D. (Rolls series.) 1874.

EDWARD THE CONFESSOR: Lives of Edward the Confessor. (Rolls series.) 1858.

ELLIOT: Life of Sydney, Earl of Godolphin, K.G. By the Hon. Hugh Elliot. 1888.

ELLIS: Original Letters illustrative of English History. By Sir Henry Ellis, K.H., F.R.S. Eleven volumes. 1860.

EVELYN: The Diary of John Evelyn, F.R.S. Four volumes. 1879.

FABIAN: The Chronicle of Fabian. 1559.

FORSTER: Historical and Biographical Essays. By John Forster. Two volumes. 1858.

FOSS: The Judges of England. By Edward Foss, F.S.A. 1870.

FOX: History of James the Second. By the Rt. Hon. C. J. Cox. 1808.

FOXE: The Acts and Monuments of the Church, etc. By John Foxe. Two volumes. 1610.

FRANCE: La Vie de Jeanne d'Arc. Par Anatole France. Two volumes. 1904.

FREEMAN: The History of the Norman Conquest. By Edward A. Freeman. Six volumes. 1867, etc.

FREEMAN: The Reign of William Rufus. By Edward A. Freeman. Two volumes. 1882.

FROISSART: Histoire et Chronique de Messire Jehan Froissart. 1574.

FROUDE: History of England from the Fall of Wolsey to the Death of Elizabeth. By J. A. Froude. Twelve volumes. 1858.

FROUDE: Short Studies. By J. A. Froude. Four volumes. 1895.

FULLER: The Church History of Britain. By Thomas Fuller. 1655.

FULLER: The History of the Worthies of England. By Thomas Fuller, D.D. 1662.

FULLER: The Holy State. By Thomas Fuller. 1648.

GALE: Rerum Anglicarum Scriptores Veteres. Edited by T. Gale. Three volumes. 1684.

GALTON: The Character and Times of Thomas Cromwell. By Arthur Galton. 1887.

GARDINER. The History of England from James I. to the Civil War. By Samuel Rawson Gardiner. Ten volumes. 1883-84.

GIBBS. The Complete Peerage. By the Hon. V. Gibbs. Five volumes. 1910-21.

GLOUCESTER: Robert of Gloucester's Chronicle. 1858.

GOODMAN: The Court of James I. By G. Goodman, Bishop of Gloucester. Two volumes. 1830.

GRAMMONT: Memoires du Comte de Grammont. Par Antoine Hamilton. Three volumes. 1812.

GREEN: History of the English People. By John Richard Green. Four volumes. 1885.

GREVILLE: The Five Years of King James. By Sir Foulk Greville. In Harleian Miscellany. vol. v.

GUIZOT: Histoire de la Révolution d'Angleterre. Par M. Guizot. Six volumes. 1854.

GUTCH: History and Antiquities of Oxford. By John Gutch. Two volumes. 1796.

HABINGTON: The Historie of Edward the Fourth. By Wm. Habington. 1640.

HALL: Hall's Chronicle. 1809.

HALLAM: The Constitutional History of England from Henry VII. to George II. By Henry Hallam. Three volumes. 1887.

HANOTAUX: Jeanne d'Arc. Par Gabriel Hanotaux. 1911.

HARDWICKE: See State Papers.

HARDYNG: The Chronicle of John Hardyng. 1812.

HARLEIAN MISCELLANY: Twelve volumes. 1808.

HAYDN: The Book of Dignities. By Joseph Haydn. 1851.

HEMMINGBURGH: Chronicon Walteri de Hemmingburgh. Two volumes. 1848.

HENRY III.: Letters of King Henry III. Edited by W. W. Shirley. Two volumes. (Rolls series.) 1862.

HENRY IV.: Annales Henrici Quarti. (Rolls Series.) 1858.

HENRY V.: Henrici Quinti Gesta. (Eng. Hist. Soc.) 1850.

HENRY V.: Memorials of King Henry V. (Rolls Series.) 1858.

HENRY VI.: Letters and Papers illustrative of the Reign of Henry VI. By Rev. J. Stevenson. Three volumes. 1861-64.

HENRY VII.: Memorials of King Henry VII. (Rolls series.) 1858.

HENRY VIII.: State Papers. 1830-52.

HERBERT: Life and Reign of King Henry VIII. By Edward, Lord Herbert. 1682.

HIGDEN: Polycronycon Ranulphi Higden. 1527.

HOLINSHED: The Chronicles of England, Scotlande and Irélande. By Raphaell Holinshed. Two volumes. 1577.

HOOK: Lives of the Archbishops of Canterbury. By the Very Rev. W. F. Hook. Twelve volumes.

HUTCHINS: History of Dorset. By John Hutchins. Three volumes. 1863.

INGRAM: Memorials of Oxford. By James Ingram, D.D. Three volumes. 1837.

INGULF: Croylandensis Historia. See Gale, vol. iii.

JESSE: Memoirs of the Court of England during the Reign of the Stuarts. By J. H. Jesse. Four volumes. 1840.

JESSE: Memoirs of the Court of England from the Revolution to 1760. Three volumes. By J. H. Jesse. 1843.

JESSE: Memorials of London. By J. H. Jesse. Two volumes. 1847.

JESSOP: William Cecil, Lord Burghley. By the Rev. Augustus Jessop. 1904.

KINGSFORD: The Song of Lewes. By C. L. Kingsford, M.A. 1890.

LANGTOFT: Peter Langtoft's Chronicle. Two volumes. 1725.

LECKY: History of England. By W. H. Lecky. Eight volumes. 1879.

LELAND: The Itinerary of John Leland. Nine volumes. 1770.

LELAND: De Rebus Britannicis Collectanea. Six volumes. 1715.

LINGARD: The History of England. By John Lingard, D.D. Ten volumes. 1888.

LOW: A Dictionary of English History. By Sidney J. Low, B.A. 1889.

LOWTH: Life of William of Wykeham. By Robert Lowth. 1759.

LYTTON: Harold. By Lord Lytton. N. d.

LYTTON: The Last of the Barons. By Lord Lytton. Edited by F. C. Romilly. 1913.

MACAULAY: The History of England. By T. B. Macaulay. Five volumes. 1849.

MACAULAY: The Works of Lord Macaulay. Eight volumes. 1871.

MALMESBURY: History of the Kings of England, and History of his own Times. By William of Malmesbury. (Stevenson's edition.) 1854.

MARÉCHAL: Histoire de Guillaume le Maréchal. (P. Meyer.) Three volumes. 1891-1901.

MARLBOROUGH: Letters and Despatches of John Churchill, first Duke of Marlborough. Five volumes. 1845.

MARLBOROUGH: Private Correspondence of Sarah, Duchess of Marlborough. Two volumes. 1838.

MATTHEW OF WESTMINSTER: Flores historiarum. 1570.

MERRIMAN: Life and Letters of Thomas Cromwell. By Roger B. Merriman. Two volumes. 1902.

MOBERLEY: Life of William of Wykeham. By G. H. Moberley. 1887.

MONSTRELET: Chroniques de Enguerran de Monstrelet. 1603.

MORE: Utopia. By Sir Thomas More. (Dibdin's edition.) 1878.

MORE: The History of Richard III. By Sir Thomas More. 1821.

MOZLEY: Henry VII., Prince Arthur and Cardinal Morton. By T. Mozley. 1878.

NAPIER: Historial Notices of the Parishes of Swyncombe and Ewelme. By the Hon. and Rev. H. A. Napier. 1868.

NAUNTON: Fragmenta Regalia. By Sir Robert Naunton. (Archer's edition.) 1870. '

NEWBRIDGE: Guillielmi Neubrigensis Historia. Two volumes. 1725.

NORTH: Lives of the Norths. By the Hon. Roger North. Three volumes. 1856.

OMAN: Warwick the Kingmaker. By Charles W. Oman. 1891,

ORDERICUS VITALIS: Historiæ Ecclesiasticæ. See Duchesne.

OSBERN. See Dunstan.

PARIS: Matthæi Parisiensis opera. 1640.

PASTON: The Paston Letters. Edited by James Gairdner. Six volumes. 1904.

PAUL: Queen Anne. By Herbert Paul. N. d.

PECK: See Desiderata Curiosa.

PEPYS: Diary of Samuel Pepys. Four volumes. 1884.

PERCY: Reliques of Ancient Poetry. By Thomas Percy. 1845.

PICCOLOMINI. See Æneas Sylvius.

POLLARD: England under Protector Somerset. By A. E. Pollard. 1900.

POLYDORE VERGIL: Angliæ Historiæ. 1546.

PROTHERO: The Life of Simon de Montfort. By G. W. Prothero. 1877.

RANSOME: A Short History of England. By Cyril Ransome. 1913.

RAPIN: The History of England. By Rapin de Thoyras. Five volumes. Tindal's translation. 1743.

RERESBY: Travels and Memoirs of Sir John Reresby, Bart. 1813.

RICKMAN : Architecture in England. By Thomas Rickman, F.S.A. 1881.

ROCHESTER: Correspondence of the Earls of Clarendon and Rochester. Two volumes. 1828.

ROMAN DE ROU: Par Wace. Two volumes. 1877–1879.

RYMER: Fœdera Angliæ. Thomas Rymer. Twenty volumes. 1727.

SEWARD: Anecdotes of Distinguished Persons. By W. Seward. Four volumes. 1804.

SIMEON OF DURHAM: Historia Ecclesiæ Dunhelmensis. 1732.

SMITH: Antiquities of the City of Westminster. By J. T. Smith. 1807.

STANHOPE: The History of England comprising the Reign of Queen Anne. By Earl Stanhope. 1870.

STANHOPE: History of England. By Lord Mahon (Earl Stanhope). Three volumes. 1839.

STATE PAPERS: 1501 to 1726. Edited by the Earl of Hardwicke. Two volumes. 1778.

STATE POEMS: Four volumes. 1703-1709.

STATE TRIALS: Cobbett's Complete Collection. Twenty-one volumes. 1809.

STEPHEN: The Acts of King Stephen. Stevenson's translation. 1858.

STOW: Annales, or a General Chronicle of England. By John Stow. 1631.

STOW: The Survey of London. By John Stow. 1633.

STRAFFORD: The Earl of Strafforde's Letters. Two volumes. 1739.

STRICKLAND: Lives of the Queens of England. By Agnes Strickland. Eight volumes. 1851.

STRUTT: The Antiquities of England. By Joseph Strutt. 1793.

STUART: Lettres de Marie Stuart. Seven volumes. 1844.

STUBBS: The Constitutional History of England. By William Stubbs, D.D. Three volumes. 1877.

STUBBS: Select Charters. By the Rt. Rev. W. Stubbs, D.D. 1870.

SURTEES: The History of Durham. By Robert Surtees. Three volumes. 1816.

SWIFT: The Works of Jonathan Swift, D.D. Nineteen volumes. 1814.

SYNGE: A Short History of Social Life in England. By M. B. Synge. 1906.

TEMPLE: The Works of Sir Wm. Temple, Bart. Four volumes. 1757.

THIERRY: Histoire de la Conquête d'Angleterre. Par A. Thierry. Four volumes. 1843.

THORNBURY: Old and New London. By Walter Thornbury. Six volumes. 1843.

TOUT: Chapters in the Administrative History of Mediæval England. By T. F. Tout, M.A. Two volumes. 1920.

TOUT: Edward the First. By Professor T. F. Tout.

TRAILL: Social England. Edited by H. D. Traill, D.C.L., and J. S. Mann, M.A. Six volumes. 1901.

TRAILL: Lord Strafford. By H. D. Traill. 1907.

TURNER: The History of the Anglo-Saxons. By Sharon Turner. Three volumes. 1852.

VETUSTA MONUMENTA: Six volumes. 1747-1842.

WALPOLE: Historic Doubts on the Life and Reign of King Richard III. By Horace Walpole. 1768.

WARWICK: Memoires of the Reigne of King Charles the First. By Sir Philip Warwick, Knight. 1701.

WAVERLEY ANNALS: See Gale, vol. ii.

WIKES: Chronicon Thomæ Wikes. See Gale, vol. ii.

WILLIAMS: Lives of the English Cardinals. By Folkestone Williams. Two volumes. 1868.

WORCESTER, William of. Annales. See Henry VI., vol. ii.

27

WORCESTER: The Chronicle of Florence of Worcester. (Church Historians.) 1853.

WOTTON: The State of Christendom. By Sir Henry Wotton, Kt. 1657.

WOTTON: The Life and Death of George Villiers, Duke of Buckingham. By Sir Henry Wotton, Kt. In Harleian Miscellany, vol. v.

WRIGHT: Political Songs. Edited by Thomas Wright. Two volumes. (Rolls series.) 1858.

WRIGHT: Queen Elizabeth and her Times. By Thomas Wright, F.S.A. Two volumes. 1838.

INDEX

The surnames of peers are omitted when identical with their titles.